DEUTERONOMY
and the Hermeneutics
of Legal Innovation

To Michael,
Fellow prowler in the
riches of ancient Israel,
with real excitement and pleasure
at having this year at the Institute
and the prospect of many talks with you)
Bernie
Princeton
11. 20. 97

DEUTERONOMY
and the Hermeneutics
of Legal Innovation

Bernard M. Levinson

New York   Oxford
OXFORD UNIVERSITY PRESS
1997

Oxford University Press

Oxford   New York

Athens   Auckland   Bangkok   Bogota   Bombay   Buenos Aires
Calcutta   Cape Town   Dar es Salaam   Delhi   Florence   Hong Kong
Istanbul   Karachi   Kuala Lumpur   Madras   Madrid   Melbourne
Mexico City   Nairobi   Paris   Singapore   Taipei   Tokyo   Toronto   Warsaw

and associated companies in
Berlin   Ibadan

Library of Congress Cataloging-in-Publication Data
Levinson, Bernard M. (Bernard Malcolm)
Deuteronomy and the hermeneutics of legal innovation / Bernard M. Levinson.
p.   cm.
Revision of the author's thesis (doctoral)—Brandeis University.
Includes bibliographical references and index.
ISBN 0-19-511280-6
1. Bible. O.T. Deuteronomy XII–XXVI—Criticism, interpretation, etc.
2. Bible. O.T. Exodus XX, 22–XXIII, 33—Criticism, interpretation, etc.
3. Law (Theology)—Biblical teaching.   I. Title.
BS1275.2.L48   1997
222'.1506—dc21   96-47389

1 3 5 7 9 8 6 4 2

Printed in the United States of America
on acid-free paper

To my father, Ulysses

PREFACE

Research for this book began with my doctoral dissertation, undertaken at Brandeis University and directed by Michael Fishbane, who first introduced me to the nature of textuality in ancient Israel and who fostered my approach to the material. His encouragement of my independence set a lasting model—not only for scholarly achievement but also for devotion to learning and commitment to family. This book represents a comprehensive rethinking and complete revision of the dissertation. The change in perspective came about as a result of a year's research leave in Germany. I am very grateful to Professor Norbert Lohfink, who first encouraged me to come to Germany and who provided extensive comments on my dissertation. I am also deeply grateful to Professor Eckart Otto of the Faculty of Protestant Theology at the Johannes Gutenberg University in Mainz for making that year possible. He generously offered me a position in the Seminar for Biblical Archaeology while freeing me to pursue my own research as we engaged in wide-ranging discussions about the field of biblical studies. That I here engage in debate with these three—whom I regard as teachers, senior colleagues, and friends—only indicates how much I have learned from them.

This book is concerned with how the authors of Deuteronomy drew on and transformed earlier literary sources in order to mandate a major transformation of religion and society in ancient Israel. In order to map that reuse, it is essential to employ the technical terms developed by biblical scholars to refer to the literary sources of the Bible. In the real hope that this book will find a wider readership, however, I would like to provide a simple primer for some of the terms, which may be obscure for nonspecialists. The classical documentary hypothesis assumes the Pentateuch to be the combination of four originally independent literary sources: the Yahwistic work, the Elohistic work, Deuteronomy, and the Priestly source, which includes the Holiness Code (Leviticus 17–26). These sources are conventionally abbreviated J (after the German term for the Yahwist), E, D, P (with H). J and E are assumed to be the oldest sources of the Pentateuch; at a relatively early stage of their literary growth they are understood to have been combined together as the work of the Jehovist, or JE. The core of Deuteronomy is normally associated with Josiah's reform, as narrated in 2 Kings 22–23, which would date to 622 B.C.E. Most scholars date the Priestly source and the Holiness Code later than Deuteronomy, to the exilic and postexilic eras, although a number of scholars, chiefly Israeli, date it prior to or contemporary with Deuteronomy.

The term "the Deuteronomistic History" (or DtrH) also requires explanation. It refers to the entirety of Joshua, Judges, 1–2 Samuel, and 1–2 Kings, viewed as the redactional achievement of one or more editors who worked under the literary influence of Deuteronomy. Most American scholars believe that a first edition of this work was completed during Josiah's reign; most European scholars believe that the work was not begun until the Exile. This editor or editors gave Deuteronomy its present introduction in chapters 1–4, which thereby provide the introduction to the Deuteronomistic History. Since the editor was also active elsewhere in Deuteronomy (and, many hold, in Exodus), scholars find it necessary to distinguish the material original to Deuteronomy, called Deuteronomic, from the later additions to this text, which are called Deuteronomistic. Many scholars also identify Deuteronomistic additions to the prophetical books, like Jeremiah, but that goes beyond the scope of this book.

Completion of this manuscript was facilitated by a one-semester teaching reduction granted by Fedwa Malti-Douglas, Martha C. Kraft Professor of the Humanities and Chair of the Department of Near Eastern Languages and Cultures at Indiana University. I am indebted to a number of colleagues and friends whose comments on previous drafts of part or all of this manuscript were invaluable and whose generosity was often heroic: Professors James S. Ackerman, Marc Brettler, Alan M. Cooper, Sam Greengus, Baruch Halpern, Stephen Katz, Gary Knoppers, Herbert Marks, Benjamin Nathans, Dina Spechler, and Stephen Weitzman. The painstaking comments by Oxford's anonymous readers were very beneficial. Cynthia Garver helped pay careful attention to demanding details of formatting while guiding the manuscript through production at Oxford. The Author Index and the Index of Scriptural and Other Citations were prepared by my student and friend Alexander Moorhead, whose meticulous work is exceeded only by his ability as a budding Hebraist and by his grace. I especially acknowledge the kindness of Professor Leah Shopkow, who taught me much about both friendship and writing.

Bloomington, Indiana   B.M.L.
June 1996

CONTENTS

ABBREVIATIONS

AB	Anchor Bible
AJBI	*Annual of the Japanese Biblical Institute*
AnBib	Analecta biblica
ANET	James B. Pritchard (ed.), *Ancient Near Eastern Texts Relating to the Old Testament* (Princeton: Princeton University Press, 1969)
AOAT	Alter Orient und Altes Testament
AOS	American Oriental Series
ATANT	Abhandlungen zur Theologie des Alten und Neuen Testaments
BBB	Bonner biblische Beiträge
BDB	F. Brown, S. R. Driver, and S. A. Briggs, *Hebrew and English Lexicon of the Old Testament* (Oxford: Clarendon, 1907)
BETL	Bibliotheca ephemeridum theologicarum lovaniensium
BFCT	Beiträge zur Förderung christlicher Theologie
Bib	*Biblica*
BJS	Brown Judaica Studies
BN	*Biblische Notizen*
BWANT	Beiträge zur Wissenschaft vom Alten und Neuen Testament
BZAW	Beihefte zur *Zeitschrift für die alttestamentliche Wissenschaft*
CAD	*The Assyrian Dictionary of the Oriental Institute of the University of Chicago*
CahRB	Cahiers de la Revue biblique
CBQ	*Catholic Biblical Quarterly*
ConBOT	Coniectanea biblica, Old Testament
CRINT	Compendia rerum iudaicarum ad novum testamentum
ErFor	Erträge der Forschung
EstBib	*Estudios bíblicos*
ETL	*Ephemerides theologicae lovanienses*

FRLANT	Forschungen zur Religion und Literatur des Alten und Neuen Testaments
GKC	E. Kautzsch (ed.), Gesenius' Hebrew Grammar, tr. A. Cowley (2d ed.; Oxford: Clarendon, 1910)
GTA	Göttinger theologische Arbeiten
HALAT	L. Koehler and W. Baumgartner et al. (eds.), *The Hebrew and Aramaic Lexicon of the Old Testament*, tr. M. E. J. Richardson (4 vols.; Leiden: E. J. Brill, 1994–97)
HAR	*Hebrew Annual Review*
HBS	Herders Biblische Studien/Herder's Biblical Studies
HSM	Harvard Semitic Monographs
HTR	*Harvard Theological Review*
HUCA	*Hebrew Union College Annual*
ICC	International Critical Commentary
IDBSup	*Interpreter's Dictionary of the Bible*, Supplementary Volume (Nashville: Abingdon, 1976)
IEJ	*Israel Exploration Journal*
Int	*Interpretation*
JAOS	*Journal of the American Oriental Society*
JBL	*Journal of Biblical Literature*
JCS	*Journal of Cuneiform Studies*
JJS	*Journal of Jewish Studies*
JNES	*Journal of Near Eastern Studies*
JPOS	*Journal of Palestine Oriental Society*
JPS	Jewish Publication Society
JQR	*Jewish Quarterly Review*
JSOT	*Journal for the Study of the Old Testament*
JSOTSup	Journal for the Study of the Old Testament Supplement Series
JTS	*Journal of Theological Studies*
KeHAT	Kurzgefasstes exegetisches Handbuch zum Alten Testament
LD	Lectio divina
LXX	Septuagint (Greek) translation of the Hebrew Bible
MT	Masoretic Text of the Hebrew Bible
NCBC	New Century Bible Commentary
NEB	New English Bible
NJPSV	New Jewish Publication Society Version = *Tanakh: A New Translation of the Holy Scriptures according to the Traditional Hebrew Text* (Philadelphia: JPS, 1988)
NRSV	New Revised Standard Version
OBO	Orbis biblicus et orientalis
OrAnt	*Oriens antiquus*
OTL	Old Testament Library
OTS	*Oudtestamentische Studiën*
PAAJR	*Proceedings of the American Academy of Jewish Research*
QD	Quaestiones disputatae
RB	*Revue biblique*

RSV	Revised Standard Version
SBAB	Stuttgarter Biblische Aufsatzbände, Altes Testament
SBLDS	Society of Biblical Literature Dissertation Series
SBLMS	Society of Biblical Literature Monograph Series
SBLMasS	Society of Biblical Literature Masoretic Studies
SBLWAW	Society of Biblical Literature Writings from the Ancient World
SBS	Stuttgarter Bibelstudien
SBT	Studies in Biblical Theology
ScrHier	Scripta hierosolymitana
SJLA	Studies in Judaism in Late Antiquity
SJOT	*Scandinavian Journal of the Old Testament*
SSN	Studia semitica neerlandica
StudBib	Studia Biblica
TBü	Theologische Bücherei
TDOT	G. J. Botterweck and H. Ringgren (eds.), *Theological Dictionary of the Old Testament* (Grand Rapids: Eerdmans, 1974–)
Tg.	*Targum*
TLZ	*Theologische Literaturzeitung*
TP	*Theologie und Philosophie*
TRE	*Theologische Realenzyklopädie*
TRu	*Theologische Rundschau*
TWAT	G. J. Botterweck and H. Ringgren (eds.), *Theologisches Wörterbuch zum Alten Testament* (Stuttgart: Kohlhammer, 1970–)
VS	Verbum salutis
VT	*Vetus Testamentum*
VTSup	Vetus Testamentum, Supplements
WMANT	Wissenschaftliche Monographien zum Alten und Neuen Testament
WZKM	*Wiener Zeitschrift für die Kunde des Morgenlandes*
ZA	*Zeitschrift für Assyriologie*
ZAW	*Zeitschrift für die alttestamentliche Wissenschaft*
ZTK	*Zeitschrift für Theologie und Kirche*

The abbreviations of biblical books and pseudepigraphical and rabbinic literature follow the conventions of *JBL*, as found most recently in the *Society of Biblical Literature Membership Directory and Handbook* (Decatur: Society of Biblical Literature, 1994) 223–40. For the sake of convenience, the abbreviations of the books of the Hebrew Bible are presented below:

Gen	Genesis	1–2 Kgs	1–2 Kings
Exod	Exodus	Isa	Isaiah
Lev	Leviticus	Jer	Jeremiah
Num	Numbers	Ezek	Ezekiel
Deut	Deuteronomy	Hos	Hosea
Josh	Joshua	Joel	Joel
Judg	Judges	Amos	Amos
1–2 Sam	1–2 Samuel	Obad	Obadiah

Jonah	Jonah	Prov	Proverbs
Mic	Micah	Ruth	Ruth
Nah	Nahum	Cant	Canticles (Song of Songs)
Hab	Habakkuk	Qoh	Qoheleth (Ecclesiastes)
Zeph	Zephaniah	Lam	Lamentations
Hag	Haggai	Esth	Esther
Zech	Zechariah	Dan	Daniel
Mal	Malachi	Ezra	Ezra
Ps (*pl.*: Pss)	Psalms	Neh	Nehemiah
Job	Job	1–2 Chr	1–2 Chronicles

DEUTERONOMY
and the Hermeneutics
of Legal Innovation

1

Textual Revision and Cultural Transformation

The Hermeneutics of Legal Innovation
in Deuteronomy

For centuries the legal corpus of Deuteronomy 12–26 has presented biblical scholars with two key difficulties. The first involves the seemingly arbitrary selection of topics within the legal corpus, their lack of coherent order, their frequent repetition, and their often tortuous philological structure. The second involves the ambiguous relationship of the corpus as a whole to the Covenant Code (Exod 20:22–23:33), a text on which it seemingly depends for both content and language but from which it nonetheless diverges in significant ways.[1] These problems, usually considered independently, have not yet found satisfactory solution. In this book I argue that they are inextricably linked. Innovation took place by means of literary reformulation in Deuteronomy; once that is recognized, the long-standing critical difficulties begin to yield. Deuteronomy represents a radical revision of the Covenant Code. The authors of Deuteronomy sought to implement a far-reaching transformation of religion, law, and social structure that was essentially without cultural precedent. They therefore turned to the earlier code in order to anchor their departure from legal convention in the very textual heritage from which they cut themselves free in substantive terms. They deliberately presented their new vision of the Judaean polity as continuous with the abrogated past and used the earlier textual material, carefully transformed, to sanction their own inde-

---

1. The Covenant Code (or Book of the Covenant) is conventionally defined as Exod 21:1–23:19, together with its preface, 20:22–26, and its homiletical conclusion, 23:20–33. There is an ongoing scholarly debate, however, concerning how much of that present textual compass is pre-Deuteronomic and how much is a result of Deuteronomistic additions. Providing a useful overview is Brevard S. Childs, *The Book of Exodus* (OTL; Philadelphia: Westminster, 1974) 451–88. Recent work has greatly increased the amount of material ceded to Deuteronomistic literary activity. On these matters, see "The Question of Deuteronomistic Revision of the Covenant Code."

3

pendent agenda. Many of the problems of coherence and structure in the legal corpus result from this revisionist activity.

The authors of Deuteronomy were sophisticated interpreters or, better, reinterpreters of texts, both Israelite and cuneiform. They were skilled scribes confronting a central problem in the history of religions: the justification of innovation.[2] Central to Deuteronomy is the question of hermeneutics. In stressing the importance of hermeneutics, I do not restrict it to the discipline of the contemporary biblical scholar or exegete, who is concerned to explicate the text philologically and raise the question of its contemporary meaning. Hermeneutics is not simply a matter of the history of reception and interpretation of Deuteronomy by ancient, medieval, or modern communities of believers or scholars. Instead, Deuteronomy was already a complex hermeneutical work from the beginning; it was the composition of authors who consciously reused and reinterpreted earlier texts to propound and justify their program of cultic and legal reform, even—or particularly—when those texts conflicted with the authors' agenda. Previous scholarship has not fully recognized, let alone conceptualized, the centrality of this hermeneutical question to Deuteronomy's authors, nor the extent to which, once recognized, it helps explain a number of long-standing problems that have otherwise resisted solution.

Deuteronomy is, on the one hand, among the most radically innovative literary units in the Hebrew Bible and, on the other, among those that most loudly silence the suggestion of innovation. The earliest literary strata of the Pentateuch, both legal and narrative, as well as the narratives of Joshua through 2 Kings, clearly contemplate sacrificial worship of Yahweh at multiple altar sites throughout the land. To select only the most familiar of examples, Abraham sacrifices at Shechem and Beth El, Jacob at Beth El, Samuel at Shiloh and Ramah, and Elijah upon Mount Carmel.[3] Contrary to this norm, the authors of Deuteronomy prohibit all sacrificial worship at the familiar local altars. They restrict legitimate sacrifice to a single, exclusive site, "the place that Yahweh shall choose," Deuteronomy's circumlocution for Jerusalem and its Temple.[4] The radically disruptive nature of that transformation of religious routine should not be underestimated. Deuteronomy's repeated emphasis on the "joy" to be experienced at the central sanctuary might well represent an attempt to pro-

2. See Jonathan Z. Smith, "Sacred Persistence: Toward a Redescription of Canon," in *Imagining Religion: From Babylon to Jonestown* (Chicago Studies in the History of Judaism; Chicago and London: University of Chicago Press, 1982) 36–52; and Bernard M. Levinson, "The Human Voice in Divine Revelation: The Problem of Authority in Biblical Law," in *Innovation in Religious Traditions* (ed. Michael A. Williams, Collett Cox, and Martin S. Jaffee; Religion and Society 31; Berlin: Mouton de Gruyter, 1992) 35–71. Note also the editors' introduction and extensive bibliography.

3. Gen 12:7–8; 35:1–7; 1 Sam 3:1; 7:17; and 1 Kgs 18:20–46.

4. The text of Deuteronomy nowhere itself specifies that the formula refers to Jerusalem. Although there is universal agreement that, in the final version of the legal corpus, the Jerusalem Temple is intended, some scholars have maintained that the formula originally functioned distributively, not exclusively. They thereby argue that, in earlier strata, the formula applied to other sanctuaries, like Shiloh or Beth El. For a more complete discussion of this issue, see chapter 2, n. 1.

vide compensation for the loss of the local cultic sites, where the people would more conventionally have gained access to the deity.[5] The rejection and transformation of the religious status quo does not stop with the institution of sacrifice alone. Already invasive and revolutionary, the implications of centralization extend still further.

The Deuteronomic proscription of local cultic activity and restriction of cultic action to the central sphere entailed the obligation to revise essentially the entire apparatus of cultic rituals and institutions that governed local cultic activity: tithes and firstlings, the festival calendar with its pilgrimages to local sanctuaries, and the Passover as an apotropaic blood rite involving a home slaughter. The authors of Deuteronomy also had to transform institutions of public life that did not directly involve the cultus. Judicial procedure, for example, had to be reorganized—because the local sanctuary had played a crucial role in the resolution of ambiguous civil and criminal legal cases. Even the conventional role of the king in Israelite society, as the highest civil and judicial authority, was fundamentally transformed on account of centralization. In this case centralization ironically led to a decrease in royal power, as the Temple eclipsed the king's authority.[6]

But the Deuteronomic authors' transformative action did not operate exclusively at the empirical level. Their profound transformation of Judah's religious and judicial institutions cannot be understood apart from the larger problem of innovation in a culture in which prestigious or authoritative texts occupy an important place. In commanding centralization, the authors and editors of the legal corpus did not create *lex ex nihilo*. They confronted existing legal texts that enshrined the legitimacy of the local altars that the Deuteronomic authors sought to prohibit. Granted, those legal texts may not yet have had the status of actual public law; they may have been only prestigious texts, part of the curriculum of scribal schools, but they were nonetheless texts that could not simply be ignored or dispensed with. The authors of Deuteronomy, in one way or another, had to take account of these texts and justify their departure from their norms.

In the innovation of centralization, therefore, the Deuteronomic authors did not only transform empirical institutions. They also rewrote literary history. Their paradoxical technique for defending their innovation was, in many cases, to appropriate and rework the earlier texts that would seem to preclude centralization. The authors of Deuteronomy coopted those texts, accommodating them to their innovations, by citing selected key words and phrases (lem-

5. Deut 12:7, 12, 18; 14:26; 15:20; 16:11, 14, 15; 26:11. For this point see Norbert Lohfink, "The Cult Reform of Josiah of Judah: 2 Kings 22–23 as a Source for the History of Israelite Religion," in *Ancient Israelite Religion: Essays in Honor of Frank Moore Cross* (ed. Patrick D. Miller, Jr., Paul D. Hanson, and S. Dean McBride; Philadelphia: Fortress, 1987) 459–75 (469); Lohfink, "Opfer und Säkularisierung im Deuteronomium," in *Studien zu Opfer und Kult im Alten Testament* (ed. Adrian Shenker; Forschungen zum Alten Testament 3; Tübingen: J. C. B. Mohr [Paul Siebeck], 1992) 15–43 (31); and Rainer Albertz, *A History of Israelite Religion in the Old Testment Period* (2 vols.; OTL; Louisville: Westminster/John Knox, 1994) 1.211.

6. See chapter 4 for the revisions both of judicial procedure and of royal authority.

mas) from their source texts and giving them new contexts and meanings. In the process, the authors camouflaged the radical and often subversive nature of their innovations, as the new textual content was often expressed, quite literally, using the terms of the older dispensation. Such learned textual recycling left in its wake a number of clear editorial markers, including citation formulas, repetitive resumption, devoicing, revoicing, and intertextual allusion. Many of the philological difficulties of the text derive from and become intelligible in light of this hermeneutical activity. They are not merely the evidence of redactional layering of pre-Deuteronomic, Deuteronomic, and Deuteronomistic strata. Rather, they represent the wake of transformative exegesis, the deliberate attempt to rework prestigious texts in light of the innovation of centralization. Standard diachronic literary criticism, although it provides the essential analysis of the philological problems of the text, lacks access to their solution unless it takes into account the hermeneutics of innovation. The scribal authors of Deuteronomy authorized their radical cultic and legal transformations by disclaiming their innovative force. Very likely, even the voicing of Deuteronomy—its attribution to Moses—points to the attempt by the text's authors to lend legitimacy to their innovations.[7] The voice of the text belies its belatedness. By means of it, the text's authors purchased a pedigree—both an antiquity and an authority—that the text properly lacked. In so doing, they borrowed pseudepigraphically from the very textual authority that they subverted.[8]

Methodological Presuppositions

In arguing that Deuteronomy revises the Covenant Code, I assume that the Covenant Code as a text chronologically precedes Deuteronomy and was known, in whole or in part, by Deuteronomy's authors. Each component of that assump-

---

7. There is no scholarly consensus about whether Deuteronomy's being garbed as Mosaic speech is original to its composition; hence, there are other ways of explaining the evidence. Contending that the Mosaic voicing of the legal corpus is not original but represents the work of its later Deuteronomistic editors is Norbert Lohfink, "2 Kön 23,3 und Dtn 6,17," *Bib* 71 (1990) 34–42; and Lohfink, "Das Deuteronomium: Jahwegesetz oder Mosegesetz? Die Subjektzuordnung bei Wörtern für 'Gesetz' im Dtn und in der dtr Literatur," *TP* 65 (1990) 387–91. Against Lohfink, Eleonore Reuter argues for the originality of the Mosaic voicing (*Kultzentralisation: Entstehung und Theologie von Dtn 12* [BBB 87; Frankfurt: Anton Hain, 1993] 213–26). In his review article, however, Lohfink maintains that Reuter misrepresents his position, which he there also amplifies ("Kultzentralisation und Deuteronomium: Zu einem Buch von Eleonore Reuter," *Zeitschrift für Altorientalische und Biblische Rechtsgeschichte*, 1 [1995] 117–48). Lohfink's review article provides a valuable assessment of the archaeological evidence for and against the historicity of Josiah's centralization of the cultus.

8. Morton Smith has demonstrated that pseudepigraphy is a literary technique characteristic of a broad range of texts within the Hebrew Bible and that Deuteronomy's attribution to Moses provides a classic example of it. See his "Pseudepigraphy in the Israelite Literary Tradition," in *Pseudepigrapha I: Pseudopythagorica—Lettres de Platon—Littérature pseudépigraphique juive* (ed. Kurt von Fritz; Fondation Hardt; Entretiens sur l'antiquité classique 18; Geneva: Vandoeuvres, 1971) 191–215.

tion is consistent with the broad scholarly consensus.[9] Some scholars have challenged the very idea of literary relation between Deuteronomy and the Covenant Code or have reversed the consensus, claiming that the Covenant Code, in whole or in part, depends upon Deuteronomy.[10] While raising valuable issues, these challenges have for good reason not won currency. There is clear precedent in the ancient Near East for subsequent legal collections directly revising earlier ones in order to articulate developments in juridical thought.[11] Moreover, the degree of the detailed lexical and syntactical correspondence between Deuteronomy and the Covenant Code is too extensive to be explained otherwise than

9. For the most recent presentations of the history of research, see Albert de Pury and Thomas Römer, "Le Pentateuque en question: Position du problème et brève histoire de la recherche," *Le Pentateuque en question: Les Origines et la composition des cinq premiers livres de la Bible à la lumière des recherches récentes* (Le Monde de la Bible 19; 2d ed.; Geneva: Labor et Fides, 1991) 9–80; and Norbert Lohfink, "Deutéronome et Pentateuque: État de la recherche," *Le Pentateuque: Débats et recherches* (ed. P. Haudebert; LD 151; Paris: Cerf, 1992) 35–64.

10. Denying any literary relation whatsoever among the biblical legal corpora is Yehezkel Kaufmann, *Toledot ha-'emuna ha-yiśre'elit* (8 vols. in 4; Jerusalem: Bialik Institute; Tel Aviv: Dvir, 1937–56) 1.113–42, 201–203 (Hebrew); abridged as *The Religion of Israel: From Its Beginnings to the Babylonian Exile* (tr. Moshe Greenberg; Chicago: University of Chicago Press, 1960) 205. Also denying dependence among the legal corpora is Rosario Pius Merendino, *Das deuteronomische Gesetz: Eine literarkritische, gattungs- und überlieferungsgeschichtliche Untersuchung zu Dt 12–26* (BBB 31; Bonn: Peter Hanstein, 1969) 401–402. Accepting dependence but reversing the sequence to argue that Exod 22:17–23:19 depends upon Deuteronomy is Gary Alan Chamberlain, "Exodus 21–23 and Deuteronomy 12–26: A Form-critical Study" (Ph.D. diss., Boston University, 1977) 129–59. Dating J postexilically, eliminating E, and therefore reversing the consensus to claim the dependence of both J and the Covenant Code upon Deuteronomy is John Van Seters, "The Place of the Yahwist in the History of Passover and Massot," *ZAW* 95 (1983) 167–82; Van Seters, "Etiology in the Moses Tradition: The Case of Exodus 18," in *Biblical and Other Studies in Memory of S. D. Goitein* (ed. R. Ahroni; HAR 9; Columbus: Department of Judaic and Near Eastern Languages and Literatures, Ohio State University, 1985), 355–61; Van Seters, "'Comparing Scripture with Scripture': Some Observations on the Sinai Pericope of Exodus 19–24," in *Canon, Theology, and Old Testament Interpretation: Essays in Honor of Brevard S. Childs* (ed. G. M. Tucker, D. L. Petersen, and R. R. Wilson; Philadelphia: Fortress, 1988) 111–30; and Van Seters, *The Life of Moses: The Yahwist as Historian in Exodus–Numbers* (Louisville: Westminster/John Knox, 1994).

11. Establishing deliberate legal revision of cuneiform legal collections, based on developments in judicial thought, are J. J. Finkelstein, *The Ox That Gored* (Transactions of the American Philosophical Society 71:2; Philadelphia: American Philosophical Society, 1981) 18–20; Barry L. Eichler, "Literary Structure in the Laws of Eshnunna," *Language, Literature and History: Philological and Historical Studies Presented to Erica Reiner* (ed. F. Rochberg-Halton; AOS 67; New Haven: American Oriental Society, 1987) 71–84; Reuven Yaron, "'Enquire Now about Hammurabi, Ruler of Babylon,'" *Legal History Review* 49 (1991) 223–38; and Eckart Otto, "Aspects of Legal Reform and Reformulation in Ancient Cuneiform and Israelite Law," in *Theory and Method in Biblical and Cuneiform Law: Revision, Interpolation, and Development* (ed. Bernard M. Levinson; JSOTSup 181; Sheffield: Sheffield Academic Press, 1994) 160–96. Denying revision but maintaining that the individual legal collections were part of a coherent literary and scholastic curriculum is Raymond Westbrook, *Studies in Biblical and Cuneiform Law* (CahRB 26; Paris: J. Gabalda, 1988) 1–8; and Westbrook, "What Is the Covenant Code?," in *Theory and Method in Biblical and Cuneiform Law: Revision, Interpolation, and Development* (ed. Bernard M. Levinson; JSOTSup 181; Sheffield: Sheffield Academic Press, 1994) 20–32.

in terms of literary dependence, while divergences can be explained in terms of terminological or legal updating. The attempts to make Deuteronomy precede the Covenant Code or the Yahwistic source do not come to grips with legal history; they overlook the evidence of historical linguistics; and they arbitrarily exclude other Pentateuchal sources from the analysis.[12]

Some scholars have proposed a "two source" theory for the composition of Deuteronomy. They hold that, in addition to the Covenant Code, an ancient "Privilege Law" source, which is identified with Exod 34:10–26, exists. These scholars have a specific view of the compositional and redactional history of the legal corpus, according to which a core of texts in Deut 12:1–16:17 represented the original Josianic Deuteronomy. The literary influence of the Privilege Law is restricted to this allegedly original section, although it operates in conjunction with the Covenant Code.[13] According to this "block model," the Josianic legal corpus was exilically expanded with "the Laws of Public Officials" (Deut 16:18–18:22), and, still later, with the final section (chs. 19–25).[14] Despite this model, I have chosen in this book to focus upon the role of the Covenant Code in the composition of Deuteronomy's legal corpus. I do not see the justification for claiming that the Privilege Law functions as an additional source. On the one hand, proponents of the block model concede that any point of literary contact between the legal corpus of Deuteronomy and Exod 34:10–26 has a corresponding parallel in the Covenant Code.[15] On the other hand, these proponents also concede that the constitutive law-giving of Deuteronomy, requiring centralization of the cult (Deut 12:4–28), finds its exclusive literary source in the altar law of the Covenant Code (Exod 20:24) and is without a parallel in Exodus 34.[16] Under these circumstances, it seems most reasonable to invoke Ockham's razor and to regard the Privilege Law as superfluous.

---

12. Refuting Kaufmann's claim of no literary contact between the pentateuchal legal sources, see Sara Japhet, "The Relationship between the Legal Corpora in the Pentateuch in Light of Manumission Laws," *Studies in Bible, 1986* (ScrHier 31; Jerusalem: Magnes, 1986) 69–70. Further disputing Kaufmann's position and those of Merendino and Van Seters, see Bernard M. Levinson, *The Hermeneutics of Innovation: The Impact of Centralization upon the Structure, Sequence, and Reformulation of Legal Material in Deuteronomy* (Ann Arbor, Mich.: University Microfilms, 1991) 88–114. Refuting Chamberlain's arguments, see Eckart Otto, *Wandel der Rechtsbegründungen in der Gesellschaftsgeschichte des antiken Israel: Eine Rechtsgeschichte des "Bundesbuches" Ex XX 22–XXIII 13* (StudBib 3; Leiden: E. J. Brill, 1988) 8.

13. That approach is maintained by Norbert Lohfink, "Deuteronomy," *IDBSup* (Nashville: Abingdon, 1976) 230; Lohfink, "Zur deuteronomischen Zentralisationsformel," *Bib* 65 (1984) 297–328, reprinted in Lohfink, *Studien zum Deuteronomium und zur deuteronomistischen Literatur II* (SBAB 12; Stuttgart: Katholisches Bibelwerk, 1991) 147–77, esp. 172–77; and Georg Braulik, *Die deuteronomischen Gesetze und der Dekalog: Studien zum Aufbau von Deuteronomium 12–26* (SBS 145; Stuttgart: Katholisches Bibelwerk, 1991) 116.

14. For a critique of this model of the redactional history of the legal corpus see Eckart Otto, "Von der Gerichtsordnung zum Verfassungsentwurf: Deuteronomische Gestaltung und deuteronomistische Interpretation im 'Ämtergesetz' Dtn 16,18–18,22," in *"Wer ist wie du, HERR, unter den Göttern?" Studien zur Theologie und Religionsgeschichte Israels für Otto Kaiser* (ed. Ingo Kottsieper et al.; Göttingen: Vandenhoeck & Ruprecht, 1995) 142–55, esp. 152.

15. See the table in Lohfink, "Zentralisationsformel," 174.

16. Lohfink, "Zentralisationsformel," 174–75.

That "double source" theory was originally invoked on the basis of older assumptions regarding the date of Exod 34:10–26, which was regarded as ancient. Since the block model was originally proposed, however, an important reorientation has taken place. An increasing number of scholars, from a variety of schools, now view that unit as a late redactional composition that presupposes Deuteronomy and that revises the Covenant Code in light of it.[17] According to this approach, the alleged Privilege Law source for Deuteronomy more properly belongs to the history of reception of Deuteronomy than to its literary prehistory. My approach poses a further challenge to the block model. In chapter 4, I show how recourse to the Covenant Code, with its laws concerning judicial oaths at the local sanctuaries, makes it inevitable that the authors of Deuteronomy will have to transform the conventional procedures for administering justice, because they abolish those sanctuaries. In contrast, for proponents of the block model, who claim Exod 34:10–26 as a source but in which there are no comparable laws, the topical shift in the legal corpus from matters of cult to matters of justice cannot be explained.

A basic core of texts in the legal corpus of Deuteronomy is associated with Josiah's centralization and purification of the cultus in 622 B.C.E., as narrated in 2 Kings 22–23. Josiah's unusual actions of restricting sacrifice to a single, exclusive sanctuary and abolishing even Yahwistic local shrines are inexplicable except with reference to Deuteronomy. Other of his actions also correspond closely to the provisions of Deuteronomy.[18] This link between the legal corpus and Josiah's reform again represents the scholarly consensus.[19] That consensus has been challenged on two counts, neither of which is finally persuasive. First, the use of 2 Kings 22–23 as a historical source has been called into question.[20] This questioning is understandable, inasmuch as the Deuteronomistic Historian does not merely narrate Josiah's reform but actively pro-

---

17. For a more detailed discussion of the older and the more recent approaches to Exod 34:10–26, with bibliography, see chapter 3.

18. For an excellent examination of the correspondences between Josiah's actions and the requirements of Deuteronomy see L. B. Paton, "The Case for the Post-Exilic Origins of Deuteronomy," *JBL* 47 [=*The Problem of Deuteronomy: A Symposium*] (1928) 322–57, esp. 325–26. Paton's article in fact refutes the postexilic date.

19. See Horst Dietrich Preuß, *Deuteronomium* (ErFor 164; Darmstadt: Wissenschaftliche Buchgesellschaft, 1982) 1–12. The preponderance of correspondences should not detract attention from points of noncorrespondence. Note the cautions properly raised by Gary N. Knoppers, *Two Nations under God: The Deuteronomistic History of Solomon and the Dual Monarchies* (2 vols.; HSM 52–53; Atlanta: Scholars Press, 1993–94) 2.179 n. 11 (with literature).

20. For the most thorough assessment of this literature, see Norbert Lohfink, "Zur neueren Diskussion über 2 Kön 22–23," in *Das Deuteronomium: Entstehung, Gestalt und Botschaft* (ed. Norbert Lohfink; BETL 68; Louvain: University Press, 1985) 24–48; translated, "Recent Discussion on 2 Kings 22–23: The State of the Question," in *A Song of Power and the Power of Song: Essays on the Book of Deuteronomy* (ed. Duane L. Christensen; Winona Lake, Ind.: Eisenbrauns, 1993) 36–61. See also Lohfink, "Cult Reform of Josiah," 459–75. For material published subsequent to Lohfink's two articles, see Steven L. McKenzie, "The Books of Kings in the Deuteronomistic History," in *The History of Israel's Traditions: The Heritage of Martin Noth* (ed. Steven L. McKenzie and M. Patrick Graham; JSOTSup 182; Sheffield: Sheffield Academic Press, 1994) 293–95.

motes and legitimates it. Indeed, it is the Deuteronomist, not any of his possible earlier annalistic sources, who first explicitly connects the accounts of the discovery of the Torah scroll in the Jerusalem temple, the national covenant ratification, and the centralization of the cult.[21] Some scholars contend that this material has no preexilic anchor whatsoever but instead represents an idealized exilic or postexilic depiction of how a righteous king ought to—and never historically did—behave.[22] But this approach does little to explain a series of problems associated with the story. Throughout the Deuteronomistic History, the editor evaluates kings according to their conformity to a standard of legal righteousness. For that same editor suddenly to confess that the lawbook that served as the basis for his evaluations was in fact completely unknown and only belatedly discovered, and then only by chance, threatens to jeopardize the credibility of the entire enterprise.[23] The later one shifts the composition of the story, the more difficult it becomes to explain it.[24] The anomaly is best explained under the premise that the narrative core of 2 Kings 22–23 is the work of a preexilic editor who sought to legitimate the introduction of a new set of laws and to sanction Josiah's cultic and political initiatives. That narrative was most likely supplemented in the exilic and postexilic periods.

Second, the nexus between Deuteronomy and Josiah's reform has been called into question by the recent claim that the Covenant Code, not Deuteronomy, precipitated Josiah's reform, with Deuteronomy the fallout of that reform rather than its impetus.[25] That argument is highly problematic. The Covenant Code could not logically have provided the legislative basis for both Josiah's centralization of the cult and his observance of a centralized Passover (2 Kgs 23:21–23): the Covenant Code refers neither to centralization of the cultus nor to the Passover, let alone to a centralized Passover! There have been other attempts as well to break the nexus between Deuteronomy and centralization or between the legal corpus and Josiah's reform. These attempts, which in defiance of the evidence date Deuteronomy to the early monarchy or even to the pre-Settlement period, are unconvincing.[26]

---

21. As noted by Lohfink, "2 Kön 22–23," 46.

22. For two recent examples among the many possible, see Hans-Detlef Hoffmann, *Reform und Reformen: Untersuchungen zu einem Grundthema der deuteronomistischen Geschichtsschreibung* (ATANT 66; Zürich: Theologischer Verlag, 1980); and Philip R. Davies, *In Search of "Ancient Israel"* (JSOTSup 148; Sheffield: JSOT Press, 1992) 40–41.

23. See the compelling arguments made by Paton, "Origins of Deuteronomy," 337–38.

24. See Knoppers, *Two Nations under God*, 2.137–38.

25. Reuter, *Kultzentralisation*, 255–58. The nearly identical position was earlier proposed by C. P. W. Gramberg, *Kritische Geschichte der Religionsideen des Alten Testaments* (2 vols.; Berlin: Duncker und Humblot, 1829–30) 1.306.

26. For a detailed critique of one such attempt to make the legal corpus the product of a single author just prior to the Conquest, see Bernard M. Levinson, "McConville's *Law and Theology in Deuteronomy*," *JQR* 80 (1990) 396–404. McConville regularly harmonizes laws that are actually inconsistent. He does not engage the arguments in favor of a neo-Assyrian setting for the treaty material in Deuteronomy, which would controvert the second millennium context he favors. Similarly problematic is the claim by Chaim Rabin that Deuteronomy belongs to the period of Elijah ("Discourse Analysis and the Dating of Deuteronomy," *Interpreting the Hebrew*

The Question of Deuteronomistic Revision
of the Covenant Code

Recent German scholarship has mounted some fundamental challenges to any simple notion of the priority of the Covenant Code to Deuteronomy. To begin with, the Covenant Code itself is viewed as having a complex redactional history. Its text is widely held to contain various secondary ethical, hortatory, and theological expansions that presuppose Deuteronomy and that align the Covenant Code, in whole or in part, with Deuteronomic thought. By these lights, Deuteronomy is no longer simply dependent upon and subsequent to the Covenant Code. The direction of literary influence becomes in effect reciprocal, as Deuteronomy also exerts, it is argued, an influence upon the language, values, and theology of the Covenant Code.[27] The most current reconstructions of the redactional history of the Covenant Code suggest, at minimum, a four stage process: (1) the compilation of the Covenant Code either from originally independent subcollections of laws of various origins (family, local courts, cult) or from separate continuous strata; (2) pre-Deuteronomic revision of the Covenant Code by way of reformulation, supplementation, and redrafting; (3) a Deuteronomistic redaction of the Covenant Code that brings it into conformity with the theology and social concerns of Deuteronomy and that is responsible for embedding it into the larger Sinai narrative (Exodus 19–24); and (4) a final priestly redaction.

Bible: Essays in Honour of E. I. J. Rosenthal [ed. J. A. Emerton and S. C. Reif; Cambridge: Cambridge University Press, 1982] 171–178). That argument overlooks the illogic of dating Deuteronomy to the ninth century, when Elijah's sacrifice on Mount Carmel blatantly contradicts Deuteronomy's demand for cult centralization. Although I disagree with Rabin's method for dating Deuteronomy, I am also not convinced by Steven L. McKenzie's recent proposal that the Elijah material in 1 Kings 17–19 represents a late, post-Deuteronomistic "prophetic supplement" to the Deuteronomistic History (*The Trouble with Kings: The Composition of the Book of Kings in the Deuteronomistic History* [VTSup 42; Leiden: E. J. Brill, 1991] 81–88, 148–49). While valuably demonstrating the redactional seams that permitted this material to be incorporated into the Deuteronomistic History, McKenzie's argument that the material must therefore be extrinsic and, thus, a late exilic or postexilic addition is not a necessary conclusion, particularly when the cultural context and the rationale for the supplement remain unclarified. Since the Deuteronomistic History is nothing if not a redactional tour de force, those textual seams might more simply be construed as pointing to the compositional techniques of an editor integrating various literary sources into a comprehensive narrative.

27. For a succinct history of the entire issue of Deuteronomistic revision of the Covenant Code see Otto, *Rechtsgeschichte des "Bundesbuches"*, 4–8, with his own conclusions at 57–60, who sees the origin of the Covenant Code in the compilation of originally independent subcollections. Arguing for separate proto-Deuteronomic, Deuteronomistic, and priestly redactions is Ludger Schwienhorst-Schönberger, *Das Bundesbuch (Ex 20,22–23,33): Studien zu seiner Entstehung und Theologie* (BZAW 188; Berlin: Walter de Gruyter, 1990) 284–417. Claiming, however, that the Covenant Code reached its final form pre-Deuteronomistically is Yuichi Osumi, *Die Kompositionsgeschichte des Bundesbuches Exodus 20,22b–23,33* (OBO 105; Freiburg, Switzerland: Universitätsverlag; Göttingen: Vandenhoeck & Ruprecht, 1991). For the most recent analysis of the issues, see Eckart Otto, "Zur Kompositionsgeschichte des alttestamentlichen 'Bundesbuches' (Ex 20,22–23,33)," a review article of *Die Kompositionsgeschichte des Bundesbuches Exodus 20,22b–23,33* by Yuichi Osumi, in WZKM 83 (1993) 149–65.

However, a number of scholars reject the claim of substantial Deuteronomistic revision of the Covenant Code. Of course, most scholars concede the existence of secondary material within the Covenant Code and the validity of diachronic analysis for discerning editorial activity.[28] That is not the issue. The crux is whether these expansions presuppose the specific language, legislation, and theology of Deuteronomy. Detailed analysis shows that the expansions do not presuppose Deuteronomy as a text, even if they begin to express related concerns, such as the social justice owed the alien, the widow, and the orphan. Since they are not textually dependent upon Deuteronomy but move in the direction of its concerns, the additions are most logically viewed as pre-Deuteronomic.[29] The further inconsistency of these expansions with Deuteronomistic language reinforces the judgment that they should be dated prior to Deuteronomy.[30] Similar arguments have been made about homiletic expansions within the older JE narratives concerning the observance of Passover and Unleavened Bread in Exodus 12–13. These expansions, too, have been classified as "proto-Deuteronomic."[31] Finally, in a crucial study that for the first time directly asks, "Did there exist a Deuteronomistic movement?," Norbert Lohfink challenges the very presupposition that underlies the tendency of many continental scholars to see extensive Deuteronomistic editorial activity throughout the entire Hebrew Bible, of which the particular arguments concerning the Cov-

28. In contrast, denying the validity of diachronic analysis altogether are Westbrook, "What Is the Covenant Code?," 15–36; and Joseph M. Sprinkle, *The "Book of the Covenant": A Literary Approach* (JSOTSup 174; Sheffield: JSOT Press, 1994). Arguing that diachronic analysis better explains the evidence are Bernard M. Levinson, "The Case for Revision and Interpolation within the Biblical Legal Corpora," Samuel Greengus, "Some Issues Relating to the Comparability of Laws and the Coherence of the Legal Tradition," Sophie Lafont, "Ancient Near Eastern Laws: Continuity and Pluralism," and Eckart Otto, "Legal Reform and Reformulation in Ancient Cuneiform and Israelite Law," all in Levinson (ed.), *Theory and Method in Biblical and Cuneiform Law*, 37–59, 60–87, 91–118, 160–96.

29. Walter Beyerlin, "Die Paränese im Bundesbuch und ihre Herkunft," in *Gottes Wort und Gottes Land: Hans-Wilhelm Hertzberg zum 70. Geburtstag* (ed. Henning Graf Reventlow; Göttingen: Vandenhoeck & Ruprecht, 1965) 9–29; Chr. Brekelmans, "Die sogennanten deuteronomischen Elemente in Gen.-Num.: Ein Beitrag zur Vorgeschichte des Deuteronomiums," *Volume du Congrès: Genève 1965* (VTSup 15; Leiden: E. J. Brill, 1966) 90–96; and, providing a systematic case using the social justice laws of the Covenant Code, Norbert Lohfink, "Gibt es eine deuteronomistische Bearbeitung im Bundesbuch?," *Pentateuchal and Deuteronomistic Studies: Papers Read at the XIIIth IOSOT Congress Leuven 1989* (ed. C. Brekelmans and J. Lust; BETL 94; Louvain: Peeters Press / University Press, 1990) 91–113. Lohfink's article provides the basis for the issues stressed here. Note, however, the challenge to this approach by Schwienhorst-Schönberger, *Das Bundesbuch*, 331–57.

30. Lohfink, "Bundesbuch," 91–113.

31. See Norbert Lohfink, *Das Hauptgebot: Eine Untersuchung literarischer Einleitungsfragen zu Dtn 5–11* (AnBib 20; Rome: Pontifical Biblical Institute, 1963) 121–22, on Exod 12:24–27a; and M. Caloz, "Exode, XIII, 3–16 et son rapport au Deutéronome," *RB* 75 (1968) 5–62. Challenging these arguments, however, and viewing both texts as presupposing Deuteronomy is Erhard Blum, *Studien zur Komposition des Pentateuch* (BZAW 189; Berlin: Walter de Gruyter, 1990) 166–69.

enant Code are just one expression.[32] The arguments on both sides are vital to our ongoing efforts to understand the complex relation of Deuteronomy to the Covenant Code.

A related problem is the complex literary and redactional history of Deuteronomy itself. It is likely, for example, that a complex chapter such as Deuteronomy 12 had a lengthy compositional history, including proto-Deuteronomic, Deuteronomic, and possibly several Deuteronomistic elements.[33] It is entirely possible, therefore, that the present form of Deuteronomy manifests several stages of interaction with the Exodus source text. Indeed, the successive reworkings of Deuteronomy may have proceeded in tandem with the redaction and reworking of the Exodus material. Moreover, I shall argue that later strata within Deuteronomy revise and transform earlier ones within Deuteronomy itself (chapter 4). My own focus, however, will be more on demonstrating the existence and the nature of the textual transformation in each case and less on assigning each a particular superscripted number denoting the hypothetical stratum to which it belongs. Too often such detailed reconstructions of the redactional history of the legal corpus become self-generating. They multiply strata on the basis of problematic criteria of originality (like rhythmically consistent original oral units), are uncontrolled by reference to the redactional techniques of cuneiform law, and do not really clarify either the meaning of the text or the motivations of its authors.[34]

Authoritative Texts and the Problem of Legal Innovation

Recent, particularly English language, scholarship concerned with the significance of texts in ancient Israel has gone in two directions: "canonical criticism"

32. Norbert Lohfink, "Gab es eine deuteronomistische Bewegung?" in *Jeremia und die "deuteronomistische Bewegung"* (ed. Walter Groß; BBB 98; Weinheim: BELTZ Athenäum, 1995) 313–82.

33. For the most recent analysis, see Reuter, *Kultzentralisation*, 42–114. Although the authors, as I argue, drew upon pre-Deuteronomic material, it is nonetheless unlikely that there was ever a pre-Deuteronomic redaction of the legal corpus. In other words, there was no Deuteronomy without cult centralization; see Reuter, *Kultzentralisation*, 189–91.

34. See most recently Fabrizio Foresti, "Storia della Redazione di Dtn. 16,18–18,22 e le sue Connessioni con l'Opera Storica Deuteronomistica," *Teresianum Ephemerides Carmeliticae* 39 (1988) 5–199; and Günter Krinetzki, *Rechtsprechung und Amt im Deuteronomium: Zur Exegese der Gesetze Dtn 16,18–20; 17,8–18,22* (Frankfurt: Peter Lang, 1994). Foresti assumes that the legal corpus of Deuteronomy derives from originally metrically consistent oral pronouncements and reconstructs eight redactional layers (pp. 181–89). His astoundingly meticulous reconstruction never once refers to the compositional norms of cuneiform literature. As such, the analysis operates in a vacuum that substantiates the author's ungrounded prior assumption that "ancient" or "original" requires syntactical simplicity and metrical consistency. Similar difficulties apply to Krinetzki's posthumous monograph. The author never articulates the criteria for his reconstruction of "original" laws, which are completely unviable both legally and syntactically (see his p. 170). By not including cuneiform literature in their purview, these works fail to recognize the degree of legal, syntactic, and redactional sophistication possessed by ancient scribes.

and "inner biblical exegesis." Canonical criticism assumes that the canon was a source of cultural identity that could be mined during times of spiritual crisis. Canonical criticism takes for granted the ability of the text to be updated in new circumstances: older narratives constitute a plenum of spiritual meaning upon which, in times of national crisis, the writers can call for spiritual renewal. This assumption of the infinite mutability of the textual patrimony in times of existential need overlooks, however, the technical and studied nature of textual reuse in Israel and the ancient Near East. It places a nearly exclusive emphasis on narrative reuse, for the sake of alleged spiritual succor, but it does not address the key role played by the deliberate reinterpretation of legal texts or the concern with matters of public polity involved in that reuse.[35] Finally, it also does not take into account the literary phenomenon of rewriting, as in the Chronicler's recourse to the Deuteronomistic History or the Deuteronomic authors' recourse to the Covenant Code, in each case to mandate an entirely new religious and social program not contemplated by the preceding literary source.

In contrast, inner biblical exegesis recognizes that the canon was not inherently flexible; rather it was, at least in intention, inflexible.[36] The canon was not simply a textual mine for subsequent creative borrowing but a problem that had to be overcome hermeneutically. The very maxim to enforce the stability of texts as timeless and unchanging—לא תספו על הדבר אשר אנכי מצוה אתכם ולא תגרעו ממנו "You must neither add to the word which I command you nor diminish from it" (Deut 4:2a; cf. 13:1)[37]—necessitated subsequent exegetical adaptation in order to accommodate older texts to newer social, economic, historical, or religious realities.[38] Of course, it is anachronistic to speak of a "canon," in the conventional sense, in ancient Israel. As technically denoting a fixed number of authoritative texts to which religious adherence is owed because of their particular status, "canon" is clearly a postbiblical concept.[39]

---

35. For a fuller presentation of my critique, see Levinson, *Hermeneutics of Innovation*, 162–68. More broadly on the impact of canonical criticism upon biblical studies, see Mark G. Brett, *Biblical Criticism in Crisis? The Impact of the Canonical Approach on Old Testament Studies* (Cambridge: Cambridge University Press, 1991), whose focus is the work of Brevard S. Childs; and Christoph Dohmen and Manfred Oeming, *Biblischer Kanon: Warum und Wozu? Eine Kanontheologie* (QD 137; Freiburg: Herder, 1992) 11–26.

36. For the most comprehensive presentation of the various types of interpretation within the Hebrew Bible, see Michael Fishbane, *Biblical Interpretation in Ancient Israel* (Oxford: Clarendon, 1985). See also James L. Kugel, "Early Interpretation: The Common Background of Late Forms of Biblical Exegesis," in *Early Biblical Interpretation* (ed. James L. Kugel and Rowan A. Greer; Philadelphia: Westminster, 1986) 9–106.

37. In English and other translations, Deut 13:1 appears as 12:32. For a fuller discussion of the hermeneutical function of Deut 13:1 and for bibliography on the canon formula, please see "Reflections upon Textuality and Exegesis in Deuteronomy 12," in chapter 2.

38. Nahum M. Sarna, "Psalm 89: A Study in Inner Biblical Exegesis," *Biblical and Other Studies* (ed. A. Altmann; Brandeis University Studies and Texts 1; Cambridge, Mass.: Harvard University Press, 1963) 34. On the dialectic in the history of religions between textual closure and exegetical transformation, see Levinson, "Human Voice in Divine Revelation," 35–39.

39. On the whole issue, see Brevard S. Childs, *Introduction to the Old Testament as Scripture* (Philadelphia: Fortress, 1979) 46–68; and James Barr, *Holy Scripture: Canon, Authority, Criticism* (Philadelphia: Westminster, 1983) 1–23.

Nonetheless, in a different sense, there did exist in the ancient Near East both concepts of a stream of learned tradition, presumably as part of the scribal curriculum, and of standardization and stabilization of the formal aspects of the text.[40] The highly formalized genre of the cuneiform legal collection was one important component of this larger scribal curriculum.[41] In the case of ancient Israel, the concepts of textual stability, prestige, and authority necessitated subsequent adaptation, interpolation, reinterpretation, and transformation.

In the end, however, inner biblical exegesis does not provide a satisfactory model to describe the achievements of the authors of Deuteronomy. The concern of the authors of Deuteronomy was not to explicate older texts but to transform them. Neither "interpretation" nor "exegesis" adequately suggests the extent to which Deuteronomy radically transforms literary and legal history in order to forge a new vision of religion and the state. Here arises the second point. If the very notion of exegesis implies the continuity of the revising text with its source, I wish to underscore the opposite: the extent to which exegesis may make itself independent of the source text, challenging and even attempting to reverse or abrogate its substantive content, all the while under the hermeneutical mantle of consistency with or dependency upon its source.[42] Exegesis is thus often radically transformative: new religious, intellectual, or cultural insights are granted sanction and legitimacy by being presented as if they derived from authoritative texts that neither contain nor anticipate those insights.[43]

40. See Francesca Rochberg-Halton, "Canonicity in Cuneiform Texts," *JCS* 36 (1984) 127–44; and Stephen J. Lieberman, "Canonical and Official Cuneiform Texts: Towards an Understanding of Assurbanipal's Personal Tablet Collection," in *Lingering over Words: Studies in Ancient Near Eastern Literature in Honor of William J. Moran* (ed. Tzvi Abusch, John Huehnergard, and Piotr Steinkeller; HSM 37; Atlanta: Scholars Press, 1990) 305–36.

41. See Raymond Westbrook, *Studies in Biblical and Cuneiform Law* (CahRB 26; Paris: J. Gabalda, 1988) 2–5; and Martha T. Roth, *Law Collections from Mesopotamia and Asia Minor* (SBLWAW 6; Atlanta: Scholars Press, 1995) 2–4.

42. See also Herbert Marks, review of *Biblical Interpretation in Ancient Israel* by Michael Fishbane, in *Yearbook of Comparative and General Literature* 35 (1986) 152–55. In fairness, Fishbane himself stresses the radical gaps between the source text and its reinterpretation at specific points; see his *Biblical Interpretation*, 263–64, 343. The overall focus of his book, however, is to emphasize continuity over discontinuity. He generally frames inner-biblical exegesis as the pious and conscientious explication of possibilities of meaning that are consistent with and latent within the source text (276–77, 537). For the same basic orientation, see Fishbane, *The Garments of Torah: Essays in Biblical Hermeneutics* (Bloomington: Indiana University Press, 1989) 17–18.

43. Postbiblical rabbinic interpretation provides a striking example of how exegesis can controvert and replace the original meaning of the source text on which it nominally depends. Within biblical law, *talion* ("measure for measure") is invoked for crimes against the person, whether bodily injury (Exod 21:23–25; Lev 24:17, 19–21) or perjury (Deut 19:19–21). In contrast, *financial compensation* is levied in the case of property damage or theft (Exod 21:36, 37; 22:3, 4, 5, 6, 11, 13). The two systems of punishment are mutually exclusive and explicitly contrasted (Lev 24:17–21). Rabbinic exegesis confutes the plain meaning of the scriptural text and rules that "an eye for an eye" means rather "[*the financial compensation for*] an eye for an eye." (See *Mekilta Exodus 21:23–24* in the edition of Jacob Z. Lauterbach, *Mekilta de-Rabbi Ishmael* [3 vols.; Philadelphia: JPS, 1935] 3.67. For very clear analyses of this reversal, see Elliot

Deuteronomy establishes that derivation itself can function as a trope, which is to say, as a ploy. Any comparison of the length, compass, and agenda of each work suggests that it is reductive to regard Deuteronomy as derived from the Covenant Code. That would be comparable to claiming that *Hamlet*, which makes agency and inwardness central to tragedy, derives from classical Greek tragedy or from Aristotle's *Poetics*, with their stress on fate as determining human action. In both cases, the later text not only goes far beyond the range of imaginative possibilities offered by the ostensible exemplar but also constructs a completely new structure of human existence. Thus, exegesis, at least as conventionally understood, does not represent an adequate way to conceptualize the literary reuse involved in Deuteronomy's recourse to the Covenant Code. While the authors of the legal corpus appropriate key lemmas from the earlier text, their concern is neither with exegesis, even through the lens of cult centralization, nor with the Covenant Code in itself.[44] Instead, their concern was to implement their own agenda: to effect a major transformation of all spheres of Judaean life—cultically, politically, theologically, judicially, ethically, and economically. The authors of Deuteronomy had a radically new vision of the religious and public polity and sought to implement unprecedented changes in religion and society. Precisely for that reason, the guise of continuity with the past became crucial. The authors of Deuteronomy sought to locate their innovative vision in prior textual authority by tendentiously appropriating texts like the Covenant Code, while freely going beyond them in programmatic and substantive terms to address matters like public administration, the role of the monarchy, and the laws of warfare.

Deuteronomy's reuse of its textual patrimony was creative, active, revisionist, and tendentious. It functioned as a means for cultural transformation. Comparable is the work of the Chronicler during the Judaean restoration. The Chronicler programmatically rewrote the Deuteronomistic History and presented the distinctive religious and political innovations of the Persian period, such as the idea of the citizen-Temple state, as if they represented the familiar

---

N. Dorff and Arthur Rosett, *A Living Tree: The Roots and Growth of Jewish Law* [Albany: State University of New York Press, 1988] 145–84; and Jacob Milgrom, "Lex Talionis and the Rabbis," *Bible Review* 12:2 [April 1996] 16, 48.) Indeed, the Rabbis were aware of their occasionally abrogating biblical law. Rabbi Yoḥanan ben Zakkai, the first president of the Sanhedrin after it moved to Yavneh (Jamniah) following the destruction of the Temple (70 c.e.), had already "enumerated instances where the *halachah* crushes the Scriptural text under heel and overthrows it" (*B. Soṭa* 16a; translated, *The Babylonian Talmud*, vol. 20, *Seder Nashim, Soṭah* [ed. I. Epstein; London: Soncino, 1936] 84. Milgrom, "Lex Talionis," 16, also adduces this citation.) For a stimulating presentation of the creativity of Second Temple rabbinic exegesis, see Simon Rawidowicz, "On Interpretation," *PAAJR* 26 (1957) 83–126, esp. 83–101; reprinted with abridged notes in Rawidowicz, *Studies in Jewish Thought* (Philadelphia: JPS, 1974) 45–80.

44. Contra Eckart Otto, who maintains that Deuteronomy represents critical exegesis of the Covenant Code in light of centralization ("Vom Bundesbuch zum Deuteronomium: Die deuteronomische Redaktion in Dtn 12–26," in *Biblische Theologie und gesellschaftlicher Wandel: für Norbert Lohfink* [ed. Georg Braulik, Walter Groß, and Sean McEvenue; Freiburg: Herder, 1993] 260–78).

norms of the preexilic Judaean monarchy.[45] In its hermeneutics of innovation, Deuteronomy is more radical than most contemporary hermeneutical theory. Deuteronomy breaks down any facile bifurcation between text and interpretation or between text composition and text reception.[46] Many recent works of literary and philosophical hermeneutics, detached from the philological method, fail to recognize the intellectual, authorial, redactional, and radically transformative nature of ancient Israelite textuality.

Editorial Devices as Cues to Textual Reformulation

That ancient Israel inherits a broad selection of literary genres and *topoi* from the Near East—the legal collection, narratives, historiographies, cultic instructions, genealogies, proverbial wisdom, theodicies, poetry—is widely recognized. Concomitant with the transmission of textual genre and topical content, both formal matters and specific redactional techniques were also inherited by Israelite scribes from their counterparts trained in cuneiform literature. In the case of the legal collections, for example, the casuistic "if . . . then" form represents one such literary feature transmitted from southern Mesopotamia through Assyria to the Hittite Empire and ancient Israel.[47] Most important for my purposes, specific techniques for collating, structuring, and annotating law were

45. For the Persian model involved, see Joel P. Weinberg, *The Citizen-Temple Community* (JSOTSup 151; Sheffield: Sheffield Academic Press, 1994). In stating that the Chronicler rewrote the Deuteronomistic History, I do not intend to gainsay the possibility that the Chronicler worked with a different and perhaps more expansive version of it than is now found in the Masoretic text (see Werner K. Lemke, "The Synoptic Problem in the Chronicler's History," *HTR* 58 [1965] 349–63) or with a no longer extant first edition of it (see Steven L. McKenzie, *The Chronicler's Use of the Deuteronomistic History* [HSM 33; Atlanta: Scholars Press, 1985] 119–58). For a concise assessment of these and other possibilities, with relevant literature, see Marc Zvi Brettler, *The Creation of History in Ancient Israel* (London: Routledge, 1995) 164–65. Despite allowing for the possibility of versional differences, my own position is that most of the Chronicler's variations from the Deuteronomistic History result from deliberate reworking.

46. R. E. Palmer develops a notion of hermeneutics as recapturing a lost oral originality (*Hermeneutics: Interpretation Theory in Schleiermacher, Dilthey, Heidegger, and Gadamer* [Northwestern University Studies in Phenomenology and Existential Philosophy; Evanston: Northwestern University Press, 1969] 13–32). He thereby fails to recognize that the (revelatory) text may actually be an original literary and intellectual composition that presupposes sophisticated hermeneutical strategems. In his reflections on Luke 24:25–27 (pp. 23–24), for example, he takes at face value the account that Jesus "interpreted" the Hebrew Bible. He fails thereby to note the extent to which that very claim was itself an interpretive construction, polemically geared to justify the early Church's Christological reading and to disenfranchise competing Jewish and sectarian interpretation. More recently, Werner G. Jeanrond still views both interpretation and reception as theological categories separate from and subsequent to the composition of the text (*Text and Interpretation as Categories of Theological Thinking* [New York: Crossroad, 1988]). In contrast, note the engaging model of hermeneutics provided by Brayton Polka, *Truth and Interpretation: An Essay in Thinking* (New York: St. Martin's, 1990).

47. R. A. F. Mackenzie, "The Formal Aspect of Ancient Near Eastern Law," in *The Seed of Wisdom* (Toronto: University of Toronto Press, 1964) 31–44; and S. Segert, "Genres of Ancient Israelite Legal Sentences: 1934 and 1974," *WZKM* 68 (1976) 131–42, together with his additional bibliography on p. 139, nn. 25, 26.

also a crucial part of the cuneiform patrimony of Israelite scribes. Likely a component of the curriculum of the scribal schools, such redactional devices include superscriptions and colophons, particular sequencing of textual material, and deictic markers for glosses.[48]

Deuteronomy is a learned text, a literary composition that is the product of skilled scribes. It is a text whose authors draw upon other texts, Israelite and cuneiform, to revise them for their own ends. The significance of this fact goes beyond the historical question of the text's origins among the scribes of Hezekiah's or Josiah's court.[49] It is also necessary to address the impact of those scribal origins upon the composition and the structure of the text. Because of this scribal background, literary reworking in Deuteronomy is frequently marked by specific scribal techniques that help identify sites of textual reformulation.

Two devices, in particular, provide evidence of editorial activity and textual reformulation: the repetitive resumption and Seidel's law. The repetitive resumption brackets a digression or interpolation by framing it with a repetition, much as a flashback in a film is often correspondingly framed, introduced by a fade-out and concluded with a fade-in.[50] In the case of the repetitive resumption, one or two clauses from the material preceding the interruption are repeated after it to mark the resumption of the original text. As such, there is a sequence of original material A B C, then the contextually disruptive X, followed by the repetition, C', after which the original sequence, D E F, resumes. The repetition in question need not be verbatim. More often it is approximate and may abridge the earlier unit. In addition, the repetition may reverse the elements of the original, in conformity with Seidel's law.[51] According to this

---

48. See Stephen A. Kaufman, "The Structure of the Deuteronomic Law," *Maarav* 1/2 (1978–79) 105–58, at 116–17, 132–33, 135, 141. See also Fishbane, *Biblical Interpretation*, 27–43 and passim. Demonstrating the influence of cuneiform redactional techniques on the editing of the Covenant Code is Eckart Otto, *Körperverletzungen in den Keilschriftrechten und im Alten Testament: Studien zum Rechtstransfer im Alten Orient* (AOAT 226; Kevelaer: Butzon & Bercker; Neukirchen-Vluyn: Neukirchener Verlag, 1991) 165–87; Otto, "Town and Rural Countryside in Ancient Israelite Law: Reception and Redaction in Cuneiform and Israelite Law," *JSOT* 57 (1993) 3–22; and Otto, "Kompositionsgeschichte des Bundesbuches," 160–64.

49. For the scribal origins of Deuteronomy, Moshe Weinfeld, *Deuteronomy and the Deuteronomic School* (Oxford: Clarendon, 1972) 57–58, provides a critical breakthrough. See further Paul Dion, "Deuteronomy 13: The Suppression of Alien Religious Propaganda in Israel during the Late Monarchical Era," in *Law and Ideology in Monarchic Israel* (ed. Baruch Halpern and Deborah W. Hobson; JSOTSup 124; Sheffield: Sheffield Academic Press, 1991) 204–205, who situates the composition of Deuteronomy 13 among Josiah's entourage.

50. For a full discussion and bibliography of this device, also called the *Wiederaufnahme*, see Levinson, *Hermeneutics of Innovation*, 142–50.

51. The principle is named after its discoverer: M. Seidel, "Parallels between Isaiah and Psalms," *Sinai* 38 (1955–56) 149–72, 229–40, 272–80, 335–55, at p. 150; reprinted, Seidel, *Hiqrei Miqra* (Jerusalem: Rav Kook Institute, 1978) 1–97 (Hebrew). Seidel's claims are often imprecise or doubtful because they are insufficiently controlled by criteria for establishing the direction of dependency. More controlled uses include Shemaryahu Talmon, "The Textual Study of the Bible—A New Outlook," in *Qumran and the History of the Biblical Text* (ed. F. M. Cross and S. Talmon; Cambridge, Mass.: Harvard University Press, 1975) 362–63; and P. Beentjes,

principle, citation within the Hebrew Bible frequently reverses the elements of the source text. As such, quotation is marked chiastically, with the original text AB often cited as B'A'. Although the repetitive resumption and Seidel's law often occur independent of each other, they may also occur in conjunction.

The repetitive resumption may function as a compositional device and need not necessarily point to editorial activity or textual reworking.[52] More generally, however, both in cuneiform and Israelite literature, the device is editorial or redactional in origin. It marks literary reuse, reformulation, or interpolation. In a narrative setting, for example, a redactor might interrupt the narrative in order to insert a genealogy that establishes the lineage of major cultural figures, as in the case of Moses and Aaron in Exod 6:14–25.[53] The function of that insertion is (1) to justify Aaron, named here for the first time in the priestly narrative, as corecipient, with Moses, of God's revelation; (2) to clarify that the two men are jointly commissioned to lead the Israelites out of Egypt; and (3) to develop the Levitical genealogy.[54] There is a carefully detailed chiastic framing of the insertion, according to Seidel's law, by the verses that precede and follow it:

(12) Moses spoke to Yahweh saying, "Seeing that the Israelites
did not listen to me, *how then should Pharaoh heed me,*   A
especially *since I am halting in speech?*   B
(13) Yahweh spoke to *Moses and Aaron,* commanding them   C
regarding the Israelites and regarding Pharaoh, king of Egypt,
to lead the Israelites out of the land of Egypt.   D
(14–25: the genealogy)   X
(27) They were the ones who spoke to Pharoah, King of
Egypt, *to lead the Israelites out of the land of Egypt,*   D'
it was *Moses and Aaron.*   C'
(28) When Yahweh spoke to Moses in the land of Egypt . . .
(30) Moses said before Yahweh, *since I am halting in speech,*   B'
how then should Pharoah heed me?   A'

Particularly within biblical law, the repetitive resumption marks interpolations or reformulations. For example, the inclusion of the Sabbath (Lev 23:3)

"Inverted Quotations in the Bible: A Neglected Stylistic Pattern," *Bib* 63 (1982) 506–23. Noting the value of Seidel's law in determining a repetitive resumption is Marc Z. Brettler, "Jud 1,1–2,10: From Appendix to Prologue," *ZAW* 101 (1989) 434.

52. Making this case for narrative is Shemaryahu Talmon, "The Presentation of Synchroneity and Simultaneity in Biblical Narrative," *Studies in Hebrew Narrative Art Throughout the Ages* (ed. J. Heinemann and S. Werses; ScrHier 27; Jerusalem: Magnes, 1978) 9–26; reprinted, Talmon, *Literary Studies in the Hebrew Bible: Form and Content, Collected Studies* (Jerusalem: Magnes; Leiden: E. J. Brill, 1993) 112–33.

53. Isaac Leo Seeligmann, "Hebräische Erzählung und biblische Geschichtsschreibung," *Theologische Zeitschrift* 18 (1962) 322 first identified Exod 6:14–25 as a "klassisches Beispiel der Wiederaufnahme." He did not, however, note the chiastic form of the device.

54. For a very clear analysis that also notes the repetitive resumption, see Georg Fohrer, *Überlieferung und Geschichte des Exodus* (BZAW 91; Berlin: A. Töpelman, 1964) 49. The genealogy's redaction into the narrative is more complex than it is possible to discuss here and

within the festival calendar of Leviticus 23 is disruptive both on topical and formal grounds.[55] That secondary inclusion, which aims at greater comprehensiveness, is marked by a repetitive resumption. The editor frames Lev 23:3 with v. 4, which repeats the verse before the interpolation (Lev 23:2) according to Seidel's law:

> (1) Yahweh spoke to Moses saying, (2) "Speak to the
> Israelites and say to them, The fixed times of
> Yahweh, *which you shall proclaim* to them,   A
> are *sacred occasions.*   B
> *These are* they—my *fixed times.*   C
> (3: Sabbath law)   X
> (4) *These are the fixed times* of Yahweh—   C'
> *sacred occasions,*   B'
> *which you shall proclaim* at their fixed time.   A'

The interpolation marks an inner-biblical tendency toward the programmatic incorporation of the Sabbath in the ritual calendar, even at the expense of distorting the original specificity of the calendar.

The Purpose and Scope of This Book

The aim of this book is to show, in depth, both how far-reaching the Deuteronomic transformation of Israelite religion and society was and how the authors of the legal corpus accomplished that program hermeneutically. The authors of Deuteronomy sought to implement a comprehensive program of religious, social, and political transformation that left no area of life untouched. Their new vision of the Judaean polity included matters of cultus, justice, political administration, family life, sexuality, warfare, social and economic justice, and theology. Treatment of this entire program is impossible. I focus here on three key units within the legal corpus, each of which has long represented a scholarly crux, in order to argue a specific thesis. The Deuteronomic program of innovation was completely without precedent. The authors of the legal corpus therefore also faced an essential hermeneutical task: to justify their innovations in light of prestigious texts like the Covenant Code that had a completely different religious orientation and that presupposed a much more traditional social structure. Precisely at the points of conflict between their agenda and the conventions of the Covenant Code, the authors of Deuteronomy ap-

---

deserves further study. There may have been a series of attempts to integrate it. Perhaps v. 26 represents the first such attempt; note that it partially repeats v. 13 and is itself partially reduplicated in v. 27. Note also that v. 29 partially repeats vv. 10–11.

55. For a thorough analysis of the secondary nature of the Sabbath in the context of this calendar, see Israel Knohl, "The Priestly Torah versus the Holiness School: Sabbath and Festivals," *HUCA* 58 (1987) 72–76. Identifying the use of the repetitive resumption to insert the Sabbath law here are Brettler, "Jud 1,1–2,10," 434; and Levinson, "Revision and Interpolation," 55–56. Much of the relevant material in Knohl's valuable article seems reprinted in Knohl, *The Sanctuary of Silence: The Priestly Torah and the Holiness School* (Minneapolis: Fortress, 1995) 14–16.

propriated the problematic laws in question and reworked them in order to erase the conflict and to further their own program. The authors of Deuteronomy employed the Covenant Code, in other words, not merely as a textual source but as a resource, in order to purchase the legitimacy and authority that their reform agenda otherwise lacked. The reuse of the older material lent their innovations the guise of continuity with the past and consistency with traditional law. The authors of Deuteronomy cast their departure from tradition as its reaffirmation, their transformation and abrogation of conventional religious law as the original intent of that law.

Each of the three chapters shows the profound changes in religion and society introduced by the authors of Deuteronomy and how their hermeneutical sophistication made the program of change possible. Everything begins, of course, with cultic centralization, which transformed the sacrificial worship of Yahweh. The familiar local altars and sanctuaries were proscribed, and new procedures had to be implemented in order to redirect all sacrifice to the central sanctuary. New procedures also had to be developed to allow for the slaughter of domestic animals for food. Deuteronomy's proscription of the local altars would otherwise have made such local slaughter impossible, since, prior to Deuteronomy, all slaughter of domestic animals, even if intended for food rather than worship, had to take place at an altar. These changes are the subject of chapter 2.

Deuteronomy's innovations affected the structure of time. Ancient Israel's festival calendar consisted of three observances, Unleavened Bread, Weeks, and Tabernacles, that were celebrated as pilgrimages to the local sanctuaries, where each Israelite male was obliged to appear before the deity (Exod 23:17). The local focus of these festivals had to be abrogated and transferred to the central sphere. The ancient rite of Passover had also to be transformed. In its original and pre-Deuteronomic form, Passover was a completely separate observance from Unleavened Bread. It involved the ritual slaughter of a lamb in the doorway of the private domicile and the smearing of its blood on the doorposts in order to protect the occupants within from the forces of irrational danger without. In this convention of Passover as a private slaughter that was completely detached from the cultus and that did not even involve an altar, the authors of Deuteronomy confronted a major challenge to their program of restricting all cultic slaughter to the central sanctuary. In chapter 3, I reconstruct this problem and show how the authors of Deuteronomy overcame it by radically transforming both Passover and the festival of Unleavened Bread.

The consequences of centralization extended beyond explicitly cultic matters, as I argue in chapter 4. Centralization entailed important changes in the administration of justice and in the conventional structures of social and political authority. The entire apparatus of local justice, both cultic and lay, had to be overturned. The local altars that the authors of Deuteronomy prohibit had conventionally played an essential role in matters of justice. The authors of Deuteronomy had to abrogate the judicial function of the local altars and establish alternative procedures. Local justice that was not associated with the sanctuary posed a different set of problems. Village justice was conventionally administered by the clan elders. That tie between justice and the lineage system of the clans was essential to maintaining the traditional structure of rural Judaean society. But with the social break and the urbanization that Hezekiah had begun to institute, the entire range of values associated with the clan networks came under attack.[56] Similarly with Deuteronomy: the authors sought to transform the very structures of traditional belief and organization that the clan system propagated. For that reason, the authors of Deuteronomy abolished the conventional role of the village elders in administering justice and substituted a professionalized judiciary. As a consequence of centralization, the conventional role of the monarch was also transformed and, paradoxically, drastically circumscribed. In the authors' attempt to elevate the Temple and to make it the sole place where ambiguous legal cases are resolved, they divested the king of one of his key functions in ancient Israel: as supreme judicial authority.

The accomplishments of the authors of Deuteronomy establish the essential connection of hermeneutics to the history of Israelite religion. The authors of Deuteronomy were writers extremely conscious of their place in Israelite literary history. In the way that they revised previous texts and previous norms of religion and law, the authors of Deuteronomy unintentionally provided a precedent for how their own composition would itself be revised by subsequent writers, no sooner than it had won authoritative status. These later revisions of Deuteronomy, which presented themselves rather as implementations of Deuteronomy, took place both inner-biblically and post-biblically. A literary dynamic of revisionist transformation—usurpation might not be too far off the mark—thus presents itself as an essential component of ancient Israelite religious and literary creativity. The final chapter suggests the implications of this perspective for a broader theory of authorship and innovation in ancient Israel.

56. See Baruch Halpern, "Jerusalem and the Lineages in the Seventh Century BCE: Kinship and the Rise of Individual Moral Liability," in *Law and Ideology in Monarchic Israel* (ed. Baruch Halpern and Deborah W. Hobson; JSOTSup 124; Sheffield: JSOT Press, 1991) 11–107.

2

The Innovation of Cultic Centralization in Deuteronomy 12

If modern biblical studies is a discipline concerned with the reconstruction of literary history, then few texts have more loudly called for such analysis, yet more successfully resisted it, than Deuteronomy 12. This introductory chapter of the legal corpus of Deuteronomy (chapters 12–26) mandates two radical transformations of Israelite religion. First, it prohibits all sacrifice at the local altars prevalent throughout the countryside. It requires the complete destruction of all such altars together with their cultic apparatus, even as it concedes the prevalence of such worship in the present (Deut 12:5). The chapter stipulates repeatedly that all sacrifice should instead take place exclusively at a single site, "the place that Yahweh shall choose," Deuteronomy's circumlocution for Jerusalem and its temple.[1] Second, although prohibiting in the strongest possible terms the

---

1. Some scholars have maintained that the formula originally functioned not exclusively but rather distributively and thus applied to a succession of earlier sanctuaries, such as at Shechem and Shiloh. This view is tied to the claim that the origins of Deuteronomy are to be found in the northern kingdom of Israel and that the formula was only secondarily respecified to apply to Jerusalem. The argument that the Deuteronomic centralization formula (as at Deut 12:14) has a distributive meaning goes back to attempts early in this century to make the origins of Deuteronomy ancient. Recent advocates of this approach include Alexander Rofé, "The Strata of Law about the Centralization of Worship in Deuteronomy and the History of the Deuteronomic Movement," in *Congress Volume: Uppsala 1971* (VTSup 22; Leiden: E. J. Brill, 1972) 221–26; and Baruch Halpern, "The Centralization Formula in Deuteronomy," *VT* 31 (1981) 20–38. Nonetheless, the attempt to assign a distributive meaning to the centralization formula cannot be defended philologically. For the early history of these attempts and refutations of their linguistic arguments, see Julius A. Bewer, "The Case for the Early Date of Deuteronomy," *JBL* 47 (1928) 305–21; and E. W. Nicholson, *Deuteronomy and Tradition* (Philadelphia: Fortress, 1967) 53–54. Indeed, there is compelling evidence that the election formula was, from its inception, centered on Jerusalem. When the formulae that include the key term בחר "choose" are examined, they always refer to Zion/Jerusalem or to the election of the Davidic dynasty resident there.

TABLE 2-1   The thematic structure of the centralization laws in Deuteronomy 12

Centralization Formula	Law no.	Unit	Addressee	Theme
Deut 12:5	1	12:2–7	plural	Cultic unity against Canaanite plurality of altars
Deut 12:11	2	12:8–12	plural	Condition for inauguration of centralization
Deut 12:14	3	12:13–19	singular	Requirement for centralization
Deut 12:18	"		singular	Concession for secular slaughter
Deut 12:21	4	12:20–28	singular	Condition for inauguration of secular slaughter
Deut 12:26	"		singular	Blood protocol

local sacrifice of domestic animals for purposes of worship, it grants permission for local secular slaughter of these animals for food. With that concession, and for the first time in Israelite religion, the chapter forges a distinction between the cultic sacrifice of animals at an altar and their secular slaughter, not at an altar.

Deuteronomy 12 is clearly composite and characterized by redundancy. It is conventionally divided into four originally independent laws, each concerned with cultic centralization (vv. 2–7, 8–12, 13–19, 20–28), and a concluding paragraph, concerned with cultic purity (vv. 29–31).[2] The formulaic command for the centralization of sacrifice occurs six different times, with some slight variations (Deut 12:5, 11, 14, 18, 21, 26). The concession for secular slaughter occurs twice (Deut 12:15, 21). The accompanying stipulation that the blood, in cases of secular slaughter, should not be consumed but rather "poured out upon the earth like water" also occurs twice (Deut 12:16, 23–24). The rationale for centralization is in each case different, and there is no obvious attempt to integrate the various repetitions into a coherent whole in substantive legal terms. Grammatical anomalies increase the sense that the chapter is disjointed. The second-person addressee of the laws shifts without explanation from primarily second-person plural (Deut 12:1–12) to singular (Deut 12:13–31), although neither section is entirely internally consistent. Two of the six repetitions of the centralization formula are found in the plural section, four in the singular section (table 2-1).[3] The four centralization laws, therefore, each have at least one occurrence of the centralization formula and vary according

---

On this issue, see Norbert Lohfink, "Zur deuteronomischen Zentralisationsformel," *Bib* 65 (1984) 297–328; reprinted in and cited according to Lohfink, *Studien zum Deuteronomium und zur deuteronomistischen Literatur II* (SBAB 12; Stuttgart: Katholisches Bibelwerk, 1991) 144–77, at 169–73. See further Eleonore Reuter's demonstration that there are no precentralization strata in Deuteronomy and that the election formula is oriented on Jerusalem (*Kultzentralisation: Entstehung und Theologie von Dtn 12* [BBB 87; Frankfurt: Anton Hain, 1993] 115–91).

2. See, for example, Gerhard von Rad, *Deuteronomy* (OTL; Philadelphia: Westminster, 1966) 89; and A. D. H. Mayes, *Deuteronomy* (NCBC; London: Marshall, Morgan & Scott, 1979) 222.

3. This table is based in part on one provided by Norbert Lohfink, "Opfer und Säkularisierung im Deuteronomium," in *Studien zu Opfer und Kult im Alten Testament* (ed. Adrian Schenker; Forschungen zum Alten Testament 3; Tübingen: J. C. B. Mohr [Paul Siebeck], 1992) 15–43, at p. 26.

TABLE 2–2 The redactional framework of Deuteronomy 12

Law no.	Unit	Number of addressee	Theme
	Deut 12:1	Singular/Plural	Superscription: *Geography and Time*
1	Deut 12:2–7	Plural	Cultic purification and centralization
2	Deut 12:8–12	Plural	*Temporal* condition for centralization
3	Deut 12:13–19	Singular	Centralization and secular slaughter
4	Deut 12:20–28	Singular	*Geographical* condition for slaughter
5	Deut 12:29–31	Singular	Conclusion: Cultic purification

to the reason given for introducing centralization and by the presence or absence of additional provisions, such as secular slaughter.

The superscription to the chapter, the work of its final editor, introduces the key organizing motifs for the four centralization laws by identifying both geographical purview and historical duration as criteria for legal adherence. The laws that follow, the superscription affirms, apply geographically in the promised land of Canaan and are historically valid while Israel inhabits that land: "These are the statutes and the laws that you shall take care to observe *in the land that Yahweh, the God of thine ancestors, has given thee to possess*—all the days that you live upon the earth" (Deut 12:1).[4] Within this superscription a shift occurs in the grammatical number of the addressee: from second-person plural at the beginning and end to second-person singular in the land donation formula in the middle (table 2-2). This shift does not entail secondary accretions; the superscription is rather a unified composition.[5] Its number change, among other functions, helps prepare the reader for the number change of the laws that follow.

In their final redaction, the laws are arranged in a chiastic structure (A B C B′ A′).[6] Laws 1 and 5 each address issues of cultic purification and polemicize

---

4. Norbert Lohfink, "Die *ḥuqqîm ûmišpāṭîm* und ihre Neubegrenzung durch Dtn 12,1," *Bib* 70 (1989) 1–29; reprinted in and cited according to Lohfink, *Studien zum Deuteronomium und zur deuteronomistischen Literatur II* (SBAB 12; Stuttgart: Katholisches Bibelwerk, 1991) 229–56. See also Lohfink, "Dtn 12,1 und Gen 15,18: Das dem Samen Abrahams geschenkte Land als der Geltungsbereich der deuteronomischen Gesetze"; and Lohfink, "Zum rabbinischen Verständnis von Dtn 12,1," both reprinted in the same volume (pp. 257–85, 287–92).

5. Lohfink, "Dtn 12,1 und Gen 15,18," 259, 265, establishes both the coherence of the superscription on juridical grounds and its text-critical originality as the *lectio difficilior* in contrast to the Septuagint, which levels the plural through the verse. This frequent number change (*Numeruswechsel*) in the Hebrew text of Deuteronomy, which occurs both in the legal corpus and in the narrative frame, still awaits satisfactory explanation. For more detailed studies see Norbert Lohfink, *Das Hauptgebot: Eine Untersuchung literarischer Einleitungsfragen zu Dtn 5–11* (AnBib 20; Rome: Pontifical Biblical Institute, 1963) 239–57; Christopher T. Begg, "The Significance of the *Numeruswechsel* in Deuteronomy—The 'Prehistory' of the Question," *ETL* 55 (1979) 116–24; Begg, "Contributions to the Elucidation of the Composition of Deuteronomy with Special Attention to the Significance of the *Numeruswechsel*" (Ph.D. diss., University of Louvain, 1987); and Yoshihide Suzuki, "The '*Numeruswechsel*' in Deuteronomy" (Ph.D. diss., Claremont Graduate School, 1982).

6. See the fine analysis by Georg Braulik, *Die deuteronomischen Gesetze und der Dekalog: Studien zum Aufbau von Deuteronomium 12–26* (SBS 145; Stuttgart: Katholisches Bibelwerk, 1991) 23–30.

against syncretism with Canaanite practices; laws 2 and 4 each present the conditions, whether historical or geographic, for the inception of centralization and secular slaughter. Thereby doubly framed and functioning as the focus of the chapter is law 3, which commands centralization and local secular slaughter. Law 5, which makes no reference to cult centralization, was most likely added by a late editor. Nonetheless, by means of the law's focus on cultic purity, the editor establishes multiple points of contact with law 1 and thereby provides the chapter with an elegant chiastic frame:[7]

A	(3)	ואשריהם תשרפון באש	You *shall burn* their sacred posts *by fire*
B	(4)	לא תעשׂון כן ליהוה אלהיכם	You *shall not do thus for Yahweh your God*
C	(5)	תדרשו	You *shall seek*
C'	(30)	ופן תדרש	Lest *thou seek*
B'	(31)	לא תעשׂה כן ליהוה אלהיך	Thou *shall not do thus for Yahweh thy God*
A'	(31)	את בניהם ואת בנתיהם ישׂרפו באש	They *burn* their sons and daughters *by fire*

As a result of such redactional design, the chapter appears simultaneously composite, redacted from five originally independent paragraphs, and cohesive, with the five paragraphs integrated into an ordered structure. This double nature of the chapter has engendered a double approach to its scholarly interpretation. The dominant approach in source-critical scholarship is to attempt by means of diachronic analysis to isolate its earliest stratum, deemed variously Deuteronomic or pre-Deuteronomic, and then to assign the other paragraphs to successive, later editors. The most recent monograph, for example, finds two preexilic, one early exilic, and one late exilic stratum.[8] Such confident precision raises more questions than it answers, since the criteria for distinguishing two preexilic Deuteronomic strata from one another, when each is Josianic and presupposes centralization—yet neither of which is Deuteronomistic—are never made clear, either linguistically or legal-historically. The problem with many such approaches is that, while properly emphasizing the composite nature of the chapter, they overlook both the evidence for the secondary imposition of an editorial structure and the difficulties that such deliberate redactional reworking pose for reconstructing literary history in the first place. Despite all such attempts, there is no direct access to a hypothetically reconstructed earliest centralization law: even the law conventionally deemed the earliest, Deut 12:13–19, has already been reworked in light of the final stage of the redaction.[9]

Conversely, a number of scholars have taken the opposite approach. Denying that the repetitions in the chapter are signs of redundancy and composite origin, these scholars reject diachronic analysis altogether. They strive

7. Note the additional parallel between "where the nations worshipped their gods" (Deut 12:2) and "how did these nations worship their gods" (Deut 12:30).

8. Reuter, *Kultzentralisation*, 109–14.

9. Norbert Lohfink, *Lectures on Deuteronomy 12–14* (Rome: Pontifical Biblical Institute, 1983) 101, 105. Professor Lohfink kindly made available to me these transcribed lectures, originally given at the Pontifical Biblical Institute, which contain a wealth of research. See also Lohfink, "Zentralisationsformel," 164.

for synchronic solutions and explain the repetitions as deliberate rhetorical em
phasis. Evidence for that position might be found in the requirement for the
septennial public reading of the law at the pilgrimage festival of Tabernacles
(Deut 31:9–13). However, almost all proponents of this synchronic approach
fail to do justice to the degree of philological difficulty in the chapter. They
restrict the difficulty, for example, to mere repetition alone, as if that problem
did not interlock with the number change of the addressee. Rhetorical emphasis might account for the former problem, but not the latter, let alone both together. Moreover, proponents of this synchronic method frequently commit a
logical error. They move from the claim of rhetorical or literary structure to
that of compositional coherence, without taking into account that such structures may, with equal justification, represent secondary editorial attempts to
impose coherence upon originally composite material. Even if a ring-pattern
or chiasm, for example, can legitimately be identified in a text, it does not follow automatically that the whole text represents the original composition of a
single author.[10] After all, that an editor has obscured textual seams does not
mean that there are no seams, no matter how adroitly the disparate material
may have been integrated through the use of redactional bridges.[11] The very
structures, in other words, that suggest compositional unity to some scholars
may actually lead to the opposite conclusion once the full degree of philological complexity of a text is recognized.[12] Each approach, both the diachronic
and the synchronic, contributes to the discussion, but neither is in itself sufficient to account for the text. A shift in perspective is necessary.

The key to the composition and redactional structure of Deuteronomy 12
is the way it engages and transforms prior Israelite literary history. The chapter is exegetical: not in the sense of a passive explication of the meaning of a
text but rather, more profoundly, in using the guise of exegesis (see Deut 1:5)
in order to sanction a major transformation of legal, cultic, and literary history
by means of literary reworking—and by ascribing the departure from convention to the authoritative tradition. Literary history presented a problem for the
authors of Deuteronomy. The authors of the legal corpus were concerned to
mandate a major transformation of Israelite religion: to institute centralization

---

10. See the due cautions of James L. Kugel, "On the Bible and Literary Criticism,"
Prooftexts 1 (1981) 217–36.

11. See the interesting discussion of "the disappearing redactor" by John Barton, *Reading the Old Testament: Method in Biblical Study* (Philadelphia: Westminster, 1984) 56–58.

12. Several analyses of Deuteronomy reason from literary design to single authorship
without considering an alternative interpretation of the evidence. For an example of baroque
chiastic analysis carried out without addressing philological issues, such as grammatical number change, which is then used to defend a claim of compositional unity, see J. G. McConville,
Law and Theology in Deuteronomy (JSOTSup 33; Sheffield: JSOT Press, 1984) 67. For a critical analysis, see Bernard M. Levinson, "McConville's *Law and Theology in Deuteronomy*," *JQR*
80 (1990) 396–404. On the synchronic approaches of Harold M. Wiener, Calum M. Carmichael,
Stephen A. Kaufman, and J. G. McConville, see Bernard M. Levinson, "Calum M. Carmichael's
Approach to the Laws of Deuteronomy," *HTR* 83 (1990) 227–57; and Levinson, *The Hermeneutics of Innovation: The Impact of Centralization upon the Structure, Sequence, and Reformulation of Legal Material in Deuteronomy* (Ann Arbor: University Microfilms, 1991) 14–60.

of the sacrificial cultus. That innovation required a transformation of the social and religious status quo, whereby sacrifices were offered throughout the land at the long-established local altars and sanctuaries. The innovation of cultic centralization entailed, moreover, a direct conflict with existing prestigious or authoritative texts that circulated within the scribal schools, even if they were not yet publicly known, and that contemplated precisely the opposite of centralization. In order for the Deuteronomic agenda to succeed, therefore, the authors and editors of the legal corpus had to find some way to justify their innovation. They had not only empirically to proscribe the local altars and sanctuaries, to which the people turned for cultic access to their God, but also to qualify the validity of the older texts whose content they contradicted and that might have jeopardized the success of their innovative agenda. In order to do so, the authors of Deuteronomy paradoxically turned to those very texts and coerced them to call for centralization.

Deuteronomy 12 does not simply represent "centralization law," as if that were some immediate positive legal requirement intended directly to act upon society. Instead, what is at stake is something broader, both theoretical and practical: not simply the innovation of centralization but also its careful justification and defense in light of previous Israelite literary history.[13] This hermeneutical issue—the impediment faced by the authors of the legal corpus and their need to defend their innovation—has not previously been recognized. Once understood, it helps to explain the problematic structure of much of the chapter. Deuteronomy 12 to a large extent represents a redactional anthology of repeated attempts not simply to command but also to justify the innovation of centralization. The chief technique for doing so employs tendentious textual exegesis: the authors turn to the very texts that threaten the validity of centralization and rework them to command the desired new content. These facts help account for the chapter's problematic redundancy and provide a new perspective for understanding the literary and hermeneutical dynamics of other key chapters in the legal corpus.

The Innovation of Centralization as Exegetical Reformulation

Widely regarded as providing the earliest stratum of the chapter, Deut 12:13–19 plays a key role in the legal corpus of Deuteronomy. In substantive terms, the unit (1) prohibits sacrificial worship at random altars (v. 13); (2) stipulates that sacrifice should take place exclusively at a single altar designated by Yahweh; (3) sanctions the secular slaughter of domestic animals, wherever and whenever desired "in each of your city-gates," that is, not at an altar (v. 15); (4) qualifies that sanction in two ways, stipulating that blood should not be con-

---

13. Morton Smith, *Palestinian Parties and Politics that Shaped the Old Testament* (2d ed.; London: SCM, 1987) broke important ground in arguing that Deut 12:8–12 represents a later exegetical harmonization between noncentralization law (Exod 20:24) and centralization law (Deut 12:4–7). In contrast to his model, however, the claim here is that the very initial formulation of the centralization law is already exegetical and intertextual. Moreover, he does not indicate why he considers Deut 12:4–7 to represent the earliest formulation of centralization.

sumed and prohibiting the making of cultic offerings and donations in the towns (vv. 16–17); (5) reiterates that all such cultic activity must take place only at the single sanctuary designated by Yahweh (v. 18); and (6) concludes with a formulaic admonition not to abandon the Levite (v. 19):

[13]השמר לך פן תעלה עלתיך בכל מקום אשר תראה [14] כי אם במקום אשר יבחר
יהוה באחד שבטיך שם תעלה עלתיך ושם תעשה כל אשר אנכי מצוך [15] רק בכל
אות נפשך תזבח ואכלת בשר כברכת יהוה אלהיך אשר נתן לך בכל שעריך הטמא
והטהור יאכלנו כצבי וכאיל [16] רק הדם לא תאכלו על הארץ תשפכנו כמים [17]
לא תוכל לאכל בשעריך מעשר דגנך ותירשך ויצהרך ובכרת בקרך וצאנך וכל נדריך
אשר תדר ונדבתיך ותרומת ידך [18] כי אם לפני יהוה אלהיך תאכלנו במקום אשר
יבחר יהוה אלהיך בו אתה ובנך ובתך ועבדך ואמתך והלוי אשר בשעריך ושמחת לפני
יהוה אלהיך בכל משלח ידך [19] השמר לך פן תעוב את הלוי כל ימיך על אדמתך

(13) Take heed lest you offer your burnt offerings in every place that you see; (14) but rather in the place that Yahweh shall choose in one of your tribes—there shall you offer your burnt offerings and there shall you do all that I command you. (15) But whenever you desire you may slaughter and eat meat in all your city-gates, according to the blessing of Yahweh your God; the impure and the pure may eat it, as of the gazelle and the hart. (16) But you must not eat the blood; you must pour it out upon the ground like water.

(17) Nor are you permitted to eat in any of your city-gates the tithes of your new grain, wine, or oil, the firstlings of your herds and your flocks, any of the votive offerings that you vow, your freewill offerings, or your donations; (18) but rather shall you eat these before Yahweh your God in the place that Yahweh your God shall choose—you, your son, your daughter, your male and your female slaves and the Levites resident in your cities—rejoicing before Yahweh your God in all of your undertakings. (19) Take heed lest you neglect the Levite as long as you live in your land.

Although Deut 12:13–19, as repetitive, may include later insertions, it has a deliberate redactional structure:[14]

(13)	השמר לך פן	Take heed lest
(14)	כי אם	but rather + centralization formula
(15)	רק	but + secular slaughter
(16)	רק	but + secular blood protocol
(18)	כי אם	but rather + centralization formula
(19)	השמר לך פן	Take heed lest

14. For a similar diagram see Gottfried Seitz, *Redaktionsgeschichtliche Studien zum Deuteronomium* (BWANT 93; Stuttgart: W. Kohlhammer, 1971) 211, who, however, arbitrarily splits v. 15b off from v. 15a to provide a focal point for his structural diagram. That half-verse cannot support such exegetical weight. For the various analyses of the literary history of the unit see Reuter, *Kultzentralisation*, 100–105.

The rhetorical formulae and the redactional structures interact with the substantive requirements in striking ways. Curiously, the opening imperative does not affirm what Deuteronomy requires—cult centralization—but rather prohibits an activity that even on the face of it seems illogical: promiscuously making sacrifices בכל מקום אשר תראה "in every place that you see" (Deut 12:13). Since under normal circumstances, sacrificial worship took place at familiar and established altars or sanctuaries, this prohibition erects a rhetorical straw man. It conceals the actual object of concern as something self-evidently to be rejected. The legal rhetoric continues to be curious in what follows. Neither of the two key substantive requirements of Deuteronomy—the centralization command that restricts all sacrifice to a single site chosen by Yahweh and the sanction for local secular slaughter—occurs as an independent imperative or affirmation. Instead, both stipulations—whereby Deuteronomy establishes its legal-historical uniqueness and independence from existing Israelite law—are shunted into the dependent syntax of opposition and qualification,[15] almost as if they were not, after all, the essential points of the authors' agenda.

Within vv. 13–15, there is a striking manipulation of syntax. In order to propound their substantive legal requirements, the unit's authors deliberately bracket the command to bring all offerings to the exclusive cultic center (v. 14) with two contrasting formulations, each of which employs the distributive pronoun כל which, depending on context, means "every" or "all." That same pronoun thereby governs both the prohibited action (v. 13) and the permitted one (v. 15). Distributive plurality cannot be applied, however, to Deuteronomy's cultic center because, by definition, it is exclusive. The syntactical play points to a triadic literary structure:

(v. 13)	בכל מקום	*in every place*
(v. 14)	במקום	*in* the *place*
(v. 15)	בכל שעריך	*in all* your city-gates

That same triadic literary structure translates into the following legal structure as it governs human action, both cultic and secular:

	Legal Status	Legal Content	Legal Locale	Form of Expression
(v. 13)	Prohibited	Random sacrifice	Multiple sites	Rhetorical deflection
(v. 14)	Prescribed	Cultic centralization	Single site	Periphrasis
(v. 15)	Permitted	Secular slaughter	Multiple sites	Metonym

Deuteronomy's authors are hardly innocent, either in the lexicon or in the conceptual background that underlies this triadic literary-legal structure. First, the very word מקום "place" that stands as the focus of attention is not a neutral term. In Hebrew, Phoenician, Aramaic, and Arabic, the word possesses, in addition, the more technical meaning of a "cult site" or "altar," as is explicit in

---

15. Lohfink, *Lectures*, 104–106.

Deut 12:2.[16] Second, the synchronic structure just isolated is quite sophisticated. It does not propound a simple binary opposition: Do not do X but rather Y. Instead, the structure is tripartite, and the logic is dialectical. Balancing and rehabilitating prohibited X, with its formulation of plurality and random action, is the newly permitted free action—ad libitum—in the plural settlements. Although sacrifice "in every place" is prohibited, noncultic slaughter "in all your city-gates" is sanctioned. At the focal point stands Deuteronomy's key requirement of cultic centralization. To express it, the authors revamp the terminology of what was prohibited to formulate what they prescribe: "not in every place . . . but in the place."

This synchronic structure originates diachronically in literary history. What the authors of Deuteronomy proscribe—sacrificial worship of Yahweh at multiple sites throughout the countryside (בכל מקום אשר "in every place that")—conforms both in substance and in formulation to the older legal norm represented by the altar law that stands now as a preface to the Covenant Code (Exod 20:24; in some printings, Exod 20:21).[17] Yahweh's first person speech there directly affirms that he provides his cultic presence and blessing consequent upon sacrifice בכל המקום אשר "in every place that" (Exod 20:24b)—precisely what Deut 12:13 proscribes as anathema. The rhetorical straw man erected by the authors of Deuteronomy thus camouflages the real point of the exercise: functionally to abrogate that law with its affirmation of multiple altar sites as legitimate for sacrifice.

16. See BDB, 880 (§ 4) and the valuable new *HALAT*, 2.627 (§ 6). S. R. Driver, *Deuteronomy* (ICC; 3d ed.; Edinburgh: T. & T. Clark, 1901) 139 adduces Gen 12:6; 28:11; 1 Sam 7:16; Jer 7:12; and Arabic *maqām* "sacred place." For evidence from Phoenician and Punic inscriptions, see R. S. Tomback, *A Comparative Semitic Lexicon of the Phoenician and Punic Languages* (SBLDS 32; Missoula: Scholars Press, 1978) 195–96. See also J. Hoftijzer and K. Jongeling, *Dictionary of the North-West Semitic Inscriptions* (2 vols.; Handbuch der Orientalistik 21; Leiden: E. J. Brill, 1995) 2.680, s.v. mqm₁ (§ 1a). Note also Aramaic אתרא.

17. The literary reconstruction of Diethelm Conrad, which makes Exod 20:24b secondary, is arbitrary (*Studien zum Altargesetz Ex 20:24–26* [Marburg: H. Kombächer, 1968]. Conrad simply assumes in his preface that second-person singular apodictic laws are directed against foreign cults. That presupposition, even though nowhere justified, nonetheless drives his subsequent literary criticism. Those sections of Exod 20:24–26 that fail to conform to it are summarily dismissed as secondary accretions to an imagined original law that constituted a polemic against foreign cults. The logic is watertight—and circular. Conrad's argument overlooks the evidence that the close literary connection in Exod 20:24 among (1) altar-building, (2) theophany, and (3) divine beneficence has clear parallels elsewhere in the Bible. See Gen 12:7–8 and 1 Kgs 3:4–5 (the first is noted in the review of Conrad's work by Henri Cazelles, *OrAnt* 11 [1972] 332–35). Indeed, the connection between a theophany and the divine's proclaiming his name in a cultic context was a convention within Israel and the ancient Near East. See Tryggve N. D. Mettinger, *The Dethronement of Sabaoth: Studies in the Shem and Kabod Theologies* (Lund: CWK Gleerup, 1982) 125–27. On the literary and redactional history of the altar law and establishing its essentially pre-Deuteronomic status are Eckart Otto, *Wandel der Rechtsbegründungen in der Gesellschaftsgeschichte des antiken Israels: Eine Rechtsgeschichte des "Bundesbuches" Ex XX 22–XXIII 13* (StudBib 3; Leiden: E. J. Brill, 1988) 54–56; and Ludger Schwienhorst-Schönberger, *Das Bundesbuch (Ex 20,22–23,33): Studien zu seiner Entstehung und Theologie* (BZAW 188; Berlin: Walter de Gruyter, 1990) 287–99.

Exod 20:24

מזבח אדמה תעשה לי וזבחת עליו את עלתיך ואת שלמיך את צאנך ואת בקרך
בכל המקום אשר אזכיר את שמי אבוא אליך וברכתיך

An earthen altar shall you make for me, and you shall sacrifice upon it
your burnt offerings and your whole offerings, your sheep and your
cattle;
In every place that I proclaim my name I shall come to you and bless
you.[18]

The authors of Deut 12:13–15 appropriate this lemma to serve their own
very different agenda. They deftly rework it to command the distinctive
innovations of Deuteronomy—both cultic centralization[19] and local, secular
slaughter:

Exod 20:24b   Deut 12:13–15

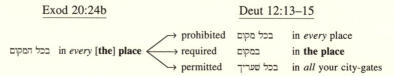

	→ prohibited	בכל מקום	in *every* place
בכל המקום in *every* [the] place ←	→ required	במקום	in **the place**
	→ permitted	בכל שעריך	in *all* your city-gates

The Deuteronomic authors skillfully break up and recast the syntax of the
older Exodus altar law. The preposition ("in") and the definite noun ("the
place") are now grouped together to designate the chosen site to which all sacrifice must be directed: "in the place." The distributive is similarly recast so
that it now refers both negatively to the prohibited multiple altar sites (which
were formerly legitimate for sacrifice) and positively to the multiple sites for
secular slaughter (which activity was previously inconceivable). By means of

18. The Hebrew of Exod 20:24b reads literally "in every [the] place." More commonly,
the idiom for "every" requires כל plus an indefinite substantive whereas כל plus a definite substantive, as here, means "all" or "the whole." Notwithstanding that convention, the correct translation here is indeed distributive "every." There are a number of other cases where כל plus the
definite substantive has a distributive function. Such a use is clear, for example, in Abraham's
self-exculpation before Abimelek: "When God caused me to wander from my father's house, I
said to her, 'Do this gracious deed for me: *in every place that* אל כל המקום אשר we come to, say
of me, "He is my brother"'" (Gen 20:13). Consequently, the discussion of Exod 20:24 and its
syntax by GKC § 127e is sorely inadequate. Gesenius argues that the use of the definite article
represents a later "dogmatic correction" and that the definite article was absent in the original
text. He considers the one other syntactical parallel he cites, Gen 20:13, similarly anomalous
"since elsewhere *every place* is always (8 times)" כל מקום (emphasis in original). Gesenius's
"always" overlooks כל המקום אשר "*every place where* the sole of your foot treads shall belong to
you" (Deut 11:24); so Brevard S. Childs, *The Book of Exodus* (OTL; Philadelphia: Westminster,
1974) 447. Moreover, that the phrase with definite *nomen rectum* means "every place"—exactly
as it does without the article—is clear from Joshua's subsequent citation of that promise using
an indefinite *nomen rectum*: כל מקום אשר "*every place where* the sole of your foot treads I have
given to you" (Josh 1:3).

19. For the ground-breaking demonstration of the relation between the "election-formula"
of Deuteronomy and Exod 20:24b, with the structure ["place" + relative clause + verb + Divine
Name] common to both, see Lohfink, "Zentralisationsformel," 167–77. See also S. Dean McBride,
"The Deuteronomic Name Theology" (Ph.D. diss., Harvard University, 1969) 209; and Michael
Fishbane, *Biblical Interpretation in Ancient Israel* (Oxford: Clarendon, 1985) 252.

this reworking, the Deuteronomic authors turn the older Exodus altar law against itself. They appropriate its syntax and lexemes to propound Deuteronomy's own innovations so that it now (1) prohibits all local sacrifice בכל מקום "in every place"; (2) mandates cultic centralization במקום "in the place"; and (3) sanctions local, secular slaughter בכל שעריך "in all your city-gates" (Deut 12:13–15).

The literary recycling allows the Deuteronomic authors to retain the ostensible validity of the older Exodus altar law or, at least, to cast their innovations in light of the older sacrificial norm and to minimize their departure from it. Nonetheless, in substantive terms, they abrogate it. Indeed, they doubly disenfranchise it. They meticulously rework it to prohibit the plurality of altars that it originally presupposed and to require the cultic exclusivity that it never contemplated.[20] The degree of technical scribal sophistication involved is remarkable. The authors of Deuteronomy have atomistically restricted the older law's authority to individual, recycled lexemes shorn from their original semantic context.

For the first time in the history of Israelite religion a distinction has been forged between cultic sacrifice (at an altar) and secular slaughter (not at an altar). That distinction would have been a contradiction in terms to the author of the altar law. Prior to Deuteronomy, all slaughter of domestic animals—even for the purposes of food—was a ritual activity necessarily carried out at an altar.[21] There was, in other words, no functional distinction between the sacrifice of sheep and cattle for cultic purposes and the slaughter of the same animals for food. Both took place at an altar. In the Exodus altar law, the same verb זבח encompassed both activities—although that verbal action could take place only at the altar. Ironically, precisely because of that double focus, the old altar law of Exod 20:24 was sufficiently polyvalent that the authors of Deuteronomy could exploit it to justify their innovations.

None of this is accidental. The Exodus altar law had the prestige of antiquity, was ascribed to Yahweh, likely circulated with the Covenant Code, and represented normative practice. Because of its prestige and normative status,

---

20. Reuter, *Kultzentralisation*, 123, maintains that the Exodus altar law shows an initial movement toward centralization in its relative clause, which she reads with a restrictive force as Yahweh's delimiting the sites where he cultically appears: "nicht jeder Ort geeignet ist, sondern nur die von JWHW dazu bestimmten." That approach makes the relative clause merely state the obvious. More problematical, it also unintentionally reinterprets the clause, nearly verbatim, in light of Deut 12:13–14—and thereby reverses legal and literary history. There is further evidence against her analysis. In its noncultic attestations, the same structure of מקום "place" + relative clause emphasizes plurality and plenitude rather than restriction or delimitation; see Gen 20:13, Deut 11:24, and Josh 1:3 (cited in previous note). Reuter is apparently unaware that her analysis of Exod 20:24 precisely recapitulates one of the harmonistic solutions employed by ancient rabbinic exegesis; see the survey collected by S. Weissblueth, "'In Every Place Where I Mention My Name I Will Come to You and Bless You,'" *Beth Miqra* 30 (1984/85) 173–78 (Hebrew).

21. This norm is presupposed by the narrative of Saul's troops who are reprimanded for slaughtering "on the ground" and eating "with the blood" (1 Sam 14:31–35. See the remarks of Roland de Vaux, *Ancient Israel* (London: Darton, Longman & Todd, 1961) 338, which represents the standard position of source criticism. See also Lev 17:1–9, which stipulates that all slaughter must take place at an altar.

the law could not be dispensed with or bypassed. In order to justify their departure from it, the authors of Deuteronomy tendentiously reworked it by means of studied, transformative exegesis, appropriating its very wording to express their own innovative agenda. Their implicit argument is that their innovation represents the actual force of that altar law, which they nevertheless replace by turning its own syntax and lexemes against it.

At issue is a problem in legal and religious history. In a culture with a curriculum of prestigious and authoritative texts, how are legal innovation and religious transformation possible? The solution is to disclaim authorship and to deny originality. Employing the technique of lemmatic citation and transformation, Deuteronomy's authors harness the lexemes of older texts, wherever possible, to formulate their own religious and legal agenda. They never speak in their own belated, seventh-century B.C.E. scribal voice. Instead, they defer to the voice of authoritative antiquity. They appropriate, and possibly create,[22] the fiction of Moses as textual speaker to make him propound their transformation of legal and literary history. Deuteronomy, in other words, is a deliberate literary pseudepigraph, designed to belie literary history by locating the innovative force of the new composition in an authoritative past. Both authorship and originality are thereby ascribed to the very textual tradition that is actually radically transformed. Looking at the material this way suggests that familiar postbiblical and Second Temple techniques of sectarian literary activity find a precedent in Deuteronomy. These include pseudepigraphy, exegesis as a technique of textual transformation, and the phenomenon of the "rewritten Bible."

The authors of Deuteronomy continue to exploit the Exodus altar law both in this unit (Deut 12:13–19) and in the following one (Deut 12:20–28). In each case, it is reworked twice. The polyvalency of its transformations is striking: the authors of Deuteronomy rework it to sponsor both cultic centralization and local secular slaughter. In order to demonstrate the techniques for textual reworking employed by the authors of Deuteronomy, I first move through each unit synchronically, showing the reuse. Then I explore the diachronic and exegetical implications of this reworking.

Lemmatic Transformation in Deut 12:13–19

In mandating their innovations, the authors of Deuteronomy transform the entire Exodus altar law, not only that portion of it which refers distributively to the מקום "place" (Exod 20:24bα). The altar law provides a textual basis not only for Deuteronomy's election or מקום "place" formula but also for the centralization command, the concession for secular slaughter, and the blood rite at the altar. There are two further examples in Deut 12:13–19. The first occurs in

---

22. Norbert Lohfink contends that the Mosaic voicing is not original but a later, Deuteronomistic addition; see chapter 1, n. 7. Were that the case, it would only strengthen my position: for Deuteronomy, at the time of its composition, like the Qumran *Temple Scroll*, would then constitute a divine pseudepigraph, with theonymy the ultimate trope of authority.

Deut 12:14, where the reference to the central sanctuary and the instructions concerning what to do there chiastically cite Exod 20:24. That altar law has two prime components:

A	You shall sacrifice	וזבחת
	upon it	עליו
	your *burnt offerings* . . .	את עלתיך . . .
B	*in every place* where . . .	. . . בכל המקום אשר

Deut 12:14 takes up those two elements in reverse order, according to Seidel's law. Here the focus is on the site of sacrifice:

B¹	*in the place*	במקום
	which Yahweh shall choose . . .	. . . אשר יבחר יהוה
A¹	there you shall offer	שם תעלה
	your burnt offerings	עלתיך

Within that reformulation, the authors of Deuteronomy locate their radical cultic and legal novum in the relative clause that, functioning like a technical gloss, redefines lemmatic [ה]מקום in terms of Deuteronomy's distinctive demand for cultic centralization: "*the place*—which Yahweh shall choose in one of your tribes."[23]

The authors of Deuteronomy reuse different segments of the same lemma in order to introduce local secular slaughter:

Exod 20:24

A	*You shall sacrifice*	וזבחת
	upon it	עליו
	your burnt offerings . . .	את עלתיך . . .
B	*in every* place where I proclaim my name	בכל המקום אשר אזכיר את שמי
	I shall come to you *and bless you*	אבוא אליך וברכתיך

The two key elements of the Exodus lemma are cited for the second time by Deut 12:15:

A²	Only, to your heart's desire	רק בכל אות נפשך
	you may slaughter	תזבח
	and eat meat	ואכלת בשר
B²	*according to the blessing*	כברכת
	of Yahweh your God	יהוה אלהיך . . .
	in each of your city-gates	בכל שעריך

In this new context the verb זבח is completely detached from its originally essential link to the altar. No longer does it denote a cultic sacrifice. The verb

---

23. Emanuel Tov, "Glosses, Interpolations, and Other Types of Scribal Additions in the Text of the Hebrew Bible," *Language, Theology, and The Bible: Essays in Honour of James Barr* (ed. Samuel E. Balentine and John Barton; Oxford: Clarendon, 1994) 40–66, urges due caution in the widespread use of the term "gloss" within the textual criticism of the Hebrew Bible. My use differs from that and does not imply a secondary addition to the text. It refers to the composition of the text, not its manuscript history.

is given a new, secular meaning: "to slaughter."[24] Its action pointedly no longer takes place in a cultic context, at an altar, but, rather, in the local settlements. The construct phrase כברכת יהוה "according to *the blessing* of Yahweh" paraphrases in the third person the lemma's original first-person divine promise וברכתיך "and *I shall bless* you." Deuteronomy thus deftly manages both to restrict the divine cultic presence to the central sanctuary and to maintain a mediated divine presence in the local, secular sphere: the land and its produce constitute divine gifts. In the lemma one receives locally the cultic blessing of Yahweh. In Deuteronomy's revision of the lemma, with the local cultic presence of Yahweh no longer a legitimate possibility, one continues to receive divine blessing and sustenance locally, albeit now in secular form, independent of any cultic activity.

Lemmatic Transformation in Deut 12:20–28

There are another two studied reformulations of the altar law in Deut 12:20–28. In the first, Deut 12:21 reformulates Exod 20:24, although with a telling ellipsis. Deuteronomy deliberately elides two elements from the Exodus altar law: the prepositional phrase עליו "upon it," which refers to the altar, and the first pair in the sacrificial list, את עלתיך ואת שלמיך "your burnt offerings and your well-being offerings."

Exod 20:24aαβ	Deut 12:21aαβ
וזבחת עליו את עלתיך ואת שלמיך	וזבחת
את צאנך ואת בקרך	מבקרך ומצאנך
	אשר נתן יהוה לך כאשר צויתך
And you shall sacrifice upon it your burnt offerings and your well-being offerings,	*And you shall slaughter* (!)
your sheep and your cattle	from *your cattle and* from *your sheep* which Yahweh has given to you as I have commanded you

Deut 12:20–21 makes the institution of secular slaughter contingent upon the expansion of the territorial boundaries, a concession to the citizenry on account of distance from the cultic center. In this context the reason for the two elisions from the lemma in the Exodus altar law is clear: the slaughter contemplated is secular rather than cultic.[25] In the technical terminology of v. 21, it is

24. This issue will be discussed in more detail in the following section, "Lemmatic Transformation in Deut 12:20–28."

25. The jurist Harold M. Wiener, *The Altars of the Old Testament* (Beigabe zur Orientalistischen Literatur-Zeitung; Leipzig: J. C. Hinrichs, 1927) 18, notes the textual relation. This synchronic insight is, however, undercut by his conservative presuppositions and his rejection of historical criticism. Assuming Deuteronomy to be Mosaic, he harmonizes Deut 12:21 with Exod 20:24—and claims that Deuteronomy does not abolish local altars. He denies altogether that Deuteronomy centralizes the cultus but never addresses Deut 12:14, where no other explanation is possible.

בשעריך "in your city-gates," that is, local, in contrast to במקום "at the place," Deuteronomy's periphrasis for the central sanctuary. Local secular slaughter by definition cannot take place עליו "upon it"—upon an altar—because Deuteronomy sanctions only the single altar at the cultic center. For the same reason, the lemma's reference to the cultic sacrifices את עלתיך ואת שלמיך "your burnt offerings and your well-being offerings" is deleted in this noncultic context.

The missing elements from the Exodus lemma, which are specific to cultic action, are restored and reworked in Deut 12:26–27, which is concerned with ritual action at the central sanctuary.

Exod 20:24a	Deut 12:27
מזבח אדמה תעשה לי וזבחת	ועשׂית עלתיך הבשׂר והדם
עליו את עלתיך ואת שלמיך	על מזבח יהוה אלהיך
	ודם זבחיך ישׁפך על מזבח יהוה אלהיך
	והבשׂר תאכל
An earthen *altar* shall you make for me, and you shall sacrifice *upon* it your *burnt offerings* and your well-being offerings	You shall offer *your burnt offerings*, both the flesh and the blood, *upon the altar* of Yahweh your God; the blood of your [other] sacrifices shall be spilled *upon the altar* of Yahweh your God but you may consume the flesh

In Exod 20:24, the adverbial phrase עליו "upon it," which followed the stipulation "you shall sacrifice," had the bound (i.e., construct) phrase מזבח אדמה "an earthen altar" as its antecedent. That phrase was distributive: any altar among the plurality of altars was legitimate so long as it was, ideally, earthen or, alternatively, of unhewn stones. In contrast, the altar reference in Deut 12:27 is bound in such a way as to become exclusive rather than distributive. The sacrifice shall take place על מזבח יהוה "upon *the* [unique] altar of Yahweh." The transformation of the original bound phrase establishes the cultic-historical distance between Deuteronomy and its predecessors.

The four-item sacrificial list of Exod 20:24 may be subdivided into two pairs. The first pair is distinctively cultic: את עלתיך ואת שלמיך "your burnt offerings and your well-being offerings."[26] The second pair, "sheep and cattle," is not necessarily cult-specific. Syntactically, since the first object marker does not have the copula, this pair may simply stand in apposition to the first pair, specifying the possible sacrificial animals rather than supplementing the first pair: את צאנך ואת בקרך "[namely,] your sheep and your cattle."[27] Only one term

---

26. I disagree with the position of Schwienhorst-Schönberger, *Das Bundesbuch*, 296, who concludes that this sacrificial list represents a secondary Deuteronomistic expansion of the original altar law. It is difficult to imagine that a Deuteronomistic interpolator would add such a list but leave unscathed the altar law's explicit reference to multiple altars as legitimate sites for cultic theophany and divine blessing.

27. Additional evidence for this syntactic rendering is that both the Samaritan Pentateuch and *Targum Pseudo-Jonathan* (E. G. Clarke, *Targum Pseudo-Jonathan of the Pentateuch: Text*

from the remaining pair is reused in this new context: עלחיך "your burnt offer-ings" (v. 27). There is a reason that the second term from the lemma, שלמיך "your well-being offerings," is not reused: with one exception, the word is never used in Deuteronomy and is not part of its vocabulary.[28]

It is striking that in this cultic context of reformulation of the Exodus altar law, its key verb—וזבחת "you shall sacrifice"—is not employed. The nonuse is the more salient inasmuch as a noun derived from the same verb—זבחיך "your sacrifices"—occurs in the same verse (v. 27). There is a clear rationale for this selectivity. In its paradoxical reuse of the Exodus altar law to sanction local *secular* slaughter, Deuteronomy has appropriated and deliberately redefined the original verb. In the new context, it no longer retains its original meaning—cultic sacrifice—but instead denotes its opposite—slaughter, but not at an altar (Deut 12:15, 21). That deliberate abrogation of the verb's conventional mean-ing is unique in the entire lexicon of the Hebrew Bible to these two verses.[29] Elsewhere, even in Deuteronomy, the verb retains its normal denotation.[30] The precision of the radical respecification of the verb admits one logical explana-tion. In both cases, the author struggles to justify the innovation of secular slaughter in terms of prior textual authority, almost as if the older Exodus altar law itself lexically sanctioned the very innovation that overturns it. But that pointed reassignment of the verb to sanction secular slaughter precludes its being used in this context also to denote cultic sacrifice. Accordingly, an alter-native idiom—in Deuteronomy, unique to this verse—becomes necessary here: עשׂה עלה "to make a burnt offering."[31]

---

and Concordance [Hoboken, N.J.: Ktav, 1984] 92) render this phrase using the partitive preposi-tion מן bound to the noun instead of the MT's object marker. Thereby the holocaust and well-being offerings would come *"from* your sheep and *from* your cattle." In both verses, the syntacti-cal change most likely reflects ancient exegetical activity that harmonizes the Exodus lemma with its revision in Deut 12:21. Thus, the Exodus altar law and the Deuteronomic centralization law were at a very early stage in the history of interpretation already read alongside one another.

28. The one exception proves the rule. The word occurs only at Deut 27:7—thus, within a chapter that is a late, secondary addition to the legal corpus. Moreover, even there, it is used within a later interpolation framed by a repetitive resumption; see Fishbane, *Biblical Interpre-tation*, 228 n. 131.

29. The verb normally has a clear cultic force—either generally "to sacrifice" or, more technically, "to offer the זבח sacrifice." Even where it does not explicitly take place in a cultic context, emulation or assertion of cultic status is involved (1 Kgs 1:9, 19, 25; 19:21). Making this point is Alfred Cholewiński, *Heiligkeitsgesetz und Deuteronomium: Eine vergleichende Studie* (AnBib 66; Rome: Biblical Institute, 1976) 151 n. 12. Independently noting the verb's anomalous use is Jacob Milgrom, "Profane Slaughter and a Formulaic Key to the Composition of Deuteronomy," *HUCA* 47 (1976) 1–11, at 2.

30. Deut 15:21; 16:2, 4, 5, 6; 17:1; 27:7; 32:17; 33:19. On the anomaly of Passover as a sacrifice (Deut 16:1–7), see chapter 3.

31. A related idiom does, however, occur in the context of Deuteronomy's festival calen-dar (Deut 16:1, 10, 13). The idiom there may be an ellipsis of חג [זבח] עשׂה "to offer the [sacri-fice] of + festival name." Elsewhere the idiom is common in the Deuteronomistic History (i.e., Judg 13:16; 2 Kgs 5:17; 10:24), P (i.e., Num 15:3, 5, 8) and the literature related to P (Chronicles and Ezekiel). The use of the verb "to do, make" in conjunction with sacrifice is also normal in Akkadian, where it may take as object *alpu* (bull), *niqê* (sacrifices), or *ududarû* (regular sheep offering); see *CAD*, 4.201–202, 214, 224, *s.v. epēšu*.

The Double Justification of Innovation in Deut 12:20–28

The altar law of Exodus figured prominently as the lemmatic source for both the secularization of slaughter and the centralization of sacrifice in Deut 12:20–28, just as it did in the previous unit (Deut 12:13–19). From this perspective, a number of widespread assumptions about Deut 12:20–28 must be reexamined. The two paragraphs contrast remarkably in their rhetorical stance. In Deut 12:13–19, secular slaughter was granted unconditionally. In contrast, the innovation is presented as doubly conditional in Deut 12:20–28. Secular slaughter is now made contingent upon both future expansion of the national boundaries and excessive distance from the cultic center (vv. 20–21). The formulation of the two verses is redundant, involving two parallel conditional clauses and two parallel concessions, each granting the consumption of meat in a nonsacrificial context.[32]

[20] כי ירחיב יהוה אלהיך את גבולך כאשר דבר לך ואמרת אכלה בשר כי תאבה נפשך
לאכל בשר בכל אות נפשך תאכל בשר [21] כי ירחק ממך המקום אשר יבחר יהוה אלהיך
לשום שמו שם וזבחת מבקרך ומצאנך אשר נתן יהוה לך כאשר צויתך ואכלת בשעריך
בכל אות נפשך

(20) *When* Yahweh your God enlarges your territory, as he has promised you, and you say, "I shall eat some meat," for you wish to eat some meat, *you may eat* meat *whenever you have the desire.* (21) *When* the place that Yahweh your God shall choose to establish his name is too distant from you, you may slaughter any of your cattle and your sheep, which Yahweh has given you, as I have commanded you; *you may eat* within your settlements *whenever you have the desire.*

There are good reasons to question the prevailing scholarly view that this unit represents a later legal reinterpretation of Deut 12:13–19, restricting secular slaughter's geographical purview.[33] Allegedly, the reference to the expansion of the boundaries refers to Josiah's extending the range of his cultic reform from Judah into Samaria, the former northern kingdom of Israel. This approach regards the unit's composition as having been triggered by an immediate, practical contingency. There is no textual justification for this claim that the double reference to the expansion of the boundaries and to distance from the cultic center reflects Josiah's expansion into the territory of the former Israel.[34] In the narrative describing his actions (2 Kgs 23:15–20), there is simply no use of

---

32. The double condition may well point to separate redactional strata, as Seitz, *Studien*, 210, maintains, believing v. 21 to be earlier. Nevertheless, it is also possible that the redactor is deliberately grouping together two different exegetical formulae to introduce his reworking of different parts of v. 15 in each case (vv. 20, 21).

33. This prevailing view is held by Cholewiński, *Heiligkeitsgesetz und Deuteronomium*, 152–53; Georg Braulik, *Deuteronomium 1–16,17* (Neue Echter Bibel 15; Würzburg: Echter, 1986) 99–100; and Lohfink, "Opfer und Säkularisierung," 16 n. 6.

34. See also Reuter, *Kultzentralisation*, 91–92. Her analysis does not clarify how she does understand the reference to operate: whether it refers to a different historical context or is merely literary.

that language or terminology and therefore no justification for claiming a connection between Deut 12:20–28 and that narrative or the event it describes. The language does not represent any form of direct historical contingency. Instead, both formulae constitute deliberate exegetical tropes that introduce and justify textual and legal revision.[35] They present the later innovation as an originally planned-for contingency, a type of *vaticinium ex eventu*. They thereby conceal the fact that prior law is actually being amended or abrogated.[36]

The second formula, which concerns distance from the cultic center, also occurs in the context of the tithes law, where it grants the citizen permission, "if the cultic center *is too distant*," to convert tithes into currency (Deut 14:24a). Such a provision directly contradicts the conventions of cultic law that prohibit the conversion of *sancta*.[37] A slight variant, using an adjectival rather than verbal construction, occurs in the war laws of Deuteronomy. In order to sanction Deuteronomy's distinctive innovation of the חרם "holy war," which calls for the killing of all the Canaanites, the earlier war law, that sanctioned taking women, children, and animals as plunder, was redactionally respecified to apply only to "all *the* [non-Canaanite] *cities which are* very distant (הערים הרחקת) from you" (Deut 20:15).[38]

It seems much more likely to connect the motifs of the expansion of the borders to the Deuteronomistic Historian's account of Solomon's hegemony, with the explicit references there to his rule over foreign powers (1 Kgs 5:1–5). There is an additional point of connection. Immediately after achieving political hegemony, Solomon initiated his plan to build the Temple: he sent his envoys to Hiram, declaring that all necessary preconditions were now met (1 Kgs 5:16–19).[39] In Deut 12:8–12, the Deuteronomistic author establishes the tem-

---

35. Alexander Rofé, *Introduction to Deuteronomy: Part I and Further Chapters* (2d rev. ed.; Jerusalem: Akademon, 1988) 16 (Hebrew); Fishbane, *Biblical Interpretation*, 157, 249.

36. This formula for the expansion of the borders also occurs in the context of the laws for the cities of refuge, in order to sanction the increase in their number from three to six (Deut 19:8). It occurs again, in the context of Deuteronomistic textual reworking, at Exod 34:24, where it marks a redactor's homiletic insertion into an earlier pilgrimage law (Exod 23:17) and is framed by a repetitive resumption. On Exod 34:24 see Fishbane, *Biblical Interpretation*, 193–94; and Erhard Blum, *Studien zur Komposition des Pentateuch* (BZAW 189; Berlin: Walter de Gruyter, 1990) 69.

37. Moshe Weinfeld, *Deuteronomy and the Deuteronomic School* (Oxford: Clarendon, 1972) 214–17. The cultic law involved would correspond to the substance of Lev 27:33, even if not to that particular text. Claiming direct textual dependence is problematic because most scholars date Leviticus 17–26 after Deuteronomy; many Israeli scholars, including Weinfeld, and some North American scholars date it contemporary with or prior to Deuteronomy. On the substantive issue of whether secularization is here involved, note the important different interpretation provided by Lohfink, "Opfer und Säkularisierung," 23–24.

38. See Fishbane, *Biblical Interpretation*, 199–200. See also his analysis of the similar adjectival construction used in the revision of the Passover law at Num 9:10 (pp. 157, 247–50).

39. Solomon's rule provided "peace from all the antagonists all about" (1 Kgs 5:4; cp. 5:18 and Deut 12:10) and thereby provided the necessary precondition for the construction of the Temple as a domicile for Yahweh's Name (1 Kgs 5:17; Deut 12:21). See further Gary N. Knoppers, *Two Nations under God: The Deuteronomistic History of Solomon and the Dual Monarchies* (2 vols.; HSM 52–53; Atlanta: Scholars Press, 1993–94) 1.7.

poral condition for the inception of centralization and points to the fulfillment of this condition of rest with Solomon's Temple (1 Kgs 8:56).[40] Similarly, Deut 12:20–28, as the geographical condition for the inception of local secular slaughter, also tags Solomonic hegemony as having satisfied the condition of the expansion of the borders.

At issue, therefore, are deliberate hermeneutical tropes that attempt to justify legal amendment or innovation. Deut 12:20–28 is not a restrictive reinterpretation of Deut 12:13–19 that was triggered by a specific historical contingency. Instead, it represents an attempt by the text's authors to justify the introduction of local secular slaughter. They were conscious of its contradicting both existing ritual practice and existing authoritative texts: the altar law of Exod 20:24.[41] That text was reworked within this unit to sponsor both the formulation of local secular slaughter and the blood ritual at the centralized altar. The trope of the expansion of the borders presents a kind of legal fiction. It suggests that the innovation of local secular slaughter does not represent a breach with legal convention. Rather, under the terms of the fictional legal trope, it grants local secular slaughter unconditional sanction—with an inception dating back effectively to the "golden age" of the Solomonic empire with its construction of the Temple. The old altar law is not explicitly abrogated. Instead, under the guise of a geographical restriction, its validity is simply made historically limited.

Now a further issue of exegetical history must be addressed. The concession for secular slaughter contains a citation tag: "If the place that Yahweh your God will choose to set his name is distant from you, then you may slaughter any of your cattle and your sheep, which Yahweh has given you, (כאשר צויתך) *as I commanded you*; you may eat in your settlements according to your heart's desire" (Deut 12:21). Almost without exception, that cross-reference has been understood to have Deut 12:15 as its antecedent.[42] According to this view, Deut 12:20–21 restrict and reinterpret Deut 12:15, making secular slaughter contingent upon the expansion of the boundaries and distance from the cultic center. On a number of grounds, that consensus position is open to question. First, since Moses in Deut 12:15 grants a free concession to Israel, permitting them locally to slaughter and eat to their heart's desire, it makes no sense to regard this verse as the antecedent of Deut 12:21, which speaks rather of a command.[43] This interpretation of the citation tag, wherein it refers to a free concession, forces

---

40. See "The Hermeneutical Function of Deut 12:8–12," which follows.

41. In contrast, Rofé argues that Deut 12:20–28 represents a late harmonization of the innovation of local secular slaughter (Deut 12:13–19) with the requirement in Lev 17:1–7 that all slaughter of domestic animals take place at the sanctuary: now secular slaughter will only apply in the geographical area where Lev 17:1–7 was never meant to apply (*Deuteronomy*, 16). Smith argues for a harmonization in the opposite direction (*Palestinian Parties*, 140).

42. Among the many examples are Driver, *Deuteronomy*, 148; Dieter Eduard Skweres, *Die Rückverweise im Buch Deuteronomium* (AnBib 79; Rome: Pontifical Biblical Institute, 1979) 71–72; Braulik, *Deuteronomium*, 100; and Reuter, *Kultzentralisation*, 80–82.

43. The difficulty of squaring the view that Deut 12:21 refers back to 12:15 with the obvious fact that v. 15 is not a command is evident in the awkward need for a gloss on v. 21: "*wie ich dir geboten* d. i. erlaubt *habe* (V. 15)"; so August Dillmann, *Die Bücher Numeri, Deuteronomium und Josua* (KeHAT; 2d ed.; Leipzig: S. Hirzel, 1886) 298 (emphasis in origi-

the verb צוה, "to command," to bear an otherwise completely unattested meaning—without ever justifying the lexicographic problem involved.[44] Second,
although there is clear linguistic similarity between the verses, v. 15 provides
no source for the emphasis in v. 21 on מבקרך ומצאנך "from your cattle and from
your sheep" as the partitive object of the verb וזבחת "you may slaughter."[45] A
new antecedent must be sought[46] However, there is a problem. There neither is
nor can be a direct textual antecedent for the verse because the innovation of
secular slaughter (Deut 12:21, 15) is unprecedented. Local secular slaughter,
like cultic centralization, represents one of the distinctive innovations of
Deuteronomy. Precisely the problem faced by the authors of Deuteronomy—
the lack of prior legal or religious warrant for their double innovation—provides a new way of approaching this crux.

Deut 12:21 is not a simple citation; it is rather a pseudocitation.[47] Reflecting
on the problem that the innovation of local secular slaughter lacked support in

---

nal). Challenging this consensus position on the antecedent of v. 21 on these grounds is Jacob
Milgrom, "Profane Slaughter and a Formulaic Key to the Composition of Deuteronomy," *HUCA*
47 (1976) 1–17, at 2–3. The similar analysis is also provided by Milgrom, "Ethics and Ritual:
The Foundations of the Biblical Dietary Laws," in *Religion and Law: Biblical-Judaic and
Islamic Perspectives* (ed. Edwin R. Firmage, Bernard G. Weiss, and John W. Welch; Winona
Lake, Ind.: Eisenbrauns, 1990) 159–91.

44. Recognizing this problem, Eduard Nielsen attempts to finesse it by proposing to translate the verb צוה as "erlauben" (permit) because it would be "viel einfacher" to do so (*Deuteronomium* [Handbuch zum Alten Testament 1.6; Tübingen: J. C. B. Mohr (Paul Siebeck), 1995]
141). That it would be much easier does not make it philologically defensible. Nielsen provides
no textual evidence in support of the new translation, which is unattested in the lexica. The only
clear modification of the verb's denotation is that it can also refer to a deathbed settling of one's
affairs, in order to prepare a legacy (Gen 50:16; 1 Kgs 2:1). The latter, established usage (see BDB,
845 [1b], *s.v.* צוה) covers the reservations expressed by Samuel A. Meier, *Speaking of Speaking:
Marking Direct Discourse in the Hebrew Bible* (VTSup 46; Leiden: E. J. Brill, 1992) 198.

45. This problem was already recognized by August Klostermann, *Der Pentateuch: Beiträge
zu seinem Verständnis und seiner Entstehungsgeschichte* (Leipzig: A. Deichert, 1907) 281.

46. Milgrom, "Profane Slaughter," 1–17 importantly opens the consensus position to reexamination. His alternative solution, however, is problematic. He argues that the citation formula in v. 21 refers to priestly rules prescribing the ritual cutting of a sacrificial animal's throat.
He thereby leaves unexplained the anomalous use of the verb זבח to govern profane slaughter in
v. 15, which lacks the citation formula. Moreover, this explanation anachronistically presupposes Second Temple and later Mishnaic systematizations for which there is no evidence in the
Bible. Unnoted by Milgrom, his own gloss on v. 21 (pp. 13–15) returns almost verbatim to the
harmonistic solution offered by the Tannaitic commentary on Deuteronomy: מה קדשים בשחיטה אף
חולין בשחיטה "Just as consecrated animals must be slaughtered in the ritual manner, so also profane animals must be slaughtered in the ritual manner"; so *Sifre on Deuteronomy, pisqa* 75 (ed.
L. Finkelstein; New York: Jewish Theological Seminary of America, 1969) 140. Precisely this
recourse to the rules for ritual slaughter, which are found only in postbiblical *halakhah*, had
earlier been rejected by David Zvi Hoffmann, *Das Buch Deuteronomium* (2 vols.; Berlin: M.
Poppelauer, 1913–22) 1.167–68, on whose work Milgrom bases his analysis in the first place.
For further details see Levinson, *Hermeneutics of Innovation*, 177–86.

47. Fishbane, *Biblical Interpretation*, 534, similarly calls it a "pseudo-ascription." His
argument, however, that the unit harmonizes Deut 12:13–19 with Leviticus 17 overlooks the
role of the Exodus altar law and raises problems by assuming the priority of the Holiness Code
to Deuteronomy.

literary history, Deuteronomy's authors attempt to give it the necessary textual pedigree. Resorting to the literary tropes that they also employ elsewhere to revise authoritative law, the text's authors present the new concession as if it embodied the intent of the altar law that is actually here abrogated. The pseudocitation tags and reworks Exod 20:24. Three facts support this interpretation. First, both the verb and the list of sacrificial animals (וזבחת מבקרך ומצאנך "you may slaughter from your cattle and your sheep") derive from Exod 20:24 (וזבחת ... את צאנך ואת בקרך "you shall sacrifice . . . your sheep and your cattle").[48] The Hebrew verb is identical in each case, as are the animals that are specified. Second, the altar law does constitute a divine command, as required by the verb of the citation tag. Third, the secularization of the Exodus altar law explains the deliberately anomalous use of the verbזבח—normally, "to sacrifice"—here as "to slaughter."

An objection to this analysis could be raised. The citation tag in Deut 12:21, where Moses is the speaker, would seem to presuppose Moses also as the issuer of the previous command—yet Yahweh is the speaker in Exod 20:24.[49] In fact, however, the promulgation formula in which Moses exhorts obedience to the law "which I command you/have commanded you" often specifies that Moses commands what Yahweh has already commanded—that Moses is the spokesperson for God. Very frequently, the promulgation formula does not refer back to something originally and independently Mosaic but to the Mosaic reiteration of divine law.[50] Moreover, the promulgation formula sometimes leaves ambiguous who is actually imposing the law in question: whether it designates Moses himself, the textual speaker, or Yahweh, for whom he speaks. On occasion it is impossible to distinguish between the two.[51] In one case (Deut 20:17), Yahweh, speaking in the first person, even seems to cite a Mosaic utterance (Deut 7:1) as his own.[52] Consequently, Moses in Deut 12:21 functions as Yahweh's spokesperson and alludes in the first person to a law originally proclaimed by Yahweh. In this case, however, the voice of Moses represents the voice of tendentious scribal hermeneutics striving to defend and justify the innovation of local secular slaughter, making a legal precedent out of necessity.

48. The sequence "cattle/sheep" (Deut 12:21) conforms to the stylistic norm of Deuteronomy (Deut 8:13; 12:17; 14:23, 26; 15:19; cf. 32:14; 7:13; 28:4, 18, 51); see J. B. Segal, *The Hebrew Passover: From the Earliest Times to A.D. 70* (London Oriental Series 12; London: Oxford University Press, 1963) 205 n. 4. It therefore cannot be construed as a chiastic citation of Exod 20:24 according to Seidel's law.

49. See Norbert Lohfink, "Fortschreibung? Zur Technik von Rechtsrevisionen im deuteronomischen Bereich, erörtert an Deuteronomium 12, Ex 21,2–11 und Dtn 15,12–18," in *Das Deuteronomium und seine Querbeziehungen* (ed. Timo Veijola; Schriften der Finnischen Exegetischen Gesellschaft 62; Göttingen: Vandenhoeck & Ruprecht, 1996) 139 n. 49.

50. For example, referring to Yahweh, Moses says to the people, "You shall observe his statutes and his commandments, *which I command you* this day" (Deut 4:40; similarly, 6:2; 8:11). An equivalent formulation is "the commandments of Yahweh and his statutes *which I command you* this day" (Deut 10:13; 11:27; similarly, 11:28; 13:19; 15:5; 27:10; 28:1, 13, 15). The most current analysis of the promulgation formula, with comprehensive bibliography, is now provided by Norbert Lohfink, *Die Väter Israels im Deuteronomium* (OBO 111; Freiburg, Switzerland: Universitätsverlag; Göttingen: Vandenhoeck & Ruprecht, 1991) 87–99.

51. See Lohfink, *Hauptgebot*, 61; and Skweres, *Rückverweise*, 71 n. 304.

52. Lohfink, *Hauptgebot*, 60–61.

The Hermeneutical Function of Deut 12:8–12

No less than the other paragraphs, Deut 12:8–10 represents an intertextual attempt to reflect upon and to justify the innovation of centralization. It represents a later, Deuteronomistic stratum of the legal corpus that has multiple ties to the Deuteronomistic History. At the same time, it is very carefully redactionally integrated into its present context. The sequence of Deut 12:2–7, commanding centralization, followed by Deut 12:8–12, reflecting upon the temporal condition for its inception, is established by Deut 12:1, which defines the purview of the Deuteronomic legal corpus in chronological and geographic terms: "These are the statutes and the laws that you shall take care to observe *in the land that Yahweh, the God of thine ancestors, has given thee to possess—all the days that you live upon the earth.*" Rhetorically, too, the unit is carefully integrated into its context. The construction of v. 8, לא תעשׂון כ, "You shall not do as," continued by כי "because" in v. 9, is nearly identical to the construction of the prior unit concerning centralization, vv. 4–7, which begins with לא תעשׂון כן "You shall not do thus" continued by כי (Deut 12:5).[53]

Whereas in the paragraphs already examined the innovation of cult centralization is justified intertextually in relation to legal history—the altar law of the Covenant Code—in this case, the editor's frame of reference is rather the Deuteronomistic History. The key to the unit is Deut 12:9–10, which has a clear programmatic function: "For you have not as yet come to *the rest and the inheritance* (אל המנוחה ואל הנחלה) that Yahweh your God is giving you. When you cross over the Jordan and settle in the land that Yahweh your God is allocating to you, *he shall grant you rest from all of your enemies round about* (והניח לכם מכל איביכם מסביב) so that you shall dwell in security." Deut 12:9 and 25:19, which provides a near verbatim repetition of the italicized clauses, form an inclusio that frames the legal corpus.[54] These verses also provide a means for the Deuteronomistic Historian to integrate the legal corpus of Deuteronomy into his larger historiographic project: to structure and periodize his theology of history into various stages of promise and fulfillment that span and unify Deuteronomy through 2 Kings.[55] The idea of God's providing "rest from the

53. In Deut 12:5, the conjunction marks disjunctive "but"; in v. 9 it functions as explanatory "because."

54. For the most careful examination of the verses' ties to the Deuteronomistic History, their programmatic function, and the inclusio, see Georg Braulik, "Zur deuteronomistischen Konzeption von Freiheit und Frieden," in *Congress Volume Salamanca 1983* (ed. J. A. Emerton; VTSup 36; Leiden: E. J. Brill, 1985) 29–39; reprinted in and cited according to Braulik, *Studien zur Theologie des Deuteronomiums* (SBAB 2; Stuttgart: Katholisches Bibelwerk, 1988) 219–30.

55. Although I refer here to the Deuteronomistic Historian, in the singular, for convenience, in point of fact there are multiple Deuteronomistic strata, the exact number and dating of which remain under discussion. For recent summaries of the discussion see Knoppers, *Two Nations under God*, 1.1–56; and Horst Dietrich Preuß, "Zum deuteronomistischen Geschichtswerk," *TRu* 58 (1993) 229–64, 341–95. Since Noth's groundbreaking work, scholars have increasingly revised his model and recognized the extent of Deuteronomistic material within the legal corpus. Instrumental in this shift is Norbert Lohfink, "Kerygmata des deuteronomistischen Geschichtswerks," in *Die Botschaft und die Boten: Festschrift für Hans Walter Wolff* (ed. J. Jeremias and L. Perlitt; Neukirchen-Vluyn: Neukirchener Verlag, 1981) 87–100; reprinted, Lohfink, *Studien zum Deute-*

enemies round about" is clearly marked as fulfilled with the idyllic meditation concerning the completion of the Conquest (Josh 21:43–45).[56] That motif of national rest is also stressed in terms of the history of the monarchy, whereby God affirms for David—immediately after he has brought the Ark to Jerusalem—that He has granted him "rest from his enemies round about" (2 Sam 7:1; cf. 11). With the completion of the Temple, as Solomon makes clear in his Temple dedication speech (1 Kgs 8:56), the nation now achieves the "rest" (מנוחה) that Yahweh had originally promised (Deut 12:9).[57] The Temple's completion, for the Deuteronomistic Historiographer, therefore provides a double fulfillment: of the Davidic dynastic oracle spoken by Nathan (2 Sam 7:13a) and of the promise to Israel spoken by Moses (Deut 12:9).[58] In the Temple, accordingly, dynastic history and cultic history, Kingship and Sacrifice, combine, as both time and national destiny find their fulfillment.

Separate from this significant integration of the Deuteronomic legal corpus into the larger historiographic scheme of the Deuteronomistic History, the unit serves another function. It provides a proleptic explanation for the inconsistency between the late innovation of cultic centralization and the entire historiographic record, in which there was no centralization and the people sacrificed at the local altars. Both the establishment of the monarchy and the construction of the Temple were the essential preconditions for centralization. This concern to explain the failure to observe centralization and to present it as a lack of centralized government whereby "each man [does] whatever is right in his own eyes" (Deut 12:8) is glossed by the Deuteronomistic Historian's more explicit editorial comment elsewhere: "In those days there was no king in Israel; every man would do whatever was right in his own eyes."[59] Within the legal corpus, the paragraph provides an exculpation for Israel's failure to observe the new standard of centralization, much as the notes by the Deuteronomistic Historian within the historiographic literature similarly attempt to excuse the nation's sacrificing at the local high places (see 1 Kgs 3:2).[60]

The cultic norm that centralization strives to displace—worship at multiple altars—becomes conveniently reinterpreted as a throwback to the pre-

---

ronomium und zur deuteronomistischen Literatur II (Stuttgart: Katholisches Bibelwerk, 1991) 125–42.

56. Josh 21:43–45 strikingly reinterprets Deut 12:10. What was originally presented as a simple divine gift, proclaimed by Moses, is reinterpreted in Joshua 21:43–45 as a divine promise to the patriarchs—with no mention of Moses. See Braulik, "Freiheit und Frieden," 222.

57. On Solomon's reign as the realization of this rest, see Gerhard von Rad, *The Problem of the Hexateuch and Other Essays* (New York: McGraw-Hill, 1966) 94–98.

58. Note the similar argument by Gary N. Knoppers that the Deuteronomistic Historian's account of the Temple dedication integrates Davidic promises and Mosaic law ("Prayer and Propaganda: Solomon's Dedication of the Temple and the Deuteronomist's Program," *CBQ* 57 [1995] 229–54).

59. Judg 17:6; 21:25; cf. 18:1; 19:1.

60. The chronological exculpation of the people for not observing the late innovation of centralization is marked in both Deut 12:10 and 1 Kgs 3:2b by the formula: כי לא + verb in perfect + עד.

monarchic period. In this deft revision of cultic and legal history, such worship was intended, from the very beginning, to have been merely contingent: a retrograde custom associated with the chaos that existed prior to the monarchy and the emergence of proper government. The hermeneutical move is bold. The authors responsible for the unit quietly restrict previously authoritative and temporally unconditional cultic law (Exod 20:24) so that it now—ex post facto—has but provisional validity and a planned obsolescence.

Reflections upon Textuality
and Exegesis in Deuteronomy 12

Through their exegetical reworking, the authors of Deuteronomy transform the Exodus altar law. They rework its key terms in such a way as finally to make it prohibit what it originally sanctioned (multiple altar sites as legitimate) and command the two innovations it could never have contemplated: cultic centralization and local, secular slaughter. Both the technique and the boldness of this hermeneutical transformation are remarkable. The lemma is viewed atomistically: legal or textual authority operates at the level of individual words that, even when recontextualized, retain their operative force. Such studied concern with textual authority, not to mention the immense meditation upon the laws that it presupposes, is astonishing in seventh-century Israel. In its reuse, the Exodus lemma is so fundamentally transformed that it commands both cultic sacrifice (at the central sanctuary) and local slaughter (voided of ritual meaning). The antithetical reworking of the original text suggests an extraordinary ambivalence on the part of the authors of Deuteronomy, who retain the old altar law only to transform it and who thereby subvert the very textual authority that they invoke.

The skilled textual manipulation presses the question of the self-understanding of the Deuteronomic authors. Did they actually believe that their transformative exegesis merely elucidated an ambiguity inherent in the Exodus altar law and therefore "was not so much rejecting the rule in Exod 20:24 as specifying its underlying intent"?[61] Their raiding of its lexemes was more likely deliberate. Ambiguity did not finally inhere in the grammar of the verse. Ambiguity was deliberately injected into that lemma in order to sponsor a radically new view of religion, law, and the social polity. Through their lemmatic transformation of the altar law, the authors and later editors of Deuteronomy found a way to maintain its formal authority, if circumscribed to the level of discrete lexemes, and to garb their innovations in the mantle of the very text that they substantively abrogate.

The hermeneutical richness of Deuteronomy is that it should subvert the force of its innovation by locating that innovation in the original revelation. The innovation is presented as a citation of what God originally required at

---

61. So Fishbane, *Biblical Interpretation*, 252; I have corrected the typo in the original, which read "Exod 20:20."

Sinai כַּאֲשֶׁר צִוִּיתִךָ "as I commanded you." Citation thereby becomes pseudo-citation: no such law was commanded at Sinai. Through their manipulation of the Exodus lemma, the authors of Deuteronomy create legal and literary history anew. Not only do they function as the authors of their new legal composition, but also they become sole mediators and arbiters of the authoritative tradition from which they depart and consistency with which they claim. It is as if the older textual dispensation itself commanded Deuteronomy's innovation of cultic centralization. Pseudocitation in turn gives way to pseudepigraphy: the authors of Deuteronomy usurp the Mosaic voice of authoritative tradition in order to authorize their own innovations.[62]

If the burden of literary history and the authority of a tradition of divine commands embedded in texts suppress innovation, one must either deny innovation or attribute it to the authoritative tradition. The first choice is one context in which exegesis emerges; the second is one basis for pseudepigraphy. In either case, the novum in literary history is denied and authorship is deflected from the writer to the authoritative tradition.[63] The late *Temple Scroll* (*11QTemple*), for example, presents its compilation of sectarian law as the original Sinaitic Torah.[64] Similarly, the Amoraim of the third through the sixth centuries C.E. authorize the Oral Law by claiming a rather ex post facto Sinaitic pedigree for it and by presenting their new legal system as merely the interpretation of older texts.[65] Moses de León confers the mantle of instant antiquity and authority for the Zohar, which he wrote in the early 1290s C.E., by pseudepigraphically ascribing it to Shimʿon bar Yoḥai, a second-century C.E. Tanna.[66] Such maneuvers, while widely recognized in postbiblical literature, have not

62. The notion of an author's deliberately misreading his literary predecessors in order to overcome the burden of an authoritative literary tradition has become a generative idea in modern literary theory. See Harold Bloom, *The Anxiety of Influence* (London: Oxford University, 1973); and Bloom, *A Map of Misreading* (Oxford: Oxford University, 1975).

63. On pseudepigraphy as a device to permit innovation in the face of an authoritative tradition, see Geoffrey H. Hartman, "On the Jewish Imagination," *Prooftexts* 5 (1985) 201–20, at 210. The prestige of the Qur'ān delayed the emergence of the novel in Muslim cultures until the turn of this century. Moreover, so problematic was originality that "the word *heresy* in Arabic is synonymous with the verb 'to innovate' or 'to begin'"; see Edward Said, *Beginnings: Intention and Method* (New York: Basic Books, 1975) 81.

64. See Yigael Yadin, *The Temple Scroll* (3 vols.; Jerusalem: Israel Exploration Society, 1977–83) 1.392; and Ben Zion Wacholder, *The Dawn of Qumran: The Sectarian Torah and the Teacher of Righteousness* (Cincinnati: Hebrew Union College Press, 1983) 222–29. Note that Wacholder (p. 3) does not accurately represent Yadin's position on the matter; their positions are closer than he suggests.

65. Martin S. Jaffee, "The Pretext of Interpretation: Rabbinic Oral Torah and the Charisma of Revelation," in *God in Language* (ed. Robert P. Scharlemann and Gilbert E. M. Ogutu; New York: Paragon House, 1987) 73–89. Robert Goldenberg, "The Problem of Originality in Talmudic Thought," *From Ancient Israel to Modern Judaism: Intellect in Quest of Understanding, Essays in Honor of Marvin Fox* (ed. Jacob Neusner, Ernest S. Frerichs, and Nahum M. Sarna; 4 vols.; BJS 159, 173–175; Atlanta: Scholars Press, 1989) 2.19–27, shows how "anxiety and ambivalence toward innovation in the realm of Torah pervade the early Rabbinic tradition" (21).

66. On the maneuver whereby authors continually ascribe new religious developments to the very tradition that they transform, see G. Scholem, "Revelation and Tradition as Religious Categories in Judaism," in his *The Messianic Idea in Judaism* (New York: Schocken, 1971)

previously been recognized as helping explain the composition and problematic structure of Deuteronomy.

It is particularly striking that the two cultic innovations of Deuteronomy 12, centralization and secular slaughter, are followed immediately by the so-called "canon formula" that prohibits any alteration of the given text: לא תסף עליו ולא תגרע ממנו "you shall neither add to it nor diminish it" (Deut 13:1b; cf. 4:2).[67] Despite the implication of the present chapter division, that formula does not function as a superscription to introduce chapter 13. Those chapter divisions are very late and originate only with the Latin Bible of the thirteenth century.[68] Instead, the ancient witnesses agree that MT Deut 13:1 actually marks the conclusion of chapter 12 and that a new unit begins with 13:2. That is clear from (1) the ancient Palestinian division of the text into סדרים "lessons" for triennial reading, where a new "lesson" begins with 13:2; (2) the Babylonian annual lection, where a(n) פסקא פתוחא "open paragraph" precedes 13:2; and (3) the Septuagint division.[69] Deut 13:1 thus functions as a colophon to the systematic reworking of the Exodus altar law in Deuteronomy 12. The sudden importuning of textual fidelity in this context suggests that the text's editors were fully aware of the chapter's radical transformation of Israelite cultic and legal history.[70] They attempted to camouflage those innovations by feigning a cunning piety with respect to the very authoritative texts that they had subverted.

282–303. On the Zohar as a late-thirteenth-century pseudepigraph and Scholem's shift from credulity to acceptance of this dating, see David Biale, *Gershom Scholem: Kabbalah and Counter-History* (Cambridge, Mass.: Harvard University Press, 1979) 115–21. Examining the recent claim that the Zohar actually does preserve an ancient oral tradition, see Hava Tirosh-Rothschild, "Continuity and Revision in the Study of Kabbalah," reviewing *Kabbalah: New Perspectives*, by Moshe Idel, *AJS Review* 16 (1991) 161–92.

67. In English and other translations, Deut 13:1 appears as 12:32, based on the Septuagint. Although the formula is an ancient one in cuneiform literature, in its present context it seems to be Deuteronomistic and secondary; see Mayes, *Deuteronomy*, 232. Adducing valuable comparative material, see Michael Fishbane, "Varia Deuteronomica," *ZAW* 84 (1972) 349–52; Eleonore Reuter, "'Nimm nichts davon weg und füge nichts hinzu': Dtn 13,1, seine alttestamentlichen Parallelen und seine altorientalischen Vorbilder," *BN* 47 (1989) 107–14; and Christoph Dohmen and Manfred Oeming, *Biblischer Kanon: Warum und Wozu? Eine Kanontheologie* (QD 137; Freiburg: Herder, 1992) 68–89. The discussions of Deut 13:1 by Reuter (p. 110) and by Dohmen and Oeming (p. 83) stress that the canon formula sanctions the centralization law, given its importance to the Deuteronomic and Deuteronomistic program. Their discussions overlook, however, what seems to be the most important point: the paradox that it is precisely in the context of cultic-legal innovation that the immutability of the textual heritage is so studiously asserted.

68. G. F. Moore, "The Vulgate Chapters and the Numbered Verses in the Hebrew Bible," *JBL* 12 (1893) 73–78; reprinted, *The Canon and Masorah of the Hebrew Bible* (ed. Sidney Z. Leiman; New York: Ktav, 1974) 815–820.

69. On the Palestinian "lessons" and the more complex Babylonian division of the Hebrew text, see B. J. Roberts, *The Old Testament Text and Versions* (Cardiff: University of Wales, 1951) 37; and, most comprehensively, Israel Yeivin, *Introduction to the Tiberian Masorah* (SBLMasS 5; Missoula: Scholars Press, 1980) 39–42.

70. Similarly, Fishbane, *Biblical Interpretation*, 263.

The Double Movement of Cultic Centralization
and Local Secularization

The authors of Deuteronomy strikingly transform and secularize both language and literary history. There are three specific points of secularization in Deut 12:13–19, 20–28. First, the very formulation of the rule for local slaughter appropriates two key terms from the lemma of the Exodus altar law—the verb זבח and the cultic list of originally sacrificial animals—and recontextualizes them, shorn of their original cultic context. Uniquely in Deut 12:15, 21, the verb, which conventionally, and everywhere else even in Deuteronomy itself, means "sacrifice," is deliberately forced to denote the secular "slaughter" that takes place locally, in the absence of an altar. The authors of Deuteronomy secularize language no less than they create a new, noncultic procedure. Second, the ritual that requires the Israelite to "*spill it* [the blood of the secularly slaughtered animal] *upon the* ground like water" כמים תשפכנו על הארץ (Deut 12:16, 24), precisely mirrors, both in language and action, the normative injunction that the blood of the sacrificial animal "be *spilled upon* the altar of Yahweh" ישפך על מזבח יהוה (Deut 12:27b). The prescribed local secular action has essentially the same structure as the cultic action at the central sanctuary. Third, the local blessing promised by Yahweh in the altar law as consequent upon sacrifice ("I shall come to you and bless you" אבוא אליך וברכתיך; Exod 20:24b) is retained—no longer, however, in the context of cultic theophany but rather in the secular context of the land's abundance that Yahweh provides the citizen (כברכת יהוה אלהיך; Deut 12:15).[71] The original cultic divine presence is retained, although now restricted to the central sanctuary where the offerings are made לפני יהוה "before Yahweh" (Deut 12:7, 12, 18).

In draining the local sphere of all cultic content, the authors of Deuteronomy do not leave it as a profane religious void. Instead, they reconceptualize it in secular terms and give it positive new content. The local sphere continues to have a fundamentally religious structure. One continues to receive divine blessing in the local sphere, although it is now mediated. The compensation for the loss of direct access to the divine, with the eradication of the local altars, does not only take place at the cultic center, with the repeated emphasis on the "joy" available there to the pilgrim.[72] That restitution is equally provided in the local sphere with this noncultic, although still religiously conceived, "blessing of Yahweh your God." In face of the dismantling of the countryside cultus begun by Hezekiah and intensified by Josiah, it was crucial for the Deuteronomic authors to establish for the citizens of Judah that the loss of the local altars did not entail complete loss of local access to God or, more seriously, that God

---

71. The reference to divine blessing is characteristic of Deuteronomy's rhetorical emphasis on the promised land and its bounty: see Deut 12:7; 15:4, 6, 10, 14, 18, etc.

72. Deut 12:7, 12, 18; 14:26; 15:20; 16:11, 14, 15; 26:11. For this point, see Norbert Lohfink, "The Cult Reform of Josiah of Judah: 2 Kings 22–23 as a Source for the History of Israelite Religion," in *Ancient Israelite Religion: Essays in Honor of Frank Moore Cross* (ed. Patrick D. Miller, Jr., Paul D. Hanson, and S. Dean McBride; Philadelphia: Fortress, 1987) 459–75 (469); and Lohfink, "Opfer und Säkularisierung," 31.

had abandoned the local sphere.[73] They went out of their way to provide the local sphere with its own integrity. Yahweh continues to be active and to grant his blessing there.

Deuteronomy's reconception of the local sphere in secular terms is radically new. The secular and the cultic are not antithetical, with only one of the two spheres constituting religious legitimacy, the other illegitimacy.[74] Rather, both spheres, local and central, are equally valid and dialectically related. Legitimacy and divine sanction adhere to both the cultic and the secular spheres. Deuteronomy's prescriptions for worship at the central sanctuary are as radically new, in terms of cultic convention and the history of religion, as are its prescriptions for local secular action.[75] Both are exegetically constituted out of the lexemes of the older altar law. Equally legitimate and jointly religiously conceived, both are also opposed to the one profane action: local sacrifice. The tripartite structure of Deut 12:13–15 explicitly distinguishes between the profane and the secular. The profane is illegitimate. The secular is legitimate and sanctioned by Yahweh's blessing:

(v. 13) local cultic action: prohibited
(v. 14) central cultic action: required
(v. 15) local secular action: permitted

This perspective challenges existing models for conceptualizing the relation between sacred and secular in Deuteronomy. Those models debate whether the primary dynamic in the legal corpus involves the secularization of prior cultic law or whether the opposite movement takes place as the authors subordinate all of life to God.[76] Both models presuppose a false dichotomy between

---

73. On the historical issue, see Baruch Halpern, "Jerusalem and the Lineages in the Seventh Century BCE: Kinship and the Rise of Individual Moral Liability," in *Law and Ideology in Monarchic Israel* (ed. Baruch Halpern and Deborah W. Hobson; JSOTSup 124; Sheffield: JSOT Press, 1991) 77–78. On the theological motif, Yahweh's judgment on Jerusalem is explicitly presented as divine abandonment: see Lam 4:20. The divine presence also abandons Jerusalem and the Temple compound in Ezekiel 10–11; see Moshe Greenberg, *Ezekiel, 1–20* (AB; Garden City, N.Y.: Doubleday, 1983) 193–205.

74. Contrast the situation in the Holiness Code where all slaughter of domestic, sacrificial animals—not at an altar—constitutes action contrary to God's will and requires excision from the community (Lev 17:3–4). Here the structure of experience involves the polar opposition between cultic and profane.

75. See Georg Braulik, "Die Freude des Festes: Das Kultverständnis des Deuteronomium— die älteste biblische Festtheorie" [1970], reprinted in Braulik, *Studien zur Theologie des Deuteronomiums* (SBAB 2; Stuttgart: Katholisches Bibelwerk, 1988) 161–218.

76. Arguing for secularization of prior cultic law and thought in Deuteronomy is Moshe Weinfeld, *Deuteronomy and the Deuteronomic School* (Oxford: Clarendon Press, 1972) 233–43. Challenging that approach with a comprehensive new interpretation that shows how Deuteronomy extends the presence of God over all of life is Lohfink, "Opfer und Säkularisierung," 15–43. Weinfeld and Lohfink provide the two most systematic and powerful alternatives. In his review article, Jacob Milgrom, "The Alleged 'Demythologization' and 'Secularization' in Deuteronomy," *IEJ* 23 (1973) 156–61, questions Weinfeld's interpretation of priestly texts. The most recent article on this issue is Eckart Otto, "Vom Rechtsbruch zur Sünde: Priesterliche Interpretationen des Rechts," *Jahrbuch für Biblische Theologie* 9 (1994) 25–52.

sacred and secular, while failing to distinguish between secular and profane. Deuteronomy's own model is more complex. The central, or cultic, and the local, or secular, are each religiously conceived. The authors of Deuteronomy transform both the central and the local sphere simultaneously; they reconceptualize each; the two are dialectically related and hermeneutically structured; each is opposed to the profane.

This double movement of Deuteronomy—cultic centralization and local secularization—operates both synchronically and diachronically. The drive to restrict cultic action to the central sphere and to secularize the local sphere provides an important synchronic insight into the composition and structure of the legal corpus. At key points, the authors of Deuteronomy work systematically to drain the local sphere of any connection with cultic action. They must do so at exactly those points where cultic centralization conflicts with norms and with texts that presuppose local cultic activity. It became necessary to establish new procedures in each case. In doing so, the authors of Deuteronomy formulate a distinctive lexicon that distinguishes between action במקום "in the place" and action בשעריך "in your city-gates"—which is to say, between the central and the local spheres, or between cultic and secular activity. The different procedures locally and at the cultic center are described in the cases of sacrifice, the festival calendar, and the administration of justice. In diachronic terms, the need to erase the contradiction between the innovation of cultic centralization and the pre-Deuteronomic texts that presupposed local sanctuaries provides the authors of Deuteronomy with a literary-historical agenda. Wherever possible, by means of lemmatic transformation, they must justify their innovations in light of existing texts. Their struggle to do so accounts for many of the *aporia* of syntax, structure, and formulation that scholars have long recognized but not yet satisfactorily accounted for.

The authors of Deuteronomy have a double program that is simultaneously legislative—to propound their new vision of religion, law, and the administration of the polity—and hermeneutical—concerned with justifying their own authority radically to overturn legal history. It is this double program that accounts for the two diverging trends in the scholarly interpretation of the legal corpus.[77] One approach has maintained that the legal corpus represents preexilic legislation designed to implement a broad-based cultic, judicial, and administrative program.[78] The other has emphasized the theoretical and impractical

77. The two diverging approaches in the history of Deuteronomy scholarship have been recognized by A. D. H. Mayes, "On Describing the Purpose of Deuteronomy," *JSOT* 58 (1993) 13–33. His ideas are taken up by Thomas Römer, "The Book of Deuteronomy," in *The History of Israel's Traditions: The Heritage of Martin Noth* (ed. Steven L. McKenzie and M. Patrick Graham; JSOTSup 182; Sheffield: Sheffield Academic Press, 1994) 192–94.

78. S. Dean McBride, "Polity of the Covenant People: The Book of Deuteronomy," *Int* 41 (1987) 229–44, reprinted in *A Song of Power and the Power of Song: Essays on the Book of Deuteronomy* (ed. Duane L. Christensen; Winona Lake, Ind.: Eisenbrauns, 1993) 62–77; and Frank Crüsemann, *Die Tora: Theologie und Sozialgeschichte des alttestamentlichen Gesetzes* (Munich: Chr. Kaiser, 1992) 235–322. Both approaches necessarily seek to establish the coherence of the legal corpus and minimize the amount of exilic and postexilic, Deuteronomistic material in it.

nature of the legal corpus, either in terms of levitical homily or as utopian theological reflection dating to the exilic or postexilic period.[79] The two discrepant approaches, when brought together at all, have been simultaneously maintained only by attributing them to separate Deuteronomic and Deuteronomistic strata of the legal corpus, a method that only emphasizes their nonrelation.[80] There has not yet been an approach that either unifies these two insights into the nature of Deuteronomy or that recognizes their common origin in the program of the text's authors. The approach taken here is that, from the very inception of the legal corpus, with the innovation of centralization, the legislative and the hermeneutical were inseparable from each other.

79. Gustav Hölscher, "Komposition und Ursprung des Deuteronomiums," *ZAW* 40 (1922) 161–255, for example, argued that the laws of Deuteronomy represented postexilic theological attempts to conform priestly law to centralization and were never meant to be implemented. From a quite different perspective, working with a "Blockmodell" of the redaction of the legal corpus, Norbert Lohfink views Deut 16:18–18:22 as a utopian, exilic, Deuteronomistic composition that never saw practical application. See his "Die Sicherung der Wirksamkeit des Gotteswortes durch das Prinzip der Schriftlichkeit der Tora und durch das Prinzip der Gewaltenteilung nach den ämtergesetzen des Buches Deuteronomium (Dt 16,18–18,22)," in *Testimonium Veritati: Festschrift Wilhelm Kempf* (ed. H. Wolter; Frankfurter Theologische Studien 7; Frankfurt: Knecht, 1971) 143–55; reprinted, Lohfink, *Studien zum Deuteronomium und zur deuteronomistischen Literatur I* (SBAB 8; Stuttgart: Katholisches Bibelwerk, 1990) 305–23. The article has been translated as "Distribution of the Functions of Power: The Laws Concerning Public Offices in Deuteronomy 16:18–18:22," in *A Song of Power and the Power of Song: Essays on the Book of Deuteronomy* (ed. Duane L. Christensen; Winona Lake, Ind.: Eisenbrauns, 1993) 336–52.

80. See Udo Rüterswörden, *Von der politischen Gemeinschaft zur Gemeinde: Studien zu Dt 16,1–18,22* (BBB 65; Frankfurt: Athenäum, 1987) 94–112; and Eckart Otto, "Von der Gerichtsordnung zum Verfassungsentwurf: Deuteronomische Gestaltung und deuteronomistische Interpretation im 'Ämtergesetz' Dtn 16,18–18,22," in *"Wer ist wie du, HERR, unter den Göttern?" Studien zur Theologie und Religionsgeschichte Israels für Otto Kaiser* (ed. Ingo Kottsieper et al.; Göttingen: Vandenhoeck & Ruprecht, 1995) 142–55. This approach has received a fundamental methodological challenge. On both approaches, see chapter 4.

3

The Transformation of Passover and Unleavened Bread in Deuteronomy 16

The festival calendar of Deut 16:1–17 goes to the very heart of the Deuteronomic program and reveals the authors' literary and religious achievements. The Deuteronomic drive to centralize the cultus did not involve a mere restriction of the location for sacrifice. It entailed a much more systematic and profound transformation of Judaean religious and social life. The authors of Deuteronomy also found it necessary to transform the festival calendar of ancient Israel together with other religious observances, most notably the Passover. Deuteronomy's proscription of the local sanctuaries meant that the ancient festivals of Unleavened Bread, Weeks, and Tabernacles could no longer be observed in the customary way. These festivals were originally "pilgrimage festivals" to the very local sanctuaries that the authors of Deuteronomy sought to abolish. Similarly, the authors' restriction of all cultic activity to the central sanctuary necessarily created a conflict with the ancient rite of the Passover. That observance involved the ritual slaughter of a sheep or goat in the doorway of the private domicile and was accompanied by a distinctive blood rite. The contradiction between such an observance and the new Deuteronomic imperative, which required that ritual slaughter take place exclusively at the central sanctuary and that all ritually significant blood be spilled at or upon the altar there, could not have been greater.

In order to implement their agenda of cultic centralization, therefore, the authors of Deuteronomy had somehow to erase the blatant contradiction between their program of cultic reform and the conventional observance of the festivals and the Passover. They could neither prohibit nor ignore these ancient observances. The festivals had immense significance: they provided a means for the people to gain cultic access to the deity, to celebrate the natural rhythms of the year, and to acknowledge the source of the land's natural bounty. Separate from the popularity of these celebrations, the authors of Deuteronomy confronted another crucial dilemma. These holy occasions were enshrined by prestigious and authoritative texts: it was a requirement of religious law that each Israelite male observe the pilgrimage festivals by appearing thrice yearly before Yahweh at the local sanctuary and that each family observe the paschal slaughter.[1] Both the popularity of these observances and, more acutely, the prestige and the authority of the texts commanding them meant that the authors of Deuteronomy were constrained to come to terms with the festival calendar and the Passover. Across the board, "the stylized nature of almost all of Deuteronomy's laws of centralization as joy-filled festivals indicates that the people had to be talked out of feeling they had lost something."[2] The question thus arises: How could the Deuteronomic authors retain these observances and acknowledge the authoritative texts concerning them without sabotaging the entire thrust of their cultic reform?

They completely coopted the older paschal rite and the festivals. Just as they had in the case of local sacrifice, which was originally sanctioned by the old altar law of Exod 20:24, so now did the authors of Deuteronomy accommodate older texts to their new vision by reworking them. In so doing, the authors of Deuteronomy profoundly transformed the very structure of Judaean religious life and ritual observance. In placing its focus upon Passover and the Festival of Unleavened Bread, this chapter follows the lead set by the authors of Deuteronomy, who devoted almost half of the entire festival calendar to these two observances (eight of the seventeen verses in Deut 16:1–17). They summarily dispatched the other two, Weeks and Tabernacles, with three formulaic and closely overlapping verses each.[3] These two festivals presented less of a problem to the authors of Deuteronomy, who essentially just diverted them to the cultic center and stressed their social focus over their original agricultural orientation.[4] In contrast, Passover and Unleavened Bread, both individually and in their conjunction, presented the authors of Deuteronomy with more far-reaching problems.

The Programmatic Origins of Deut 16:1–8

It has long been held that the festival calendar of Deut 16:1–8 involves "a process of growth . . . in the course of which two separate festivals, Passover and

---

1. Exod 23:14, 17 and 34:23; 12:3, 21.
2. Norbert Lohfink, "The Cult Reform of Josiah of Judah: 2 Kings 22–23 as a Source for the History of Israelite Religion," in *Ancient Israelite Religion: Essays in Honor of Frank Moore Cross* (ed. Patrick D. Miller, Jr., Paul D. Hanson, and S. Dean McBride; Philadelphia: Fortress, 1987) 459–75, at 469, citing Deut 12:7, 12, 18; 14:26; 15:20; 16:11, 14, 15; 26:11. Note also Georg Braulik, "Die Freude des Festes: Das Kultverständnis des Deuteronomium—die älteste biblische Festtheorie," in Braulik, *Studien zur Theologie des Deuteronomiums* (SBAB 2; Stuttgart: Katholisches Bibelwerk, 1988) 161–218.
3. Deut 16:11 // Deut 16:14 + 15aβ; Deut 16:10b // Deut 16:15aα.
4. On Deuteronomy's conception of Weeks and Tabernacles see Georg Braulik, "Leidensgedächtnisfeier und Freudenfest: 'Volksliturgie' nach dem deuteronomischen Festkalender (Dtn 16, 1–17)," *TP* 56 (1981) 335–57; reprinted in and cited from Braulik, *Studien zur Theologie des Deuteronomiums* (SBAB 2; Stuttgart: Katholisches Bibelwerk, 1988) 95–121.

Unleavened Bread (Mazzot), have been combined."[5] According to this approach, the text achieves its form as the result of prior cultic or tradition history, which it reflects. Allegedly, the gradual shift from nomadic to settled life leads to the obsolescence of such ancient nomadic customs as the paschal slaughter, and the festival calendar thus mirrors already achieved, de facto, empirical development. Despite its popularity, that hypothesis has no real supporting evidence except for the very text that the reconstruction of external history both derives from and attempts to explain. The circular argument obscures its unexamined presupposition, which I dispute: that Deuteronomy's festival calendar passively reflects the external cultic and economic history problematically reconstructed to account for it. By this account, the authors of Deuteronomy were merely playing catch-up, bringing law into conformity with existing practice.

The dubious historical assumptions of the circular argument create further difficulties when it comes to analyzing the blend of Passover and Unleavened Bread in Deut 16:1–8. With literary history viewed as a mirror of empirical events, the analysis of Deut 16:1–8 becomes a simplistic, either/or issue. The critic only attempts to resolve whether the text's editor interpolated Passover into preexisting Unleavened Bread legislation or whether the editor did the reverse by interpolating Unleavened Bread legislation into preexisting Passover texts.[6] Much of the scholarship on Deuteronomy's festival calendar has been devoted to that question. The forced choice restricts the analytical question to simple diachrony alone. Such an approach fails to do full justice to either the historical or the literary issues that underlie the composition and the structure of this unit.

The conventional approach fails to recognize the programmatic nature and the intentional composition of Deuteronomy's festival calendar. It views history as taking place as if there were no actors, and texts as if they had no authors capable of originality. Deuteronomy's festival calendar was not an update but

---

5. A. D. H. Mayes, *Deuteronomy* (NCBC; London: Marshall, Morgan & Scott, 1979) 254. This view of the "Zusammenmischung von Passah u. Mazzoth" in Deut 16:1–8 is already explicit in August Dillmann, *Die Bücher Numeri, Deuteronomium und Josua* (KeHAT; 2d ed.; Leipzig: S. Hirzel, 1886) 311. More broadly, for a valuable analysis of the importance of Deuteronomy's festival calendar to the history of pentateuchal scholarship, see Timo Veijola, "The History of Passover in the Light of Deuteronomy 16, 1–8," *Zeitschrift für Altorientalische und Biblische Rechtsgeschichte* 2 (1996) 53–75, which arrived just as this manuscript was in press. I do not agree, however, with his redactional reconstruction, which views the material as post-priestly and situates it in the late postexilic period. For a critique of this and similar approaches, see Jan Christian Gertz, "Die Passa-Massot-Ordnung im deuteronomischen Festkalender," in *Das Deuteronomium und seine Querbeziehungen* (ed. Timo Veijola; Schriften der Finnischen Exegetischen Gesellschaft 62; Göttingen: Vandenhoeck & Ruprecht, 1996) 56–80.

6. For a detailed presentation of the scholars following each alternative, see Alfred Cholewiński, *Heiligkeitsgesetz und Deuteronomium: Eine vergleichende Studie* (AnBib 66; Rome: Pontifical Biblical Institute, 1976) 179–81; or Mayes, *Deuteronomy*, 254–55. Eckart Otto, "פסח *pāsaḥ/paesaḥ*," *TWAT* 6 (1989) 659–82, at 675, seeks to find a way out of the traditional either/or approach by suggesting that each is true from its own perspective: diachronically, the Unleavened Bread legislation is prior, but synchronically, Passover legislation provides the current frame. Even so, the tenets of the existing model are still affirmed.

a revolution. The truth of the matter is that, prior to and independent of Deuteronomy, Unleavened Bread was not joined to Passover, nor was Passover, prior to Deuteronomy, anything other than a rite in the private home. The issue is not priority in genetic terms. Posing the question in that way is futile, since it is impossible to move behind the texts to establish the relative priority of either Passover or Unleavened Bread. There is no prior text that can be reconstructed as "original."[7] Nor is it a matter of the interpolation of either Passover or Unleavened Bread legislation into the other. Neither legislation is preserved intact; each is transformed in light of the other.

What is prior is neither Passover nor Unleavened Bread, in itself, but rather the innovation of centralization and the historical program of Deuteronomy's authors. In Deut 16:1–8, the authors of Deuteronomy construct and sanction an entirely new observance that supplants both the original Passover and the original Unleavened Bread and that is now consistent with the Deuteronomic program. The complex structure of the text reflects intentionality, not prior cultic history. The innovation of cultic centralization compelled the authors of Deuteronomy to create new texts. They had to eclipse the authority of existing texts that did not contemplate centralization in order to authorize their innovation. Paradoxically, it was precisely to those older texts that the Deuteronomic authors turned—deliberately, creatively, and tendentiously raiding them for their prestigious lemmas, which they then reconstituted in order to accomplish their own religious and social agenda.

Although it contains much arcane material, Deuteronomy's festival calendar therefore reveals the capacity of the text's authors for radical religious and legal innovation, as well as the techniques of studied textual transformation used to accomplish their program. The authors of Deuteronomy apply lemmas to the new Passover, whose original reference was the Feast of Unleavened Bread. This reformulation transforms the Passover, originally a local domestic observance, into a pilgrimage festival in everything but name. Unleavened Bread is similarly transformed, but in a different direction. Unleavened Bread originally involved a pilgrimage to the local sanctuary; Deuteronomy's version is completely shorn of the pilgrimage element to become a static local observance. Both transformations involve the larger dynamic that I demonstrated in chapter 1: cultic centralization and local secularization. In order to demonstrate these arguments, I provide a reconstruction of the pre-Deuteronomic Passover and Unleavened Bread festival, showing how each conflicted with the Deuteronomic program. Then I show how the authors of Deuteronomy transformed both observances in light of centralization.

---

7. Unconvincing is the reconstruction offered by Eleonore Reuter, *Kultzentralisation: Entstehung und Theologie von Dtn 12* (BBB 87; Frankfurt: Anton Hain, 1993) 255–58. She claims that the Unleavened Bread legislation is original; the Passover legislation, a later accretion. Her own valuable insistence elsewhere that there is no Deuteronomy without cult centralization (pp. 189–91) contradicts that claim. To reconstruct a festival calendar with Unleavened Bread legislation as original (p. 170) but in which neither cult centralization nor pilgrimage to the sanctuary plays a role then becomes illogical.

The Pre-Deuteronomic Passover

Passover originally had nothing whatsoever to do with the Festival of Unleavened Bread, מצות.[8] It was not technically a "festival" (חג), that is, an observance requiring that the worshiper undertake a pilgrimage to one of the local sanctuaries to pay homage to the deity (Exod 23:17).[9] Nor did the Passover ritual involve, in the technical sense of the term, a normal cultic sacrifice. The rite bore no connection to the public or official cultus. Instead, in its original form, prior to Deuteronomy, the paschal slaughter was a ritual activity that took place entirely within the context of the clan. The Yahwistic legislation (J) uses the distributive to stipulate that each family unit was required to slaughter its own small cattle: צאן למשפחתיכם "sheep for your families" (Exod 12:21), a requirement and construction retained by the later Priestly (P) source: שׂה לבית אבת שׂה לבית "a lamb to a family, a lamb to a household" (Exod 12:3).[10] This emphasis on the clan is widely recognized as owing to the Passover's origin in the nomadic culture of the pre-Settlement period.[11] In sociological terms, the family

8. Inevitably, all the possible positions have been argued. Thus, the claim that the two rites represented an original unity, only secondarily presented as separate, is not supported by the language of the texts involved; contra J. B. Segal, *The Hebrew Passover: From the Earliest Times to A.D. 70* (London Oriental Series 12; London: Oxford University Press, 1963) 175. Nor does either rite simply represent a logical, traditio-historical development from the other. Specifically, the Unleavened Bread ritual does not originate in the Passover, contra Jörn Halbe, "Erwägungen zu Ursprung und Wesen des Massotfestes," *ZAW* 87 (1975) 324–46; nor, conversely, does Passover represent a Deuteronomic development of the Unleavened Bread festival, contra B. N. Wambacq, "Les Maṣṣot," *Bib* 61 (1980) 31–54. Refuting these positions and demonstrating the independence of the two rites is Eckart Otto, *Das Mazzotfest in Gilgal* (BWANT 107; Stuttgart: W. Kohlhammer, 1975) 175–84; and Otto (with Tim Schramm), *Festival and Joy* (Nashville: Abingdon, 1980) 13, 195–96.

9. There was a scholarly fashion during the 1960s and 1970s to regard the Deuteronomic view of Passover as a pilgrimage as a carryover from the premonarchic period. Allegedly, Passover was an important celebration of the early tribal league that involved a pilgrimage or "ritual conquest" to the "central" sanctuary at Gilgal. One reconstruction in this vein is provided by Frank Moore Cross, who casts the net as widely as possible by referring to "the spring festival ('Passover' or 'Maṣṣōt')"; see his *Canaanite Myth and Hebrew Epic: Essays in the History of the Religion of Israel* (Cambridge: Harvard University Press, 1973) 79–85, 103. All such reconstructions appear highly problematic in light of recent studies of Israelite origins, which dispute the notion of a tribal league or amphictyony.

10. It is quite possible, however, that the priestly source does not passively retain the original family nexus of the J source (Exod 12:21). P's בית אבות (Exod 12:3) may actually refer to a quite different social institution of the postexilic period: the units of approximately one thousand males into which *Yehûd* as a civic-and-temple community may have been organized, following the model of Persian agnatic groups. See Joel P. Weinberg, "Das *bêit 'abōt* im 6.–4. Jahrhundert v.u.Z.," *VT* 23 (1973) 400–414; Weinberg, *The Citizen-Temple Community* (JSOTSup 151; Sheffield: Sheffield Academic Press, 1992); and Paul E. Dion, "The Civic-and-Temple Community of Persian Period Judaea: Neglected Insights from Eastern Europe," *JNES* 50 (1991) 281–87. On these grounds Joseph Blenkinsopp concludes that the priestly account of the passover ritual is distinctly postexilic rather than preexilic in its orientation (*The Pentateuch: An Introduction to the First Five Books of the Bible* [New York: Doubleday, 1992] 156).

11. Alternatively, the text may not be retaining a primitive rite unchanged but imaginatively creating it as part of a larger construction of a national prehistory. For a valuable chal-

setting points to the origin of the stipulations in a *Gemeinschaft* rather than a complex, national *Gesellschaft*.[12]

Despite the biblical text's presentation of the paschal observance as originating in Egypt in the context of the divine sparing of the Israelites from the final plague, the Passover actually originated as an apotropaic ritualized slaughter with no inherent connection to the plagues or to the events of the Exodus. The etymology of the word פסח—properly, "protection," not "pass over"— also makes this clear.[13] The apotropaic origin of the Passover is particularly evident in the blood ritual that is central to the observance. Using a branch of hyssop, the paterfamilias daubs fresh blood from the sheep just slaughtered upon the threshold onto each of the two door posts and the lintel of the doorway. Both the hyssop and the daubing are apotropaic.[14] The fourfold framing of the entrance with blood—top, bottom, and sides, thus marking totality[15]—protects the household from the demonic agent of destruction, barring his entrance: ולא יתן המשחית לבא אל בתיכם לנגף "and not permit the Destroyer to enter and smite your home" (Exod 12:23, J).[16] By framing the doorway with blood, the head

---

lenge to traditio-historical assumptions of Passover's antiquity, see John Van Seters, *The Life of Moses: The Yahwist as Historian in Exodus–Numbers* (Louisville: Westminster/John Knox, 1994) 114. Recent historiography has seriously challenged all older models of the nomadic origins of ancient Israel and complicated the very notion of how nomadism should be defined. See Thomas L. Thompson, "Palestinian Pastoralism and Israel's Origins," *SJOT* 6 (1992) 1–13; and Thompson, *Early History of the Israelite People: From the Written and Archaeological Sources* (Studies in the History of the Ancient Near East 4; Leiden: E. J. Brill, 1992) 21–22, 177–300.

12. For the classical formulation of the two sociological categories, see F. Tönnies, *Community and Society* [1887] (New York: Harper & Row, 1957); for the community setting of the Passover see Otto, "*pāsaḥ/paesaḥ*," 672.

13. On the original independence of the Passover rite see Samuel E. Loewenstamm, *The Evolution of the Exodus Tradition* (Jerusalem: Magnes, 1992) 189–218. On the rite's nomadic and apotropaic origins, note also Menahem Haran, *Temples and Temple-Service in Ancient Israel: An Inquiry into the Character of Cult-Phenomena and the Historical Setting of the Priestly School* (Oxford: Clarendon, 1978) 318–21, esp. 320 n. 7. For the most recent analyses of the meaning of the verb, see Loewenstamm, *Exodus Tradition*, 197–202, 219–21; and Otto, "*pāsaḥ/paesaḥ*," 659–82, who provides a concise reconstruction of the rite's origins and development.

14. On hyssop and its apotropaic function, see Haran, *Temples*, 319 n. 5.

15. The symbolic requirement that the protective daubing be fourfold and thereby comprehensive is equally preserved in the use of the paleo-Hebrew *taw*, shaped like an "X," as apotropaic mark inscribed by a scribal angel on the foreheads of the righteous in Ezek 9:4–6. That text marks a symbolic inversion of Exodus 12: the angelic destroyer is now set loose against those who do not recognize Yahweh's authority within Jerusalem; those who reject God are internal rather than external to the nation. The current Samaritan observance of the Passover combines the apotropy of that protective mark with that of blood's power of sympathetic substitution. The celebrants smear an "X" (recalling the paleo-Hebrew *taw* of Ezek 9:4–6) upon the foreheads of their children by using the blood of the paschal lamb (personal observation, Samaritan Passover, Nablus/Schechem, spring, 1980).

16. Note the later reformulation by P, deanimating this personification to a simple abstract verbal noun, "there shall not be upon you smiting to destruction" לְמַשְׁחִית (Exod 12:13). The intertextual dimensions of the Priestly version of the Passover, as a revision of sources, is stressed by Van Seters, *Life of Moses*, 123, while using different examples and assumptions about dating.

of each Israelite family establishes a liminal barrier between "within the house"—as a refuge—and ביתו מפתח "outside the door of his house" (Exod 12:22)—as the realm of otherwise uncontrolled demonic energies. The ritual works by the magic of sympathetic substitution: the token of the lamb's blood on the doorway averts the spilling of further blood—that of the house's occupants.[17]

Most standard translations obscure the location of the blood ritual, incorrectly rendering בסף אשר הדם as "the blood which is *in the basin*" (Exod 12:22).[18] The phrase should more properly be rendered as "the blood which is upon the threshold."[19] Granted, the lexeme סף may have two meanings, one of which refers to basins as receptacles for liquids, although that definition has received an important challenge.[20] More accurately, it denotes the threshold or sill of a doorway, a meaning also reflected in one of the guilds of temple functionaries, the door-keepers.[21] The double meaning of the word from very early times gave rise to a double exegetical tradition. The ancient textual versions divide, with the Septuagint (τοῦ παρὰ τὴν θύραν) and Vulgate (*sanguine qui est in limine*) reflecting "doorway," while the Syriac *Peshiṭta* and the Targums reflect "vessel" (בדמא דבמנא in *Targum Onqelos*; בדמא דבמן פחרא in *Targum Pseudo-Jonathan*; באדמה די במנה in *Targum Neofiti I*).[22] Ancient rabbinic exegesis similarly divides, with the competing meanings debated in the Tannaitic midra-

---

17. The apotropaic use of blood against a demonically threatening divine power recalls the incident of Exod 4:24–26, where Zipporah places the bloody prepuce of the infant upon the "legs" (a euphemism for the genitalia) of Moses to divert a hostile God. In both cases, blood by sympathetic substitution magically averts the further demonic spilling of blood.

18. So the RSV, the NJPSV, NRSV, and, equivalently, the German revised Luther Bible (1984).

19. See A. M. Honeyman, "Hebrew סף 'Basin, Goblet'," *JTS* 37 (1936) 56–59. The attempt by Segal, *The Hebrew Passover*, 53, 157–58 to deny this interpretation is untenable. His analogy (158 n. 1) to Exod 24:6 is forced. Moreover, his claim that "basin" applies—even if "threshold" represents the actual meaning—amounts to special pleading.

20. The texts normally cited are 2 Sam 17:28; 1 Kgs 7:50; 2 Kgs 12:14; Jer 52:19. Rejecting the validity altogether of that definition for the word is Honeyman, "Basin, Goblet," 56–59.

21. The word denotes the doorway or threshold at Judg 19:27; 1 Kgs 14:17; Isa 6:4; Ezek 40:6, 7; 41:16 [bis], 43:8 [bis]; Amos 9:1; 2 Chr 3:7. The guild of doorkeepers is mentioned at 2 Kgs 12:10; 22:4 = 2 Chr 34:9; Jer 35:4, and so on.

22. The Vulgate of Exod 12:22 is cited according to *Biblica Sacra Iuxta Vulgatam Versionem; I: Genesis-Psalmi* (ed. Bonifatius Fischer et al.; 3d ed.; Stuttgart: Deutsche Bibelgesellschaft, 1983) 93. For the Syriac see *The Old Testament in Syriac According to the Peshiṭta Edition* (ed. Peshiṭta Institute; 1.1; Leiden: E. J. Brill, 1977) 143. *Targum Onqelos* is widely printed in Rabbinic Bibles; see also Alexander Sperber, *The Bible in Aramaic Based on Old Manuscripts and Printed Texts; 1: The Pentateuch According to Targum Onkelos* (Leiden: E. J. Brill, 1959) 108. *Targum Pseudo-Jonathan* Exod 12:22 is cited according to E. G. Clarke, *Targum Pseudo-Jonathan of the Pentateuch: Text and Concordance* (Hoboken, NJ: Ktav, 1984) 79. *Neofiti* is cited according to Alejandro Díez Macho, *Neophyti 1*, vol. 2, *Éxodo* (Madrid: Consejo Superior de Investigaciones Científicas, 1970) 73. No commentary on the verse is preserved in the *Fragmentary Targum*; see *The Fragment-Targums of the Pentateuch* (ed. Michael L. Klein; AnBib 76; Rome: Pontifical Biblical Institute, 1980).

shim.[23] In his longer commentary on Exod 12:22, Abraham ibn Ezra (1089–1164) presents both of these exegetical traditions as equally valid, without explicitly stating his preference: ‏ויש אומרים כי הפסח היו שוחטין אותו בסף השער‎, ‏ומבל האזוב בו ויגיעו אל המזוזות . . . ואחרים אמרו, כי הוא כלי‎ "There are those who say that the paschal offering used to be slaughtered *upon the threshold of the doorway*; the hyssop would be dipped in it [i.e., that blood] and applied to the door posts. . . . Others say that it refers to a vessel."[24] The former translation, to which ibn Ezra grants pride of place, is the only logical one: the stipulation intends that the entire doorway—top, sides, and bottom—be framed with blood.[25] The contrary rendering of the Syriac and Targums is best understood as an attempt to mask or revise the anomaly of a ritual slaughter detached from an altar.

In every respect, the paschal rite contradicted the conventions of the Israelite cultus. As represented by the literary sources of the Bible, normative sacrifice took place at an altar (Exod 20:24; Lev 1:3; 17:4; 1 Sam 14:31–35). By contrast, the Passover slaughter took place on the threshold of the family doorway. Moreover, common to all the pentateuchal literary sources is the expectation or stipulation that the blood of the sacrificial victim ritually be dashed against the altar or at its base. JE requires that the animal be slaughtered at an altar (Exod 20:24); its narrative of the covenant ratification ceremony specifies the sprinkling of blood upon the altar (Exod 24:6). This requirement is explicitly formulated in each of the other literary strata of the Pentateuch. Deuteronomy (Deut 12:27), the Priestly source (e.g., Lev 1:5), and the Holiness Code (Lev 17:6) consistently require that the blood be spilled in the direction of the altar or upon its base.[26] This consigning of the blood—which symbolizes the life force of a sentient being (Gen 9:4; Lev 17:11, 14; Deut 12:23)—to the altar has an important function in the cult. It symbolically drains the blood of the power to work autonomous magic and subordinates its effi-

23. See both *Mekilta De-Rabbi Ishmael* (ed. J. Z. Lauterbach; 3 vols.; Philadelphia: JPS, 1933) 1.84 and *Mekhilta D'Rabbi Šimʿon b. Jochai* (ed. J. N. Epstein and E. Z. Melamed; Jerusalem: Mekitze Nirdamim, 1955) 25–26. In the first instance, R. Ishmael argues that the word means threshold; in both cases it is R. Aqiba' who argues that the word means ‏כלי‎ "vessel." On the double exegetical tradition engendered by the word, see Alexander Rofé, *Introduction to Deuteronomy: Part I and Further Chapters* (2d rev. ed.; Jerusalem: Akademon, 1988) 41–42 (Hebrew).

24. Rabbi Abraham ibn Ezra, *Commentary on the Torah* (ed. A. Weiser; 3 vols.; Jerusalem: Rav Kook Institute, 1977) 2.81 (Hebrew).

25. The Hebrew Bible preserves other apotropaic rituals whose focus is the threshold. Indeed, the formulas for apotropaic avoidance of the entrance or threshold are strikingly similar in each case: "pass over the entrance" (Exod 12:23; J); "tread on the threshold" (1 Sam 5:5); "leap over the threshold" (Zeph 1:9); cf. "but if you do not do right, sin crouches at the door" (Gen 4:7).

26. Whereas MT Deut 12:27 seems to require that the blood be spilled in the direction of the altar, the LXX of that verse makes a harmonization with Lev 17:6, requiring that the blood be spilled upon the base of that altar. The similar embedding of later halakhic norms is evident in the *Temple Scroll* (11QTemple 52:21). On this issue see P. E. Dion, "Early Evidence for the Ritual Significance of the Base of the Altar," *JBL* 106 (1987) 487–90. The same issues emerge at 2 Chr 30:16; 35:11; and Jub 49:20.

cacy to that of Yahweh. The contradiction between that cultic norm and the blood apotropy of Passover could not be greater.

Both the specification of the animal and the method of cooking it also contradicted the conventions of the Israelite cultus. The restriction of the animal to be slaughtered to small cattle, such as sheep or goats, that are members of the *flock*, common to J and P in the verses cited, derives from the nomadic origins of Passover. The restriction stands in striking contrast to the normal sacrificial protocol that includes both large domestic cattle from the *herd*, such as cows or oxen, and small ones from the flock (Exod 20:24; Lev 1:2; 17:3; Num 22:40; 28:11, etc.).

As regards the animal's preparation, the situation is more complex. The earliest Passover regulations focus exclusively on the apotropaic force of the blood rite (Exod 12:21–23, J; vv. 24–27a, proto-Deuteronomic).[27] They make no mention whatsoever of eating: neither of unleavened wafers nor of the slaughtered lamb! In contrast, P regards the lamb's consumption as central: it preserves the stipulation that the paschal lamb be roasted and prohibits its being either boiled or eaten raw (Exod 12:8–9). There thus arises a methodological difficulty in knowing how to interpret the preservation by a late stratum (P) of an ostensibly ancient rite (the roasting of the lamb) for which there is no evidence in the earliest literary stratum—J. The latter's nonmention of the consumption of the lamb raises the real possibility that Passover was indeed originally only an apotropaic blood rite, with the lamb not subsequently consumed.[28] Nevertheless, if the stipulations of P concerning the preparation and consumption of the paschal lamb were only a late and secondary addition, it is difficult to understand why the Priestly editor would here tolerate such a contravention of P's own normal protocol for sacrificial meals. Boiling—not roasting, as with the paschal lamb—is the normative means for preparing sacrificial meat, both in P and more broadly.[29] It therefore seems likely that P here

---

27. The literary analysis is based on B. S. Childs, *The Book of Exodus* (OTL; Philadelphia: Westminster, 1974) 184. I have corrected his typo for J as "12:2–23" to 12:21–23. The isolation of the proto-Deuteronomic text follows Norbert Lohfink, *Das Hauptgebot: Eine Untersuchung literarischer Einleitungsfragen zu Dtn 5–11* (AnBib 20; Rome: Pontifical Biblical Institute, 1963) 121–22. Note, however, the challenge by Erhard Blum, *Studien zur Komposition des Pentateuch* (BZAW 189; Berlin: Walter de Gruyter, 1990) 166–69. See also n. 30 in this chapter. For the argument that the entirety of Exod 12:1–28 is P, see Van Seters, *Life of Moses*, 114–19.

28. For scholarly literature maintaining this position, see Haran, *Temples*, 320 n. 7. Although valuable for its explication of cultic phenomenology, Haran's literary analysis and reconstruction of the Passover (pp. 316–48) are problematic. He asserts that no contradictions exist between the J Passover (Exod 12:21–27) and the P account (Exod 12:1–14). His harmonization of the two accounts employs a conventional strategy of erasing crucial textual difference: "Both refer to the same happening, but neither of them has all the details, which means that they actually complement one another" (p. 320). This classical harmonistic approach (equivalent in its presuppositions to Tatian's *Diatessaron*) "fills in" what each text allegedly omits— and thereby levels all legal-historical and religious-historical differences between the texts involved. This methodology removes the criteria that would be necessary for Haran to demonstrate the antiquity of P, although doing so is one of the avowed purposes of the book (p. v).

29. Exod 29:31; Lev 6:28; 8:31; Num 6:19 (all, P); 1 Sam 2:15; Zech 14:21; and in Ezekiel's vision of the restored Temple, the "boiling-places" (Ezek 46:20, 24); so S. R. Driver, *The Book of Exodus* (Cambridge Bible for Schools and Colleges; Cambridge: University Press, 1911) 91.

actually preserves ancient stipulations concerning the preparation of the paschal lamb. If similar stipulations had once been part of J's account of the Passover, the redactor might have omitted them as redundant in light of his granting priority to the P Passover account in Exod 12:1–13.

This apotropaic use of blood within the Passover rite thus completely contradicted the norms of the Israelite cultus in four respects: (a) the specification of the animal (only members of the flock rather than either members of the herd or the flock); (b) the location of the slaughter (doorway rather than altar); (c) the disposition of the blood (daubing at the threshold as liminal site rather than being consigned to the altar); and (d) the method of cooking the animal (roasting rather than boiling). All of these—the very phenomena that grant the paschal slaughter its distinctiveness—make it absolutely anomalous within the normative sacrificial protocol of ancient Israel. The anomaly of the Passover was also linguistically marked. Neither the legislation of J in Exod 12:23 nor that of P in 12:1–14 speak of a paschal *sacrifice* (זבח). Instead, each technically mandates a paschal *slaughter*: ושחטו הפסח "Slaughter the paschal offering" (Exod 12:21, J), ושחטו אתו "Slaughter it" (Exod 12:6, P).[30] The paschal *slaughter*, in the home and without an altar, represented the antithesis of the normal cultic *sacrifice*. The conflict with the Deuteronomic program that restricted all cultic slaughter and all cultic blood rites to the central sanctuary could not have been greater.

The Conflict between Centralization and the Pre-Deuteronomic Passover

The intent of the Deuteronomic reform, and of Josiah's drive for cultic and political renewal, was to create a unified, centralized, essentially homogeneous cult and to assert the authority of Jerusalem, simultaneously political and religious, over all of Judah and Israel. Most likely, cultic centralization made a religious virtue out of a political necessity. In the period following Sennacherib's expeditions, Jerusalem was forced to retrench; it became a rump state, protected by its fortress cities. As a strategic response to the neo-Assyrian incursions, Hezekiah largely abandoned the countryside to the invaders and sought to urbanize Judah's population. In so doing, he dismantled both the extensive rural cultus and the familiar clan structure that supported it. What resulted was a massive disruption of popular forms of religion.[31] Notwithstanding Hezekiah's

30. Most likely, the assimilation of the Passover *slaughter* to the normative cultic protocol already begins to become apparent in the proto-Deuteronomic redaction that asserts: "It is a paschal *sacrifice* for Yahweh" (Exod 12:27a). Nevertheless, that designation by itself may require reconsideration of Lohfink's argument that Exod 12:24–27a is proto-D (*Das Hauptgebot*, 122). His argument is based on the passage's vocabulary but does not address either this phrase or the cult-historical issue it raises.

31. For a far-reaching analysis of the archaeological and literary evidence and of Deuteronomy's connection to the immense social change wrought by Hezekiah and Josiah, see Baruch Halpern, "Jerusalem and the Lineages in the Seventh Century BCE: Kinship and the Rise of Individual Moral Liability," in *Law and Ideology in Monarchic Israel* (ed. Baruch Halpern and Deborah W. Hobson; JSOTSup 124; Sheffield: JSOT Press, 1991) 11–107, at 27, 74–75.

attempts, there is archaeological evidence that popular religion not only sur-
vived but actually flourished in the final decades of the Judaean state. Archaeology attests the existence of a "distributed" and "non-conformist cultus,"
located in individual domiciles, that burst into expression in the seventh century.[32] Cultic materials found in domestic stratigraphy are iconic and suggest
the popularity of private, domestic shrines that included, among others, female
figurines (often set into pillars and most likely representing Asherah), horse
and rider figures, and zoomorphic figures.[33] These distributed, or private, shrines
differ notably from the primarily aniconic relics of the public cult, as preserved
at Temple sites. The archaeological evidence thus points to a sharp contrast
between popular piety, centered in the family domicile, and "establishment"
religion as the latter is represented both in Temple archaeology and in the literary sources of the Hebrew Bible.[34]

It is particularly striking that the distributed cultus seemed to flourish in
the final decades of the Judaean state. That chronology overlaps with the conventional dating of Deuteronomy to the Josianic period. On that basis, it is
suggestive to view Deuteronomy, on the one hand, with its centralizing and
anti-iconic drive, and the burgeoning popular piety, with its iconic recourse to
the *dea nutrix*, on the other, as two competing emergency responses to Judah's
national crisis under neo-Assyrian hegemony. Each response seems, moreover,
to involve an appropriation of the past in order to inject new life and meaning
into the present. In the case of Deuteronomy, that recourse to an idealized
reconfiguration of the past represents an elite literary construction with parallels to neo-Assyrian classicizing tendencies evident in Ashurbanipal's library.[35]
In the case of the distributed religion, it involves a popular return to Syrian
and Canaanite deities that seem to have been out of fashion for a period.[36]

32. For both the data cited here and the valuable distinction between a "distributed" or
"nonconformist" cultus and an "establishment" cultus, see John S. Holladay, Jr., "Religion in
Israel and Judah under the Monarchy: An Explicitly Archaeological Approach," in *Ancient
Israelite Religion: Essays in Honor of Frank Moore Cross* (ed. Patrick D. Miller, Jr., Paul D.
Hanson, and S. Dean McBride; Philadelphia: Fortress, 1987) 249–99, at 275–81.

33. See Holladay, "Religion in Israel and Judah," 274–78, discussing the evidence at Hazor,
Stratum V (in the North), and Tell Beit Mirsim and Lachish, Level IV (in Judah).

34. In his very stimulating Endnote, Holladay, "Religion in Israel and Judah," 295–99,
attempts to grapple with the inconsistency of popular religion with both temple sites and the
literary account of the Bible.

35. See Halpern, "Jerusalem and the Lineages," 87–88.

36. For the literary recourse to the past as a model to transform the present and the consequent growth of literary canons see Halpern, "Jerusalem and the Lineages," 87–91; and Halpern,
"Sybil, or the Two Nations? Archaism, Kinship, Alienation, and the Elite Redefinition of Traditional Culture in Judah in the 8th–7th Centuries B.C.E.," in *The Study of the Ancient Near East
in the Twenty-First Century: The William Foxwell Albright Centennial Conference* (ed. Jerrold
S. Cooper and Glenn M. Schwartz; Winona Lake, Ind.: Eisenbrauns, 1996) 291–338. For the
sudden bursts of popular piety and of iconic objects in the archaeological remains see Holladay,
"Religion in Israel and Judah," 278–80. The analogy between the two, as competing although
having a common structure, is my own hypothesis. In this context Jeremiah 44 raises fascinat-
ing issues: popular nostalgia for the past involves the desire to restore the worship of the Queen
of Heaven.

There is an additional matter. If the distributed cultus was not official, neither could Deuteronomy, at its composition, have represented either normative or official religion. Quite the opposite. It was hardly normative, because centralization directs itself against the prevailing assumptions of the pre-Deuteronomic texts. More likely, it represented something closer to a sectarian reconceptualization of religion. This does not mean, however, that Deuteronomy was popular in origin. Although there is an immense commitment to improving the lot of all those living at the fringes of society, its studied literary nature and language suggest its scribal origin in the Judaean court.[37] These reflections are conjecture, of course. But central to Deuteronomy as a text is its own bid for authority. In order to implement their own new vision of religion and law, the authors of Deuteronomy had to displace both established norms of worship and the texts that enshrined those norms. They began by proscribing the formerly valid local sanctuaries (as they do in Deuteronomy 12). They also found it essential to penetrate into the private domicile. The paschal rite that took place there involved the private, domestic manipulation of blood independent of any form of social control. Precisely because it was detached from the altar and the public cultus, the manipulation of blood by the paterfamilias or clan elder threatened the Deuteronomic attempt to construct a centralized cultus and a uniform state religion.[38] Within such family or clan-based activities, centrifugal forces could emerge, permitting religious difference (private religiosity) to perpetuate itself.[39] Consequently, it became necessary for the Deuteronomic authors to abrogate and wrest the pre-Deuteronomic Passover out of the private domain. Blood became a "controlled substance," whose ritual use the authors of Deuteronomy restricted to the central sanctuary (Deut 12:27). Deuteronomy's Passover (Deut 16:1–8) remarkably makes no mention whatsoever of the blood originally essential to the rite: the better to silence its threat. The result of these changes was homogenization—but thereby the creation of a national religion.

37. On the social focus see Norbert Lohfink, "Das deuteronomische Gesetz in der Endgestalt —Entwurf einer Gesellschaft ohne marginale Gruppen," *BN* 51 (1990) 25–40. On the scribal origins see Moshe Weinfeld, *Deuteronomy and the Deuteronomic School* (Oxford: Clarendon, 1972) 158–78.

38. That conflict between the legal norms of the pre-Deuteronomic Passover and Deuteronomy's drive for centralization remains the crucial point. I do not mean to imply that the pre-Deuteronomic Passover directly represents either popular piety or the distributed cultus. That it is represented in the pentateuchal literary sources already suggests otherwise. All that can be safely said is that it represents one prestigious norm of religious law that contradicted Deuteronomy's new vision and that the authors of Deuteronomy had to revise in order to implement their vision.

39. See the analysis of Deut 13:2–6 in the following chapter. From a different perspective than the one taken here, Rainer Albertz, *Persönliche Frömmigkeit und offizielle Religion: Religionsinterner Pluralismus in Israel und Babylon* (Stuttgart: Calwer, 1978) 169–78 was the first to address the transformation of popular piety and its integration into the official religion by the Deuteronomic authors. See further Albertz, *A History of Israelite Religion in the Old Testament Period* (2 vols.; OTL; Louisville: Westminster/John Knox, 1994) 1.210–16.

The Originality of Deuteronomy's Transformation and Blend of Passover and Unleavened Bread

Despite the blend represented by Deut 16:1–8, the pilgrimage festival of Unleavened Bread originally bore no relation to the Passover. Prior to Deuteronomy, the two observances were entirely independent of and unrelated to each other, both in religious-historical terms and in literary representation. The authors of Deuteronomy were responsible for both the transformation of each observance and their literary integration. In order to prove this, having reconstructed the pre-Deuteronomic Passover, it is also necessary to reconstruct the pre-Deuteronomic Festival of Unleavened Bread. After this, I argue that textual material claimed by some scholars to be a source for Deuteronomy's festival calendar actually presupposes it.

Just as the J and proto-D accounts of the Passover (Exod 12:21–23 + 24–27a) make no mention of the eating of unleavened bread, so the earliest literary strata of the Pentateuch—in the context of the Feast of Unleavened Bread—never refer to the Passover. The two calendrical observances are never presented as contiguous ritual events. It is the authors of Deuteronomy who are responsible for the combination of the two. In order to reconstruct the pre-Deuteronomic form of this festival, two passages are important to examine: the Covenant Code's festival calendar (Exod 23:14–19; cf. 34:18–26) and the account of the Festival of Unleavened Bread in Exod 13:3–10, given in the context of the Exodus narrative.

Exod 23:14–19

Deuteronomy draws on the festival legislation of Exod 23:14–19 as a literary source. That unit is ancient and bears clear evidence of linguistic and redactional coherence with the rest of the Covenant Code.[40] It is possible that the unit had an originally independent circulation prior to its incorporation into the Covenant Code.[41] Nonetheless, if so, that redactional incorporation took place at a pre-Deuteronomic stage. Neither in language nor in substantive law

---

40. See Bernard R. Goldstein and Alan Cooper, "The Festivals of Israel and Judah and the Literary History of the Pentateuch," *JAOS* 110 (1990) 21, emphasizing the structural coherence of Exod 23:10–19.

41. Maintaining the original redactional independence of Exod 23:14–19 are Eckart Otto, *Wandel der Rechtsbegründungen in der Gesellschaftsgeschichte des antiken Israel: eine Rechtsgeschichte des "Bundesbuches" Ex XX 22–XXIII 13* (StudBib 3; Leiden: E. J. Brill, 1988) 58; and Ludger Schwienhorst-Schönberger, *Das Bundesbuch (Ex 20,22–23,33): Studien zu seiner Entstehung und Theologie* (BZAW 188; Berlin: Walter de Gruyter, 1990) 22–23, 29–30, 37, 401–406. Both authors maintain that the unit is pre-Deuteronomic in content, although they diverge in their analysis of when it was redactionally incorporated into the Covenant Code. Otto argues that the unit was first integrated into the Covenant Code quite late, with the Covenant Code's incorporation into the Sinai pericope. In contrast, Schwienhorst-Schönberger maintains its pre-Deuteronomic redaction into the Covenant Code, a position that I follow. For further details, please see the next note.

does that unit betray any signs of Deuteronomistic or later editing.[42] Nor does this unit presuppose Deuteronomy as a literary source.[43] That claim, which reverses dependence and reception, involves special pleading and has not found wide acceptance.[44]

42. Contra Eckart Otto, who maintains that the Covenant Code originally concluded with Exod 23:13. More commonly, scholars understand the Covenant Code to extend to Exod 23:19, with 23:20–33 viewed as an epilogue. Otto develops his arguments in *Wandel der Rechtsbegründungen*, 10–11, 52–56; Otto, "שבע/שבעות *šaeba'/šābû'ôt*," *TWAT* 7 (1992) 1022–23; and Otto, "Zur Kompositionsgeschichte des alttestamentlichen 'Bundesbuches' Ex 20,22b–23,33," *WZKM* 83 (1993) 149–65. The latter article provides an important review of current scholarship on the Covenant Code. Otto's proposal that a Deuteronomistic or later redactor had final disposition of Exod 23:14–19, viewed as secondary, is unlikely. Such a redactor would be expected to update this calendar just as he did at Exod 34:25b, in order to harmonize Unleavened Bread with Passover. The text betrays, however, no signs of such updating and remains free of the type of Deuteronomistic incursions that Otto identifies in Exodus 34. Indeed, Otto himself elsewhere establishes the priority of the Unleavened Bread legislation of Exod 23:15, which lacks any reference to Passover, to that of Exod 34:24, which secondarily adds it (*Mazzotfest in Gilgal*, 248). Consequently, Otto can only argue from silence in support of his claim that this unit has undergone secondary revision. For example, he suggests that Exod 23:14–19 originally contained a sabbath law, on analogy with Exod 34:21a. He maintains that the late redactor who allegedly joined Exod 23:14–19 to the Covenant Code proper (Exod 21:1–23:12) and who then incorporated the newly expanded Covenant Code into the Sinai pericope (Exodus 19–24) deleted this original sabbath law in order to avoid redundancy with Exod 23:12 (*Wandel der Rechtsbegründungen*, 58; and "*šaeba'/šābû'ôt*," 1023). But this insertion of an "original" Sabbath law into Exod 23:14–19, merely on the basis of the parallel with Exodus 34, begs the question of the priority of Exodus 34 to the Covenant Code, which is precisely the question. Both the reconstruction of an original form of Exod 23:14–19 (with Sabbath law added) and the claim of a subsequent editorial deletion (necessary to account for its absence) require special pleading, since there is no textual evidence, versional or otherwise, to support either assertion. Strikingly, this claim that the festival calendar of the Covenant Code represents a late addition jeopardizes Otto's compelling arguments elsewhere that Deuteronomy owes its redactional structure to the Covenant Code ("Vom Bundesbuch zum Deuteronomium: Die deuteronomische Redaktion in Dtn 12–26," *Biblische Theologie und gesellschaftlicher Wandel: Für Norbert Lohfink* [ed. Georg Braulik, Walter Groß, and Sean McEvenue; Freiburg: Herder, 1993] 266, 269; and Otto, "Aspects of Legal Reforms and Reformulations in Ancient Cuneiform and Israelite Law," in *Theory and Method in Biblical and Cuneiform Law: Revision, Interpolation, and Development* [ed. Bernard M. Levinson; JSOTSup 181; Sheffield: Sheffield Academic Press, 1994] 188, 194). Given Otto's point-by-point derivation of the structure of the Deuteronomic legal corpus from the Covenant Code, why does Deuteronomy's festival calendar alone hover without a tether to the Covenant Code? At this point his redactional analysis of the Deuteronomic legal corpus (as an exegetical revision of the Covenant Code under the influence of cult centralization) and his redactional analysis of the Covenant Code (which regards the calendar of Exod 23:14–19 as secondary) become mutually inconsistent. Given the importance of the celebration of the centralized Passover to the Josianic setting of Deuteronomy, this matter will warrant further study.

43. Contra Gary Alan Chamberlain, "Exodus 21–23 and Deuteronomy 12–26: A Form-Critical Study" (Ph.D. diss., Boston University, 1977) 152–55. Also contra John Van Seters, "The Place of the Yahwist in the History of Passover and Massot," *ZAW* 95 (1983) 167–82, who offers a new source analysis of Exodus 12–13, based on his claim of J as late, and posits that "the earliest statement on passover is in Deuteronomy" (p. 179). Similarly, Van Seters, *Life of Moses*, 113–27.

44. Otto, *Wandel der Rechtsbegründungen*, 8, provides a concise refutation of Chamberlain's arguments. Challenging the claim by Van Seters that the Yahwist presupposes Deuteronomy, see Bernard M. Levinson, *The Hermeneutics of Innovation: the Impact of Centralization upon the*

The festival calendar with which the Covenant Code concludes (Exod 23:14–17), together with its coda of related ritual rules (vv. 18–19), lists the three festivals during the year when male Israelites were required to make a pilgrimage to the local sanctuary: Unleavened Bread, Harvest, and Ingathering.[45] Exod 23:14 + 17 redactionally frame the itemization of the specific festivals within vv. 15–16. Of course, the three festivals specified by vv. 15–16 were not the only events of ritual importance within the Israelite calendar: both Sabbaths and New Moons, for example, were observed by special sacrifices (see Num 28:9–10, 11–15). These three festivals, however, were the only ones that required the lay Israelite to undertake a pilgrimage to the local sanctuary. "Pilgrimage festival" is thus the specific denotation of the technical term חג, the regulations concerning which are this unit's focus.[46]

Two features distinguish the stipulations for Unleavened Bread, in Exod 23:15, from the stipulations for the other two festivals, Harvest and Ingathering, in v. 16. First, alone of the three, Unleavened Bread contains a textual cross-reference to an earlier divine promulgation. The festival should be celebrated, Yahweh requires in the first person, כאשר צויתך "as I commanded you" (Exod 23:15), which reference can apply only to Exod 13:6.[47] The stipulation in Exod 23:15 that requires שבעת ימים תאכל מצות "seven days shall you eat unleavened bread" is an exact citation of the latter lemma.[48] This citation of Exod 13:6 by the Covenant Code provides important evidence that ancient stipulations remain at the core of Exod 13:3–10 (see next section) and that the proto-Deuteronomic redaction consists primarily of the parenetic framework, not substantive law.

Second, Unleavened Bread is the only one of the three festivals to be specified both calendrically ("at the appointed time in the month of Abib") and as

---

Structure, Sequence, and Reformulation of Legal Material in Deuteronomy (Ann Arbor, Mich.: University Microfilms, 1991) 106–14.

45. I employ the term "festival calendar" to stress (1) the focus of these units upon the three major pilgrimage festivals and (2) that the units intentionally span the calendar year. These points are not made sufficiently clear by Donn Farley Morgan, *The So-Called Cultic Calendars in the Pentateuch: A Morphological and Typological Study* (Ann Arbor, Mich.: University Microfilms, 1974) 159 in his form-critical argument that Exod 23:14–17, 34:18–26, and Deut 16:1–17 each represents "not a [cultic] calendar but a list of festal prescriptions."

46. See Driver, *Exodus*, 242; and Haran, *Temples*, 289–94, with valuable bibliography.

47. The claim by Schwienhorst-Schönberger that this cross-reference must be a late Deuteronomistic addition is arbitrary (*Das Bundesbuch*, 402–404). There is no reason that the textual cross-reference must presuppose the incorporation of the Covenant Code into the Sinai pericope. The reference could just as easily have been made prior to and independent of the present redaction of both texts. By analogy, Deuteronomy's reuse of the Covenant Code does not presuppose the latter's incorporation into the Sinai pericope.

48. So also H. L. Ginsberg, *The Israelian Heritage of Judaism* (New York: Jewish Theological Seminary of America, 1982) 47. In contrast, the claim by U. Cassuto, *A Commentary on the Book of Exodus* (Jerusalem: Magnes, 1967) 303 that the citation tag refers to Exod 12:15 cannot be sustained. The clauses differ in syntax and verbal number; further, Cassuto does not address any of the diachronic and source-critical issues involved in making Exod 12:15, as a P text, function as a literary source for the Covenant Code.

having an historical justification, commemorating the Exodus: כי בו יצאת ממצרים "for in it you went forth from Egypt" (Exod 23:15). In contrast, the other two festivals are marked only by the stages of the agricultural year. The Festival of the Harvest marks the firstfruits of the field while the Festival of Ingathering marks the completion of the harvest season (Exod 23:16).

Exod 13:3–10

Earlier literary critics identified this unit as deriving from the Yahwist and understood it to represent the latter's account of Unleavened Bread in contrast to the Priestly account of Exod 12:14–20.[49] The trend more recently is to identify the unit as proto-Deuteronomic.[50] As such, the unit provides insight into the nature of the pre-Deuteronomic Festival of Unleavened Bread. The festival is from the beginning rationalized in terms of its marking the date of the exodus from Egypt: היום אתם יצאים בחדש האביב "This day you go free, in the month of Abib" (Exod 13:4).[51] Apart from this exact commemoration of the Exodus (see Exod 12:29–30), the date of the given day is not further calendrically specified.

The celebration of Unleavened Bread lasts seven days and involves the removal of both sourdough starter and risen loaves (Exod 13:6–7). The seventh of these days is distinguished from the first six: "Seven days shall you eat unleavened bread, and on the seventh day there shall be a (חג ליהוה) pilgrimage festival for Yahweh" (Exod 13:6). As a "pilgrimage festival," the observance of Unleavened Bread was crowned with a sacrifice at the local sanctuary.

---

49. August Dillmann, *Die Bücher Exodus und Leviticus* (ed. V. Ryssel; KeHAT; 3d ed.; Leipzig: S. Hirzel, 1897) 139; and Driver, *Exodus*, 106.

50. Lohfink, *Das Hauptgebot*, 121–24; and M. Caloz, "Exode, XIII, 3–16 et son rapport au Deutéronome," *RB* 75 (1968) 5–62. Note the disagreement of Blum, *Komposition des Pentateuch*, 166–69.

51. As an alternative translation, "on the *new moon* of Abib," or even, glossing Abib as referring to newly ripe grain, "on the new moon of milky ears of corn." The issue is that the word חדש can mean either "month" or "New Moon" (BDB, 294). This ambiguity creates a vexing difficulty in the exegesis of passages such as this one; Exod 23:15; 34:18; and the double occurrence of the word at Deut 16:1. In Exod 13:4, the convention is to translate it as "month" (so BDB, 294, 2b). Nonetheless, there is good reason to translate it here as "new moon." For the justification, see Otto, *Mazzotfest in Gilgal*, 182 and n. 5; and Ginsberg, *Israelian Heritage*, 44. Note the helpful summary by Braulik, "Leidensgedächtnisfeier und Freudenfest," 102 n. 19. The rendering "new moon" requires the additional postulate that, postexilically, P shifts the original date of Unleavened Bread from being a New Moon observance (allegedly preserved by Exod 13:4) to a Full Moon observance on the fifteenth of the month, as at Num 33:3; see Ginsberg, *Israelian Heritage*, 78–79. A now widely held position is that the word always means "new moon" preexilically, and "month" postexilically; see E. Auerbach, "Die Feste im alten Israel," *VT* 8 (1958) 1–14, at 1. That claim is refuted by Cholewiński, *Heiligkeitsgesetz und Deuteronomium*, 183–84; and by William S. Morrow, "The Composition of Deuteronomy 14:1–17:1," (Ph.D. diss., University of Toronto, 1988) 214–15 (the expanded revision, *Scribing the Center: Organization and Redaction in Deuteronomy 14:1–17:13* [SBLMS 49; Atlanta: Scholars Press, 1995] has just appeared). Suggesting that the word has a different meaning depending upon whether the calendars are Israelite or Judaean are Goldstein and Cooper, "The Festivals of Israel and Judah," 21.

This connection between the Festival of Unleavened Bread and the local sanctuaries constitutes its challenge to the authors of Deuteronomy. The Deuteronomic program of cult centralization involved the extirpation of the very local sanctuaries that provided the festival with its home. That conflict required that the authors of Deuteronomy find a way to transform Unleavened Bread. In principle, two options were open to them: either to divert its celebration from the local to the central sanctuary or to secularize it, by deleting altogether its connection to the sacrificial cultus and the altar. I argue that they elected the latter option. It is Passover that they diverted to the central sphere, leaving Unleavened Bread to be celebrated locally, with the original pilgrimage element entirely voided.

The Secondary Status of the Passover Reference in Exod 34:25b

Exodus 34, which narrates the renewal of the covenant between God and Israel following the Golden Calf incident, contains a divine proclamation of law that includes a religious calendar (Exod 34:18–26). Within that passage, which parallels certain parts of the Covenant Code, there is a command: "the sacrifice of the Festival of Passover (זבח חג הפסח) shall not be left lying until morning" (Exod 34:25b). That reference presents Passover as a technical pilgrimage festival (חג). Were it pre-Deuteronomic, it would undermine my claim that Deuteronomy is responsible for the transformation of Passover. However, there is broad scholarly agreement that the phrase is a late, Deuteronomistic interpolation in the verse.[52] As such, Deuteronomy represents the real source for that passage, and not vice versa. Passover material does not otherwise appear in Exod 34:18–26, and the unit's regulations for Unleavened Bread are otherwise essentially identical to those found in the Covenant Code (Exod 23:15a//34:18). Accordingly, in discussing the festival calendar, I shall treat Exod 34:25 as belonging to the history of reception of Deuteronomy's festival calendar.

Very likely, an isolated, later addition is not the issue in Exod 34:25b. Instead, a much more programmatic revision of prior law is at stake. The verse is arguably a deliberate attempt to revise and update the festival legislation of the Covenant Code (Exod 23:18) specifically in light of Deuteronomy's distinctive blend of Passover and Unleavened Bread (Deut 16:1–8).[53] The notion that the change involved is not isolated but programmatic represents one component of a broader debate concerning Exod 34:18–26. Classical source-criticism regarded the unit as an ancient "cultic Decalogue" ascribed to the Yahwist.[54]

52. See Julius Wellhausen, *Prolegomena to the History of Ancient Israel* [1878] (New York: Meridian, 1957) 85 n. 1. More recently, Jörn Halbe, *Das Privilegrecht Jahwes Ex 34,10–26: Gestalt und Wesen, Herkunft und Wirken in vordeuteronomischer Zeit* (FRLANT 114; Göttingen: Vandenhoeck & Ruprecht, 1975) 195–97; Otto, *Mazzotfest in Gilgal*, 177 n. 1, 247; and Braulik, "Leidensgedächtnisfeier und Freudenfest," 101 n. 110. Each of the latter three scholars provides extensive further bibliography.

53. Most clearly, Ginsberg, *Israelian Heritage*, 64–65.

54. Classically, J. Wellhausen, *Die Composition des Hexateuchs und der historischen Bücher des Alten Testaments* (4th ed.; Berlin: Walter de Gruyter, 1963) 84–86, especially 329–35.

Traditio-historical scholarship viewed the unit as yet more ancient: as a pre-monarchic Privilege Law.[55] On that assumption of its antiquity, the unit has sometimes been viewed, conjointly with the Covenant Code, as providing a literary source for Deuteronomy, including its festival legislation.[56]

Despite this older view, Exod 34:18–26 does not constitute a literary source for Deuteronomy's festival calendar. Increasingly within scholarship, the tendency has been to move away from the older source-critical and traditio-historical dating of the unit and to regard it as post-Deuteronomic. Indeed, a more profound paradigm shift has taken place. Many scholars now no longer regard the unit as an independent literary or traditio-historical source but rather see it as itself a deliberate redactional conflation of prior literary sources (including the Covenant Code, Exodus 13, and Deuteronomy 16) that attempts forcibly to read later legal and textual developments back into the Sinai pericope.[57] This approach provides the best explanation for the actual sequence and structure of the laws and hortatory material within Exodus 34. In this light, with the unit seen as a post-Deuteronomic redactional composition, it becomes methodologically problematic to seek to reconstruct a pre-Deuteronomistic core for the chapter, as if the Deuteronomistic material were simply secondary accretions added to an original source.[58]

Deuteronomy as Responsible for the Transformation of the Calendar

The originality of Deuteronomy's combination of Passover and Unleavened Bread has recently been challenged by Bernard R. Goldstein and Alan Cooper, who claim that Deuteronomy introduces no significant structural change into

---

55. On the Privilege Law see Halbe, *Das Privilegrecht Jahwes*, 502–505 for whom the unit also represented a source for the Covenant Code. In contrast, Otto, *Mazzotfest in Gilgal*, 241–54, maintains that neither Exodus 34 nor Exodus 23 depends upon the other but that both embody an ancient, preliterary tradition joining covenant, Unleavened Bread, and Conquest.

56. Norbert Lohfink, "Zur deuteronomischen Zentralisationsformel," *Bib* 65 (1984) 297–328, republished in and cited after Lohfink, *Studien zum Deuteronomium und zur deuteronomistischen Literatur* II (SBAB 12; Stuttgart: Katholisches Bibelwerk, 1991) 147–77, at 173–77; Lohfink, "Deuteronomy," *IDBSup* (1976) 230; and Georg Braulik, *Deuteronomium 1–16,17* (Neue Echter Bibel 15; Würzburg: Echter Verlag, 1986) 10.

57. Ginsberg, *Israelian Heritage*, 62–66; Michael Fishbane, *Biblical Interpretation in Ancient Israel* (Oxford: Clarendon, 1985) 194–97; William Johnstone, "Reactivating the Chronicles Analogy in Pentateuchal Studies, with Special Reference to the Sinai Pericope in Exodus," *ZAW* 99 (1987) 16–37; Erik Aurelius, *Der Fürbitter Israels: Eine Studie zum Mosebild im Alten Testament* (ConBOT 27; Stockholm: Almqvist & Wiksell, 1988) 116–26; and Blum, *Komposition des Pentateuch*, 67–70, 369–77. Note the astute early analysis by N. M. Nicolsky, "Pascha im Kulte des jerusalemischen Tempels," *ZAW* 45 (1927) 174–75.

58. Otto's careful attempt at literary separation does not draw the full implications of the very redactional models that he cites ("Kompositionsgeschichte des alttestamentlichen 'Bundesbuches,'" 154–55). It is not clear that the text he reconstructs ever had any pre-Deuteronomic independent existence.

the festival calendar. They assign the key transformation of the calendar to a radically redefined R^JE, whom they describe as a northern redactor operating in Judah during the early eighth century.[59] While their position offers a valuable rethinking of the evidence, some methodological difficulties arise in shifting the innovative force of Deuteronomy's festival legislation back to this pre-Deuteronomic redactor. The major one is that they derive the festival legislation of Exod 34:18–26 from this same, *pre*-Deuteronomic R^JE, with the result that the designation there of Passover as a חג "festival" (Exod 34:25) also becomes pre-Deuteronomic. That understanding of the calendar in Exodus 34 then constitutes evidence for claiming that Deuteronomy is not responsible for significant structural change in the festival calendar. Goldstein and Cooper's argument is problematic. They base their view of Exodus 34 as a redactional reworking of the Covenant Code and their assumption of the northern origins of proto-Deuteronomy on the work of H. L. Ginsberg.[60] In particular, they defend their reconstruction of the literary history of the calendar in light of "Ginsberg's characterization of the festival legislation in Exodus 34 as proto-deuteronomic."[61] Ginsberg's actual position was the opposite. He argued that Exodus 34 was a post-Deuteronomic revision of Exodus 23 in light of Deuteronomy's festival calendar.[62] With that error, their diachronic scheme loses its essential support. Their argument is further weakened because they assume the priority of P to D, without noting that such a sequence is highly contested and that Ginsberg himself rejected it in favor of the prevailing view that P is later than Deuteronoy.[63]

Prior to Deuteronomy, Passover and Unleavened Bread were therefore independent of each other, both religiously and textually. Passover involved an apotropaic blood ritual; Unleavened Bread, a pilgrimage to the local sanctuary. All that changed with Deuteronomy.

---

59. Goldstein and Cooper, "The Festivals of Israel and Judah," 27, 29, 31; and Cooper and Goldstein, "Exodus and *Maṣṣôt* in History and Tradition," *Maarav* (Stanley Gevirtz Memorial Volume) 8 (1994) 15–37, at 17, 27.

60. In claiming that Deuteronomy's origins are northern and in emphasizing the strikingly close ties of the legal corpus to the oracles of Hosea, Ginsberg, *Israelian Heritage* (1982), 19–24, overlooks the similar arguments long ago made by Adam C. Welch, *The Code of Deuteronomy: A New Theory of Its Origin* (New York: George H. Doran [1924]) 31–34, 128–31, 184–90.

61. Cooper and Goldstein, "Exodus and *Maṣṣôt*," 17. Contrast the accurate representation in Goldstein and Cooper, "The Festivals of Israel and Judah," 24, although there dismissing Ginsberg's dating without engaging with any of his specific textual arguments.

62. Ginsberg, *Israelian Heritage*, 62–66. With respect to the incongruous designation of Passover as a festival in Exod 34:25, Ginsberg's position was implicitly already proposed by August Dillmann, *Deuteronomium* (1886), 311.

63. Goldstein and Cooper, "The Festivals of Israel and Judah," 27, 30–31; Cooper and Goldstein, "Exodus and *Maṣṣôt*," 25 n. 35; and Ginsberg, *Israelian Heritage*, 100–117. Ginsberg tentatively allowed only Deut 15:12–18 as an exception. Now even that exception has been refuted: see Stephen A. Kaufman, "Deuteronomy 15 and Recent Research on the Dating of P," in *Das Deuteronomium: Entstehung, Gestalt und Botschaft* (ed. Norbert Lohfink; BETL 68; Louvain: University Press, 1985) 273–76.

Deuteronomy's Double Transformation
of Passover and Unleavened Bread

The authors of Deuteronomy radically transformed the original observances of Passover and Unleavened Bread. In a striking reversal of cultic and literary history, Passover, originally a local, family based slaughter, becomes in everything but name a pilgrimage festival, to be performed, as all sacrifices must, at the central sanctuary.[64] Even the initial purpose of the paschal slaughter, the apotropaic blood ritual—which is to be observed annually in perpetuity (Exod 12:24–27a, proto-D)—is rejected in total silence.[65] Precisely the ritual that gives the Passover its distinctive identity—and that militates against Deuteronomy's restricting the cultic use of blood to the altar at the central sanctuary—is absolutely suppressed. The Passover slaughter loses its ritual distinctiveness and, but for the specification that it take place at night (Deut 16:1, 6), becomes assimilated to the standard sacrificial protocol.[66]

So thorough is this routinization of the Passover that both the selection of animals and their preparation are equally transformed.[67] If, reflecting the ritual's nomadic origins, the paschal slaughter was originally restricted to small cattle from the flock, either sheep or goats (Exod 12:21; cf. Exod 12:3, 5), that restriction is now effectively canceled. The animal becomes standardized to include both small and large cattle (Deut 16:2), as is conventional for sacrifice (Deut 12:21; Exod 20:24; Lev 1:2; Num 22:40).[68] Similarly, the nomadic routine that specifies the roasting of the lamb is accommodated to the normal sacrifi-

---

64. Baruch A. Levine, *Leviticus* (JPS Torah Commentary; Philadelphia: JPS, 1989) 266. In contrast, to argue, "The earliest statement on Passover is in Deuteronomy," while also maintaining that "Deuteronomy (Dtn) historicized it . . . and he centralized it," leaves unexplained what the "it" was that Deuteronomy reacted against. For this reason, Van Seters, *Life of Moses*, 123–24, opens his argument to question.

65. For Deuteronomy's excision of other ancient features of the Passover, see Moshe Weinfeld, "The Reorientation in the Understanding of the Divinity and of the Cultus in the Book of Deuteronomy," *Tarbiz* 31 (1961–62) 5 (Hebrew); and Haran, *Temples*, 321.

66. Note also Braulik, "Leidensgedächtnisfeier und Freudenfest," 101–103; and Ginsberg, *Israelian Heritage*, 57.

67. See Moshe Weinfeld, "Deuteronomy—The Present State of Inquiry," *JBL* 86 (1967) 259–60; reprinted in *A Song of Power and the Power of Song: Essays on the Book of Deuteronomy* (ed. Duane L. Christensen; Winona Lake, Ind.: Eisenbrauns, 1993) 31–32.

68. Contra Segal, who notes the problem but attempts to explain away "large cattle" as a scribal error (*The Hebrew Passover*, 205). Lacking all versional support, Segal makes his case on the sole basis that, elsewhere in Deuteronomy, "large cattle" precedes "sheep," whereas here it follows it. Segal thereby overlooks that in the Passover texts which the author inherits, the focus is exclusively on "sheep" (Exod 12:21, J; cf. 12:3, P), which explains its priority here, before the extension of the prescription to include large cattle. That the sequence is not anomalous is clear from its conformity to Exod 20:24. Rosario Pius Merendino (*Das deuteronomische Gesetz: Eine literarkritische, gattungs- und überlieferungsgeschichtliche Untersuchung zu Dt 12–26* [BBB 31; Bonn: Peter Hanstein, 1969] 128) and Jörn Halbe ("Passa-Massot im deuteronomischen Festkalender: Komposition, Entstehung und Programm von Dtn 16, 1–8," *ZAW* 87 [1975] 152) similarly avoid the issue by deleting "large and small cattle" as a later addition. This, too, lacks versional support. Moreover, as Morrow notes, excluding the phrase makes the verse redundant alongside 16:5–6 ("Deut 14:1–17:1," 216).

cial protocol that involves the boiling of those parts in which the celebrant and priest share (Deut 16:7; cf. 1 Sam 2:13–16).[69] The attempts to deny this deliberate transformation by claiming either that the verse contains an interpolation or that the verb בשל does not mean "boil" are untenable.[70]

All these transformations of legal and religious history cohere in the command שם שמו לשכן יהוה יבחר אשר במקום ובקר צאן אלהיך ליהוה פסח וזבחת "You shall sacrifice the paschal offering to Yahweh, your God—sheep or cattle—in the place that Yahweh shall choose to establish his name" (Deut 16:2). That command expresses *in nuce* the complete Deuteronomic transformation of Passover. The correct idiom was conventionally הפסח ושחטו "You shall *slaughter* the Passover."[71] The change in formulation represents a radical innovation by the authors of Deuteronomy. The application of the technical verb "sacrifice" (Deut 16:2, 5, 6)[72] to the paschal slaughter signals the complete abrogation of the old rite and its assimilation into the public cult. This represents as bold a reworking of language as does the paradoxical use of the same verb to denote local secular slaughter, completely detached from any altar, in Deut 12:15, 21.[73]

69. Concerning the shift in animals and preparation, see G. von Rad, *Deuteronomy* (Philadelphia: Westminster, 1966) 112.

70. Claiming an interpolation are Merendino, *Das deuteronomische Gesetz*, 133–34; and Halbe, "Passa-Massot im deuteronomischen Festkalender," 152. Claiming that the verb בשל means only "cook," not "boil," are Segal, *The Hebrew Passover*, 205–206; and J. G. McConville, *Law and Theology in Deuteronomy* (JSOTSup 33; Sheffield: JSOT Press, 1984) 117–18. For a more detailed critique of these positions, see Morrow, "Deuteronomy 14:1–17:1," 130, 220; and Bernard M. Levinson, "McConville's *Law and Theology in Deuteronomy*," *JQR* 80 (1990) 396–404. Interestingly, Segal's and McConville's claim returns precisely to the harmonistic solution of ancient Rabbinic exegesis; see *Mekilta de-Rabbi Ishmael* (ed. Jacob Z. Lauterbach; 3 vols.; Philadelphia: JPS, 1933–35) 1.49. Seeking to erase the manifest contradiction between Exod 12:9 and Deut 16:7, the *Mekilta* paradoxically cites the earlier inner-biblical harmonization represented by 2 Chr 35:13 as if it represented an independent use of the verb. On 2 Chr 35:13, see further chapter 5. On the rabbinic linguistic harmonizations involved, see Fishbane, *Biblical Interpretation*, 135–36. On rabbinic exegesis as "harmonizing inconcinnities," see Jon D. Levenson, "The Hebrew Bible, the Old Testament, and Historical Criticism," in his *The Hebrew Bible, the Old Testament, and Historical Criticism* (Louisville: Westminster/John Knox, 1993) 2–3.

71. Exod 12:21 (JE); similarly, Exod 12:6 (P).

72. The verb designates the sacrifice as one "whose meat is eaten by the worshiper," an essential feature if this rite is to replace the original paschal family ritual. For the definition, see Jacob Milgrom, *Leviticus 1–16* (AB 3; New York: Doubleday, 1991) 218. Recognizing the transformation from paschal rite to offering, Braulik, "Leidensgedächtnisfeier und Freudenfest," 101.

73. Contra Reuter, *Kultzentralisation*, 167, who maintains that the verb is used in Deut 16:2, 5, 6 merely in its conventional cultic sense, without noting the anomaly involved. The same problem arises with Samuel Amsler, "Les Documents de la loi et la formation du Pentateuque," in *Le Pentateuque en question: Les Origines et la composition des cinq premiers livres de la Bible à la lumière des recherches récentes* (ed. Albert de Pury; Le Monde de la Bible 19; 2d ed.; Geneva: Labor et Fides, 1989) 251. Amsler contradictorily explains the verb on the basis of Exod 23:18 (where it applies to the festival of Unleavened Bread, not the paschal slaughter) and Exod 34:25 (which he himself regards as Deuteronomistic, and therefore post-Deuteronomic). Although Amsler valuably stresses the importance of biblical law for pentateuchal theory, his analysis overlooks the basic distinction between Passover and Unleavened Bread.

In each case, the anomalous use of the verb integrates into normative religion that which was formally incompatible with it.

Language here becomes a means of hegemony, as the public cult asserts its control over the distributed cult. Not only the conversion of Passover into a normative sacrifice but also the syntactical conjunction of Passover and Deuteronomy's centralization formula establish the extraordinary capacity of Deuteronomy's authors for innovation. The insistence that the Passover should be a sacrifice performed at the central sanctuary—of all places—completely annuls its original identity as a slaughter that took place at the threshold of the family domicile. The authors of Deuteronomy remove the rite's original clan focus to make it instead the constitutive national holiday, with each family observing it simultaneously at the central sanctuary. Passover, as the holiday in which the family members were originally forbidden from leaving their residence (Exod 12:22b), under pain of death, now becomes an observance which the citizens are forbidden to celebrate at home:

> You must not sacrifice the paschal offering in any of your city-gates
> which Yahweh your God is giving you; but rather, at the place where
> Yahweh your God shall choose to establish his name, there shall you
> sacrifice the paschal offering in the evening. . . . (Deut 16:5–6)

Deuteronomy's Passover completely abrogates earlier authoritative law. The formula for prohibition—לֹא תוּכַל לִזְבֹּחַ אֶת הַפֶּסַח בְּאַחַד שְׁעָרֶיךָ "You must not sacrifice the paschal offering in any of your city-gates"[74]—is an all but explicit polemic against the pre-Deuteronomic laws regulating the Passover. The prohibition transforms the Passover not only in the place of its observance but also in form and social structure. The prohibition voids the Passover of its original clan nexus by shunting each individual family to the Temple in a single national convocation. So profoundly do the authors of Deuteronomy transform the Passover that it essentially becomes the pilgrimage festival par excellence as they integrate it into their formulaic language for all Temple pilgrimages.[75]

---

74. The Hebrew literally translates as "in one of your [city]-gates" (Deut 16:5). The function of the "one" in this case is distributive and indicates completely random or arbitrary choice (as at Deut 23:17). The German *Einheitsübersetzung* (Stuttgart: Katholische Bibelanstalt, 1980) captures the idea perfectly: *irgendeinem* ("just any, any one or other"). Reuter's claim that Deut 16:5 conflicts with Deut 12:13 because of the different use of "one" in each case is therefore unconvincing (*Kultzentralisation*, 168–69). She moves prematurely from recognizing different lexical choices to claiming inconsistency and contradiction. The same word used differently in two different cases hardly implies that the authors of Deut 16:1–8 failed to take into account the distinction between local and central forged by Deut 12:13–15.

75. The pilgrimage scheme involves the consistent structure of language and thought employed by the Deuteronomic author to represent cultic action at the central sanctuary and travel to it. That scheme was discovered by Norbert Lohfink, who presents it most comprehensively in "Opfer und Säkularisierung im Deuteronomium," in *Studien zu Opfer und Kult im Alten Testament* (ed. Adrian Schenker; Forschungen zum Alten Testament 3; Tübingen: J. C. B. Mohr [Paul Siebeck], 1992) 15–43.

Lemmatic Reformulation in Deut 16:1–8

In order to accomplish their program, the authors of Deuteronomy apply to the new Deuteronomic Passover lemmas whose original reference is the Feast of Unleavened Bread. Conversely, the authors of Deuteronomy transform Unleavened Bread into a neutered local observance: they remove its original connection to the local sanctuaries and thus void it of the very pilgrimage element originally essential to it. Table 3-1 and its subsequent textual analysis demonstrate Deuteronomy's lemmatic recontextualizations. Particularly important is the way that the text's authors draw upon and revise the festival legislation that concludes the Covenant Code.

Exod 23:15, in the context of the Covenant Code's festival calendar, commands את חג המצות תשמר "The [Pilgrimage] Festival of Unleavened Bread shall you observe." The same verb is retained by the calendar of Deuteronomy. In its new application, however, that verb is remarkably detached from its original grammatical object. Whereas the lemma stressed that object by means of a *casus pendens* that placed it in an initial, marked position, the authors of Deuteronomy stress the verbal action instead. They shift the verb from its original final position now to an introductory infinitive absolute: "*Observe* the month of Abib." The authors of Deuteronomy thereby avoid emphasizing the object of the verb—which they have pointedly revised from "the Festival of Unleavened Bread" (Exod 23:15) to חדש האביב "the month of Abib" (Deut 16:1).[76] The transformation of the verbal object, brought up from the adverbial phrase in the lemma, permits in turn the more radical shift: a pilgrimage—no longer in order to observe the Festival of Unleavened Bread but rather in order to "offer the passover sacrifice" (ועשית פסח, Deut 16:1). The incongruity of the resulting literary unit, let alone of the sacrificial rite involved, cannot be too highly stressed. Both the conclusion to the Covenant Code, Exod 23:15–18, and Deut 16:1–17, in its overall orientation, present a festival calendar that lists the three pilgrimages which each male Israelite is bound to observe. The reformulation of Exod 23:15–16 by Deut 16:16 substantiates this point. The inclusion, therefore, of what is quintessentially a local home rite, the Passover, in the context of a festival calendar whose concern is rather pilgrimage to the sanctuary, points to Deuteronomy's radical reworking of cultic and literary history.

If Deuteronomy marks its deletion of the lemma's original object—Unleavened Bread as the pilgrimage festival—so it marks its striking addition to that lemma—Passover as the Abib observance. The striking interpolation of the paschal slaughter into the lemma is distinguished by a repetition within Deut 16:1. The double reference to the festival date as "[in] the month of Abib" frames the Passover command and marks a repetitive resumption within the verse:

Frame (A):   Observe *the month of Abib* חדש האביב
Passover Command: and offer a passover sacrifice to Yahweh your God,

---

76. Alternatively, "the new moon of Abib"; see n. 51.

TABLE 3-1 Textual sources for Deuteronomy's Passover legislation

Deut 16:1–4	Exod 23:15+18	Exod 13:3–10
[1] שָׁמוֹר אֶת חֹדֶשׁ הָאָבִיב וְעָשִׂיתָ פֶּסַח לַיהוה אֱלֹהֶיךָ	[15] אֶת חַג הַמַּצּוֹת תִּשְׁמֹר שִׁבְעַת יָמִים תֹּאכַל מַצּוֹת כַּאֲשֶׁר צִוִּיתִךָ	
כִּי בְּחֹדֶשׁ הָאָבִיב הוֹצִיאֲךָ יהוה אֱלֹהֶיךָ מִמִּצְרַיִם לָיְלָה	לְמוֹעֵד חֹדֶשׁ הָאָבִיב כִּי בוֹ יָצָאתָ מִמִּצְרַיִם	[4] בְּחֹדֶשׁ הָאָבִיב [9] הוֹצִאֲךָ יהוה מִמִּצְרַיִם
	וְלֹא יֵרָאוּ פָנַי רֵיקָם	
[3] לֹא תֹאכַל עָלָיו חָמֵץ	[18] לֹא תִזְבַּח עַל חָמֵץ דַּם זִבְחִי	
שִׁבְעַת יָמִים תֹּאכַל עָלָיו מַצּוֹת לֶחֶם עֹנִי . . .		[6] שִׁבְעַת יָמִים תֹּאכַל מַצֹּת וּבַיּוֹם הַשְּׁבִיעִי חַג לַיהוה
[4] וְלֹא יֵרָאֶה לְךָ שְׂאֹר בְּכָל גְּבֻלְךָ שִׁבְעַת יָמִים		[7] וְלֹא יֵרָאֶה לְךָ שְׂאֹר בְּכָל גְּבֻלְךָ
וְלֹא יָלִין מִן הַבָּשָׂר אֲשֶׁר תִּזְבַּח בָּעֶרֶב בַּיּוֹם הָרִאשׁוֹן לַבֹּקֶר	וְלֹא יָלִין חֵלֶב חַגִּי עַד בֹּקֶר	

(1) *Observe* the month of Abib and offer a passover sacrifice to Yahweh your God,	(15) The Festival of Unleavened Bread shall you *observe*: seven days shall you eat unleavened bread, as I commanded you, at the appointed time	
for *in the month of Abib Yahweh your God led you out of Egypt,* at night.	*in the month of Abib,* for in it you went *out of Egypt.*	(4) *in the month of Abib* (9) *Yahweh* [your God][a] *led you out of Egypt*
	None shall appear before me empty-handed.	
(3) *You shall not* eat *anything leavened with* it	(18) *You shall not* offer *anything leavened with* the blood of my sacrifice;	
Seven days shall you eat unleavened bread with it— bread of distress . . .		(6) *Seven days shall you eat unleavened bread* and on the seventh day—a Pilgrimage Festival to Yahweh.
(4) *No sourdough shall be seen with you in all your territory* for seven days, *nor shall any of* the flesh which you sacrificed on the evening of the first day *remain until the morning.*	*nor shall any of* the fat of my Festival offering *remain until the morning.*	(7) *No sourdough shall be seen with you in all your territory.*

a. Septuagint plus.

Frame (A'):   for in *the month of Abib* בְּחֹדֶשׁ הָאָבִיב
Motive Clause.   Yahweh your God led you out of Egypt
Adverbial Accusative: by night

The insertion of the Passover command into the frame, whose original focus was Unleavened Bread, manifests the dexterity of the authors of Deuteronomy: textual transformation is essential to their transformation of legal and cultic history. By means of the repetitive resumption, they transform the original Passover from a local domestic slaughter into a centralized cultic sacrifice. The motive clause similarly applies to the Passover observance a lemma that originally belonged to the Unleavened Bread observance (see Exod 13:9; similarly, 23:15).

In order to reassign that lemma to their reconceived Passover, the authors of Deuteronomy complete it with an adverbial accusative asserting that the Exodus took place לַיְלָה "by night." In the context of the motive clause, which derives from Unleavened Bread, the nocturnal reference is inappropriate.[77] Despite the assertion of the lemma, the dominant biblical tradition is that the Exodus took place dramatically in broad daylight, the better to *épater les Egyptiens*.[78] The trope of "night" properly belongs to the Passover, whose distinctive doorway slaughter and blood rite both took place at sunset.[79] The adverb's strategic addition to the lemma signals the Deuteronomic authors' exegetical legerdemain. It effects the transition from the lemma's original focus—Unleavened Bread—to its reuse in their reformulation of the Passover. This "night" motif is amplified and integrated more specifically into the Passover regulations as the time of the paschal sacrifice in Deut 16:6.

Far more is involved than merely making a deft literary transition. At stake is the complete transformation by the Deuteronomic author of the original

77. It is absent both in the Covenant Code (Exod 23:15–18) and in the proto-Deuteronomic Unleavened Bread legislation (Exod 13:3–10).

78. "They set out from Rameses in the first month, on the fifteenth day of the first month; *on the morrow of the passover offering the Israelites went out highhandedly in the sight of all the Egyptians*" (Num 33:3; P). This emphasis on the dramatic daylight departure for the Exodus is consistent with the divine command in the instructions concerning the Passover that prohibits the Israelites from exiting their domiciles until daybreak (Exod 12:22b; J). The biblical traditions are inconsistent on this point, however. The narrative of Exod 12:30–31 (J), implies that the departure occurs the very night of the Passover. The inconsistency most likely represents originally independent traditions or, perhaps, the contamination of one tradition (daylight Exodus) by another (nocturnal Passover) in the context of their literary redaction. Loewenstamm, *Exodus Tradition*, 222–25, convincingly isolates two distinct traditions: (1) that of the paschal sacrifice by night, which requires a daytime departure (Exod 12:22b); and (2) that of the firstborn plague, which struck at midnight and which implies a departure as soon as possible thereafter that same night. Israel Knohl, "The Priestly Torah versus the Holiness School: Sabbath and the Festivals," *HUCA* 58 (1987) 65–117, at 77–81, also demonstrates the weak connection between the Exodus and the night motif. Once the tradition of the daytime departure became the dominant one within the Bible, early Jewish exegesis revised Deut 16:1 to make the explicit night reference no longer apply to the Exodus but rather to the paschal sacrifice (so *Tg. Pseudo-Jonathan Deut 16:1* [ed. Clarke, *Targum Pseudo-Jonathan*, 228]) or to the performance of divine wonders (so *Tg. Onqelos Deut 16:1*); see also Loewenstamm, *Exodus Tradition*, 223.

79. Exod 12:22b, J; and Exod 12:6b, P.

signification of the Passover. Deut 16:1 asserts that the Passover commemorates the Exodus.[80] There is no evidence whatsoever for that assertion in
Deuteronomy's sources. The original cultic commemoration of the Exodus is
not the Passover but the Festival of Unleavened Bread. Passover properly commemorates the deliverance of the Israelites from the plague directed against
the first-born.[81] Deuteronomy's contrary assertion—that the Passover commemorates the Exodus—is thus an innovation that lacks any direct basis in literary history. The transformation is not a natural traditio-historical development but rather a creative solution to a hermeneutical problem. Their program
of cult centralization required the authors of Deuteronomy to abrogate the
doorway slaughter and blood apotropy originally essential to the paschal rite.
To do this, they transformed the noncultic slaughter into a normative sacrifice
at the Temple, where the blood would, as with all sacrifices, be poured against
the base of the altar (Deut 12:27b). That transformation, however, completely
drained Passover of its distinctive identity. The Deuteronomic assertion that
Passover commemorates the Exodus is therefore nearly an admission of de-
spair: how else to retain the Passover altogether but by giving it renewed
significance, however tendentiously predicated?

This reapplication of the Exodus material to Passover is also evident in
Deut 16:6. What was originally an adverbial phrase to specify the *date* of the
Festival of Unleavened Bread becomes recontextualized rather to specify the
hour of the performance of the Passover slaughter! In this recontextualization,
the term מועד "appointed time, sacred season," which conventionally refers
to significant dates within the lunar or solar calendar, becomes respecified
to denote the time of day. Whereas Exod 23:15 refers to the seven days of
Unleavened Bread as occurring למועד חדש האביב כי בו יצאת ממצרים *"at the
appointed time* in the month of Abib, for in it you went forth from Egypt," Deut
16:6 stipulates that the Passover sacrifice should occur בערב כבוא השמש מועד
צאתך ממצרים "in the evening, at sundown, *the time* [*of day*] when you went forth
from Egypt." The night motif, added to the lemma in Deut 16:1, now so thoroughly controls the lemmatic reformulation that the paschal slaughter at
sunset—rather than, as the lemma contemplates, the seven-day eating of unleavened bread during Abib—commemorates the Exodus. Remarkably, in
Deuteronomy, the Passover proper—the deliverance from the tenth plague—
remains entirely without cultic commemoration!

The most striking addition to Deut 16:1, framed by the repetitive resumption, is the application of Deuteronomy's technical language for sacrifice to
the Passover, originally a noncultic slaughter. Deuteronomy's addition to the
lemma—ועשית פסח ליהוה אלהיך "You shall offer a paschal sacrifice to Yahweh,

---

80. On this memorial aspect of Deuteronomy's festival calendar, see Braulik, "Leidensgedächtnisfeier und Freudenfest," 95–121.

81. The difference between the two is made clear in the instructions to the Israelite father
on how to instruct his children concerning the significance of each observance (Exod 12:26–27;
13:8; both, proto-D). The Covenant Code's Unleavened Bread legislation (Exod 23:15) and the
narrative anchoring of Unleavened Bread in the story of the Exodus (Exod 12:33, 39) confirm
that the Exodus originally has its commemoration exclusively in the Unleavened Bread festival.

your God" (Deut 16:1aβ)—deliberately reverses cultic and legal history. The verb involved does not merely exhort abstract observance; hence, it is misleading to render it simply as *"keep* the Passover" (RSV; similarly, NRSV).[82] Instead, the verb represents Deuteronomy's technical term for cultic sacrifice at the centralized altar (see Deut 12:27).[83] Just that technical idiom interpolated into the lemma by itself expresses *in nuce* the whole of Deuteronomy's fundamental transformation of the Passover. In rejecting the earlier idiom of local, paschal slaughter (ושחטו הפסח "Slaughter the passover offering" [Exod 12:21, JE]) for the terminology of cultic sacrifice, Deuteronomy forcibly assimilates the Passover to the normative sacrificial protocol.

Deuteronomy will tolerate no cultic ritual but at the Temple, as the continuation and expansion of this clause in Deut 16:2 makes clear: וזבחת פסח ליהוה אלהיך צאן ובקר במקום אשר יבחר יהוה לשכן שמו שם "You shall sacrifice the passover offering for Yahweh your God, sheep and cattle, in the place where Yahweh your God shall choose to make his name dwell." The Passover—an anomaly in terms of Deuteronomy's creation of the local sphere as the realm of the secular and its restriction of cultic activity to the central Temple—is here relocated in its phenomenology from the private to the central sphere. The Passover is no longer a slaughter in the doorway of the individual family's home, and the apotropaic daubing of blood is excised from the rite. Extraordinarily, the Passover becomes a festival pilgrimage to the central Temple in order to perform a routine cultic sacrifice. The normative objects of sacrifice, both small and large cattle, are to be sacrificed upon an altar; the blood will be spilled on the base of the altar, according to protocol (Deut 12:27); and the parts of the animal to be eaten are, as normal, boiled (Deut 16:7), rather than roasted (inconsistent with the older norm retained by Exod 12:8–9, P).

The appropriation of the paschal slaughter into the centralized sacrificial system thus involves an extensive series of normalizations: (1) of the slaughtered animal, from formerly just sheep to both sheep and cattle; (2) the abolition of blood apotropy—Deuteronomy 16 avoids even mentioning blood; (3) the shift from roasting to cultically routine boiling as the means for the preparation of the offering; (4) and, preeminently, the prohibition of precisely the local, domestic context for the ritual (Deut 16:2b, 5–6a) that formerly distinguished the Passover.[84] The Festival of Unleavened Bread becomes equally transformed. It retains its local focus but loses its distinctive identity as a pilgrimage to a local altar. In fact, the Passover pilgrims are now commanded to

---

82. Contra Morrow, "Deut 14:1–17:1," 126, 215, who considers that the idiom involves "holding" the Passover festival. Mayes, *Deuteronomy,* 258, follows the RSV in its rendering.

83. See chapter 2, n. 31 for the verb's use in the other literary sources of the Bible and for the similar sacrificial uses of its cognate in Akkadian.

84. For a different compositional analysis, see Morrow, "Deut 14:1–17:1," 231–32. Morrow's methodology of structural linguistics explicitly subordinates textual content to the meticulous mapping of syntactical form (p. 23). Such a move takes the text largely as a given and as essentially cohesive. By removing matters of content from consideration, this approach a priori precludes recognizing the programmatic aspects of a text: of authors seeking, through their literary composition, to effect changes in religion or society.

return home from their pilgrimage to observe the prescription to eat unleavened bread for a seven-day period. Unleavened Bread is thereby completely shorn of its original identity as a pilgrimage festival.

The changes demonstrated here in the festival calendar are consistent in their structure with the transformation of sacrifice (Deut 12:1–28). The deliberate assimilation of the originally domestic paschal slaughter to the central sanctuary conforms to Deuteronomy's transfer of sacrifice from the local to the central sphere. In both cases, textual reworking becomes the means to overcome and coopt a fundamental challenge to the innovative program of the Deuteronomic authors. The structural parallel goes further. The authors of Deuteronomy 12 paradoxically retain and transform what they proscribe: local sacrifice, albeit now secularized as a local slaughter and completely detached from the cultus and from the altar (Deut 12:15–16, 20–25). Analogously, in the case of the festival legislation, the Deuteronomic authors retain Unleavened Bread as a local observance but shear its original nexus with the now proscribed local sanctuary. What remains then is the public assembly and the eating of unleavened cakes, now detached from any explicit connection to the cultus. The local realm is thereby not made into a religiohistorical or a textual void; it is given new content and integrity.

This analysis of how both observances are so profoundly transformed sheds new light on the reason why the authors of Deuteronomy do not employ the term חג "pilgrimage festival" to refer either to Passover or to Unleavened Bread in Deut 16:1–8. That omission is striking because the term is correctly applied, as expected, to both Weeks (Deut 16:10) and Booths (Deut 16:13), and to the traditional three, including Unleavened Bread, in the colophon (Deut 16:16). Most likely, the nonuse is studied and deliberate. The Deuteronomic authors withhold this designation not simply because of ritual difference[85] but because their transformations are completely without precedent. They are consciously departing from literary convention. It is therefore entirely proper that the authors of Deut 16:1–8 refrain from designating as a חג "pilgrimage festival" either Unleavened Bread (which no longer involves a pilgrimage to a sanctuary) or Passover (which, despite its origins, they have transformed into a pilgrimage in all but name).[86] To invoke the

---

85. Contra Nicolsky, "Pascha," 182–83; and Braulik, "Leidensgedächtnisfeier und Freudenfest," 101.

86. The term "pilgrimage festival," pointedly missing from the Hebrew of Deut 16:1–8, is restored by the Samaritan version, arguably as a harmonization with Exod 13:6b, the very text that the authors of Deuteronomy were constrained to revise. Conversely, both the Samaritan and the Septuagint harmonize the numerical scheme of Exod 13:6 to make it conform to that of Deut 16:8 ("*six* days shall you eat unleavened cakes and on the seventh . . ."). This reading in the LXX and the Samaritan Pentateuch of Exod 13:6 therefore does not represent a more original text than the MT; contra B. N. Wambacq, "Les *Maṣṣôt*," *Bib* 61 (1980) 31–54, at 46. Instead, it is simply an example of the versions' attempt to eliminate inconsistencies between parallel texts. There is no evidence to support the reconstruction of MT Deut 16:8 by Peter Laaf, *Die Pascha-Feier Israels: Eine literarkritische und überlieferungsgeschichtliche Studie* (BBB 36; Bonn: Peter Hanstein, 1970) 79. He makes up his own eccentric idiom, for which there is neither biblical attestation nor support from the textual witnesses.

conventional reference to the pilgrimage festival at this point would only call attention to the paschal lamb's new clothes.

The innovation of centralization represents the driving force that accounts for the problematic structures evident in both the centralization law of Deuteronomy 12 and the cultic calendar of Deut 16:1–8. Deuteronomy's transformation of the Passover renders illegitimate what formerly was required: לא תוכל לזבח את הפסח באחד שעריך "You must not sacrifice the Passover offering in any of your city-gates" (Deut 16:5). In the antithesis, the authors of Deuteronomy assert as exclusively legitimate that which is both religiously and textually unprecedented: כי אם אל המקום אשר יבחר יהוה אלהיך לשכן שמו שם תזבח את הפסח בערב "but rather at the place where Yahweh shall cause his name to dwell, there shall you sacrifice the passover offering, in the evening" (Deut 16:6; similarly, 12:18, 5, 14). The analogy with the prohibition of the local consumption of *sancta* in the case of Deuteronomy's centralization law is striking. In both cases the prohibition –לא תוכל ל "You must not" signals the Deuteronomic authors' ruling against current or anticipated practice while simultaneously, if covertly, rejecting the authority of their textual patrimony.[87] The similar prohibition in Deut 12:17 does not simply prohibit the cultic activity that, pre-Deuteronomically, would have taken place at the local altars. It also directs itself against the pre-Deuteronomic laws that require local sacrifice and the local offering of tithes, firstfruits, and firstlings[88]—and forbids them. Both laws prohibit obedience to prior religious law. Here the authors of Deuteronomy do not merely abrogate the prior dispensation that enshrines cultic activity at the local altars. They polemically engage it. They avoid identifying it as previously normative and instead stigmatize it as anathema, as contrary to the divine revelation that Moses now mediates. Horeb, as reiterated at Moab, subverts Sinai.

When Texts Collide: The Hermeneutics of Prepositional Reduplication

Scholars have long identified *aporia* of grammar, syntax, and meaning in Deuteronomy's blend of Passover and Unleavened Bread (Deut 16:1–8). There have been many attempts to account for these difficulties, which have, for the most part, not been successful. They include claims that errors in the transmission of the text caused dittography or that words are used in this text with meanings elsewhere unattested for them. These philological problems are better explained as a by-product of the deliberate redactional composition of the festival calendar. As the Deuteronomic authors transform Passover into a normative sacrifice, their

---

87. Whether this formula consistently in Deuteronomy signals a polemic, direct or indirect, warrants further investigation. Unconvincing, for example, is the suggestion by David Daube that the formula's use in the law of the king (Deut 17:15) represents a direct textual allusion to the story of Abimelech's kingship in Judges 9 ("'One from among Your Brethren Shall I Set King over You,'" *JBL* 90 [1971] 480–81). There are insufficient linguistic ties between the texts involved to support his proposal.

88. Exod 20:24; 22:27–29; 23:19.

technique for doing so involves the recontextualization of originally unrelated lemmas into a new text. As a result, the now centralized Passover is forcibly adjoined to the new Festival of Unleavened Bread, which itself is transformed so as no longer to involve a pilgrimage. The forced conjunction of the two is preeminently a textual reformulation born of hermeneutical necessity.

The degree of transformation of the lemmas concerned with each observance accounts for the structural and philological difficulties long identified but hitherto not resolved. The authors' redactional work creates textual "fault lines" where originally unrelated lemmas abut. Deut 16:3a represents one such critical textual seam. Both its α and β portions raise complex syntactic and literary-critical issues.

Deut 16:3aα—לא תאכל עליו חמץ—is conventionally understood as a regulation that "concerns the passover sacrifice at night."[89] The new Jewish Publication Society Version embeds this exegesis in its translation: "You shall not eat anything leavened with it."[90] Such translations presuppose that, as object of the preposition, the word "*it* refers to the sacrificial animal."[91] Neither the translation of the verse nor the claim that the preposition refers back to the paschal offering in the previous verse (Deut 16:2) is tenable:

[2] וזבחת פסח ליהוה אלהיך צאן ובקר במקום אשר יבחר יהוה לשכן שמו שם
[3] לא תאכל עליו חמץ . . .

(2) You shall sacrifice the passover offering for Yahweh your God,
from the flock or the herd, in the place where Yahweh shall choose
to establish his name.

(3) You shall not eat anything leavened *upon/with it* . . .

Contextually, the pronominal suffix on the preposition, עליו "upon *it*" (v. 3), must have the פסח "paschal offering" of v. 2 for its antecedent. That antecedent in turn, however, points to the lack of logic in the placement of the prohibition in v. 3aα. After all, v. 2, with its centralization formula, prescribes only the proper location for the paschal sacrifice; the proper ritual preparation of the sacrifice is not addressed. The intrusive force of the prohibition against eating an offering (so v. 3aα)—the instructions concerning the cooking of which have yet to be given—becomes clear by contrasting it with the more logical sequence that follows in vv. 5–7a.

[5] לא תוכל לזבח את הפסח באחד שעריך אשר יהוה אלהיך נתן לך
[6] כי אם אל המקום אשר יבחר יהוה אלהיך לשכן שמו
שם תזבח את הפסח בערב כבוא השמש מועד צאתך ממצרים
[7] ובשלת ואכלת במקום אשר יבחר יהוה אלהיך בו . . .

(5) You must not sacrifice the passover offering in any of your city-
gates which Yahweh your God is giving you;

---

89. So Rofé, *Deuteronomy*, 39 (my translation).

90. *Tanakh: A New Translation of the Holy Scriptures according to the Traditional Hebrew Text* (Philadelphia: JPS, 1988) 300.

91. Mayes, *Deuteronomy*, 259 (emphasis in the original).

(6) but rather, at the place where Yahweh your God shall choose to establish his name, there shall you sacrifice the passover offering in the evening, at sundown, at the time of day that you came forth from Egypt.

(7) You shall cook and eat it in the place which Yahweh your God shall choose . . .

Verse 5 provides the negative formulation and, arguably, the logical continuation of v. 2, while v. 6a restates the centralization formula, which specifies the proper location of sacrifice. From this specification, v. 6b logically follows, prescribing the proper time for the sacrifice, as does v. 7a, stipulating the proper method of its preparation. In contrast, however, to the logical sequence of vv. 5–7a, the conjunction of vv. 2 + 3aα is illogical. It proscribes eating leavened bread עליו "with it"—with the as yet uncooked paschal sacrifice!

Not only does v. 16:3aα fail to make contextual sense but its proper literary-historical derivation is also problematic. A. D. H. Mayes has argued, "This is a Passover regulation; *it* refers to the Passover sacrificial animal. Leaven was not permitted with the Passover sacrifice." He adduces as sole support for his argument Exod 23:18 and 34:25, two texts that have no original connection to the Passover.[92] The first of these texts derives rather from the Covenant Code's coda of rules that apply to the pilgrimage festival sacrifices.[93] The second, as I have already argued, is Deuteronomistic: it represents a post-Deuteronomic revision of Exod 23:18 in light of Deuteronomy's festival calendar—the very passage in question. Mayes's argument is thus circular. He has read Exod 23:18 as if it meant the same thing as Exod 34:25—and thus missed the literary-historical distance between the two passages.

Another possible explanation for Deut 16:3aα, which prohibits the consumption of leaven with the paschal offering, is that it represents a negative formulation of the Priestly stipulation that the lamb be consumed with unleavened cakes and bitter herbs. Indeed, even the use of the preposition על to indicate accompaniment and the verbal root are common to both contexts: ומצות על מררים יאכלהו "[with] unleavened cakes and *with* bitter herbs they shall eat it" (Exod 12:8; cf. Num 9:11).[94] This approach is also problematic. With rare

---

92. Mayes, *Deuteronomy*, 258, who bases his analysis upon Halbe, "Passa-Massot im deuteronomischen Festkalender," 150, 153.

93. Contra Haran, *Temples*, 327–31, who, although not explicitly, follows the harmonization of *Targum Onqelos* Exod 23:18 and reads the Passover specification of Exod 34:25 back into Exod 23:18. In other words, he subordinates the pre-Deuteronomic source to its later, Deuteronomistic reformulation. For the original meaning of Exod 23:18 as a general festival prescription, see Dillmann, *Exodus*, 279.

94. Neither the grammar nor the syntax of Exod 12:8 is straightforward. Traditional Rabbinic exegesis, disregarding the אתנחתא (disjunctive accent) under בלילה הזה "this night," construes the verse as "They shall eat the meat during this night roasted by fire *and* [with] unleavened cakes; with bitter herbs they shall eat it." Nachmanides renders it, "They shall eat the meat during this night roasted by fire; they shall eat it [with] unleavened cakes and bitter herbs." See Nachmanides (Ramban), *Commentary on the Torah* (2 vols.; Jerusalem: Rav Kook Institute, 1975–76) 1.228 (Hebrew). On the range of traditional renderings, note H. M. Orlinsky, *Notes on the New Translation of the Torah* (Philadelphia: JPS, 1970) 164–65.

exception, even the minority of scholars who date P prior to or contemporary with D usually do not assert direct literary influence between the two sources.[95] Second, there remains the problem of the logic of the text's organization. In the context of the P prescriptions for the Passover (Exod 12:1–13), the stipulation to consume the offering together with unleavened cakes and bitter herbs logically follows the references to the offering's being slaughtered, cooked, and eaten (Exod 12:6–8a). Precisely that logical coherence of textual sequence is absent in Deut 16:1–3aα. Hence, the attempt to derive Deut 16:3aα from Passover legislation founders because no such stipulation can be cited in a Passover context and because the derivation fails to explain the textual disorder.

Not less contextually incoherent than the first עליו is the second in v. 3.[96] Like the first, the preposition in the phrase under discussion—שבעת ימים תאכל עליו מצות "seven days shall you eat unleavened cakes *with* it"—grammatically requires the paschal offering of v. 2 as the antecedent for its pronominal suffix. That grammatical antecedent, however, would require the law's addressee to eat unleavened bread for seven days עליו "with it"—with the passover offering which, according to v. 4b, must not be retained beyond the morning following the evening slaughter (similarly, Exod 12:8; Num 9:12). To observe Unleavened Bread would thereby require abrogation of the Passover law. Such a command makes no sense.[97]

Various attempts have been made to resolve this illogic both of grammar and ritual law. None have been successful. For example, a synchronic attempt

---

In fact, Exod 12:8b is a casus pendens with a double adverbial accusative, the first of which is צלי אש "roasted by fire," the second of which is the phrase ומצות על מררים "[with] unleavened cakes and with bitter herbs," both of which accusatives are governed by the verb in final position יאכלהו "they shall eat it." Adverbial accusative clauses such as this normally (1) are anarthrous (lack the definite article) and (2) occur in inverted word order; see R. J. Williams, *Hebrew Syntax: An Outline* (2d ed.; Toronto: University of Toronto Press, 1976) 14 (§ 60), 81–82 (§ 491). The verse as a whole is thus most accurately translated: "They shall eat the flesh that same night, *eating it roasted, with unleavened cakes and bitter herbs*"; so Childs, *Exodus*, 179. The preposition על in context thus marks accompaniment ("with" or "and"). For this usage, with a citation to this passage, see Williams, *Hebrew Syntax*, 52 (§ 293).

The syntactical ambiguities of Exod 12:8b are removed in the citation which occurs in the exegetical context of the second Passover in Num 9:11: על מצות ומררים יאכלהו (note the cross-reference in Num 9:3). The adverbial accusative is broken and a prepositional phrase substituted; the *waw*, rather than marking the second object, becomes a simple copula. For the exegetical nature of Num 9:6–14, see Fishbane, *Biblical Interpretation*, 99. The linguistic analysis here confirms his argument that Num 9:6–14 must represent a later stratum within P.

95. See Sara Japhet, "The Relationship between the Legal Corpora in the Pentateuch in Light of Manumission Laws," *Studies in Bible, 1986* (ed. Sara Japhet; ScrHier 31; Jerusalem: Magnes, 1986) 68–78. Her own important article rejects that view of the nonrelation of the sources. Nonetheless, I disagree with her conclusion that the manumission law of Lev 25:39–46 presupposes that of Deut 15:12–18. See also Levinson, *Hermeneutics of Innovation*, 90–106, 113–14. For an analysis of Jacob Milgrom's argument that D cites P, see chapter 2, n. 46.

96. See Halbe, "Passa-Massot," 150 n. 14; and Cholewiński, *Heiligkeitsgesetz und Deuteronomium*, 182–83 (n. 19), 187, for the many previous attempts to explain the preposition.

97. Morrow, "Deut 14:1–17:1," 128, 218, defends this reading but provides no clear account of what the phrase means, given its antecedent in v. 2.

is implicit in the translation of the new Jewish Publication Society Version, which renders the problematic prepositional phrase, "for seven days *thereafter*" and thus severs the connection between this rule and that concerning the paschal offering.[98] Such a ruse of translation is untenable; it lacks any justification in lexicography.[99] The temporal signification it assigns the preposition is not defended in the accompanying footnote, which concedes, "Lit. 'upon it.'" That the identical preposition in two adjacent phrases should have such starkly inconsistent translations—in the first case, "with it"; in the second, "thereafter"—is intrinsically problematic. No more effective are text-critical solutions: the textual witnesses attest the prepositional phrase. The failure of a harmonizing, synchronic solution and the lack of justification for a text-critical emendation suggest that a diachronic interpretation is called for.

Although they are contiguous, the two clauses (vv. 3aα + β) do not constitute a coherent text. Their contiguity is rather by means of the forced appropriation of texts. Deut 16:3aβ, which refers to the Festival of Unleavened Bread, bears no original relationship to the immediately preceding clause (v. 3aα), which is concerned rather with the Passover ritual. Deut 16:3aβ–4a are widely regarded as an original Unleavened Bread unit, into which a Passover unit consisting of Deut 16:3aα + 4b was interpolated.[100] This analysis of the text is strengthened by the recognition that the contextually disruptive section concerned with the Festival of Unleavened Bread, vv. 3aβ–4a, both begins and closes with the adverbial accusative phrase שבעת ימים "seven days." The repetition frames the insertion and marks the problematic text as a repetitive resumption. This insertion is not diachronically "secondary"; rather, the text is itself an original redactional composition that uses prior lemmas in the process of its formulation.

Once the preceding analysis is recognized as accounting for the problematic structure of the verse, the literary history and the exegetical reworking of each half can separately be traced. Prior to the interpolation of the Unleavened Bread unit, vv. 3aα + 4b were continuous. With this observation, the original context in literary history for the difficult 3aα can be recovered:

לא תאכל עליו חמץ [3aα]

ולא ילין מן הבשר אשר תזבח בערב ביום הראשון לבקר [4b]

(3aα) You must not eat anything leavened with it;

(4b) None of the flesh which you sacrifice on the evening of the first day shall be allowed to remain until morning.

98. *Tanakh*, 300.

99. Such a rendering for the preposition is absent in S. R. Driver's detailed analysis in BDB, 752–759, *s.v.* Nor does it find any support in Williams, *Hebrew Syntax*, 51–52 (§ 285–96) or, most recently, in Bruce K. Waltke and M. O'Connor, *An Introduction to Biblical Hebrew Syntax* (Winona Lake, Ind.: Eisenbrauns, 1990) 216–18.

100. So Halbe, "Passa-Massot," 150–54; and Mayes, *Deuteronomy*, 254–55, 258. Note the structural analysis of Otto, "*pāsah/paesah*," 674–75. Disputing the chronological priority of the Unleavened Bread unit is Cholewiński, *Heiligkeitsgesetz und Deuteronomium*, 181.

Although in its present context v. 3aα deals with Passover, such a derivation is impossible in terms of its lemmatic history. Similarly, however, it is
impossible to derive Deut 16:4b from Passover stipulations. Despite the temp-
tation of an analogy with the priestly regulation ולא תותירו ממנו עד בקר "You
shall not leave any of it over until morning" (Exod 12:10, cf. Num 9:12), it is
unclear why v. 4b should include a temporal specification (אשר תזבח בערב "which
you sacrifice *on the evening*"), when the stipulation about how and the time
when to perform the sacrifice in the first place is not positively formulated until
v. 6aβ,b–7.

Neither of the two clauses in question can logically derive from Passover
legislation. Instead, Deuteronomy's regulation for the Passover observance
(Deut 16:3aα + 4b) paradoxically derives from the laws for pilgrimage festival sacrifices found in the Covenant Code (Exod 23:18b).[101] Given Deuteronomy's drive to centralize the Passover and transform it into a pilgrimage
festival in all but name, such a lemmatic origin makes sense, even as it stands
prior law on its head. The verse in question from the Covenant Code accounts
for many features of Deuteronomy's Passover regulation: the sequence of two
negatives joined by a copula (ולא . . . לא), the formulation involving an initial
second person singular verb resumed by third person singular, and even the
specific verb used by the prohibition, "let there not remain until the morrow":

Deut 16:3aα + 4b	Exod 23:18
לא תאכל עליו חמץ . . .	לא תזבח על חמץ דם זבחי
ולא ילין מן הבשר אשר תזבח בערב	ולא ילין חלב חגי
ביום הראשון לבקר	עד בקר

You shall not eat *anything leavened
with* it
Nor shall any of the flesh which
you sacrifice on the evening of the
first day
be allowed to remain to *morning.*

You shall not offer *anything leavened
with* the blood of my sacrifice
Nor shall the fat of my pilgrimage
festival offering
be allowed to remain until *morning.*

The authors of Deuteronomy respecify the coda to the Covenant Code,
concerned with regulations for the festival sacrifices, so that it now governs
the originally local paschal slaughter.[102] This hypothesis that the verse was
originally concerned to prohibit leaven in the context of festival sacrifices, not
in the context of the Passover, avoids the present incoherence of the text, which
prohibits the consumption of the just slaughtered but not yet cooked paschal

101. S. R. Driver, *Deuteronomy* (ICC; 3d ed.; Edinburgh: T. & T. Clark, 1901) 192 places
the texts parallel but does not analyze the exegetical reformulation.

102. Contra Morrow, "Deut 14:1–17:1," 228. Here there are two problems. First, he char-
acterizes both Exod 23:18 and 34:25 as Passover regulations. He thereby reads Exod 34:25 back
into 23:18, although they are independent and the former is Deuteronomistic. Second, Morrow
notes the differences between the texts but does not consider the possibility of the tendentious
reworking of a source text as one form of textual relationship. His method, a descriptive structural linguistics that sees relation in terms of cohesion or similarity, rules it out.

offering.[103] The hypothesis raises, however, a further issue. The verb of the original prohibition concerns not the eating of leaven but rather the sacrifice of a festival offering with leaven. Although the lemma specifies לא תזבח על "You shall not *sacrifice* with," the reformulated text in Deuteronomy specifies לא תאכל על "You shall not *eat* with." How may this shift be understood? It seems most likely that the original verb was changed in order to effect the transition from the frame of the repetitive resumption, concerned with Passover (Deut 16:3aα + 4b), to the insertion (Deut 16:3aβ-4a), concerned rather with the Festival of Unleavened Bread. The verbal substitution facilitated the integration of the two units.

As a result of the change, the sacrificial rule of the lemma is assimilated to the eating motif of the interpolation. The editor creates a lexical analogy between the leaven upon which the Passover offering is not to be sacrificed and the leaven that the community is prohibited from eating during Unleavened Bread.[104] The forced assimilation of the two prescriptions expresses itself in the redundancy of the verse: לא תאכל עליו חמץ שבעת ימים תאכל עליו מצות "You shall not eat *with it* anything leavened; seven days shall you eat *with it* unleavened cakes" (Deut 16:3a). The pleonasm of the preposition is thus not a mechanical error resulting from dittography.[105] Instead, it derives from the forced combination of two originally independent regulations.

The repetitive resumption establishes that the original continuation of 16:3aα is v. 4b. This permits the restoration of the lemma's original verb, תזבח "You shall sacrifice," on analogy with Exod 23:18a. That missing verb, first observed in v. 2a, reappears in the continuation: הבשר אשר תזבח בערב "the flesh which you *sacrifice* in the evening" (Deut 16:4b). That regulation applies to the paschal offering a rule whose literary-historical origin is rather the general pilgrimage festival regulations of Exod 23:18b.

This raises an interesting question of cultic history. I have earlier noted that the earliest (J) regulations concerned with Passover do not specify that it was eaten: they mention neither the consumption of the paschal slaughter nor the requirement that it be consumed before morning (Exod 12:21–23).[106] They stipulate only that, following the rite of blood apotropy, no one leave the domicile עד בקר "until the morning" (Exod 12:22). In contrast, the post-Deuteronomic regulations for the Passover not only stipulate the blood apotropy but also specify that the paschal lamb should be eaten by night and not be allowed to remain עד בקר "until the morning" (Exod 12:8, 10; P). It is therefore

---

103. The prohibition of leaven in the cultus extended to all cereal offerings (Lev 2:11; 6:10) except for the thanksgiving offering (Lev 7:13) and the loaves for the priests (Lev 23:17); see Cassuto, *Exodus*, 304.

104. This maneuver is loosely comparable to the formalized Rabbinic exegetical technique of interpreting a problematic word in light of its usage in another context (*gezerah shavah*). On that technique see Saul J. Lieberman, *Hellenism in Jewish Palestine* (2d ed.; New York: Jewish Theological Seminary of America, 1962) 58–62; and Menahem Elon, *Jewish Law: History, Sources, Principles* (4 vols.; Philadelphia: JPS, 1994) 1.351–55.

105. Contra Halbe, "Passa-Massot," 150.

106. See p. 61.

possible that Deuteronomy, which stands between these two literary sources,[107] is responsible for the transformation of the Passover from strictly a rite of blood apotropy, in which the lamb was not eaten, into a communal meal.

In its second appearance in v. 3, the problematic prepositional phrase— עליו "upon it"—must be recognized as having no original role in the legislation concerning the Festival of Unleavened Bread. Rather it arises, either intentionally or from contamination by the first half of the verse, as part of the combination by the Deuteronomic author of the originally separate rituals concerning Passover and Unleavened Bread. In this passage, the Deuteronomic author appropriates key lemmas from the proto-Deuteronomic legislation concerning Unleavened Bread:

Deut 16:3aβ–4a	Exod 13:6–7
שבעת ימים תאכל עליו מצות	שבעת ימים תאכל מצת
	וביום השביעי חג ליהוה
לחם עני	מצות יאכל את שבעת הימים
כי בחפזון יצאת מארץ מצרים . . .	ולא יראה לך חמץ
ולא יראה לך שאר בכל גבלך	ולא יראה לך שאר בכל גבלך
שבעת ימים	

Seven days shall you eat	*Seven days shall you eat*
unleavened cakes **upon it**,	*unleavened cakes;*
the bread of affliction	and on the seventh day there shall be a
—for you departed from the	pilgrimage festival for Yahweh.
land of Egypt in haste . . .	Unleavened cakes shall be eaten for
	the seven days;
	No leavened bread shall be seen
	with you,
Nor shall sourdough be seen	*nor shall sourdough be seen*
with you in all your territory	*with you in all your territory.*
for seven days.	

107. The date of the Priestly source in relation to Deuteronomy (and P's relation to the Holiness Code) remains in dispute. I follow the consensus that considers P and H, in their present redaction, to follow Deuteronomy. A number of scholars, however, especially those following Yehezkel Kaufmann, maintain that P precedes Deuteronomy and, independently of it, presupposes centralization. Among those dating P before Deuteronomy are Haran, *Temples*, 132–48; Avi Hurvitz, *A Linguistic Study of the Relationship between the Priestly Source and the Book of Ezekiel* (CahRB 20; Paris: J. Gabalda, 1982; Richard Elliott Friedman, *Who Wrote the Bible?* (Englewood Cliffs, N.J.: Prentice Hall, 1987) 161–216; and Milgrom, *Leviticus*, 13–35. Note the review of Milgrom's work by Victor Avigdor Hurowitz, "Ancient Israelite Cult in History, Tradition, and Interpretation," *AJS Review* 19 (1994) 213–36. Israel Knohl proposes a multilayered approach (*The Sanctuary of Silence: The Priestly Torah and the Holiness School* [Minneapolis: Fortress, 1995] 199–226. He argues that preexilic priestly material, dating from the time of Solomon's Temple, underwent a process of later redaction by the authors of the Holiness Code, whose latest layers date to the beginning of the Persian period. While I accept his arguments for the priority of P to H, the Solomonic dating of P is unconvincing. Knohl's argument seems to represent a compromise position between Yehezkel Kaufmann's preexilic and Wellhausen's postexilic dating of

Deuteronomy's reuse of the lemma is highly selective: deliberately so. The authors retain only the dietary requirement that can be observed independent of the local altar and delete the pilgrimage that requires that altar. The force of the reworking is completely to transform Unleavened Bread from a pilgrimage festival (חג) into a local observance completely removed from the sanctuary and distinguished only by its flat diet. It therefore becomes inevitable that the concluding day of the nonfestival can only be marked bloodlessly. Thus in contrast to the lemma וביום השביעי חג ליהוה "and on the seventh day there shall be a *pilgrimage festival* for Yahweh" (Exod 13:6b), Deut 16:8 can require only וביום השביעי עצרת ליהוה אלהיך לא תעשה מלאכה "and on the seventh day there shall be a *solemn assembly* for Yahweh your God; you shall do no work."[108]

In the end, there is no simple blend of Passover and Unleavened Bread in Deuteronomy's festival calendar. It is not a matter of the two observances' being sutured together or of one being interpolated into the other, as if each were otherwise retained intact. To the contrary, the authors of Deuteronomy already radically transform each of the two in the act of bringing them into conjunction. Both Passover and Unleavened Bread emerge newly conceived. Passover becomes a pilgrimage sacrifice in all but name, while Unleavened Bread has the pilgrimage element entirely deleted from it. So forcibly does the new Passover usurp that original identity of Unleavened Bread that the pilgrim who paradoxically goes *to the Temple for the Passover offering* must immediately make a pilgrimage *away* from the sanctuary in order to return home to celebrate Unleavened Bread: ופנית בבקר והלכת לאהליך "And *in the morning* you shall turn back and go to your tents" (Deut 16:7b).[109] The hapless pilgrim's double movement marks the Deuteronomic authors' double reworking of the cultic observances involved.

---

the priestly material. Knohl's historical arguments would be strengthened by an analysis that directly addressed the important matter of the relation of P and H to Deuteronomy.

108. The coherence and inevitability of Deut 16:8 call into question Cholewiński's claim that the verse represents a third stratum within the unit (*Heiligkeitsgesetz und Deuteronomium*, 184–86). On the replacement of the key term in Deut 16:8, see Caloz, "Exode XIII, 3–16," 57. The argument here would also rule out attempts to view Deut 16:8 as a priestly or even later post-priestly interpolation; see, most recently, Veijola, "History of Passover," 66–72. For a detailed critique, see Gertz, "Die Passa-Massot-Ordnung im deuteronomischen Festkalender," 56–80. More broadly on the importance of septads for the redaction of this calendar and the legal corpus, see Georg Braulik, "Die Funktion von Siebenergruppierungen im Endtext des Deuteronomiums," in *Ein Gott—eine Offenbarung: Festschrift Notker Füglister* (ed. Friedrich V. Reiterer; Würzburg: Echter, 1991) 37–50; and Otto, "Šaeba'/Šābû'ôt," 1017–22 (with literature).

109. A. B. Ehrlich, *Mikra ki-Pheschuto* (3 vols.; Berlin: M. Poppelauer, 1899–1901; reprinted, New York: Ktav, 1969) 1.338 (Hebrew), defends the clear sense of the text against the postbiblical halakhah, which prohibits travel on festivals and holy days. Nonetheless, he then inconsistently reinstates the halakhic norm of the Mishnah and Tosephta, maintaining that the only travel contemplated here is *within Jerusalem*, to the pilgrims' temporary tents, not back to their homes in the outlying cities.

The Transformation of Law and Religion in Deut 16:16–17

Deuteronomy's festival calendar, Deut 16:1–17, concludes with two verses, the first of which summarizes the three pilgrimage festivals and the second of which is a general exhortation to cultic generosity. Deut 16:16 chiastically cites Exod 23:15–17, consistent with Seidel's law, and, by means of the interpolation of the centralization formula, completely transforms that lemma in light of Deuteronomy's distinctive ideology.

<u>Exod 23:15–17</u>

[15] את חג המצות תשמר ...

A   ולא יראו פני ריקם

[16] וחג הקציר ... וחג האסף ...   B

[17] שלש פעמים בשנה יראה כל זכורך אל פני האדן יהוה   C

        (15) You shall observe the Festival of Unleavened Bread . . .

A   and *none shall appear before me empty-handed*;

  B   (16) And the Festival of Harvest . . . and the Festival of Ingathering

C   (17) Three times a year shall all your males

        appear before the Lord Yahweh

<u>Deut 16:16–17</u>

[16] שלש פעמים בשנה יראה כל זכורך את פני יהוה אלהיך   C'

במקום אשר יבחר   +X

בחג המצות ובחג השבעות ובחג הסכות   B'

ולא יראה את פני יהוה ריקם   A'

[17] איש כמתנת ידו כברכת יהוה אלהיך אשר נתן לך

C'   (16) Three times a year shall all your males

        appear before Yahweh your God

+X   *in the place that he shall choose*:

B   on the Festival of Unleavened Bread, on the Festival of Weeks, and on the Festival of Booths.

  A'   None shall *appear before Yahweh empty-handed*;

     (17) each man [shall give], as he is able, according to the blessing that Yahweh your God has bestowed upon you.

The authors of Deuteronomy revise the formula from the Covenant Code that mandates the appearance of the male Israelite at the originally local sanctuary (C) by interpolating the centralization formula: C'+X. With that interpolation, the Israelite is now required exclusively to make his cultic appearance before Yawheh at the central sanctuary; all festival pilgrimages (to the local sanctuary) thereby become Temple pilgrimages. That transformation abrogates the norm of older law while seeming to be only a restatement of it. The transformation involved has far-reaching consequences. In the Covenant Code, the command to appear thrice yearly before Yahweh was a distributive command; it could be fulfilled at any of the multiple altars or sanctuaries throughout Judah and Israel. Each male would observe it at the nearest sanctuary; many such observances would therefore take place simultaneously, with Unleavened Bread celebrated at every local altar by the clans in the adjacent area. Very likely, given variations in climate and growing season throughout the land and the fact that the festival observances were not calendrically fixed, the same observance would even have taken place at different times at different sanctuaries.

The authors of Deuteronomy reject all this. They introduce uniformity and systematization where they did not previously exist. They abrogate the original intimate connection between the formula to appear before Yahweh and the multiple local sanctuaries that were its home. Compliance with that command now requires an unprecedented pilgrimage to the central sanctuary. There is no cultic access to Yahweh, the authors of Deuteronomy insist, but at the central sanctuary. That transformation asserts hegemony by the national and public cult over the local cult. The restriction of site (and of sight) creates a religious monopoly that involves power and exclusivity. The very assertion that there is no cultus but the Jerusalem Temple cultus implies that there is no valid religious law but the law of Deuteronomy.

The Israelite would originally have observed the festivals at the local sanctuary, which would have been part of his community and where he would have been known. Deuteronomy's command to undertake a pilgrimage to the central sanctuary to observe these festivals had to involve immense social displacement; not only would the new site have been unfamiliar, but the celebrant would himself be unknown in the Temple precincts. He would be surrounded by others alien to him, themselves feeling equally alien. The new command, therefore, would contribute to a breakdown of the local cultus and to a decrease in the dominance of the clan networks in conventional religious life. Deuteronomy replaces these with a corporate religion. The citizenry becomes constituted as a national religious polity as it now begins to celebrate the festivals at a single time, at a single place, and as a single body.

A different issue arises as the authors of Deuteronomy also attempt to solve a problem regarding the original celebration of Unleavened Bread. In Deut 16:16, the introductory positive injunction of יראה "shall appear" is framed by the concluding negative ולא יראה "shall not appear." Originally, however, the latter prohibition against appearing before Yahweh empty-handed was specific to Unleavened Bread (in the lemma, A). The authors of Deuteronomy void its original specificity to make it a general coda applying to all three festivals (A').[110] There is a reason that it is no longer necessary in its original context.

In the Covenant Code, that admonition was necessary because of a problem associated with observing the Festival of Unleavened Bread. Although pilgrimage to the sanctuary required an offering, the early date of the observance within the agricultural season precluded having produce ripe enough to be presented on the altar. Despite the older opinion that understood Unleavened Bread to mark the beginning of the barley harvest, the month of Abib

---

110. This change of application, although not the more detailed chiastic citation, was also observed by Morgan, *Cultic Calendars in the Pentateuch*, 150.

was too early for a harvest festival. Neither barley nor wheat would be sufficiently mature to permit flour to be made from them, which might in turn be
used to bake unleavened cakes.[111] Later in the season, produce would be available as an offering, and thus no such prohibition against appearing empty-
handed accompanies the injunctions to observe the Festivals of Harvest and
Ingathering: both are followed by clauses relating the observance to the progress
of the agricultural year (Exod 23:16). Of necessity, then, in the case of Unleavened Bread, the legislator could only lamely require that the celebrant not
appear before God empty-handed; he could not suggest what produce the celebrant might offer.

That problem is redactionally solved in the context of Deuteronomy's festival calendar. The Unleavened Bread festival of Deut 16:16 contextually can
only mean that union of Passover and Unleavened Bread prescribed in Deut
16:1–8. As such, there is now no doubt about what to bring: וזבחת פסח ליהוה
אלהיך צאן ובקר "You shall sacrifice the passover offering to Yahweh your God,
sheep and cattle" (Deut 16:2). The paschal offering, now reworked into a normative sacrifice, fills the void and becomes the Unleavened Bread offering.

The sheep and cattle in question may well be specifically the firstlings of
each (Deut 15:19–23), as suggested by the legislation that immediately precedes the festival calendar. Deuteronomy 15 represents a redactional association of two originally separate types of legislation, each of which was concerned
with the seventh year: the law of the year of release (Deut 15:1–11) and the
law concerning manumission of slaves (Deut 15:12–18). In the context of that
assemblage of units with a common septennial cycle (Deut 15:1, 12), to add a
unit that mandates the annual presentation of firstlings of cattle and sheep to
Yahweh at the central sanctuary is disruptive (Deut 15:19–23). The most logical reason for its placement is that it serves as a redactional gloss upon the festival calendar that immediately follows. Firstlings, the redactor implies, constitute the logical offering for the Deuteronomically transformed Passover/
Unleavened Bread sacrifice of sheep and cattle (Deut 16:2).[112] The same redactional association of Firstlings and Unleavened Bread evident here is also

---

111. The erroneous assumption about the growing season is almost universally reflected
in the commentaries. See Driver, *Exodus*, 242; M. Noth, *Exodus* (Philadelphia: Westminster,
1962) 191; and J. P. Hyatt, *Exodus* (NCBC; Grand Rapids: Eerdmans, 1971) 248. Recognizing
that the month of Abib is too early for a harvest festival are Otto, *Mazzotfest in Gilgal*, 173;
Halbe, "Erwägungen zu Ursprung und Wesen des Massotfestes," 324–46; and, overlooking the
earlier work of Otto and Halbe, Ginsberg, *Israelian Heritage*, 44 n. 60, 58–59. All three depend
upon the crucial insight on the growing season provided by G. Dalman, *Arbeit und Sitte in
Palästina 1.2: Jahresablauf und Tagesablauf: Frühling und Sommer* (BFCT 2.17; Gütersloh:
Bertelsmann, 1928) 453. Note, however, the important cautions raised by Veijola, "History of
the Passover," 61.

112. My analysis of the redactional logic for the conjunction of Firstlings and Unleavened Bread / Passover thus differs with Alexander Rofé, "The Arrangement of the Laws in
Deuteronomy," *ETL* 64 (1988) 265–87, at 280, who understands the connection to be based on
direct or indirect references to the Exodus.

found elsewhere in the Hebrew Bible.[113] The contiguity of the two units here may also be predicated on the homophony of the verbal adjective פִּסֵּחַ "is lame" (Deut 15:21) and the noun פֶּסַח "passover offering" (Deut 16:1).[114]

Conclusions

The double transformation of Passover and Unleavened Bread reveals the same dynamic structure that was evident in Deuteronomy's transformation of sacrifice in chapter 12. Cultic centralization and local secularization were essential to the success of the Deuteronomic program. That program was simultaneously legal, striving to transform social reality, and hermeneutical, striving to transform prior textual authority and to justify innovation. Cultic centralization accounts for the transformation of the Passover into a pilgrimage festival in all but name, as the authors of Deuteronomy restricted all religiously significant blood rituals to the central sanctuary. Just as sacrifice at the local sanctuaries was prohibited (Deut 12:17) and redirected to the central sanctuary (Deut 12:14, 18), so was Passover prohibited in the local sphere (Deut 16:5) and redirected to the central sanctuary (Deut 16:2, 6). There is a single structure of language and thought that operates consistently in both cases.

In extirpating the local sanctuaries, Deuteronomy's authors also had to secularize all religious activities that formerly adhered to those altars. Just as the innovation of secular slaughter took the convention of sacrifice at those local altars, deleted the connection to the altar, and retained the slaughter, so did the authors of Deuteronomy shear Unleavened Bread of its originally essential pilgrimage to the local sanctuaries. The neutered observance that resulted was a pale imitation of the original: with the pilgrimage elided, all that remained was a weeklong local observance distinguished only by its unleavened diet and by its final assembly and work stoppage.

Deuteronomy's transformation of Unleavened Bread produced an interesting anomaly. On the one hand, the observance is no longer a pilgrimage festival, although that was its original identity, as enshrined in previous religious law. The pilgrimage command (Exod 23:17) cannot be retained, since the Deuteronomic authors have just banned the local sanctuaries that were the festival's original home. On the other hand, the burden of textual memory clearly still operates, despite the obscuring of the festival's original identity: Unleavened Bread becomes nearly an antipilgrimage festival. The evasion points straight to the repression, as the pilgrim to the Temple for Passover is commanded immediately, on the morrow, to undertake a reverse pilgrimage to the home precincts, there to observe Unleavened Bread (Deut 16:7).

---

113. Both Exod 34:18–20 and Exod 13:1–2 + (3–10) + 11–16 redactionally associate Unleavened Bread with Firstlings. For an analysis of the redactional logic involved see Fishbane, *Biblical Interpretation*, 195–97.

114. See Stephen A. Kaufman, "The Structure of the Deuteronomic Law," *Maarav* 1/2 (1978–79) 105–58, at 132.

Rendering—perhaps denaturing is the better word—Passover as a pilgrimage sacrifice and Unleavened Bread as a nonpilgrimage, the Deuteronomic authors radically transformed both the institutions and the texts associated with the festival calendar. Most likely, the authors of Deuteronomy were fully conscious of just how anomalous was their subversive new creation. This awareness of themselves as authors and as transformers provides the most logical explanation for how punctiliously they avoided designating their hybrid of Passover and Unleavened Bread as a חג "pilgrimage festival" (Deut 16:1–8). They knew the contrary facts too well. Only where the issues were not so pressing, as at Weeks and Tabernacles (Deut 16:10, 13–14) or in the summarizing colophon that chastely avoids reference back to the Passover (Deut 16:16), did the authors feel free to invoke that term.

Deuteronomy's festival calendar reveals the extraordinary capacity of the authors of Deuteronomy to innovate. They implemented centralization as a far-reaching transformation of Judaean life and acted in complete independence of the very traditions of textual authority to which they ostensibly deferred. Their reuse of older texts is creative: the authors of Deuteronomy went beyond anything that was in those texts to implement a new vision of religion and the social polity. For these reasons the festival calendar represents an important chapter in the cultural history of authorship and textuality. The radical creativity evident in Deuteronomy's transformation of the Passover challenges prevailing models used within biblical studies to understand authorship. Deuteronomy's transformation of Passover and Unleavened Bread confutes the history of traditions model because the calendar does not involve any natural development, nor did its authors simply play catch-up with already completed, external cultic history. The calendar is not an evolution but a revolution. The festival calendar equally challenges the model of textuality associated with Inner Biblical Exegesis. If exegesis means explication, derivation, and deference, then the authors of Deuteronomy were rather subverters of the texts that they inherited. They exploited those texts for convenient lexemes, the more effectively to deny those texts their semantic coherence and legal integrity and the better to implement an entirely new program of religion and social change. With the reuse, the older texts do not speak in a new voice; nor is there traditio-historical *Vergegenwärtigung*. The older texts are silenced, and there is only the voice of the authors of Deuteronomy. In the end, textual authority is not a given that resides in the pre-Deuteronomic tradition to which the Deuteronomic authors must defer. Instead, textual authority represents an ideological and programmatic construction to which, the Deuteronomic authors insist, previous texts must defer. It then becomes an irony of literary history that the very texts that the authors of Deuteronomy sought to replace were nonetheless redacted with it in the Pentateuch.

The authors of Deuteronomy used older texts only to buttress their own agenda. Their revisions of those texts completely changed the significance and practice of the major festivals, which retained little of their original character. If implemented according to Deuteronomy's festival calendar, Passover and Unleavened Bread would bear scant, if any, resemblance to the ancient practices. The Passover is no longer family based and characterized by blood apotropy in the private domicile; rather, it requires a pilgrimage to the Temple, where it becomes the constitutive national holiday, in which all families are incorporated into a single polity. The original requirement in the festival superscription and coda of the Covenant Code that all males appear thrice yearly before Yahweh no longer functions distributively, sending those men to the local sanctuaries. Instead, in its Deuteronomic revision, it too creates a new, uniform polity, as all males must now appear simultaneously at a single site, the exclusive sanctuary (Deut 16:16).

The textual reuse allowed the Deuteronomic authors to associate their new legislation with earlier, authoritative legislation. Hence, their text has the guise of familiarity and consistency with tradition, even as that tradition is subverted. The hermeneutical screw continues to turn in precisely the same way once Deuteronomy itself wins normative status. The Deuteronomistic Historian wants the reader to understand the Josianic reforms as the triumph of Deuteronomic law; and so, too, has it been understood by most scholars, as implementing Deuteronomy's norms. The actual story is more complex, for Deuteronomy's norms are implemented by the Deuteronomistic Historian in a completely non-Deuteronomic way.[115] The Deuteronomistic account of the national celebration of the Passover in Jerusalem, the high point of the account of Josiah's reform, radically revises the Deuteronomic Passover, which it ostensibly enacts to the letter (2 Kgs 23:21–23). In Deuteronomy, the festival calendar is addressed to each citizen who is commanded to observe it (see Deut 16:11, 14). It is not supervised by any official or public authority, not even the highest of them, the King. Textually speaking, the Passover law within the festival calendar (Deut 16:1–17) is detached from the Laws of Public Officials (Deut 16:18–18:22). Conversely, Deuteronomy's Law of the King scrupulously denies the king active participation in all matters that, according to biblical and Near Eastern convention, were part of his bailiwick: leadership in war, supreme judicial authority, and sponsorship of the cult.[116]

This double denial by the Deuteronomic author that there should be any connection between king and cult is completely revoked by the Deuteronomistic Historian. In narrating the first ever centralized celebration of the Passover,[117]

---

115. Gary N. Knoppers, *Two Nations under God: The Deuteronomistic History of Solomon and the Dual Monarchies* (2 vols.; HSM 52–53; Atlanta: Scholars Press, 1993–94) 2.223–25 shows the transformation of Deuteronomic law involved in Josiah's Passover. See also Knoppers, "The Deuteronomist and the Deuteromic Law of the King: A Reexamination of a Relationship," *ZAW* 108 (1996) 329–46. In speaking in the singular about the Deuteronomistic Historian, I do not mean to level the differences among the various strata and the complexity of dating involved; see chapter 2, n. 55. It is simply necessary to speak schematically in order to make some broader observations about authorship and literary history.

116. See the more extensive analysis in the following chapter.

117. Roland de Vaux, *Ancient Israel* (London: Darton, Longman & Todd) 487–88, understands the syntax of 2 Kgs 23:22 to presuppose an early centralized observance of the Passover during the period of the tribal league, with Josiah's observance marking its reinstatement. That analysis can be supported neither syntactically nor historically. The parallel between the syntax of comparison in v. 22 and the subsequent note about Josiah—"that like him there was no king before him . . . nor arose [one] like him after him" (v. 25)—suggests that the Deuteronomist in both cases uses the language of comparison to express absolute difference: both Josiah and

the Deuteronomistic Historian made Josiah the royal patron of the cult who assiduously supervised the celebration of the Passover. He it is, then, standing ceremoniously before the assembled people, who solemnly commands: עשׂו פסח ליהוה אלהיכם ככתוב על ספר הברית הזה "Offer the passover sacrifice to Yahweh, your God, *as it is written* upon this scroll of the covenant" (2 Kgs 23:21). The formula ככתוב points to the king's near verbatim citation of the Deuteronomic command ועשׂית פסח ליהוה אליהיך "You shall offer the passover sacrifice to Yahweh, your God" (Deut 16:1aβ). Despite the royal insistence upon conformity to law, Josiah's very invocation of that law transforms it. The narrative introduction to the royal citation already raises the interplay of voice and authority as the Deuteronomist cannily observes that Torah is here implemented under royal aegis: ויצו המלך את כל העם *"The king commanded* all the people . . ." (2 Kgs 23:21aα). In one deft stroke the Deuteronomistic Historian revokes and redefines both the Deuteronomic Passover, now enacted under royal command, and Deuteronomy's Law of the King, since the king now leads the cultus. The Deuteronomistic Historian subordinates normative Deuteronomic law to his own revisionist view of the proper relation between king and cult. The king's pious affirmation of textual fidelity is thus rather self-serving: as the monarch presides over the Passover, Mosaic law becomes embedded in royal speech, and Zion coopts Sinai.[118]

There is an additional irony involved in the Deuteronomic transfer of the Passover to the Temple, and then of the Deuteronomistic Historian asserting that Josiah's Passover, celebrated at Jerusalem, represents the letter of that law. The affirmation that the Jerusalem Temple represents the proper site for the commemoration of the Exodus from Egypt is curious. The same link between Temple and Exodus is elsewhere evident in the Deuteronomistic History, where the editor affirms that the construction of the Temple marks the four hundred and eightieth anniversary of the Exodus (1 Kgs 6:1). In both cases, the link between Temple and Exodus is tendentious. Neither in tribal disposition nor in historical context did Jerusalem bear any original connection to the Exodus. The editor is far less concerned with chronology and the commemoration of freedom than he is with constructing a decidedly non-Deuteronomic royal ideology that sanctions what pentateuchal law could not have anticipated: both the construction of the Temple (1 Kgs 6:1b) and the celebration of the major cultic festivals, Tabernacles (1 Kgs 8:2) and Passover (2 Kgs 23:21–23) alike, under royal initiative and aegis.[119]

---

the Passover were unique. Historically, there is no evidence to support any premonarchic tribal unity under an amphictyony; see the critique of the latter notion in A. D. H. Mayes, "The Period of the Judges and the Rise of the Monarchy," in *Israelite and Judaean History* (ed. J. H. Hayes and J. M. Miller; Philadelphia: Westminster, 1977) 297–304. J. G. McConville, *Law and Theology in Deuteronomy* (JSOTSup 33; Sheffield: JSOT Press, 1984) 108 follows de Vaux in the misunderstanding of 2 Kgs 23:22.

118. On the dynamic relationship between Sinai and Zion in other biblical traditions, see Jon D. Levenson, *Sinai and Zion: An Entry into the Jewish Bible* (Minneapolis: Winston, 1985).

119. That Josiah's Passover involves more than piety has been conceived in different ways. Suggesting that Passover provided a timely political ploy to win support for Josiah's ensuing

Nothing could be more Deuteronomic in spirit than for the Deuteronomistic Historian to subordinate Deuteronomy, which he claims to implement, to his own independent agenda. The Deuteronomistic Historian uses both Josiah and the anonymity of the narrator to deflect his own vocal transformation of authoritative texts, much as the Deuteronomic author employs the voice of Moses to camouflage his innovations. The literary history of the festival calendar reveals a cascade down of voice, or in the rank of the speaker, as one moves from the Covenant Code to Deuteronomy to the Deuteronomistic History:

Observance	Textual Speaker	Textual Source
Unleavened Bread as festival	Yahweh	Covenant Code
Passover as pilgrimage sacrifice	Moses	Deuteronomy
Royal sponsorship of Passover	Josiah + anonymous narrator	Deuteronomistic History

Nevertheless, there is an attendant cascade up in the autonomy of the author, who obliquely transforms previous textual authority. If the Deuteronomic author both revises and expands the Covenant Code with new notions of religion and the social polity, so, too, is Deuteronomy itself revised and expanded in the Deuteronomistic Historian's reconfiguration of the ties between cult and monarchy. In each case, continuity with tradition is both claimed and breached. As authors speak through the masks of Mosaic authority, royal speech, or anonymity, the pseudepigraphic deflection of authorial voice provides an important means to purchase a more profound originality and conceptual independence. It enables successive authors to assert their autonomy in relation to their forbears.

---

campaign against Egypt is Nicolsky, "Pascha," 171–90. Addressing rather the way that the Passover advances the programmatic aims of the Deuteronomistic Historian is Knoppers, *Two Nations under God*, 2.223–25. Knoppers also demonstrates how Solomon's allusion to the Temple as the fulfillment of Mosaic law (1 Kgs 8:56) is similarly tendentious (1.112–18).

4

The Transformation of Justice in Light of Centralization

In systematically working out the implications of cultic centralization, the authors of Deuteronomy would also have had to take up issues that seem entirely unrelated to the cultus. Foremost among these would have been the impact of their innovation upon justice. Centralization required a revision both of conventional forms of judicial procedure and of conventional sources of judicial authority. In the local sphere, the important judicial function conventionally played by the local altar or sanctuary could no longer be tolerated; moreover, if the innovations of the Deuteronomic authors were to succeed, the judicial authority of the elders, the bearers of precedent, would in some way have to be circumscribed or curtailed. Finally, in the central sphere, the role played by the king as the final arbiter of justice also had to be transformed. That role, conforming to Israelite and broader ancient Near East convention, had to be radically revised in order to permit the central sanctuary to occupy its new place in the judicial administration. This hypothesis permits a cluster of long-standing problems associated with the sequence and order of the legal corpus to find their solution.

As a case in point, Deut 16:18–17:13 represents one of the most problematic "case studies" available within the legal corpus for the entire range of ordering issues: topic selection, sequencing, and ostensible redundancy. The initial problem with the unit arises at the global level of the organization of the legal corpus. Essentially, all critical commentaries note that the first section of the legal corpus, Deut 12:1–16:17, has the Israelite cultus as its primary concern and that a new unit begins with Deut 16:18 and extends to Deut 18:22; this unit is generally entitled "Office-bearers of the theocracy."[1] That ostensibly

---

1. S. R. Driver, *Deuteronomy* (ICC; 3rd ed.; Edinburgh: T. & T. Clark, 1901) 135. Almost identical is the description of A. D. H. Mayes, *Deuteronomy* (NCBC; London: Marshall, Morgan & Scott, 1979) 261: "Officials in the Theocratic State."

simple description, however, begs a series of prior questions. First, what motivates the ostensible shift in topic altogether from cultic to administrative issues? In other words, is there any logic to the transition from the last cultic issue, the festival calendar of Deut 16:1–17, to the initial focus of the new section, local judicial officials (Deut 16:18–20)? Indeed, precisely because the transition seems so abrupt, as if an entirely new unit were beginning that lacks substantive relation to what precedes, some scholars have argued that the original Deuteronomic law book concluded with Deut 16:17.[2] According to this "block model" of the redaction of the legal corpus, a later, Deuteronomistic edition begins with Deut 16:18. That approach translates the synchronic problem—the apparent thematic discontinuity between the first and the second sections of the legal corpus—into a diachronic hypothesis: the new section represents a later stratum, discontinuous both topically and compositionally with the earlier section.[3] Although I disagree with that redactional model, it arose in the attempt to solve a clear problem. In this chapter, I provide an alternative analysis: the same hermeneutical issue that I have highlighted as operating in the first section of the legal corpus continues to operate in this section as well. Both sections of the legal corpus cohere as its authors continue to work out the implications of cultic centralization.

The unit contains a second, fundamental problem that has not previously been solved, despite repeated attempts over the past century. It has often been argued that one of the paragraphs in this section of the legal corpus, concerned with apostasy, does not belong in its present context and should be relocated into the first section. In fact, scholars view an entire section of text, concerned with cultic issues (Deut 16:21–17:1, 17:2–7) as intrusive in a context otherwise concerned with public officials and judicial procedure. For that reason, these scholars maintain that the unit belongs more properly in the previous section of the legal corpus, which is concerned with matters of cult. Nonetheless, the text is coherent. The key to its logic is the very paragraph normally

---

2. Stressing the "abrupt" transition and ascribing an exilic date to the redaction of Deut 16:18–18:22 is Norbert Lohfink, "Die Sicherung der Wirksamkeit des Gotteswortes durch das Prinzip der Schriftlichkeit der Tora und durch das Prinzip der Gewaltenteilung nach den Ämtergesetzen des Buches Deuteronomium (Dt 16,18–18,22)," in *Testimonium Veritati: Festschrift Wilhelm Kempf* (ed. H. Wolter; Frankfurter Theologische Studien 7; Frankfurt: Knecht, 1971) 143–55; reprinted and cited according to Lohfink, *Studien zum Deuteronomium und zur deuteronomistischen Literatur I* (SBAB 8; Stuttgart: Katholisches Bibelwerk, 1990) 305–23, especially pp. 306, 313–14. The article has been translated as "Distribution of the Functions of Power: The Laws Concerning Public Offices in Deuteronomy 16:18–18:22," in *A Song of Power and the Power of Song: Essays on the Book of Deuteronomy* (ed. Duane L. Christensen; Winona Lake, Ind.: Eisenbrauns, 1993) 336–52.

3. Georg Braulik, *Die deuteronomischen Gesetze und der Dekalog: Studien zum Aufbau von Deuteronomium 12–26* (SBS 145; Stuttgart: Katholisches Bibelwerk, 1991) 115–18. Note that an earlier version of one chapter of this book is translated as "The Sequence of the Laws in Deuteronomy 12–26 and in the Decalogue," in *A Song of Power and the Power of Song: Essays on the Book of Deuteronomy* (ed. Duane L. Christensen; Winona Lake, Ind.: Eisenbrauns, 1993) 313–35. For a succinct analysis of the different redactional models, see Eckart Otto, *Theologische Ethik des Alten Testaments* (Theologische Wissenschaft 3.2; Stuttgart: W. Kohlhammer, 1994) 177–79.

viewed either as intrusive or as belonging to a later redactional stratum: Deut 17:2–7. In that paragraph, the text's authors are concerned to work out the implications of centralization for judicial procedure. Once that fact is recognized, the coherence of the text can emerge.

Deut 16:18–17:13: The Problematic of Textual Sequence

Deut 16:18–17:13 has long been thought to be marred by disruption and interpolation. The unit begins with three verses (Deut 16:18–20), the first of which inaugurates a system of judicial officials to be located throughout the land, the second two of which exhort judicial probity.

> (18) Judges and officials shall you appoint in each of your cities that Yahweh your God is giving to you, according to your tribes. They shall judge the people with righteous justice. (19) Do not pervert justice, do not show partiality, and do not take bribes, for bribes blind the eyes of the wise and pervert the plea of those who are in the right. (20) Justice, only justice shall you pursue, so that you may live and retain possession of the land that Yahweh your God is giving you.

Given that introductory focus, it is contextually problematic that the three verses immediately following (Deut 16:21–17:1) bear no relationship whatsoever to justice. They deal with cultic issues—the topic of the previous section of the legal corpus (Deut 12:1–16:17).

> (16:21) You shall neither set up any pole as a sacred pillar (Asherah) beside the altar that you make to Yahweh your God; (16:22) nor shall you erect a stone pillar—things that Yahweh your God detests! (17:1) You shall not sacrifice to Yahweh your God an ox or a sheep that has any kind of serious defect, for that is abhorrent to Yahweh your God.

This section already raises at least three questions concerning its sequence. First, why are cultic regulations—already presented in the first section of the legal corpus—reintroduced in this new section, which is rather concerned with judicial administration? Second, why does the redactor begin with justice in Deut 16:18–20 only to shift back to cultic issues in which neither justice nor administration plays any role? Third, what is the reason for the prohibition of the sacrifice of blemished animals? That prohibition is redundant given the similar prohibition of Deut 15:21–23. Whereas the latter prohibition made sense, since it is found in the context of a law requiring the sacrifice of firstborn animals, the rationale for repeating such a prohibition here, in a judicial context, is unclear.[4]

---

4. The secondary nature of Deut 17:1 is suggested on two grounds. First, in literary terms, it cites 15:21 according to Seidel's law. The AB sequence of Deut 15:21 ("*If it has a defect, . . . any serious* defect, **you shall not sacrifice** it **to Yahweh your God**") recurs chiastically A'B' in 17:1 ("**You shall not sacrifice to Yahweh your God** an ox or a sheep *if it has a defect, any serious* matter"). Second, in legal terms, Deut 17:1 universalizes the application of 15:21 from its original specific prohibition against sacrificing blemished *firstlings* into a general rule gov-

The textual sequence becomes even more problematic with the next paragraph, whose focus is the stoning of the apostate (Deut 17:2–7). That paragraph does not focus on any official, judicial or otherwise. Only one verse of it bears any relation to the judicial topos established by Deut 16:18–20. Deut 17:6 establishes the rule that two witnesses are required to convict someone of a capital offense. If the larger unit (Deut 16:18–18:22) is properly entitled "Office-bearers of the theocracy," then this paragraph bears little clear relation to that topos.

> (2) If there is found in your midst, in one of your city-gates that
> Yahweh your God is giving you, a man or a woman who does what is
> evil in the sight of Yahweh your God by transgressing his covenant; (3)
> and he goes and worships other gods, prostrating himself to them—
> whether to the sun or the moon or to any of the heavenly host, which I
> never commanded—(4) and if it is reported to you or you hear of it,
> then you shall conduct a thorough inquiry. If indeed it is true—the case
> is established—this abomination was performed in Israel, (5) then you
> shall take that man or that woman who performed this wicked act out to
> your city-gates and you shall stone them—man or woman—to death!—
> (6) On the testimony of two witnesses or three witnesses shall a person
> be executed; a person must not be executed on the testimony of a single
> witness.—(7) The hands of the witnesses shall be first against him to
> execute him, and the hands of all the people thereafter. Thus shall you
> purge evil from your midst!

This focus on apostasy seems even more disruptive in relation to the paragraph that follows. Deut 17:8–13 returns to the original topos of judicial organization and provides a protocol for the resolution of problematic cases through recourse to a type of High Court at the central sanctuary.

> (8) If a legal case exceeds your ken—whether distinguishing between
> one category of homicide and another, one category of civil law and
> another, one category of bodily injury and another, any kind of legal
> dispute within your city-gates—then you shall proceed up to the place
> that Yahweh your God shall choose, (9) and come and inquire before
> the levitical priests and the judge who is in office at that time. When
> they proclaim to you the verdict of the case, (10) you must implement
> the verdict that they proclaim to you from that place which Yahweh
> shall choose. Be sure to do all that they instruct you. (11) You must
> fully implement the instruction that they teach you and the verdict
> that they proclaim to you. You may deviate neither right nor left
> from the verdict that they announce to you. (12) Should a man act
> presumptuously so as to disobey the priest appointed there to serve

---

erning all sacrificial animals. For both points, see the fine analysis by Jan Christian Gertz, *Die Gerichtsorganisation Israels im deuteronomischen Gesetz* (FRLANT 165; Göttingen: Vandenhoeck & Ruprecht, 1994) 58. I have added the identification of the citation as conforming to Seidel's law.

Yahweh your God, or the judge, that man shall die. Thus shall you purge evil from Israel! (13) And all the people will take heed and be afraid and not act presumptuously again.

The array of topics is difficult to explain. The two paragraphs that logically ought to be adjacent, because they share the theme of judicial administration—Deut 16:18–20 (local judicial officials and judicial probity) + 17:8–13 (the "High Court" at the central sanctuary)—are instead separated by two paragraphs—Deut 16:21–17:1 (cultic issues) + 17:2–7 (apostasy)—each of which is anomalous in the context of the larger unit. The disruptiveness of these two paragraphs is marked linguistically and thematically. Their only links to their context are superficial, second-order ones involving verbal associations that are not based on meaning or legal context. Such associations do not point to compositional design.[5] In the case of Deut 16:21–17:1, the three cultic prohibitions in these verses echo the three moral ones addressed to the judiciary in 16:19. The association thus seems to be based on verbal assonance (לא תטה 16:19; לא תטע 16:21) and similar morphology (second person prohibition).[6] Similarly, in the case of Deut 17:2–7, the relation of the paragraph to the larger unit seems superficial. The idiom נעשׂתה התועבה הזאת בישׂראל (Deut 17:4) confirming that the apostasy, characterized as an "abomination," has definitely occurred, echoes the cultic terminology of the verse that immediately precedes this paragraph. That verse prohibits sacrificing a blemished animal "because it is an *abomination to Yahweh* (תועבת יהוה) your God" (Deut 17:1). As already noted, however, Deut 17:1 is itself dependent upon Deut 15:21 and intrusive in the context of the unit's larger concern with the administration of justice. Consequently, Deut 17:2–7 seems to have only superficial lexical ties to its context: the verbal association of a single word—"abomination"—with a preceding verse that is itself redundant and contextually disruptive. No substantive or thematic relation seems to exist.

Even more striking, Deut 17:2–7, as the following table illustrates, reduplicates the topos, form, and terminology of the sequence of three paragraphs

---

5. The explanation of a textual join in terms of verbal association confuses means and ends: it may account for the technique used to make a join but not the intent of the join, let alone whether the join is original or secondary. Two scholars have attempted to use the association of ideas or of words to account for the problematic organization of the legal corpus of Deuteronomy: Harold M. Wiener, "The Arrangement of Deuteronomy 12–26," *JPOS* 6 (1926) 185–95; republished in Wiener, *Posthumous Essays* (ed. H. Loewe; London: Oxford, 1932) 26–36; and Alexander Rofé, "The Arrangement of the Laws in Deuteronomy," *ETL* 64 (1988) 265–87. Neither attempt provides a convincing analysis of compositional design as opposed to indicating how redactors might have added secondary material, as Rofé acknowledges. Recourse to association often overlooks inner-Israelite literary tradition, such as inherited legal sequences, that might more directly explain a given textual join. For a fuller analysis of each of these attempts, see Bernard M. Levinson, *The Hermeneutics of Innovation: The Impact of Centralization upon the Structure, Sequence, and Reformulation of Legal Material in Deuteronomy* (Ann Arbor, Mich.: University Microfilms, 1991) 16–36.

6. Stephen A. Kaufman, "The Structure of the Deuteronomic Law," *Maarav* 1/2 (1978–1979) 155 n. 87; and Rofé, "Arrangement," 270–71.

concerned with apostasy in Deut 13:2–19.[7] Deut 13:2–6 concerns incitement to apostasy by a mantic prophet or oneiromancer; vv. 7–12, by a member of the same kinship group as the legal addressee; vv. 13–18 by a band of rogues who successfully incite an entire city to apostasy (v. 19 is a general conclusion). Both Deut 17:2–7 and chapter 13 thus address the topos of apostasy and mandate that the community take concerted action to remove any such threat from its midst.

Deut 17:2–7	Deut 13:2–6, 7–12, 13–18
[2] כי ימצא בקרבך	[2] כי יקום בקרבך
[13] באחד שעריך אשר יהוה אלהיך נתן לך ...	באחת עריך אשר יהוה אלהיך נתן לך ...
[3] וילך ויעבד אלהים אחרים ...	[14=7]נלכה ונעבדה אלהים אחרים
[4] והגד לך ושמעת	[13] כי תשמע ...
ודרשת היטב	[15] ודרשת וחקרת ושאלת היטב
והנה אמת נכון הדבר	והנה אמת נכון הדבר
נעשתה התועבה הזאת בישראל	נעשתה התועבה הזאת בקרבך
[5] וסקלתם באבנים ומתו	[11] וסקלתו באבנים ומת
[7] יד העדים תהיה בו בראשנה להמיתו	[10] ידך תהיה בו בראשנה להמיתו
ויד כל העם באחרנה	ויד כל העם באחרנה
ובערת הרע מקרבך	[6] ובערת הרע מקרבך

(2) *If there* is found *in your midst, in one of your* gates *which Yahweh your God is giving you* . . .

(3) *and* he *goes and worships other gods* . . .

(4) and it has been reported to you, or *you hear, then you shall thoroughly inquire;*

and if indeed it is true— the case is established— this abomination was performed in Israel,

(5) *then you shall stone* them *to death with stones.*

(7) *The hand* of the witnesses *shall be first against him to execute him; thereafter, the hand of all the people. Thus shall you extirpate the evil from your midst.*

(2) *If there* arises *in your midst,* . . .

(13) *in one of your* cities *which Yahweh your God is giving you*

(7) "*Let us go and worship other gods*"

(13) *If you hear* . . .

(15) *then you shall thoroughly inquire,* investigate and interrogate;

and if indeed it is true— the case is established— this abomination was performed among you,

(11) *then you shall stone* him *to death with stones.*

(10) Your *hand shall be first against him to execute him; thereafter, the hand of all the people.*

(6) *Thus shall you extirpate the evil from your midst.*

---

7. Note the similar table provided by G. Seitz, *Redaktionsgeschichtliche Studien zum Deuteronomium* (BWANT 93; Stuttgart: Kohlhammer, 1971) 154.

Each case is formulated in the distinctive Deuteronomic casuistic form, with protasis introduced by כִּי "if," followed by a second-person addressee. In each case the incitement to apostasy is technically formulated in the idiom הלך ועבד אלהים אחרים "to go and worship other gods."[8] In chapter 13 the incitement is consistently presented as a hypothetical citation introduced by לאמר and continued with first-person plural cohortative נלכה ונעבדה/ונעבדם "Let us go so that we may worship [them]" (vv. 3, 7, 14). The same idiom for apostasy recurs in Deut 17:2–7 where, however, the offense is presented as actual apostasy, not mere incitement. Further, in each of chapter 13 and 17:2–7 there is detailed attention to legal process involving common technical formulae both for investigation and for execution by means of the collective stoning of the apostate. The requirements for the corroboration of the accusation are formulated nearly identically (Deut 13:15; 17:4). In both cases, too, the text specifies in nearly identical terms the procedure for the stoning: the addressee or witnesses initiate the action, which is then followed by the participation of the entire community (Deut 13:10–11; 17:5+7). Finally, the formula that concludes 17:2–7, ובערת הרע מקרבך "you shall extirpate the evil from your midst," is also employed in the conclusion to 13:2–6.[9] It emerges that Deut 17:2–7, concerned with apostasy and seemingly disruptive in its present context, bears very close linguistic and topical ties to chapter 13, concerned with incitement to apostasy. Thus, the paragraph's closest literary relationship is ostensibly to the previous section of the legal corpus, whose focus is the cult.

Deut 17:2–7: The Standard Argument for Textual Relocation

With very few exceptions, scholars of all methodologies have attempted to resolve the disruptiveness of Deut 17:2–7 by relocating the problematic unit to the context of chapter 13. With a single literary critical stratagem, therefore, a double exegetical problem—the contextual disruptiveness of Deut 17:2–7 and its duplication in a new section of the legal corpus of the topos, form, and formulae of chapter 13—is ostensibly resolved. This solution originates with

---

8. This idiom seems to conflate two separate ones whose origin lies in the treaty terminology of the Near East. The first is ללכת אחרי [אלהים] אחרים = Akkadian *alāku arki* found in the Amarna letters. The second is עבד . . . אחרים, to which compare Akkadian *arādu, ardūtu*. For complete citations to both the Deuteronomic and the later Deuteronomistic use of each formula, see Moshe Weinfeld, *Deuteronomy and the Deuteronomic School* (Oxford: Clarendon, 1972) 320. For their origin in cuneiform and Aramaic treaty terminology see his p. 83 (with literature). The full conflation of the two idioms is evident in Deut 13:3: . . . . נלכה אחרי אלהים אחרים ונעבדם "Let us go after other gods . . . in order that we may worship them" (cf. Deut 28:14). Mayes, *Deuteronomy*, 233, points out that the idiom of הלך אחרי "to go after" always takes "other gods" as its object within the legal corpus—except for Deut 13:5, which is formulated as a stressed antithesis to Deut 13:3.

9. The formula appears elsewhere in Deut 19:19; 21:21; 22:21, 24; 24:7. The formula occurs also with "from Israel" substituted for "from your midst" in Deut 17:12; 22:22; see J. L'Hour, "Une législation criminelle dans le Deutéronome," *Bib* 44 (1963) 1–28 and Mayes, *Deuteronomy*, 233–34.

August Dillmann's suggestion more than a century ago that Deut 16:21–17:1 and 17:2–7 should conjointly be relocated between 12:31 and 13:2.[10] Dillmann's rearrangement of the text rapidly won broad acceptance. S. R. Driver, for example, follows Dillmann's analysis, noting the separation of the two units concerned with judicial administration (16:18–20 + 17:8–13) that would more naturally be conjoined. Thus he too restores Deut 16:21–17:7 to a claimed original context before Deut 13:2 in order to achieve the double topical coherence: (1) a single unit consistently concerned with apostasy (Deut 17:2–7+ 13:2–19), and (2) a single unit consistently concerned with "judges" (Deut 16:18–20 + 17:8–13).[11] Karl Budde concludes his own important analysis claiming the restoration to be incontrovertible: "In sum, it is not subject to any doubt: 13:2–19 never existed without 17:2–7."[12] Perhaps most striking in the history of this text-critical restoration is its acceptance even by scholars who otherwise reject the diachronic analysis of biblical law. Harold Wiener claimed to demonstrate the perfect coherence of the entire legal corpus of Deuteronomy on the basis of "the association of ideas." He found only a single clear exception—Deut 17:2–7—which, he maintained, belonged more properly in chapter 13.[13]

With essential agreement won early in this century, and with assent gained even from opponents of diachronic analysis, it is no wonder that a consensus rapidly emerged that the problematic material (Deut 16:21–17:1 + 17:2–7) should be relocated to chapter 13. This consensus, the essential elements of which were all in place a century ago, remains dominant even in the most recent work. It provides a rare note of near unanimity within biblical scholarship and joins scholars of all methodological persuasions, whether synchronic or diachronic, whether literary-critical, legal-historical, form-critical, redaction-historical, or comparativist, whether European, American, or Israeli.[14] Until recently, dissent was all but nonexistent.[15]

---

10. August Dillmann, *Die Bücher Numeri, Deuteronomium und Josua* (KeHAT; 2d ed.; Leipzig: S. Hirzel, 1886) 319.

11. Driver, *Deuteronomy*, 135, 201.

12. K. Budde, "Dtn 13 10, und was daran hängt," *ZAW* 36 (1916) 187–97; citation from p. 194 (my translation).

13. Wiener, "Arrangement of Deuteronomy 12–26," 33. In contrast, Kaufman, "Structure of the Deuteronomic Law," 134, provides an explanation of Deut 17:2–7 in its context and does not call for the paragraph's transposition. He does not however note the paragraph's close similarities to chapter 13. Moreover, he contends that the legal corpus is coherent in its redaction and the product of a single author, allowing only Deut 24:1–4 as a disruption (pp. 112, 144–47). The synchronic reading provided by Robert Polzin, *Moses and the Deuteronomist: A Literary Study of the Deuteronomic History* (New York: Seabury, 1980) 43–69, does not discuss Deut 17:2–7 and thereby avoids an important challenge to his arguments defending the unity of the text.

14. George Ernest Wright, "Deuteronomy," *IB* (Nashville: Abingdon-Cokesbury, 1953) 2.436–37; P. Buis, *Le Deutéronome* (VS 4; Paris: Beauchesne, 1969) 273; Seitz, *Redaktionsgeschichtliche Studien*, 201; Weinfeld, *Deuteronomy and the Deuteronomic School*, 92 n. 2; 95; Horst Dietrich Preuß, *Deuteronomium* (ErFor 164; Darmstadt: Wissenschaftliche Buchgesellschaft, 1982) 134; Yoshihide Suzuki, "Deuteronomic Reformation in View of the Centralization of the Administration of Justice," *AJBI* 13 (1987) 22–58; Fabrizio Foresti, "Storia della

Some scholars have, however, advocated a different approach. Norbert Lohfink, in particular, introduced a revolutionary shift in the discussion with his argument that Deut 16:18–18:22 represents a utopian draft constitution put together by the second Deuteronomistic Historian during the Babylonian exile.[16] Rather than try conventionally to reconstruct the unit's complex literary history, which he conceded, Lohfink instead raised a question that had, astonishingly, never previously been asked: Given that complexity, what is the redactor trying to say? What, in other words, is the significance of the text as it currently stands? With the coherence of the text now made the point of departure, however, the entire question of the textual relocation was shunted aside. In this approach, the present position of Deut 17:2–7 is assumed as a given. Whether that context is original or secondary, let alone what compositional or legal-historical issue, if any, accounts for the paragraph's inclusion, is not addressed.

Similar issues arise in subsequent work. Georg Braulik, for example, presupposing Lohfink's analysis, does not so much argue for the compositional integrity of Deut 17:2–7 to its context as demonstrate the ways it now coheres by means of lexical and associational links. Whether those linkages are original or secondary is not directly addressed: whether they embody an original compositional logic or are the means redactionally to incorporate a passage that originated elsewhere is not distinguished. With his focus on the "final form" of the text, he deliberately does not seek any reconstruction of its composi-

---

Redazione di Dtn. 16,18–18,22 e le sue Connessioni con l'Opera Storica Deuteronomistica," in *Teresianum Ephemerides Carmeliticae* 39 (1988) 5–199, at pp. 22–76; Rofé, "Arrangement," 278, 286; and Horst Seebaß, "Vorschlag zur Vereinfachung literarischer Analysen im dtn Gesetz," *BN* 58 (1991) 83–98. This scenario was simply reversed by Rosario Pius Merendino, *Das deuteronomische Gesetz: Eine literarkritische, gattungs- und überlieferungsgeschichtliche Untersuchung zu Dt 12–26* (BBB 31; Bonn: Peter Hanstein, 1969) 80–81, for whom Deut 13:2–19 originally followed Deut 17:2–7. For Günter Krinetzki, *Rechtsprechung und Amt im Deuteronomium: Zur Exegese der Gesetze Dtn 16,18–20; 17,8–18,22* (Frankfurt: Peter Lang, 1994) 124, the entire unit is so extrinsic that it is altogether omitted from any kind of consideration, one way or the other, in his extensive posthumous monograph.

15. The rejection by Mayes, *Deuteronomy*, 230, of the relocation is only an apparent exception. On the one hand, he importantly recognizes that Deut 17:2–7 involves apostasy that has been committed, while chapter 13, only incitement. For that reason, he opposes transposition. On the other hand, Mayes concedes that Deut 17:2–7 makes no sense in its present context. He attempts to mitigate the difficulty by reconstructing an original version of the law concerned not with apostasy but with "those who do 'what is evil in the sight of the Lord your God'" (pp. 263, 266). That idiom, however, cannot be used to reconstruct an earlier version of the law. It is much better attested in the later Deuteronomistic literature than in Deuteronomic strata. Against fifty attestations in Deuteronomistic contexts, there are only four in Deuteronomy; see Weinfeld, *Deuteronomy and the Deuteronomic School*, 339. Mayes's reconstruction is contradicted by his own demonstration that, this passage aside, each of the three other attestations of the idiom in Deuteronomy belongs to the later, Deuteronomistic stratum (Deut 4:25; 9:18; 31:29; see pp. 148, 195, 379).

16. Lohfink, "Ämtergesetze," 305–23. In the postbiblical reception of the text, Deuteronomy was from ancient times viewed as a constitutional model by Jews. The rabbinic patriarchate in Israel during the second century C.E. and the exilarchate in Babylon were organized in the spirit of Deuteronomy; see Daniel J. Elazar, *Covenant and Polity in Biblical Israel: Biblical Foundations and Jewish Expressions* (New Brunswick: Transaction, 1995) 196.

tional or redactional history.[17] If the descriptive analysis restricts itself, however, to the *Endgestalt*, it does not automatically follow that the observations, however fine, apply to an earlier form of the text.[18] It is difficult, in other words, to draw diachronic conclusions from synchronic observations.[19]

While such approaches valuably posit the coherence of Deut 17:2–7 within its present context as a theoretically possible reading, they do not justify that claim either by refuting the arguments to the contrary or by providing the rationale for the paragraph's inclusion in the first place. On linguistic grounds, too, it has been suggested that Deut 17:2–7 is a Deuteronomistic composition that reuses material from chapter 13 and therefore should not be relocated.[20] That insight has not been developed, however, to provide a clear reason for the textual reuse. A recent monograph summarily dispatches the paragraph, viewed as secondary and extrinsic, in two sentences.[21] In all these cases, therefore, the basic problem of the paragraph's function remains unsolved. The arguments in favor of the standard solution have never, to the best of my knowledge, been directly engaged and refuted.[22] Nor has a clear counterargument for the contextual function and legal-historical role of Deut 17:2–7 been provided. In what follows, I attempt to do both.

A Critique of the Standard Solution

The relocation of Deut 17:2–7 to chapter 13 creates topical coherence but involves two fundamental presuppositions. The first is that Deut 17:2–7 com-

17. Braulik, *Die deuteronomischen Gesetze*, 46.

18. The same applies to Braulik's larger thesis that the redaction of Deuteronomy 12–26 is based upon the Decalogue; see Eckart Otto, review of *Die deuteronomischen Gesetze und der Dekalog* by Georg Braulik, *TLZ* 119 (1994) 15–17.

19. Recent scholarship has turned away from Lohfink's insight and dissolved the premise of a redactionally coherent unit. Rather than see Deut 16:18–18:22 as a unit concerned with the Laws of the Public Officials and as outlining a draft constitution, the unit is seen as expressing the theological concerns of the Deuteronomistic Historian. For a valuable critical assessment of this literature, see Udo Rüterswörden, "Der Verfassungsentwurf des Deuteronomiums in der neueren Diskussion: Ein Überblick," in *Altes Testament Forschung und Wirkung: Festschrift für Henning Graf Reventlow* (ed. Peter Mommer and Winfried Thiel; Frankfurt: Peter Lang, 1994) 313–28.

20. First noted by Udo Rüterswörden, *Von der politischen Gemeinschaft zur Gemeinde: Studien zu Dt 16,18–18,22* (BBB 65; Frankfurt: Athenäum, 1987) 32–38. The arguments are presented most comprehensively, on the basis of careful linguistic analysis, by Paul E. Dion, "Deuteronomy 13: The Suppression of Alien Religious Propaganda in Israel during the Late Monarchical Era," in *Law and Ideology in Monarchic Israel* (ed. Baruch Halpern and Deborah W. Hobson; JSOTSup 124; Sheffield: JSOT Press, 1991) 147–216. Dion establishes that Deut 17:2–7 does not represent a broken off piece of Deuteronomy 13 but rather represents a later "derivative" of that chapter. With his focus on the language and historical context of chapter 13, however, Dion does not investigate the textual or legal-historical function of Deut 17:2–7 in its context.

21. Eleonore Reuter, *Kultzentralisation: Entstehung und Theologie von Dtn 12* (BBB 87; Frankfurt: Anton Hain, 1993) 176.

22. Braulik, "Die deuteronomischen Gesetze," 20 n. 36, 31 n. 17, for example, disagrees with the restoration, which he associates only with Rofé, "Arrangement," but does not refute it.

pletes an apostasy series in chapter 13, to which it originally belonged. Second, the relocation assumes that both Deut 17:2–7 and chapter 13 derive from the same literary stratum. Neither assumption can be maintained. The section "Deut 17:2–7 as a Revision of Deut 13:7–12" addresses the literary stratification; here the analysis focuses on the matter of textual sequence. The "restoration" of the allegedly misplaced paragraph (Deut 17:2–7) only transfers the problem of disorder from one context to another and makes matters worse. It introduces a redundancy into the newly reconstituted chapter, saddling the new chapter 13 with two cases, each of which treats apostasy by an individual (13:7–12; 17:2–7).[23] In addition to this redundancy, there is another problem. The "restored" sequence (Deut 12:29–13:1 + 16:21–17:1 + 17:2–7 + 13:2–19) is incoherent. Why should the two cases that each deal with action by lay individuals (17:2–7; 13:7–12) have the case of incitement by a prophet illogically wedged between them? The alleged solution thus mirrors the very same problem that triggered it in the first place: the disruption of cases that seem to belong together. Nor does inserting Deut 17:2–7 immediately before 13:7–12, so as to group together the two cases involving apostasy by an individual, provide an adequate solution.[24] This arrangement simply creates another difficulty, equally serious. It disrupts an ordered series of cases, all dealing with incitement, with a single case, Deut 17:2–7, concerned with the *fact* of apostasy, in which there is no incitement and in which the grammar involves past action rather than quoted provocation.[25]

Conventional literary criticism can identify the problem—the contextual problematic of Deut 17:2–7—but, in its attempts to solve the problem, substitutes a superficial topical coherence that breaks down upon more careful analysis. The ostensibly critical solution unknowingly repeats the similar precritical solution found earlier in the history of interpretation. The redactor of the Qumran *Temple Scroll*, consistent with his proclivity to regroup biblical laws, has Deut 16:18–20 begin a section on the judicial system (11QTemple 51:11–16). He follows that unit with a broad collection of cult laws culled from the Tetrateuch (11QTemple 51:16–54:7), then adds the apostasy laws of Deut 13:1–18 (11QTemple 54:8–55:14), *with his revision of Deut 17:2–7 deftly conjoined* (11QTemple 55:15–56:[ ]).[26] Only after this broad excursus does the redactor of the *Temple Scroll* continue with the original biblical sequence from which he had departed: Deut 17:8–13, on the central court at the Temple (11QTemple 56:[ ]–11) and Deut 17:14–20, the unit on the king (11QTemple 56:12–21). The modern solution, therefore, shares with the ancient one an approach that is harmonistic. This yearning for topical coherence at any cost

---

23. Rofé, "Arrangement," 278, is one of the few scholars to address this difficulty. He claims that Deuteronomy 13 is incomplete for omitting an instance of apostasy by a general individual, while including apostasy by a close kin (Deut 13:7–12). Contrary to his proposal, however, that case is not restricted to the kinship group but extends to the "friend" who is not kin (Deut 13:7).

24. Wiener, "Arrangement of Deuteronomy 12–26," 29–30.

25. Note Mayes, *Deuteronomy*, 230.

26. The top lines of column 56 are unfortunately not preserved.

replaces an attempt to come to grips with a challenging textual sequence. On these grounds, then, the meaning of the text as it stands, with its *ordo difficilior*,[27] may be probed.

The Rewriting of Legal History:
The Coherence of Deut 17:2–7 and 8–13

The integrity of Deut 17:2–7 to the larger unit becomes clear with the recognition that the consequences of Deuteronomy's reform, cultic centralization, extend beyond the cultic to the legal realm.[28] A fundamental literary dynamic underlies the legal corpus. All local cultic activity, hitherto legitimate, presents a double problem in light of the Deuteronomic reform. Given the prohibition of the local altars, indeed, of all local cultic activity (including the pre-Deuteronomic paschal slaughter, originally a home rite), not only must existing cultic practice be revised, but authoritative Israelite texts contemplating such local cultic activity must also be reformulated in order to justify innovation.

The authors of Deuteronomy redirect and restrict to the cultic center the sacrifices that were formerly valid in the local sphere. This transformation involves innovation at two levels. First arises the creation of new cultic protocols—and texts to describe them. Second arises the necessity, as a consequence of centralization, of transforming the local sphere into a realm where customary cultic rites, such as sacrifice, are prohibited. Cultic centralization thus involves a double dynamic: the restriction of cultic activity to the central sphere and the secularization of the local sphere. This double transformation is not simply empirical but also, and more importantly, literary-historical. The transformation involves not merely the revision of existing normative practice but also the legitimation of that empirical reform in light of existing authoritative texts.

Accordingly, the prevalent claim that Deut 16:18 begins a new section of the legal corpus, whether classically understood as "The Administration of the Theocracy" or as a draft constitution, overlooks a fundamental issue. The same

27. For the felicitous Latin coinage, as applied to postbiblical law, see David Daube, "The Civil Law of the Mishnah: The Arrangement of the Three Gates," *Tulane Law Review* 18 (1943–44) 351–407.

28. The following arguments for the coherence and legal-historical function of Deut 17:2–7 were first presented in my dissertation: Bernard M. Levinson, *The Hermeneutics of Innovation: The Impact of Centralization upon the Structure, Sequence, and Reformulation of Legal Material in Deuteronomy* (Ann Arbor, Mich.: University Microfilms, 1991) 325–432. Other scholars have since accepted these arguments: Eckart Otto, "Rechtsreformen in Deuteronomium XII–XXVI und im Mittelassyrischen Kodex der Tafel A (KAV 1)," in *Congress Volume: Paris, 1992* (ed. J. A. Emerton; VTSup 61; Leiden: Brill, 1995) 264; Otto, "Vom Bundesbuch zum Deuteronomium: Die deuteronomische Redaktion in Dtn 12–26," *Biblische Theologie und gesellschaftlicher Wandel: Für Norbert Lohfink* (ed. Georg Braulik, Walter Groß, and Sean McEvenue; Freiburg: Herder, 1993) 262; Otto, "Aspects of Legal Reforms and Reformulations in Ancient Cuneiform and Israelite Law," in *Theory and Method in Biblical and Cuneiform Law: Revision, Interpolation, and Development* (ed. Bernard M. Levinson; JSOTSup 181; Sheffield: Sheffield Academic Press, 1994) 190–91; Otto, *Theologische Ethik*, 194–95; and Rüterswörden, "Der Verfassungsentwurf des Deuteronomiums," 327.

literary-historical concerns that motivate the text's authors in the first section of the legal corpus (Deut 12:1–16:17), continue to engage them in this allegedly new section.[29] The transformation of existing norms of action in light of centralization and the textual defense of that innovative activity continue to operate and account for the structure and sequence of Deut 17:2–7 + 8–13. The problematic sequence of legal topoi in this unit becomes intelligible only with the recognition of the unit's true topos, which is not immediately empirical—an ancient administrative flowchart—but, rather, hermeneutical—the necessity of transforming judicial procedure as a consequence of cultic centralization. An analysis of judicial procedures prior to Deuteronomy will clarify why Deuteronomy's authors were constrained to introduce the changes that they made.

Pre-Deuteronomic Judicial Procedures in the Local Sphere

According to the most recent reconstructions, there were four major contexts for the administration of justice in ancient Israel: family and clan law, in the hands of the paterfamilias; local or town law, administered by the elders; sacral law, dispensed by the priests; and royal judicial authority.[30] These four spheres most likely overlapped historically and competed with one another. I reserve treatment of the king's role in justice for the conclusion of this chapter, in conjunction with the law of the king in Deut 17:14–20. My focus here is on local justice and on the role of the cultus in justice.

Local justice had its home in important public locales such as the city gate (Deut 21:19; 22:15; 25:7; Ruth 4:11) or the threshing-floor (Ruth 3:10–14;

---

29. From a different perspective, Lothar Perlitt also challenges the separation of this unit from the preceding one ("Der Staatsgedanke im Deuteronomium," *Language, Theology, and The Bible: Essays in Honour of James Barr* [ed. Samuel E. Balentine and James Barton; Oxford: Clarendon, 1994] 182–98). He argues that the unit is not concerned with political administration but continues the same concern with religious reform found in Deut 12:1–16:17.

30. A. Phillips, *Ancient Israel's Criminal Law: A New Approach to The Decalogue* (New York: Schocken, 1970) 17–35; G. C. Macholz, "Zur Geschichte der Justizorganisation in Juda," *ZAW* 84 (1972) 314–40; Keith W. Whitelam, *The Just King: Monarchical Judicial Authority in Ancient Israel* (JSOTSup 12; Sheffield: JSOT Press, 1979) 39–69. Attempting to reconstruct the premonarchic judicial system on the basis of sociological models is Robert R. Wilson, "Enforcing the Covenant: The Mechanisms of Judicial Authority in Early Israel," in *The Quest for the Kingdom of God: Studies in Honor of George E. Mendenhall* (ed. H. B. Huffmon, F. A. Spina, and A. R. W. Green; Winona Lake, Ind.: Eisenbrauns, 1983) 59–75; and, similarly, Wilson, "Israel's Judicial System in the Preexilic Period," *JQR* 74 (1983) 229–48. Reconstructing the history of justice at the local courts, see L. H. Köhler, *Hebrew Man* (London: SCM, 1956) 149–75; D. A. McKenzie, "Judicial Procedure at the Town Gate," *VT* 14 (1964) 100–104; Hans Jochen Boecker, *Law and the Administration of Justice in the Old Testament and Ancient East* (Minneapolis: Augsburg, 1980) 27–40; Herbert Niehr, *Rechtsprechung in Israel: Untersuchungen zur Geschichte der Gerichtsorganisation im Alten Testament* (SBS 130; Stuttgart: Katholisches Bibelwerk, 1987) 50–54, 63–66; and Eckart Otto, "שער *Ša'ar*," *TWAT* 8 (1995) 358–403. Disputing the usual reconstruction of the judicial role of the elders at the gate, see Frank Crüsemann, *Die Tora: Theologie und Sozialgeschichte des alttestamentlichen Gesetzes* (Munich: Chr. Kaiser, 1992) 80–113. Note the important review of the latter: Eckart Otto, "Die Tora in Israels Rechtsgeschichte," *TLZ* 118 (1994) 903–10.

1 Kgs 22:10).[31] The agents for judicial deliberation in such "civic centers" were the elders, most commonly, or the public assembly.[32] These public bodies combined the function of judge and jury in a legal proceeding. This formalization, which specified or presupposed a public hearing, served to delimit the right of the paterfamilias to take independent legal action against his wife or minor children.[33] In addition, judicial oracles seem to have been proclaimed (Judg 4:4–5) by the charismatic שפטים "judges" who may also have functioned as traveling "circuit-court" judges (1 Sam 7:15–17).[34]

In contrast to the lay dispensation of justice stand the sundry cultic contexts for judicial decision making. The various literary genres of the Bible, including each of the pentateuchal literary strata, point to the important role played by the altar, the gate of the local sanctuary, the priesthood, and the priestly lots in judicial activity.[35] Perhaps the most dramatic image of the interconnection in Israelite thought between justice and the cultus is the tradition, preserved by the Priestly stratum, that the vestments of the Priest include the חשן המשפט "breastplate of justice," within which were stored the Urim and Thummim, the lots by means of which the priests made their legal rulings (Exod 28:15–30; Lev 8:8). The Blessing of Moses assigns pride of place to the Urim and the Thummim as the preeminent attributes of Levi (Deut 33:8).

The cultus provided a significant site for judicial procedure at the gate of the local sanctuary or directly before the altar. Such locations constituted authoritative sites wherein legal proceedings could take place numinously in the presence of the divine: אל האלהים (Exod 21:6; 22:7) or עד האלהים (Exod 22:8), both, "before God," or לפני יהוה "before Yahweh" (Num 5:16, 18, 30; 27:5). In addition to its providing an authoritative setting and access to di-

---

31. Victor H. Matthews, "Entrance Ways and Threshing Floors: Legally Significant Sites in the Ancient Near East," *Fides et Historia* 19 (1987) 25–40. Matthews does not address the difficult question of Ruth's dating and consequently its reliability for legal-historical reconstruction. My assumption is that Ruth is late but accurately archaizes in stressing the judicial role of the elders at the city gate.

32. On the elders, see Moshe Weinfeld, "Elders," *Encyclopaedia Judaica* (Jerusalem: Encyclopaedia Judaica, 1972) 6.578–80; Whitelam, *The Just King*, 42–44. Several studies focus on the role of the elders in Deuteronomy. Leslie J. Hoppe, *The Origins of Deuteronomy* (Ann Arbor, Mich.: University Microfilms, 1978) argues that they—not the levitical priests or a scribal school—are responsible for the composition of the text. Despite his valuable critique, Hoppe does not defend his presupposition that the text's authors would in some direct way reflect themselves in their composition. His similar argument, "Elders and Deuteronomy," *Église et théologie* 14 (1983) 259–72, asserts cultic centralization to be a completely postexilic institution but does not address the evidence that the pre-Deuteronomistic Deuteronomy is preexilic; nor does it engage archaeological evidence. The most recent treatments are Joachim Buchholz, *Die Ältesten Israels im Deuteronomium* (GTA 36; Göttingen: Vandenhoeck & Ruprecht, 1988); and Gertz, *Gerichtsorganisation Israels*, 173–225.

33. Wilson, "Judicial System," 233–34.

34. For the difficulties of historical reconstruction involved, see Whitelam, *The Just King*, 47–69.

35. Whitelam, *The Just King*, 45, correctly rejects the claim by Phillips, *Ancient Israel's Criminal Law*, 22, that "the priests appear to have exercised no judicial role in early Israel." He points out that Phillips omits reference to the lots in premonarchical narratives.

vine judicial knowledge, the temple gate seems to have been thought particularly appropriate for the performance of certain legal rituals marking a transition in legal or social status. A case in point is the asseveration by an indentured servant that he voluntarily relinquishes manumission (Exod 21:5–6).[36] This ceremony is to occur in the gateway of the local sanctuary: והגישו אדניו אל האלהים והגישו אל הדלת או אל המזוזה "his master shall bring him before God; his master shall bring him before the doorway or the door post" (Exod 21:6a).[37] The liminal ceremony, involving the transition from contractually limited to permanent slavery, requires a liminal context: the gateway of a temple or sanctuary, which marks the transition point between the divine and the human realms.

Legal proceedings in this cultic context seem to have taken a number of forms. The Hebrew Bible preserves all of the following forms of cultically mediated judicial resolution: (1) the judicial oath;[38] (2) the judicial ordeal;[39]

---

36. See the recent study by Åke Viberg, *Symbols of Law: A Contextual Analysis of Legal Symbolic Acts in the Old Testament* (ConBOT 34; Stockholm: Almqvist & Wiksell, 1992) 77–87.

37. The ancient versions preserve diverging exegetical traditions concerning the meaning of אלהים in this and related judicial contexts (Exod 22:7, 8). In each case the LXX renders the term in its conventional sense of "God," whereas *Targum Onqelos* renders דיניא "judges" (see Ps 138:1, which is not explicitly a legal setting, for the same divergence). The latter meaning is frequently represented in traditional translations. Nevertheless, the inadmissibility of "judges" as an accurate rendering for the word was established by Cyrus H. Gordon on the basis of the use of the cognate *ilāni* "gods" in Nuzi legal texts; see his "*Elohim* in its Reputed Meaning of Rulers, Judges," *JBL* 54 (1935) 134–44. With the question of translation resolved, however, a more complex issue arises. The testamentary literature at Nuzi provides clear evidence that the *ilāni* denoted family gods that were worshipped in home shrines and that were transferred as part of the private estate; see the meticulous presentation by Karlheinz Deller, "Die Hausgötter der Familie Šukrija S. Ḫuja," *Studies on the Civilization and Culture of Nuzi and the Hurrians in Honor of Ernest R. Lacheman* (ed. M. A. Morrison and D. I. Owen; Winona Lake, Ind.: Eisenbrauns, 1981) 47–76. Clearly, it is to be expected that the family gods, as part of the inheritance, should figure in the private wills preserved in the Nuzi archives. It goes beyond the evidence, however, to transfer that meaning into the Covenant Code, which belongs to a different literary genre, and to assume that the judicial oaths of Exod 21:6 and 22:7, 8 take place in the context of a home shrine, as maintained by A. E. Draffkorn, "*ILĀNI/ELOHIM*," *JBL* 76 (1957) 216–24; and Meir Malul, *Studies in Mesopotamian Legal Symbolism* (AOAT 221; Kevelaer: Butzon & Bercker; Neukirchen-Vluyn: Neukirchener Verlag, 1988) 86 n. 30. The casuistic material in the Covenant Code much more closely resembles the cuneiform legal collections, in which the judicial oath and the appearance before the deity takes place at the local sanctuary, not in the private domicile.

38. Of course, a wider range of oath forms exists in the Hebrew Bible, not all of which were sworn in a cultic context: note Gen 24:1–3. For a useful study of the terminology and form of biblical oaths, with reference to broader Near Eastern conventions, see M. R. Lehmann, "Biblical Oaths," *ZAW* 81 (1969) 74–92. Vows are a separate category; for the most recent study, see Tony W. Cartledge, *Vows in the Hebrew Bible and the Ancient Near East* (JSOTSup 147; Sheffield: Sheffield Academic Press, 1992).

39. Moshe Weinfeld, "Ordeal of Jealousy," *Encyclopaedia Judaica* (Jerusalem: Encyclopaedia Judaica, 1972) 12.1449–50; Tikva Frymer-Kensky, *The Judicial Ordeal in the Ancient Near East* (Ann Arbor, Mich.: University Microfilms, 1977) 474–80; and Frymer-Kensky, "The Strange Case of the Suspected Sotah (Numbers v 11–31)," *VT* 34 (1984) 11–26.

(3) the priestly manipulation of oracular paraphernalia, such as the lots[40] in order to issue a judicial ruling; (4) and priestly oracular rulings, apparently without recourse to the lots. It is not the cultic locale alone or the participation of priestly functionaries that distinguishes these cases from those administered in a lay context by the elders or the public assembly. Rather, it is a question of the nature of the case. Obviously, the priests are to be involved in all questions related to ritual purity and impurity, as the divine commission of Aaron and his sons makes clear (Lev 10:10–11). This role is presupposed in the regulations associated with afflictions of skin or cloth (Lev 13:1–59), leprosy (Lev 14:1–32), and fungal infestation of dwellings (Lev 14:33–55); elsewhere, too, the priesthood rules on questions involving the communicability of purity or contagion (Hag 2:10–13).

Less obvious, and most important, the cultus played an essential role in justice, even with respect to cases that had nothing whatsoever to do with cultic or ritual matters. Under certain conditions, secular cases of civil or criminal law had to be adjudicated cultically. Where a dearth of evidence—the absence of either testimony by witnesses or material proof—deprives human reason of the possibility of making a determination, the cultus granted the community access to a suprahuman agency of judicial decision making.[41] Under such circumstances, the parties to the dispute would repair to the local altar or sanctuary, there, in the symbolic presence of the deity, to swear a judicial oath or to submit to the ordeal.[42] With human reason unable to make a ruling, the deity, whose judicial insight was free of empirical constraint, would determine the guilty party: אֲשֶׁר יַרְשִׁיעֻן אֱלֹהִים יְשַׁלֵּם שְׁנַיִם לְרֵעֵהוּ "he whom God indicts shall pay double to his neighbor" (Exod 22:8b).[43] In cases involving trial by ordeal, the divine determination of guilt became also, in effect, a death sentence.

40. For a useful overview of the latter two, with a different organization than here presented, see P. J. Budd, "Priestly Instruction in Pre-Exilic Israel," *VT* 23 (1973) 1–14. For the first study of the priestly proclamation as a *Gattung* (literary form), see J. Begrich, "Die priesterliche Torah," in *Werden und Wesen des Alten Testaments* (BZAW 66; Berlin: Walter de Gruyter, 1936) 63–88; reprinted in his *Gesammelte Studien zum Alten Testament* (TBü 21; Munich: Chr. Kaiser, 1964) 232–60.

41. For the most comprehensive analysis of recourse to divine means for the resolution of legal disputes, see Frymer-Kensky, *The Judicial Ordeal in the Ancient Near East*; and Frymer-Kensky, "Suprarational Legal Procedures in Elam and Nuzi," *Studies on the Civilization and Culture of Nuzi and the Hurrians in Honor of Ernest R. Lacheman* (ed. M. A. Morrison and D. I. Owen; Winona Lake, Ind.: Eisenbrauns, 1981) 115–31.

42. On the religious and forensic function of oaths, see Karel van der Toorn, *Sin and Sanction in Israel and Mesopotamia: A Comparative Study* (SSN 22; Assen/Maastricht: Van Gorcum, 1985) 45–55.

43. The plural verb in the Hebrew has sometimes been understood as referring to the judges, an interpretation that I have refuted in n. 37. Alternately, some scholars maintain that a pre-Israelite notion of arbitration by "the gods" accounts for the plural verb, while others explain it as merely a plural of majesty that should be translated as a singular. For scholars taking both sides in that debate, see Ludger Schwienhorst-Schönberger (*Das Bundesbuch* [*Ex 20,22–23,33*]: *Studien zu seiner Entstehung und Theologie* [BZAW 188; Berlin: Walter de Gruyter, 1990] 200 n. 25), although he does not indicate his opinion on the matter. Since the label "plural of majesty" risks being a circular argument, simply explaining away an otherwise unexplained plural,

This norm that even secular disputes having nothing directly to do with the cultus were nonetheless resolved by means of recourse to the local altar or sanctuary represents a literary convention within both biblical and cuneiform law. This convention would have been presupposed by the authors of Deuteronomy, who would also have been constrained to transform it as a result of cultic centralization. It was specifically the recourse to the local sanctuary or altar for the resolution of such ambiguous cases that necessitated the transformation of this procedure by the authors of Deuteronomy. Prior to Deuteronomy, in all cases of evidentiary insufficiency—the unavailability of witnesses or evidence that would permit a normal judicial ruling—the case would be cultically resolved. For example, in cuneiform law, even in such noncultic cases as those involving the deposit of chattels in someone's house for safekeeping or livestock entrusted to a shepherd, if the depositor accuses the recipient of misappropriation and the recipient claims in turn that he is not guilty of the loss but that some third party stole it, with neither side able to produce witnesses, the only recourse is to repair to the local sanctuary where the guilty party swears a judicial oath to exculpate himself: *bēl bītim ina bāb* (*KÁ*) *ᴰTišpak nīš ilim izakkaršuma* "the owner of the house shall in the gate of Tišpak swear an oath to him [his accuser] by god" (*Laws of Eshnunna* § 37).[44] Both the legal topos of deposits and the technical terminology associated with the judicial oath

---

I prefer to avoid it. In my judgment, the text should be translated as a singular on both comparative and syntactical grounds. Cuneiform law illuminates the context. The judicial oath is sworn, after all, at the temple or altar of a particular god, who would then provide the oracular ruling (see the *Laws of Eshnunna*, § 37, discussed later). In terms of Hebrew grammar, the coordination of אלהים with a plural verb is not exceptional: see Gen 20:13; 31:53; 35:7; Josh 24:19; and 2 Sam 7:23. In all cases (except the double subject of Gen 35:7), the reference seems unambiguously to "God," understood as a single deity. Note the formulation יהוה כי אלהים קדשים הוא "Yahweh—for he is a holy God" (Josh 24:19), where the adjective "holy" occurs in the plural in order to agree with the morphologically plural form for "God," even though both "he" and "Yahweh" are singular. The anomalous plural form therefore seems to reflect morphological conformity between the verb or adjective and the plural ending of אלהים but need not imply that the given phrase is plural in meaning. For the converse phenomenon, where formal consistency requires a single verb when the plural is more logically expected, see n. 54.

44. See R. Yaron, *The Laws of Eshnunna* (2d ed.; Jerusalem: Magnes; Leiden: E. J. Brill, 1988) 64–65 (col. B iii 3) or Martha T. Roth, *Law Collections from Mesopotamia and Asia Minor* (SBLWAW 6; Atlanta: Scholars Press, 1995) 65. The normalization of the Akkadian is my own. A iii 20 preserves an interesting variant. Instead of the reference to the gate, the latter refers to the *bīt* "house" of Tišpak as the locus for the ceremony. The two alternative readings, independently preserved and functionally synonymous, explain a problematic redundancy in Exod 21:6. That verse coordinates two clauses, each with identical verb and preposition, both of which specify the locus for the divine oath whereby the indentured slave relinquishes his right to manumission: והגישו אדניו אל האלהים והגישו אל הדלת או אל המזוזה "His master *shall take him before* God; *shall take him before* the gate or before the door post." It is unnecessary to resolve the redundancy by claiming that the latter clause is a later (Deuteronomistic) addition, as does, most recently, Schwienhorst-Schönberger, *Bundesbuch*, 308. More likely, the Hebrew text preserves two variant readings alongside one another, corresponding to the two separately preserved in the cuneiform text: one specifying the presence before the divine (at the altar or sanctuary), the other, the location in the gate. On the phenomenon of conflated variants elsewhere, see S. Talmon, "Double Readings in the Massoretic Text," *Textus* 1 (1960) 144–84.

at the local sanctuary were taken over by the redactors of the Covenant Code: ונקרב בעל הבית אל האלהים "the owner of the house shall approach God" in order to swear שבעת יהוה "an oath by Yahweh" (Exod 22:7, 10).[45]

Within the Covenant Code, the Israelite legal draftsman structures the text to establish a binary opposition between a secular and a cultic context for the resolution of the dispute, contingent upon evidentiary ambiguity. The legal draftsman first introduces the major case with protasis marked by כי "if": כי יתן איש אל רעהו כסף או כלים לשמר וגנב מבית האיש "if a man deposits silver or vessels with his neighbor for safekeeping which are then stolen from the man's residence . . ." (Exod 22:6a). The two alternative subordinate clauses, a contrasting matched pair each introduced by the dependent protasis marker אם "if," make cultic resolution of the dispute contingent upon the absence of evidence—the failure to apprehend a third party with the stolen goods in his possession.[46]

<u>Exod 22:6b-7</u>

[A] אם ימצא הגנב ישלם שנים

[B] אם לא ימצא הגנב ונקרב בעל הבית אל האלהים אם לא שלח ידו במלאכת רעהו

(A) if the thief is apprehended, he shall pay double;
(B) if the thief is not apprehended, the owner of the house shall approach God [to take an oath] that he did not appropriate his neighbor's property.

In the second case (B), neither the depositor nor the bailee can prove or refute the accusation of theft. With secular arbitration by definition impossible, the two litigants must refer their case to divine arbitration: עד האלהים יבא דבר שניהם "unto God shall go the case between the two of them" (Exod 22:8).[47] The accused takes a judicial oath asserting his innocence in the divine

---

45. The literary-legal topos of deposits is an ancient one in the cuneiform legal collections and is appropriated by Israelite legal draftsmen. See the comprehensive analysis by Eckart Otto, "Die rechtshistorische Entwicklung des Depositenrechts in altorientalischen und altisraelitischen Rechtskorpora," *Zeitschrift der Savigny-Stiftung für Rechtsgeschichte, Romanistische Abteilung*, 105 (1988) 1–31; and, most recently, his "Diachronie und Synchronie im Depositenrecht des 'Bundesbuches,'" *Zeitschrift für Altorientalische und Biblische Rechtsgeschichte* 2 (1996) 76–85.

46. On the structure see G. Liedke, *Gestalt und Bezeichnung alttestamentlicher Rechtssätze: Eine formgeschichtlich-terminologische Studie* (WMANT 39; Neukirchen-Vluyn: Neukirchener Verlag, 1971) 32–34; Eckart Otto, *Wandel der Rechtsbegründungen in der Gesellschaftsgeschichte des antiken Israel: Eine Rechtsgeschichte des "Bundesbuches" Ex XX 22–XXIII 13* (StudBib 3; Leiden: E. J. Brill, 1988) 16–17; Yuichi Osumi, *Die Kompositionsgeschichte des Bundesbuches Exodus 20,22b–23,33* (OBO 105; Freiburg, Switzerland: Universitätsverlag; Göttingen: Vandenhoeck & Ruprecht, 1991) 93–101.

47. Otto, *Wandel der Rechtsbegründungen*, 14–19; and Otto, "Depositenrechts," 17–28, maintains that the cultic oath here (and at Exod 22:10) represent secondary interpolations. He reconstructs an entirely different text in which there is no oath but simple compensation of the lost property. There is no versional support for that reconstruction. Nor, turning to cuneiform legal history, does the simple compensation mandated by the *Laws of Eshnunna* § 36 suggest that such a clause was original here, which would then overload the Covenant Code topos with two cases requiring compensation (double and then single)—but no guidelines as to when the

presence, possibly in the gate of the local sanctuary (Exod 21:6) or before the altar. The technical formula for the judicial oath whereby each litigant formally asserts his innocence is שבעת יהוה "an oath by Yahweh" (Exod 22:10). The substantive denoting the asseveration is grammatically bound to Yahweh as the source of its authority and as the one who would fulfill it.[48] This formula is the exact Hebrew equivalent of the Akkadian *nīš ilim* "[oath by] the life of the god." The Hebrew formula for remanding the case to a cultic context such that the disputants appear אל האלהים "before God" (Exod 22:7; 21:6) is the exact interdialectical equivalent of the Akkadian *ina maḫar ilim*.[49]

In the law under discussion, the redactional structure providing the two paradigmatic alternatives in the case of a dispute regarding deposits may well have been inherited by the Israelite legal draftsmen from cuneiform law. The example from the *Laws of Eshnunna* §§ 36–37, already discussed, provides the same double conditional formulation (*šumma* "if" . . . *šumma* "if" . . .). The first law, based upon satisfactory evidence, requires restitution, and the second, in which there is a deadlock, mandates recourse to the temple for a judicial oath. The redactor of the Covenant Code uses a similar redactional structure: again the alternatives are formulated in two parallel subordinate clauses (אם . . . אם "if . . . if . . . ; Exod 22:6b–7). The first, in which the thief is apprehended and the requirements for evidence satisfied, requires restitution, and the second, in which there is no evidence, mandates recourse to the altar.

That redactional structure provides an important clue to the problematic sequence of Deut 17:2–7 + 8–13 that has not previously been noticed. Here, too, the redactor assembles two parallel, conditionally formulated laws (. . . כי . . . כי "if . . . if . . ."). The first involves secular resolution (Deut 17:2–7) based upon incontrovertible evidence (the testimony of two witnesses) and the second, in which there is ambiguity, mandates cultic resolution (Deut 17:8–13). The innovation of cultic centralization made it necessary, however, for the authors of Deuteronomy to transform the convention of repairing to the local sanctuary for the resolution of such ambiguous legal cases. This binary structure links the two paragraphs and begins to establish their legal-historical logic. Deut 17:2–7 had to be part of this redactional structure from the beginning. Its function is to define the conditions for evidentiary certainty.

---

judicial oath must be sworn. The redactional logic of both the *Laws of Eshnunna* §§ 36–37 and the Covenant Code (Exod 22:6–7) is to provide a paradigmatic case distinguishing, in the case of lost deposits, when compensation is called for and when a judicial oath must be sworn.

48. This observation establishes that the translation of Exod 22:10 provided by the NJPSV, "an oath *before* the LORD" (my emphasis) is philologically incorrect. Comparative evidence for my assertion is found in Akkadian, which has both the exact interdialectical equivalent, *nīš ilim* "oath by god," and the alternative, *nīš šarrim* "oath by the king." For a comprehensive study of Israelite oath forms, see M. Lehmann, "Biblical Oaths," *ZAW* 81 (1969) 74–92. Schwienhorst-Schönberger, *Bundesbuch*, 201–202, also notes this meaning.

49. See, for example, Hammurapi's Laws, §§ 9, 23, 107, 120, 126, 266, in the context of judicial oaths. For the most recent translation, see the superb edition by Martha T. Roth, *Law Collections from Mesopotamia and Asia Minor* (SBLWAW 6; Atlanta: Scholars Press, 1995) 71–142.

The Implications of Centralization for Israelite Justice

The cultic innovations of Deuteronomy—centralization of sacrifice and the concomitant prohibition of local altars—make local resolution of ambiguous legal cases impossible. By definition, with all cultic activity relegated to the central sanctuary, so must those judicial cases that hitherto required local cultic resolution be transferred to the central context. No longer was it possible to swear a judicial oath "before God" at the local sanctuary. Clearly, the implications of centralization were not restricted to such cultic issues as sacrifice (Deuteronomy 12), tithes and firstlings (Deut 14:22–29; 15:19–23), or the festival calendar (Deut 16:1–17). Centralization equally transformed judicial procedure. The extirpation of local altars created a "judicial vacuum in the provincial cities."[50]

The innovation of centralization thus involved a double agenda for the authors of this section of Deuteronomy: (1) they needed to fill the local legal vacuum created by centralization, and (2) they needed to find a means to adjudicate the ambiguous legal cases formerly tried at the local sanctuary. This working out of the implications of centralization for judicial procedure took place both empirically and at the level of the text and its structure. Most often, it is only the former that is recognized. Moshe Weinfeld, for example, correctly points out the Deuteronomic authors' double historical response to fill the local legal vacuum: first, "the appointment of state judges in every city (Deut 16:18–20)" and, second, the use of the central tribunal in Jerusalem for cases too problematic for the local courts (Deut 17:8–13).[51] In his focus on the historical issue, however, Weinfeld does not address the textual issue: the implications of the Deuteronomic reform for the sequence and the structure of the legal corpus. His historical reconstruction presupposes the standard literary-critical position whereby Deut 17:2–7, deemed disruptive, is "restored" to chapter 13. His analysis of the judicial reform moves directly from Deut 16:18–20 (the innovation of local, professional judicial officials) to Deut 17:8–13 (the combination of priests and magistrates at the central tribunal).[52] There remains for Deut 17:2–7, accordingly, neither legal-historical nor textual function.

Other questions remain. What precisely is the relation of the central to the local courts? What are the precise conditions for determining the venue where a given case will be heard? What precisely are the criteria whereby cases "must be submitted to the adjudication of the central tribunal in Jerusalem (17:8–13)"?[53] Categorizing such cases as those where "the provincial magistrate was unable to render a decisive verdict" involves a circular argument:

---

50. Weinfeld, *Deuteronomy and the Deuteronomic School*, 234.

51. Weinfeld, *Deuteronomy and the Deuteronomic School*, 234–35. Weinfeld attempts to reconstruct the historical role and broader background of the professional appointees in "Judge and Officer in Ancient Israel and in the Ancient Near East," *Israel Oriental Studies* 7 (1977) 65–88.

52. Weinfeld, *Deuteronomy and the Deuteronomic School*, 92 n. 2; 95 n. 1; 234–35.

53. Weinfeld, *Deuteronomy and the Deuteronomic School*, 235.

remanded to the central court are those cases too difficult to solve locally. The prior, essential question is by what criteria some cases were permitted and others denied local competence. The key to resolving these questions is the recognition that cultic centralization was not merely a matter of the cult. The innovation required a transformation of conventional judicial procedure. With the penetration of the state and its judicial administration into the local sphere, centralization was both cultic and political.

Deut 17:2–7 as a Revision of Deut 13:7–12

The function of Deut 17:2–7 is to demarcate the domain of local justice. The authors' concern is not the explicit topos of apostasy but rather evidentiary procedure. They rework a topos ostensibly involving cultic law, which they appropriate from the apostasy series found in chapter 13. Their transformation of that topos makes conviction in cases of apostasy conditional upon the availability of two witnesses. As a result, they restrict local jurisdiction to those cases that can be empirically resolved. The authors select the particular case of apostasy precisely because of its gravity and in order to drive home two essential points: (1) the priority of witness law over summary execution and (2) the secularization of judicial procedure in the local sphere. Deut 17:2–7 belongs to a separate and later literary stratum than does chapter 13 and exegetically reworks Deut 13:7–12, both of which paragraphs focus on the individual.

Deut 13:7–12 is concerned with incitement to apostasy by a single individual who is an immediate member of the kinship group of the law's addressee (Deut 13:7). In the case of such a provocation, the person to whom the incitement is addressed must take summary action to execute the inciter, acting in self-defense on behalf of the entire community to defend it from a mortal threat. The lemma, Deut 13:10–11a, commands:

[A] ידך תהיה בו בראשונה להמיתו ויד כל העם באחרנה

[B] וסקלתו באבנים ומת

(A) Your hand shall be first against him to execute him;
  thereafter, the hand of all the people;[54]
(B) You shall stone him to death!

---

54. The construction both here and at Deut 17:7 initially appears ungrammatical, with the singular "hand" bound to a collective ("people") or plural ("witnesses") noun. This construction, however, is characteristic of classical Hebrew syntax. In all such cases, the construction suggests that the singular "hand" is construed as having a distributive force: Gen 19:16 (וביד שתי בנתיו) ... ויחזקו האנשים בידו "The men seized his hand ... *and the hand* of his two daughters"); Exod 29:9; Lev 8:24; Deut 1:25; Judg 7:20 (*bis*). These references are found in BDB, 389 (1a), *s.v.* יד. The linguistic rationale for such a construction is that plurality does not in fact apply to the noun in question: each person, whatever the number, employs but one of his pair of hands to hurl the stone. Surprisingly, this semantic issue is overlooked by the most recent textbook: Bruce K. Waltke and M. O'Connor, *An Introduction to Biblical Hebrew Syntax* (Winona Lake, Ind.: Eisenbrauns, 1990). The Septuagint and the Targums normalize the construction, substituting the logical plural for the distributive.

That lemma is cited nearly verbatim by Deut 17:5b–7.[55] The citation is chiastic, according to Seidel's law. This reversal of the elements of the original explains an incongruity in the sequence of instructions for the trial and execution of the apostate in Deut 17:4–6. A number of scholars have questioned why the ruling that the apostate should be executed at the city gate, in v. 5, precedes the condition for reaching that verdict: the requirement that conviction in capital cases be based upon the testimony of two or more witnesses, first stated in v. 6. This incongruity in the order of the verses has led some scholars to claim that v. 6 is a late addition to the text, disrupting its order.[56] Despite that claim, the disorder is to be explained not in terms of a secondary interpolation but rather in terms of Seidel's law, as an editorial technique marking textual reuse:

Deut 17:5b-7

[B′] וסקלתם באבנים ומתו

[X] על פי שנים עדים או שלשה עדים יומת המת לא יומת על פי עד אחד

[A′] יד העדים תהיה בו בראשנה להמיתו ויד כל העם באחרנה

(B′) You shall stone them to death!

(X) On the testimony of two witnesses or three witnesses shall a person be executed; he shall not be executed on the testimony of a single witness;

(A′) The hand of the witnesses shall be first against him to execute him; thereafter, the hand of all the people.

In his reformulation, the editor interpolates the requirement, nowhere found in chapter 13, that the conviction be based upon the testimony of a minimum of two witnesses. In light of that interpolation, the chiastically cited second element of the lemma is strikingly transformed so that the plural witnesses, rather than the single accuser, are the ones required to initiate the capital punishment that results from their testimony.[57] The rejection of the lemmatic ידך

---

55. Bernard M. Levinson, *The Hermeneutics of Innovation: The Impact of Centralization upon the Structure, Sequence, and Reformulation of Legal Material in Deuteronomy* (Ann Arbor, Mich.: University Microfilms, 1991) 381–82. Note also, very similarly, Georg Braulik, *Deuteronomium II: 16,18–34,12* (Neue Echter Bibel 28; Würzburg: Echter Verlag, 1992) 125.

56. So Rüterswörden, *Gemeinschaft zur Gemeinde*, 37; and Foresti, "Dtn. 16.18–18.22," 27.

57. The recent attempt by Eckart Otto to claim that there is no contradiction between the two laws is unconvincing ("Gerichtsordnung," 153). In claiming that the addressee of Deut 13:10–11a "ist einer der Zeugen in 17,7," he overlooks the emphatic assertion to the contrary by the author of Deut 13:7–12, who stipulates that the enticement took place בסתר "in secret" (Deut 13:7): without witnesses. Otto's harmonization of the two contradictory laws unintentionally repeats nearly verbatim a prior harmonization by Rabbi Abraham ibn Ezra (1089–1164). Glossing the lemma of ידך תהיה בו "Your hand shall be upon him" (Deut 13:10a), he wrote: היה נראה כי הוא משנים עדים "It would appear that this refers to each of the two witnesses [specified in 17:6–7]" (*Commentary on the Torah* [ed. Asher Weiser; Jerusalem: Rav Kook Institute, 1977] 3.253 [Hebrew; my translation]). No textual basis is evident for such eisegesis, which in effect rewrites Deut 13:7–12 (where it is specified that there are no witnesses) to make it conform to Deut 17:5b–7 (which specifically invokes witness law).

"your hand" for the reformulation העדים יד "the hand of the witnesses" establishes the legal-historical distance between the two texts.[58]

The concern of Deut 13:10–11a is with summary execution: the singular addressee of the law, as the one to whom the incitement had been addressed (Deut 13:7), must subordinate feelings of kinship and mercy (Deut 13:9b), even in the case of intimate kin (Deut 13:7), to a prior responsibility: the defense of the community from the threat of apostasy.[59] As such, immediate summary execution—a form of community self-defense—is called for: תהרגנו הרג כי "But you shall surely kill him!" (Deut 13:10).[60] Following cuneiform treaty precedents, summary execution is the proper punishment for disloyalty.

In contrast, Deut 17:5–7 subordinates punishment to due process and highlights the witnesses as the agents of justice. This underscoring of their role works both through the interpolation, which specifies that there should be no convic-

---

58. For linguistic and other evidence independently confirming that Deut 17:2–7 represents a later reuse of material from chapter 13, see Dion, "Deuteronomy 13," 159–62, 191–92; Rütersworden, *Gemeinschaft zur Gemeinde*, 37; Rütersworden, "Der Verfassungsentwurf des Deuteronomiums," 326–28; and Gertz, *Gerichtsorganisation Israels*, 45–52. In contrast, Eckart Otto has recently sought to level the diachronic difference between Deuteronomy 13 and 17:2–7 by reconstructing an allegedly original Deuteronomic core, common to both, from which he excises ostensibly secondary Deuteronomistic accretions ("Von der Gerichtsordnung zum Verfassungsentwurf: Deuteronomische Gestaltung und deuteronomistische Interpretation im »Ämtergesetz« Dtn 16,18–18,22," in *"Wer ist wie du, HERR, unter den Göttern?" Studien zur Theologie und Religionsgeschichte Israels für Otto Kaiser* [ed. Ingo Kottsieper et al.; Göttingen: Vandenhoeck & Ruprecht, 1995] 149, 153). To support his reconstruction of this essential Deuteronomic core for Deuteronomy 13, Otto (p. 149 n. 36) cites Dion's redactional analysis of the chapter. The problem is that Dion's actual conclusions controvert Otto's enterprise, since Dion denies that any Deuteronomic core is recoverable for either Deuteronomy 13 or 17:2–7. Indeed, he insists that "Deut. 13.2–18 *in its entirety is a dtr composition*" and disallows that it is "a D composition" ("Deuteronomy 13," 190, 191; my emphasis).

59. On Deut 13:7–12 as a test case that trenchantly sets loyalty to Yahweh over ties of kinship and love, see Bernard M. Levinson, "Recovering the Lost Original Meaning of תכסה ולא עליו (Deuteronomy 13:9)," *JBL* 115 (1996) 601–20.

60. Despite the nearly absolute scholarly consensus to the contrary, the MT reading, not a retroversion based on the Septuagint variant ἀναγγελλῶν ἀναγγελεῖς περὶ αὐτοῦ "You shall report him" (LXX Deut 13:9), is original. The LXX is but one of a chorus of mutually inconsistent versional attempts to revise the MT and make it conform to due process. Moreover, the neo-Assyrian treaties employed to support the LXX variant actually support the MT and require summary execution of traitors. See Bernard M. Levinson, "'But You Shall Surely Kill Him!': The Text-Critical and Neo-Assyrian Evidence for MT Deut 13:10," in *Bundesdokument und Gesetz: Studien zum Deuteronomium* (ed. Georg Braulik; HBS 4; Freiburg: Herder, 1995) 37–63. The recent defense of the Septuagint reading by Anneli Aejmelaeus is unconvincing ("Die Septuaginta des Deuteronomiums," in *Das Deuteronomium und seine Querbeziehungen* [ed. Timo Veijola; Schriften der Finnischen Exegetischen Gesellschaft 62; Göttingen: Vandenhoeck & Ruprecht, 1996] 19–21). Her article implies that the other textual witnesses, the history of interpretation, and the cuneiform material are all irrelevant to establishing the original text in question. Her analysis avoids the evidence that consonantal metathesis was a widely attested hermeneutical technique used by the Septuagint translators as well as by the Qumran sectarians and rabbinic exegesis (see Levinson, "'But You Shall Surely Kill Him!,'" 53). It also concedes that it cannot explain the absence from the Septuagint of the very adversative particle that is essential to the reconstruction (p. 20 n. 65.).

tion on the basis of a single accuser (similarly, Deut 19:15), and through the requirement that the witnesses themselves initiate the punishment that follows from their testimony. Their direct involvement in the execution entails a legal safeguard: it may well intimate the consequences of false accusation or false testimony to the perpetrators. Confirming this hypothesis, the one place where Deuteronomy cites the law of talion is in specifying the judicial penalty for false accusation (Deut 19:19).

Strikingly, the requirement of a minimum of two witnesses becomes a precondition to conviction even in the case of the most heinous offense imaginable, apostasy as the breach of the first commandment of the Decalogue (cf. Deut 13:3; Exod 20:5 = Deut 5:9; Exod 23:24).[61] Even in such a case, normative witness law must be scrupulously implemented. In the context of Deut 17:2–7, therefore, the selection of the particular case seems to function less for its specific than for its paradigmatic value. That the formulation of the case involves the reuse of prior lemmas and, but for the recontextualization, is quite formulaic lends weight to the argument that the true topos of the paragraph is not apostasy but the rules of evidence.

This introduction of the laws concerned with evidentiary procedure corresponds closely to the pride of place that the drafters of Hammurapi's Laws grant to the same topos, setting it at the very beginning of the legal corpus. In the context both of Deut 17:2–7 and the cuneiform corpus (§§ 1–5), therefore, not only does justice functionally mean freedom from false accusation, but the initial laws—in a unit whose topos is justice—become remarkably self-reflexive, regulating judicial procedure (adjective law) more than actual delicts per se (substantive law). That capital offenses, even in the gravest of cases (apostasy in Deut 17:2–7; accusations of murder or sorcery in Hammurapi's Laws §§ 1–2) are subordinated to a general law of evidence clearly gives a powerful theme-setting demonstration of the injunction with which the unit as a whole opens: ושפטו את העם משפט צדק "they shall judge the people with righteous justice" (Deut 16:18).[62]

---

61. Later Jewish tradition makes the relation between the passages more explicit. The Tiberian Massorah uses a theological vocalization to draw an exegetical analogy between the case of apostasy in Deut 13:3 and the Decalogue's prohibition. The grammatically anomalous *hophal* of the verb עבד "to serve, worship" is, but for these cases, completely unattested. A comparable instance of grammatically anomalous theological vocalization occurs in Num 7:89; Ezek 2:2; 43:6. In all these instances divine speech is vocalized as an intransitive reflexive (*hithpael*) of דבר. See the analysis by Moshe Greenberg, *Ezekiel, 1–20* (AB; Garden City, N.Y.: Doubleday, 1983) 62, who identifies them as "a later linguistic conceit."

62. For a valuable explanation of the logic of Hammurapi's Laws §§ 1–5, see Herbert Petschow, "Zur Systematik und Gesetzestechnik im Codex Hammurabi," *ZA* 57 (1965) 148–49. Medieval rabbinic exegesis already recognized the theme-setting role of initial laws within a legal collection. Nachmanides (1194–1270) made the analogous claim about the otherwise problematic placement of laws concerned with manumission of slaves (Exod 21:2–11) at the very beginning of the Covenant Code (Exod 21:1–19)—prior even to a cluster of apodictic capital cases (Exod 21:12–17). He argues that this placement is intelligible only as reflecting the first verse of the Decalogue, both in its topos (manumission) and in its language: הוצאתיך ... עבדים "led you out ... slaves" (Exod 20:2) is chiastically echoed (see Seidel's law) by עבד ... יצא "slave ... shall go out" (Exod 21:2). See Nachmanides (R. Moses ben Nachman), *Commentary on*

Whereas the topos of chapter 13 is incitement to apostasy, the actual topos of Deut 17:2–7 is the innovation it makes in legal history: the evidentiary requirement of two witnesses.[63] The topos, form, and terminology of chapter 13 are appropriated by the drafter of Deut 17:2–7 in order to transform the earlier judicial protocol. This reinterpretation extends the range of examples of textual transformation demonstrated within Deuteronomy. Previous examples have revealed Deuteronomy's tendentious revision of pre-Deuteronomic literature (the Covenant Code and JE material). This case raises a different issue. It suggests that earlier strata within the legal corpus achieved sufficient authoritative status that subsequent editors made new law through the reinterpretation of earlier texts deriving from the same legal-scribal school.

This trajectory of textual revision within the legal corpus is highly nuanced and multilayered. In its revision of Deuteronomy 13, Deut 17:2–7 revises a text that is itself already a revision of earlier law, both biblical and cuneiform. First, Deuteronomy 13 is very much of a literary text: a deliberate composition in which Josianic authors appropriate the literary and the political model of the neo-Assyrian state treaties, with their requirement for exclusive allegiance to the secular lord, and transfer that loyalty oath (*adê*) to Yahweh. No discrete literary strata, corresponding to alleged transformations in the nature of Israelite piety, moving from a pristine clan-based immediacy that embodies a "primitive-archaic naïveté" to a more complex form of social and religious organization, can legitimately be isolated.[64] Such attempts, presupposing a specious

---

the Torah (ed. Charles B. Chavel; 2 vols.; Jerusalem: Rav Kook Institute, 1959) 1.412–13 (Hebrew; translated in 5 vols., New York: Shilo, 1971). Nachmanides was preceded in his analysis by the ninth-century *Midraš Exodus Rabbah* 30:15, which may have served him as a source. The best edition of this text is *Midrash rabbah ha-mevu'ar*, vol. 2, *Shemot rabbah* (2 vols.; Jerusalem: Makhon ha-midrash ha-mevu'ar, 1983) 2.90 (Hebrew). For the translation, see *Midrash Rabbah Exodus* (tr. S. M. Lehrman; London: Soncino, 1983) 363.

63. This witness law is a Deuteronomic innovation, which is then presupposed by the Priestly source in Num 35:30. There is no evidence for such witness law to be pre-Deuteronomic. Anachronistically set in the ninth century, the narrative of the kangaroo court set up by Jezebel (1 Kgs 21:10–13) constitutes a very late Deuteronomistic literary composition that presupposes the witness law of Deuteronomy. Establishing by virtue of language and content that 1 Kgs 21:1–16 dates to the Persian period and knows all four collections of pentateuchal law (BC, D, H, and P) is Alexander Rofé, "The Vineyard of Naboth: The Origin and Message of the Story," *VT* 38 (1988) 89–104.

64. Contra Martin Rose, *Der Ausschließlichkeitsanspruch Jahwes: Deuteronomische Schultheologie und die Volksfrömmigkeit in der späten Königszeit* (BWANT 106; Stuttgart: W. Kohlhammer, 1975), 19–50. Rose's source-critical reconstruction of the earliest stage of the text of Deut 13:2–19; 17:2–7, is ineluctably linked to his postulate of the stage it is supposed to represent in terms of the history of religions: "Es ist die Stufe archaisch-primitiver Naivität, die von der Gemeinschaft der Stammeseinheit her denkt" (p. 46). He claims that the text's original focus was less on allegiance to a particular God (pp. 20–21, 33) than on the rejection of unfamiliar gods in order to maintain the intimacy of the ethnic community. Naming the deity to whom exclusive allegiance is owed thus represents a secondary development and a fall from original immediacy (pp. 40–41). Parenesis is added only at the tertiary level. The neo-Assyrian vassal treaties controvert Rose's reconstruction. The Vassal Treaty of Esarhaddon requires the subject's exclusive allegiance specifically to Esarhaddon and to his son Ashurbanipal; each is identified by name and appropriate royal title; and admonitory parenesis is inseparable from the requirement for loyalty.

understanding of the history of religions, are controverted by the fact that Deuteronomy 13 is from the outset a literary composition, most likely a product of the Josianic court, deliberately transferring the neo-Assyrian model to an Israelite context and incorporating earlier Deuteronomic language and literary motifs.[65]

Second, Deuteronomy 13 revises and replaces the prohibition against sacrifice to foreign gods found in the Covenant Code (Exod 22:19).[66] The assumption is that the latter text's stipulation that such transgressors be "consecrated to destruction" (יחרם) would additionally have involved the collective destruction of the entire family, together with its material goods.[67] As such, Deut 13:7–12 represents a restrictive reinterpretation of Exod 22:19, limiting the punishment to the individual, while Deut 13:13–18 would limit collective punishment to those cases where the wrongdoing was actually collective, as in the case of the city that succumbs to apostasy. On the one hand, Deut 13:7–12 mitigates the severity of Exod 22:19, abrogating its original requirement for collective punishment. On the other hand, the original law is also made more severe: now mere incitement, and not the fact of apostasy, becomes a capital offense.

The Hermeneutical Function of Deut 17:2–7

Deut 17:2–7 reformulates Deut 13:7–12 in order to introduce the requirement for a minimum of two witnesses for conviction in capital cases. The inclusion

---

65. See Dion, "Deuteronomy 13," 147–216. Arguing that despite the intimate ties to neo-Assyrian treaty language, the chapter should nonetheless be dated to a postexilic redactional layer is Timo Veijola, "Wahrheit und Intoleranz nach Deuteronomium 13," *ZTK* 92 (1995) 309–10. The author's argument for a late Deuteronomistic redaction, motivated by covenant theology, does not provide a clear explanation of its premise that the neo-Assyrian material first entered Deuteronomy only in the Persian period, not during the neo-Assyrian hegemony over Judah while the treaty was a live issue, nor even during the subsequent Babylonian hegemony. The most recent analysis of the chapter provides a comprehensive argument for the reuse of the neo-Assyrian material in the context of the Josianic court. See Eckart Otto, "Treueid und Gesetz: Die Ursprünge des Deuteronomiums im Horizont neuassyrischen Vertragsrechts," *Zeitschrift für Altorientalische und Biblische Rechtsgeschichte* 2 (1996) 1–52.

66. Norbert Lohfink, "חרם *ḥāram*," *TDOT* 5 (1986) 198; and Seebaß, "Vorschlag," 83–98. The clearest arguments are provided by Schwienhorst-Schönberger, *Bundesbuch*, 316–20, providing the strongest, if indirect, case for literary dependence; and, extending his earlier idea, Norbert Lohfink, "Opfer und Säkularisierung im Deuteronomium," in *Studien zu Opfer und Kult im Alten Testament* (ed. Adrian Schenker; Forschungen zum Alten Testament 3; Tübingen: J. C. B. Mohr [Paul Siebeck], 1992) 39–40. For the Near Eastern context, see Philip D. Stern, *The Biblical Ḥerem: A Window on Israel's Religious Experience* (BJS 211; Atlanta: Scholars Press, 1991) 67–110, who, however, does not address the literary-critical and redactional issues in his analysis of Deut 13:13–18 (p. 106) and assumes, rather than demonstrates, a relation to Exod 22:19 (pp. 123–25).

67. So G. Schmitt, *Du solst keinen Frieden schließen mit den Bewohnern des Landes: Die Wegweisung gegen die Kanaanäer in Israels Geschichte und Geschichtsschreibung* (BWANT 91; Stuttgart: Kohlhammer, 1970) 141–42. However, there is no conclusive evidence that the punishment does extend to the family in Exod 22:19. Making this point and adducing other difficulties in the formulation by Seebaß, see Rüterswörden, "Der Verfassungsentwurf des Deuteronomiums," 326–27.

of this paragraph in the larger unit serves a double purpose. First, the requirement of two or more witnesses defines the case as one where a legal ruling is intrinsically possible on the basis of empirical evidence and human reason alone. As such, this evidentiary requirement is restrictive so far as the demarcation of legal authority is concerned: *only* those cases, the authors assert, that permit of secular resolution may be tried locally. Second, if the authors prohibit local *cultic* justice as a consequence of centralization, they do not prohibit local justice altogether. Consistently for the authors of Deuteronomy, centralization involves a double transformation—cultic exclusivity in the central sphere and local secularization. With respect to sacrifice, for example, the authors of Deuteronomy restrict legitimate cultic slaughter to the central sanctuary while sanctioning secular slaughter of animals in the local sphere. The same principle holds true for the two cases in question here. Cultic justice is restricted to the central sanctuary in Deut 17:8–13; concomitantly, the local sphere, in Deut 17:2–7, is legitimated as the site of secular justice.

The function of Deut 17:2–7 is to serve paradigmatically to define and to legitimate the role of the local sphere in judicial administration. Gustav Hölscher was thus close to the mark in claiming that the case of apostasy served as "merely a paradigm of a criminal case" and as "a school example."[68] The problem is his "merely." That the case indeed functions paradigmatically does not mean that, at the time of its composition, it was only so intended. Far more likely, it was part of a far-reaching program to implement centralization through all of life, cultically and judicially. The text's authors drive home the point that the local sphere need not totally relinquish its authority to the Jerusalem revisionists. Its lay personnel can continue to try even capital cases. Since those cases requiring cultic resolution were always beyond the scope of local lay authority, the shift merely in cultic venue—from the local to the central sanctuary—does not, at least in principle, diminish local lay jurisdiction. Even the gravest of possible offenses, apostasy, by definition capital, may be tried locally, contingent upon the case's satisfying the evidentiary requirement.

Whether, in sanctioning local justice, the authors of Deuteronomy also intended to sanction the continued authority of the local clan elders is less clear. The Deuteronomic authors impose a system of judicial professionals (Deut 16:18–20) upon the older system of city-gate justice and restrict ambiguous cases requiring cultic recourse to the judiciary at the central sanctuary (Deut 17:8–9). The text's authors do not specify how or whether the professional judiciary is to function alongside the older system of the clan justice. It is, after all, precisely at the gate where the older system of clan justice, in the hands

---

68. Gustav Hölscher, "Komposition und Ursprung des Deuteronomiums," *ZAW* 40 (1922) 198 ("nur Musterbeispiel eines Kriminalvergehens," "Schulbeispiel"; my translation). Hölscher's denial of the practicability of the law is part of his larger argument against the Josianic dating of the legal corpus: he maintains that it merely represents post-exilic scholastic theologizing. That argument is very unlikely. Centralization was a late pre-exilic concern. Postexilic *Yehud* took it for granted and was more concerned with the role of Jerusalem and the construction of a citizen-Temple state along Achaemenid models.

of the elders, operated (Deut 21:19; 22:15; 25:7; Job 29:7; Ruth 4:1, 11; Lam 5:14). Consequently the imposition of professional judges at the local level may have initiated a conflict over spheres of judicial authority. Weinfeld recognizes this conflict. However, he attempts to negate the problem by reconstructing separate jurisdictions for each of the professional judiciary and the clan elders, as if each operated simultaneously alongside the other, with the elders now restricted to matters of family law.[69] Such a synchronic harmonization overlooks diachronic issues involved in the composition of the legal corpus. It is doubtful that the two systems of judicial administration—that of the elders and that of the professional judicial appointees of Deut 16:18–20—ever coexisted historically.[70]

The authors begin the unit concerned with the implications of centralization for judicial procedure with paragraphs that deny, by means of polemical silence, any role for the elders. Indeed, the authors impose their professionalized judicial system upon the city gate as if it were a tabula rasa without traditional legal-historical occupants: שׁפטים ושׁטרים תתן לך בכל שׁעריך "Judges and judicial officers shall you appoint for yourself in each of your city-gates" (Deut 16:18)!

69. M. Weinfeld, "Elders," 6.578–80; Weinfeld, *Deuteronomy and the Deuteronomic School*, 234. Similarly, Jacob Milgrom, "The Ideological and Historical Importance of the Office of Judge in Deuteronomy," in *Isac* [sic] *Leo Seeligmann Volume: Essays on the Bible and the Ancient World* (ed. Alexander Rofé and Yair Zakovitch; 3 vols.; Jerusalem: E. Rubinstein, 1983) 3.129–39 (138). Unfortunately, this entire question concerning the respective spheres of authority of the elders and the official judicial system is not addressed by Hanoch Reviv, *The Elders in Ancient Israel: A Study of a Biblical Institution* (Jerusalem: Magnes, 1989) 61–70. By discussing neither the installation of the judicial officials (Deut 16:18–20) nor the law of the king (Deut 17:14–20), he avoids challenges to his claim that Deuteronomy retains the institution of the elders essentially intact in its presettlement form.

70. Most commonly, scholars view those laws in which the elders are active as an earlier and pre-Deuteronomic stratum of the legal corpus. See Alexander Rofé, "The Law about the Organization of Justice in Deuteronomy (16:18–20; 17:8–13)," *Beth Mikra* 65 (1976) 199–210, esp. 200–201 (Hebrew; English abstract); and Mayes, *Deuteronomy*, 284–85, 304. That widely held position has recently come under challenge from two different perspectives. First, Eckart Otto has argued that these laws are Deuteronomic and that the professionalized judiciary coexisted with the administration of justice by the elders. See Otto, *Ša'ar*, 375–76; and Otto, "Soziale Verantwortung und Reinheit des Landes: Zur Redaktion der kasuistischen Rechtssätze in Deuteronomium 19–25," in *Prophetie und geschichtliche Wirklichkeit im alten Israel: Festschrift für Siegfried Hermann* (ed. Rüdiger Liwak and Siegfried Wagner; Stuttgart: W. Kohlhammer, 1991) 290–306. His argument that their redaction is now Deuteronomic is compelling. The claim of the coexistence of the two systems, however, strikes me as harmonistic: Deut 16:18 installs the professionalized judiciary precisely at the site where the elders would exercise their public function, pulling the bench out from under them. Second, Jan Christian Gertz has recently reversed the conventional view to argue that the laws involving the elders (Deut 21:18–21; 22:13–21; and 25:5–10) actually are *post*-Deuteronomic and exilic in origin (*Gerichtsorganisation Israels*, 173–225). As such, they would be later than—not earlier than or contemporary with—the Deuteronomic system of a professionalized judiciary. Gertz was anticipated in his late dating of the elder material by Hoppe, *Origins of Deuteronomy*, 257–356. His proposal leads to some difficulties. Why should post-Deuteronomic tradents subvert Deuteronomic law by overturning the leading judicial role assigned to a professionalized judiciary in 16:18–20? Why only in the exilic period would an ancient motif of cuneiform law, the casuistic law of the disrespectful son (see *Hammurabi's Code* § 195) enter the legal corpus (Deut 21:18–21) as a late straggler, when other cuneiform motifs (adultery and rape law) were already present (Deut 22:22–29)?

What the text here presents as simple installation actually involves the replacement of one system of justice with another, as the elders are silently evicted from their customary place of honor.[71] The deliberate nonmention of the elders in the very site where they customarily exercised their judicial function can only constitute a deliberate polemic. As such, legal history is rewritten by means of the textual strategy of exegetical silence.

The authors of Deuteronomy radically transform the authority structures of public life. Mere seniority within the clan is no longer requisite to the task of exercising judicial authority. This conventional role of the elders had been based upon their social position and inherent status. The elders were thus neither appointed by nor answerable to the larger community. The authors of Deuteronomy disrupt that old clan lineage judicial system and instead make exercise of the judicial function conditional, first, upon appointment to the office and, second, upon professionalization. In breaking the nexus between justice and clan status, the authors of Deuteronomy push further to create a fully independent judiciary that is equally free of royal control. The king does not appoint the local judiciary.[72] Just as there is no mention of the monarch in the context of judicial procedure (Deut 17:2–7, 8–13), so is there no mention of his judicial authority or even of his right to appoint judicial officials in the law of the king (Deut 17:14–20). The texts are perfectly consistent in sundering any connection between justice and monarchy.[73]

---

71. Also arguing that the elders are displaced are Rofé, "Organization of Justice," 200–201; Niehr, *Rechtsprechung in Israel*, 96–97; and Suzuki, "Administration of Justice," 34, 38. Milgrom, "Judge in Deuteronomy," 129–39, recognizes the usurpation but harmonizes, maintaining that the elders retain their authority in the domestic sphere. Wilson, "Israel's Judicial System," 246, accepts that the system of clan lineage justice is abrogated but maintains that the professionalization of the judiciary precedes the Deuteronomic reform. Deut 16:18–20, in his analysis, merely extends the existing system of judicial appointees in cities under royal control, as established by Jehoshaphat's judicial reform, to all towns. But the only evidence for Jehoshaphat's judicial reform is the narrative of 2 Chronicles 19—and Wilson himself establishes that the narrative is not historical (pp. 246–48). See further n. 73.

72. Arguing that the king is not given the power of judicial appointment are S. Dean McBride, Jr., "Deuteronomium," *TRE* 8 (1982) 531–43 (534); Rüterswörden, *Gemeinschaft zur Gemeinde*, 92–93; and Patrick D. Miller, *Deuteronomy* (Louisville: John Knox, 1990) 143. Suzuki, "Administration of Justice," 22–58, argues for royal appointment. His argument is predicated, however, upon problematic legal-historical distinctions between laws formulated in the second-person singular and the plural. His analysis of the law of the king does not differentiate between Deuteronomic and Deuteronomistic elements and, in describing the king's authority, seems to describe the viewpoint of the text's authors instead (41–43).

73. Only postexilically, under the influence of Achaemenid models of royal authority, is the monarch's right to judicial appointment restored to him. The Chronicler's programmatic narrative of Jehoshaphat's judicial reform anachronistically revises Deut 16:18–20; 17:2–7 (and other texts) in order to reassert royal judicial authority (2 Chronicles 19). That text, despite the very influential article by Albright, is not historical. It is a deliberate compilation of other texts and provides reliable information only about the Chronicler's vision for a reconstruction in the Persian Age. Establishing the text's nonhistoricity are Rofé, "Organization of Justice," 199–210; Wilson, "Israel's Judicial System," 246–48; Rüterswörden, *Gemeinschaft zur Gemeinde*, 15–19; and, most extensively, Gary N. Knoppers, "Jehoshaphat's Judiciary and 'the Scroll of YHWH'S Torah,'" *JBL* 113 (1994) 59–80. Rofé's article has been widely overlooked.

This new vision radically transforms Israelite and ancient Near Eastern precedent, whereby central to the royal ideology is the monarch's role in the administration of justice. The authors of Deuteronomy have created a fully independent judiciary, chosen by and answerable to the population at large (Deut 16:18).[74] But, more complexly, these new judicial officials also owe their commission to the new Deuteronomic initiative. They must conform to and implement Deuteronomy's own principles of sapiential justice (Deut 16:19–20), using the paradigmatic cases of the legal corpus as the final arbiters of justice. Rejecting both the conventional privilege of the elders and the conventional power of the king, the authors of Deuteronomy substitute a new structure of judicial and public authority: the Deuteronomic Torah.[75]

The Contextual Function of Deut 17:8–13

The Deuteronomic program of cultic centralization also provides the key to the judicial role of the central sanctuary. Even civil cases that could not be empirically resolved because of evidentiary insufficiency were referred to the cultus for an oracular responsum. Within the Covenant Code, the terminology for appearing before the divine to make a judicial oath is ונקרב . . . אל האלהים "to draw near to God" (Exod 22:7) or עד האלהים יבא דבר שניהם "unto God shall come the case between the two of them" (Exod 22:8). Centralization necessitated the transfer of that originally local cultic access to the central sphere. Because that legal-historical convention already existed, the authors needed not to abrogate but merely to respecify the existing norm. Just such reworking is apparent in the protasis of Deut 17:8. Consistent with earlier protocol, that verse refers any case that defies empirical resolution "to the cultic site" where an oracular responsum may be obtained: אל המקום.[76] As a consequence of centralization, therefore, it becomes necessary to respecify the cultic reference: אל המקום אשר יבחר יהוה אלהיך בו "to the place *which Yahweh your God shall choose*" (Deut 17:8). The reformulation works like a lemma with its gloss. The relative clause restricts the מקום site where cultic access is achieved to the central sanctuary: the location of the one legitimate altar. The originally local oracular resolution of the דבר "case" granted in Exod 22:8 is now centrally granted by the levitical priests or judge: והגידו לך את דבר המשפט "they will proclaim to you the sentence of judgment" (Deut 17:9b).

The authors of the text take pains to stress that the cultic center does not function as a Supreme or appellate court.[77] Instead, its authority operates by

---

74. My formulation follows S. Dean McBride, Jr., "Polity of the Covenant People: The Book of Deuteronomy," *Int* 41 (1987) 229–44 (240); reprinted in *A Song of Power and the Power of Song: Essays on the Book of Deuteronomy* (ed. Duane L. Christensen; Winona Lake, Ind.: Eisenbrauns, 1993) 62–77.

75. See also the reflections of Lohfink, "Ämtergesetze," 319–20.

76. See chapter 2, n. 16. Given the connection between the cultus and justice, as stressed here, it is relevant that in 1 Sam 7:16, the Septuagint reads "sanctified places" for MT מקומה. The reading thus assumes that Samuel's judicial oracles are proclaimed at the sanctuaries listed in the verse.

77. As noted by Lohfink, "Ämtergesetze," 307. I thus disagree with Suzuki, "Administration of Justice," 35–36.

default, in cases defined by the absence of witnesses or evidence. Only in cases that defy empirical resolution—herewith local judicial authority receives its sanction as the tribunal of first choice—must the litigants transfer the venue of the case from the local to the central sphere: כי יפלא ממך דבר למשפט בין דם לדם בין דין לדין ובין נגע לנגע לנגע דברי ריבות בשעריך "If a legal case exceeds your ken— whether distinguishing between one category of homicide and another, one category of civil law and another, one category of bodily injury and another, any kind of legal dispute within your city-gates . . ." (Deut 17:8).

What is the function of the three pairs of delicts found in the protasis, each of which is formulated as a double prepositional phrase, ‏בין __ ל-__ "between __ and __"? The intent seems to be to raise the issue of judicial classification in terms of binary opposition: whether a particular case belongs in the category of a culpable or nonculpable offense. For example, the distinction intended by בין דם לדם, literally, "between blood and blood," means, as Abraham ibn Ezra (1089–1164) correctly glosses, recovering the original meaning against the halakhah: בין דם נקי לדם חייב "between innocent blood-spilling and culpable blood-spilling."[78] Samuel ben Meir (Rashbam, 1080/85–c. 1174) similarly rejects the conventional halakhic meaning: בין דם לדם: לפי פשוטו בין רציחה לרציחה, בין שוגג למזיד "between blood and blood: according to its literal meaning, between [one form of] murder and [another form] of murder, between [the] homicide and the murderer."[79] As these members of both the Spanish and the French schools recognized, the syntax signals the crucial judicial distinction as to whether a given homicide constitutes murder or manslaughter. This distinction is forged by the law, found in the three legal strata of the Pentateuch, that grants refuge from the blood avenger to the unintentional killer but denies it to the murderer: the Covenant Code (Exod 21:12, 14 versus v. 13), the Priestly stratum (Num 35:16–21 versus vv. 22–23), and Deuteronomy (Deut 19:4–7 versus vv. 11–13). That indeed the syntax in question signals this distinction is suggested by the Priestly text that requires the community to adjudicate between the competing claims of the homicide—that it was not murder—and of the blood avenger—that the death in fact requires avenging: ושפטו העדה בין המכה ובין גאל הדם "the congregation shall adjudicate between the slayer and the blood avenger" (Num 35:24).

In the absence of witnesses or evidence, there were no rational or empirical grounds for a human ruling concerning intent or probable cause: thus, whether the case constituted murder or manslaughter. This requirement for access to a capacity for discernment that exceeds finite and empirically condi-

78. Abraham ibn Ezra, *Commentary on the Torah*, 3.266 (Hebrew; my translation).

79. R. Samuel ben Meir (Rashbam), *Commentary on the Pentateuch* (ed. David Rosin; Breslau: Schottelaender, 1881) 216 (Hebrew; my translation). This edition is frequently reprinted and is more accurate than the edition by A. I. Bromberg (1965). For a very interesting, comparative study of ibn Ezra and Samuel ben Meir, showing the emergence during the twelfth century of nonhalakhic biblical exegesis, see Martin I. Lockshin, "Tradition or Context: Two Exegetes Struggle with Peshat," *From Ancient Israel to Modern Judaism: Intellect in Quest of Understanding, Essays in Honor of Marvin Fox* (ed. Jacob Neusner, Ernest S. Frerichs, and Nahum M. Sarna; 4 vols.; BJS 159, 173–175; Atlanta: Scholars Press, 1989) 2.173–86.

tioned human knowledge is precisely what the key verb of the protasis signals: כִּי יִפָּלֵא מִמְּךָ דָבָר לַמִּשְׁפָּט "if a legal case exceeds your ken" (Deut 17:8).[80] That the case refers to one in which human reason cannot operate because it lacks all the facts is confirmed by Job's finally recanting his legal case against God on account of the overwhelming disproportion between divine and human knowledge: לָכֵן הִגַּדְתִּי וְלֹא אָבִין נִפְלָאוֹת מִמֶּנִּי וְלֹא אֵדָע "Thus I spoke without under-standing—*things too wondrous for me*, which I did not know" (Job 42:3). Job's recantation employs the same grammatical formula found in the protasis of Deut 17:8, the niphal of פלא + prepositional מִן bound to a divine or human refer-ence. As Job drops his legal case consequent upon a divine theophany, so con-versely in the context of Deut 17:8–13, in the absence of the two witnesses that would permit empirical adjudication, the legal case must be referred to the Temple for divine arbitration.

The apodosis requires that the litigants proceed to the cultic center where alone they may seek a legal ruling (Deut 17:8b–9). Scholars remain unclear about who is understood actually to travel to the cultic center to receive the judgment: the litigants themselves, to receive an oracular responsum (as in Exod 22:6–8, 9–10) or the judicial authorities responsible for trying them. The rhetoric of Deuteronomy clouds the issue, since at times the second-person-singular addressee represents the judicial authorities of the community who are respon-sible for both criminal investigation and execution (Deut 17:4–5, 8a). This might suggest that the judicial authorities, not the actual parties to the dispute, travel to the Temple to receive an advisory responsum that permits them—this needs to be assumed—to return to the local sphere to complete the legal hearing.[81]

Such an interpretation is unlikely. The litigants themselves appear before the altar. First, the legal-historical antecedent for the cultic recourse, the judi-cial oath (שְׁבֻעַת יהוה / *nīš ilim*), requires the *accused*'s self-exculpatory assev-eration in the divine presence (אֶל הָאֱלֹהִים / *ina maḫar ilim*). Second, the am-biguous second person formulation of Deut 17:9 (וּבָאתָ אֶל הַכֹּהֲנִים הַלְוִיִּם וְאֶל הַשֹּׁפֵט אֲשֶׁר יִהְיֶה בַּיָּמִים הָהֵם "you shall come to the levitical priests and the judge who shall officiate at that time") has a third-person counterpart in Deut 19:17 that removes the ambiguity: וְעָמְדוּ שְׁנֵי הָאֲנָשִׁים אֲשֶׁר לָהֶם הָרִיב לִפְנֵי יהוה לִפְנֵי הַכֹּהֲנִים וְהַשֹּׁפְטִים אֲשֶׁר יִהְיוּ בַּיָּמִים הָהֵם "the two parties to the dispute shall stand *before* Yahweh—*before* the priests and the judges who shall officiate at that time." This formulation makes clear the editor's presupposition that the litigants them-selves are present at the Temple to receive the judicial ruling. The second לִפְנֵי "before" clause constitutes a gloss upon the first. The asyndetic gloss accom-modates what may have been an older formula for the judicial oath sworn in

---

80. Note Ps 131:1. Note further הֲיִפָּלֵא מֵיהוה דָבָר "Is anything too wondrous for Yahweh?" (Gen 18:14). The latter passage is the exact antithesis of the protasis of Deut 17:8, both of which include in the formula the substantive דבר (word, case, matter, thing). In Deut 17:8 that sub-stantive has a technical legal force, whereas in Gen 18:18 it has a more general denotation. On the verb, note Weinfeld, *Deuteronomy and the Deuteronomic School*, 235 n. 1; 258–60; and Rüterswörden, *Gemeinschaft zur Gemeinde*, 44, with literature.

81. So both Mayes, *Deuteronomy*, 267, and, most recently, Rüterswörden, "Der Verfas-sungsentwurf des Deuteronomiums," 316.

an originally noncentralized cultic context (cf. Num 5:16, 18) to Deuteronomy's cultic centralization. Finally, the Deuteronomistic History knows this convention of the now centralized altar as the site of judicial oath taking. The very first petition in Solomon's Temple inauguration prayer confirms that the accused "shall come (ובא) . . . before your altar in this Temple" to swear his innocence and receive divine vindication (1 Kgs 8:31–32).

Toward a Coherent Reading of Deut 17:2–7 and 8–13

The scholarly attempts to relocate Deut 17:2–7 to chapter 13 overlook the paragraph's dialectical function. It works in conjunction with 17:8–13 to express the fundamental concern of the authors to define and frequently to redefine those activities that are legitimate in both the local and the central spheres as a consequence of centralization. The two paragraphs dialectically cohere both topically and in their terminology. The two cases interlock: they restrict the local sphere to secular legal activity (which they define through a paradigmatic empirically soluble case), and they restrict cultic recourse for ambiguous legal cases to the central sanctuary.

Just as in the case of the disputed deposit (Exod 22:6–7), the sequence of Deut 17:2–7 + 8–13 functions to establish as a coherent whole the separate conditions for lay resolution and for cultic resolution. Lay resolution of judicial disputes, as was the case with Exod 22:6b, is contingent upon evidentiary sufficiency. Deut 17:2–7 by definition satisfies this requirement. By stipulating the presence of two or more witnesses, the case leaves no room for ambiguity or legal deadlock: it is not a matter of one man's word against another's. In contrast, cultic resolution, as was the case with Exod 22:7, is required for those cases that exceed the powers of human knowledge because they require a ruling in the absence of decisive evidence, as in Deut 17:8.

The logic of the two paragraphs is dialectical. Together, Deut 17:2–7 and 17:8–13 combine to form a merism for *all* categories of judicial activity, secular and cultic. Paradoxically, however, the redactor selects in the first instance an ostensibly cultic case to define the conditions for local secular authority while, equally paradoxically, selecting in the second instance ostensibly secular cases to define the conditions for recourse to the cultic center. As such, the redactor has selected in Deut 17:2–7 the most heinous cultic offense conceivable: עבד אלהים אחרים the *sacrificial worship* of other gods (Deut 13:3, 7, 14; 17:3). Precisely that paradigmatic case, however, establishes the condition for a legitimate secular and now (in light of Deut 16:18–20) professionally conducted trial: evidentiary certainty, the corroboration of a capital accusation by means of the testimony of two witnesses. The local is thus dialectically defined as the realm of the secular. Not only capital but also cultic offenses may be tried locally—on condition that they leave no room for empirical doubt and thus require no cultic recourse.

Conversely, the sphere in which cultic law operates is similarly dialectically defined in terms of those ostensibly noncultic cases, all belonging to the realm of criminal or civil law, that do not permit empirical resolution. The two judicial venues are terminologically contrasted. The protasis defines the local realm, restricted to secular judicial procedure and the rules of evidence, by means of the metonym בשעריך "in your city-gates" (Deut 17:8a). The apodosis defines the central sphere, where alone cultic access may be granted, by means of the periphrasis for the Temple: המקום אשר יבחר יהוה אלהיך בו "the place which Yahweh your God shall choose" (Deut 17:8b).

The technical reference to the local sphere in the protasis marks this legal paragraph (Deut 17:8–13) as the direct continuation of the previous one (Deut 17:2–7) where the locus was similarly באחד שעריך "in one of your city-gates" (Deut 17:2; also the site of the execution in v. 5) and in which a profession-alized—secular—system of judicial protocol was to be instituted: שפטים ושטרים תתן לך בכל שעריך "judges and judicial officers shall you appoint in each of your city-gates" (Deut 16:18). The terminology is technical: Deuteronomy inno-vates at the local sphere—demanding judicial professionalization and secular-ization (evidentiary sufficiency defined as at minimum two witnesses for conviction in capital cases)—no less than it innovates at the central sphere, restricting all cultic activity to a single, legitimate site. The very distinction between the two spheres—topography here becomes a hermeneutical trope—is itself a Deuteronomic innovation: the local is created as exclusively the realm of the secular, cultic activity is restricted to the central sphere, as the two, both secular and cultic, become dialectically defined in terms of each other.

From the preceding analysis, it emerges that the distinction between במקום "in the place" and בשעריך/בכל שעריך "in [all] your city-gates" plays an impor-tant role in the legal corpus of Deuteronomy. These two terms are more than polar opposites and more, too, than a way for the text's redactor to organize different kinds of religious activity.[82] The distinction is not simply termino-logical or procedural but more profoundly conceptual: each reference, both the periphrasis and the metonym, functions as a trope for the cultic and the secular respectively. The interplay of the two terms embodies textual and religious transformation. That the sequence of Deut 17:2–7 + 8–13 becomes coherent only when that dialectic is grasped means that the sequence of the legal corpus reflects hermeneutical issues confronted by the text's authors as a consequence of innovation.

My argument concerning the technical terms and dialectical structure of Deut 17:2–7 + 8–13 provides additional confirmation that the literary-critical attempts to "restore" Deut 17:2–7 to chapter 13 finally break down on their own terms. That Deut 17:2–7 belongs to a different redactional stratum of the legal corpus than chapter 13 is clear on three counts. First, only in 17:2–7 is the punishment of the apostate restricted by the rule of evidentiary procedure, itself a reformulation of an original lemma found in chapter 13, as I have dem-onstrated. Second, the casuistic protasis of Deut 17:2 begins with כי "if" plus third-person-imperfect Niphal; in contrast, each of the three casuistic protases

---

82. For the former position, see Seitz, *Redaktionsgeschichtliche Studien*, 192. For the latter position, see William S. Morrow, "The Composition of Deuteronomy 14:1–17:1" (Ph.D. diss., University of Toronto, 1988) 493.

in chapter 13 begins with כִּי plus an active verb (13:2, 7, 13). Third, the technical metonym for the local sphere found throughout this unit is totally absent from Deuteronomy 13: שֹׁפְטִים וְשֹׁטְרִים תִּתֶּן לְךָ בְּכָל שְׁעָרֶיךָ "Judges and judicial officers shall you appoint *in each of your city-gates*" (Deut 16:18); דִּבְרֵי רִיבֹת בִּשְׁעָרֶיךָ "disputed cases *in your city-gates*" (Deut 17:8).

Despite the standard text-critical relocation of Deut 17:2–7 to chapter 13 for its alleged disruption of the continuity of Deut 16:18–20 with Deut 17:8–13, Deut 17:2–7 in fact shares a technical vocabulary with those two paragraphs that chapter 13 lacks. The different vocabulary involved itself militates against the transposition. Governing Deut 16:18–20, 17:2–7, and 17:8–13 is the structural distinction between the local sphere, marked by the metonym "in your gates" (Deut 16:18; 17:2, 5, 8), and the central sphere, marked by the centralization formula (Deut 17:8, 10). That structuring principle, together with its distinctive terminology, is completely absent from Deuteronomy 13. The consistent designation for the locus of the incitement to apostasy in chapter 13 is, instead, בְּקִרְבְּךָ / מִקִּרְבְּךָ "in your midst / from your midst," found in each of its three paragraphs (Deut 13:2 and 6, which form an inclusio, framing the first paragraph; v. 12, which concludes the second paragraph; and vv. 14, 15, in the third paragraph). This term is distinct from the local/central distinction that operates elsewhere; it most likely renders *ina birtukūnu* from the neo-Assyrian treaties that provide the literary model after which Deuteronomy 13 is patterned.[83] Nor can the reference in Deut 13:13 to בְּאַחַת עָרֶיךָ "in one of your cities," which is otherwise unattested in Deuteronomy, be conflated with the standard metonym elsewhere for the local sphere בְּ(כָל) שְׁעָרֶיךָ "in (all) your gates." The terms are not synonymous and have very different rhetorical functions.[84] The reference to "in one of your cities" does not function to distinguish local as opposed to central action. Instead, the reference marks the incremental progression from incitement of an individual by a prophet (13:2–6) to incitement of an individual by a family member or neighbor (13:7–12) to the successful incitement to apostasy of an entire city by a band of rogues (13:13–18).

In this context, Deut 17:2 is strikingly redundant in juxtaposing the two contrasting forms of geographic reference: בְּקִרְבְּךָ בְּאַחַד שְׁעָרֶיךָ "in your midst— in one of your gates." The redundancy suggests that the redactor of Deut 17:2–7 added his own distinctive terminology—בְּאַחַד שְׁעָרֶיךָ "in one of your gates"— to an earlier text that derived from the apostasy series of Deuteronomy 13, employing בְּקִרְבְּךָ "in your midst." Modern translations inaccurately render the duplicated reference in synchronic terms, as if the second form were appositional to the first (RSV, NEB, NJPSV, NRSV). More likely, however, the redundancy of Deut 17:2 involves the juxtaposition of two sets of terms that

---

83. Levinson, "'But You Shall Surely Kill Him!,'" 61 n. 51. To be sure, the reference with קרב "midst" is frequent in Deuteronomy; see Driver, *Deuteronomy*, lxxxiii (#58) for a complete list.

84. Contra Rose, *Der Ausschließlichkeitsanspruch Jahwes*, 43 n. 1, who assigns both terms to a single stratum, considering them synonymous. A similar position is implied by Rüterswörden, *Gemeinschaft zur Gemeinde*, 32. Dion's contextual explanation ("Deuteronomy 13," 182) conflicts with his insight on p. 156.

originally derive from separate literary strata.[85] As I have already demonstrated, the first paragraph of chapter 13, where the distinctive Deuteronomic metonym is absent, is framed by an inclusio: בקרבך/מקרבך "in your midst/from your midst" (Deut 13:2, 6). Once the redundant Deuteronomic metonym is removed, the identical inclusio frames Deut 17:2–7: [באחד שעריך] בקרבך *"in your midst* [in one of your gates]" // ובערת הרע מקרבך *"you shall purge the evil from your midst"* (Deut 17:2 // 7).[86]

This terminological analysis provides independent corroboration that Deut 17:2–7 reformulates the apostasy series of chapter 13 in two ways. First, it interpolates witness law. Second, it introduces the distinction between local (Deut 17:2–7) and central (Deut 17:8–13) judicial protocol. Justice is thereby made consistent with the structuring principle of the first section of the legal corpus, which regulated the cultus. The common structure involves local secularization and cultic centralization.

Apostasy as the Transgression against the Text

In Deuteronomy 13, the offense is consistently apostasy: the sacrificial worship of deities other than Yahweh (Deut 13:3, 7, 14).[87] At least in its present redaction, the text stands in relation to the innovation of cultic centralization (Deuteronomy 12) as point and counterpoint: the requirement of conformity to the new cultic protocol and the requirement of fidelity to Yahweh, who sponsors the new cultic regime. Together they function as a kind of primary commandment, from which all else follows.[88] Sacrifice at a single exclusive site

---

85. The juxtaposition of divergent editorial terms also points to separate redactional layers elsewhere; see the analysis of the additive על preserved alongside מלבד in Numbers 28 by Israel Knohl, "The Priestly Torah versus the Holiness School: Sabbath and the Festivals," *HUCA* 58 (1987) 89.

86. Evidence in support of this analysis is the fact that Deut 17:2 is the single case in Deuteronomy where "in one of your gates" is juxtaposed with the alternative formula "in your midst." This unique juxtaposition is the more salient because of the frequency of the metonym "in [one/each of/all] your gates," which occurs twenty-six times in Deuteronomy (Deut 12:12, 15, 17, 18, 21; 14:21, 27, 28, 29; 15:7, 22; 16:5, 11, 14, 18; 17:2, 8; 18:6; 23:17; 24:14; 26:12; 28:52, 55, 57; 31:12; and Deut 5:14 = Exod 20:10; for this list, see Driver, *Deuteronomy*, lxxix). The Septuagint translator seems to have recognized the redundancy inasmuch as it reads only one of the two terms: ἐν μιᾷ τῶν πόλεών σου "in any one of your cities."

87. Later theological redactors extended this original concern to require exclusive loyalty to Yahweh as the primary religious requirement (*das Hauptgebot*; Exod 34:14; 22:19; 23:13) and oriented it specifically on the text of the Decalogue. The most explicit allusions to the text of the Decalogue, as at Deut 13:6, seem to derive from the later theological expansions of the Deuteronomistic redactor. On Deut 13:6, see Georg Braulik, "Die Ausdrücke für 'Gesetz' im Buch Deuteronomium," *Bib* 51 (1970) 39–66; reprinted and cited after Braulik, *Studien zur Theologie des Deuteronomiums* (SBAB 2; Stuttgart: Katholisches Bibelwerk, 1988) 11–38, at p. 22. On the theological expansion see Dion, "Deuteronomy 13," 192. More generally on Deuteronomy 13 and the Decalogue, see Georg Braulik, *Deuteronomium 1–16,17* (Neue Echter Bibel 15; Würzburg: Echter Verlag, 1986) 101–102.

88. See Otto, "Legal Reforms and Reformulations," 190–91. For a diverging analysis, see Veijola, "Deuteronomium 13," 308.

has for its counterpart the exclusive loyalty owed to Yahweh. In chapter 13, the text's authors clearly drew upon the neo-Assyrian vassal treaties and transferred the penalty for disloyalty from the Assyrian overlord to Yahweh, just as they strove to replace the vassal treaty that bound Judah to Assyria with Deuteronomy itself as a new covenant binding Judah to the Great King.[89] The common punishment for enticing others into acts of disloyalty, with political sedition now reconfigured as religious apostasy, is capital. In circumstances where, by definition, there are no witnesses, even immediate summary execution—taking the law into one's own hands—is mandated: only so does the subject establish his absolute allegiance to the lord, political or divine.[90]

In contrast, in Deut 17:2–7, apostasy is now redefined. No longer is it simply a matter of worshiping other gods. Instead, apostasy becomes reinterpreted as a breach of faith with a text: the violation of the first commandment of the Decalogue. No longer is the offense the invitation to worship foreign gods (Deut 13:3, 7, 14) but rather, "if there is found in your midst, in one of your city-gates, which Yahweh your God is about to give you, a man or a woman who would do evil in the opinion of God *by transgressing his covenant* (לעבר בריתו)" (Deut 17:2). The apostate transgresses not simply against God, by worshiping other gods; the transgression is specifically against the Decalogue as the central commandment of the Torah.[91] "His covenant" (בריתו) means, for all intents and purposes, the Decalogue, already here presupposed as a text.[92] After all, it is distinctively Deuteronomy that construes the relationship between God and Israel, forged at Horeb with the proclamation of the Decalogue, in covenantal terms (Deut 4:13; 5:2).

In the following clause, the editor takes over from his source text in chapter 13 the conventional notion of apostasy as the worship of foreign deities:

---

89. On Deuteronomy 13, see Weinfeld, *Deuteronomy and the Deuteronomic School*, 91–100; and Dion, "Deuteronomy 13," 147–216. On Deuteronomy as a substitute for the vassal treaty, see R. Frankena, "The Vassal-Treaties of Esarhaddon and the Dating of Deuteronomy," *OTS* 14 (1965) 153; and A. D. H. Mayes, "On Describing the Purpose of Deuteronomy," *JSOT* 58 (1993) 13–33. The conservative scholar Meredith G. Kline, *Treaty of the Great King: The Covenant Structure of Deuteronomy* (Grand Rapids: Eerdmans, 1963) also posits the substitution but maintains the Mosaic dating of Deuteronomy. No longer tenable is the position of Rose, who rejected any direct literary influence of cuneiform material on Deuteronomy (*Der Ausschließlichkeitsanspruch Jahwes*, 28–31). See the argument made by Hans Ulrich Steymans, after a careful review of the evidence pro and con, that the curses of Deut 28:20–44 directly depend on neo-Assyrian treaties, whether in cuneiform original or Aramaic translation ("Eine assyrische Vorlage für Deuteronomium 28,20–44," in *Bundesdokument und Gesetz: Studien zum Deuteronomium* [ed. Georg Braulik; HBS 4; Freiburg: Herder, 1995] 119–41).

90. Levinson, "'But You Shall Surely Kill Him!,'" 54–63.

91. Lohfink, "Ämtergesetze," 320.

92. A number of passages refer to contraventions of the "covenant" and thereby specifically refer to breach of the first commandment of the Decalogue (Deut 4:23; 17:2; 29:24; 31:16, 20). The breach in question occurs through the worship of "other gods" (Deut 17:3; 29:25; 31:16, 20) or of their images (Deut 4:23)—precisely as forbidden by the Decalogue (Deut 5:7–8). The comments here follow the analysis provided by Braulik, "Ausdrücke für 'Gesetz,'" 15–16. In other contexts in Deuteronomy, of course, as Braulik also notes, "covenant" may not have so specific a denotation.

"and he went and worshipped them" (Deut 17:3aα; see Deut 13:3, 7, 14). In reusing that source text, the editor appends a clause that extends the original notion of apostasy to include astral worship: "and he prostrated himself before them, and to the sun or the moon or the entire heavenly host—which I did not command (אשר לא צויתי)" (Deut 17:3bβ). Moses had earlier emphasized, speaking for Yahweh to the nation, that the Decalogue constitutes "his covenant which he commanded (בריתו אשר צוה) you to do: the Ten Commandments" (Deut 4:13). Now Yahweh himself stresses that the transgression against the covenant represents "that which I did not command" (Deut 17:3b).[93] The divine voice represents the incursion into the text of the perspective of the Deuteronomistic editors, who construe the Decalogue, in addition to the legal corpus, as the covenant. It is they who represent apostasy as breach of the covenant that they have forged between the nation and its God: the text of Deuteronomy, whose redactors and defenders they are.

The Dialectic of Coherence

Just as the coherence of Deut 17:2–7 + 8–13 is dialectical, so, more broadly, does this section of the legal corpus, concerned with justice, cohere dialectically with the previous section, concerned with the cult. In both cases, the primary concern of the text's authors is to confront the implications of centralization for sacrifice as well as for justice. It is not simply conventional practice that must be revised but also formerly authoritative texts that must be reformulated. The transition from the first section of the legal corpus, concerned with the cultus, to the present section, concerned with judicial procedure, is therefore not "abrupt."[94] Precisely at the point of transition, the editors deliberately interweave the two subject areas, cultus and justice, in order to mark their inner coherence:

---

93. The identity of the first person speaker of that negative command formula is ambiguous. Normally Moses is the primary speaker in the legal corpus and refers to Yahweh in the third person, as in the immediately preceding reference to "his covenant" (Deut 17:2). Further suggesting that Moses remains the speaker here is that the negative command alludes to an earlier warning against astral worship by Moses: "[Beware] lest you raise your eyes heavenward and see the sun and the moon and the stars, the entire heavenly host, and be thrust away and prostrate yourself before them and worship them" (Deut 4:19a). (See Dieter Eduard Skweres, *Die Rückverweise im Buch Deuteronomium* [AnBib 79; Rome: Pontifical Biblical Institute, 1979] 73.) That passage is a Deuteronomistic meditation upon the first commandment of the Decalogue. (See Georg Braulik, *Die Mittel deuteronomischer Rhetorik erhoben aus Deuteronomium 4,1–40* [AnBib 68; Rome: Pontifical Biblical Institute, 1978].) Nonetheless, other evidence argues in favor of Yahweh as the speaker of this interjection. The phrase "which I did not command" is otherwise absent in Deuteronomy but occurs in Deuteronomistic material in the prophetical books (Jer 7:31; 19:5; 32:35, in each case in connection with worship at the high places and child sacrifice), where it is explicitly presented as direct Yahwistic speech. This consideration seems the more decisive, and the formula in Deut 17:2 seems to mark a direct interjection by Yahweh into the speech of Moses.

94. Contra Lohfink, "Ämtergesetze," 306.

A   Cultus (Deut 12:1–16:17)
B   Justice (Deut 16:18–20)
A′   Cultus (Deut 16:21–17:1)
B′   Justice (Deut 17:2–7 + 8–13)

This redactional bridge was first discovered by Udo Rüterswörden.[95] Georg Braulik elaborated this insight, demonstrating how elegantly the editors of the legal corpus reprise key terms and motifs as they make the transition from cultic law (Deut 12:1–16:17) to the *Ämtergesetze* "Laws of Office-holders" (Deut 16:18–18:22).[96] He showed how the redactional bridge at Deut 16:21–17:1 both repeats and anticipates key terms of the preceding and following blocs of law. At the same time, this very emphasis on the redactional bridge and the recurrence of language only raises the larger problem of textual coherence more forcefully. By focusing on these technical connections, Rüterswörden and Braulik have unintentionally perpetuated the notion that there was no substantive coherence between the two major sections of the legal corpus. In effect, the connection was comprehended as merely external: a formal redactional lattice whose parts overlap but do not truly join.

In contrast, the connection between the two sections of the legal corpus is actually substantive and intellectual. The redactional bridge establishes their dialectical relation. In both sections, the text's editors have a single, constant concern: to work out the implications, both practical and hermeneutical, of centralization. They justify their innovations by exegetically transforming prior Israelite texts, preeminently the Covenant Code. The topical shift to address the judicial and public personnel therefore marks no disjunction from the preceding section of the legal corpus but rather represents a logical consequence of the Deuteronomic program of centralization. Deuteronomy's innovation is accordingly not simply a matter of cultic unity and purity (*Einheit und Reinheit*), as conventionally understood, nor is it one that is addressed only in the first section of the legal corpus. The authors work out the implications of centralization not only for sacrifice and the cultic calendar but also for judicial procedure and the public administration, both of which are transformed. The text mandates centralization as the constitutive feature of Israelite life: that charter accounts for the coherence of this section with the previous one.[97]

---

95. Rüterswörden, *Gemeinschaft zur Gemeinde*, 30 (seeing the initial unit only as Deut 14:22–16:17).

96. Braulik, *Die deuteronomischen Gesetze*, 46–61.

97. I concede a methodological difficulty, the resolution of which requires further research. On the one hand, the evidence gathered here calls into question the notion that a redactionally distinct and independent unit of the legal corpus begins with Deut 16:18, as proponents of the block model maintain (see the compelling arguments of Otto, "Gerichtsordnung," 152). To the contrary, the new unit continues to elaborate the Deuteronomic agenda of centralization. On the other hand, assigning Deut 17:2–7 to a later stratum than Deuteronomy 13 approximates one part of the block model analysis (which has not systematically addressed the literary relation of the two texts), although I disagree that Deut 17:2–7 is exilic in its orientation. Hence the difficulty: Is Deut 17:2–7 Deuteronomistic because, in my analysis, it is a later stratum than Deut 13:7–12? Or is it, on substantive grounds, Deuteronomic, because it furthers the Deu-

The transformation of public life was indeed utopian, as Lohfink contends, in subordinating each office to the ultimate authority of Torah. At the same time, however, the program was also profoundly practical, pointedly departing from the legal model provided by the Covenant Code to address the judicial and administrative structure of public life systematically. To that extent, the old literary critical label of this unit as concerned with the theocratic administration may justifiably be reclaimed and reconciled with the newer model of the unit as an ideal draft constitution. It is both simultaneously, not originally one and then secondarily the other.[98] The Deuteronomic agenda is thus both cultic and judicial, both utopian and practical; it is concerned both with the rewriting of texts and with the transformation of public life. The deliberateness of this program is such that, just as the two paragraphs concerned with local and central judicial procedure mutually interlock (Deut 17:2–7 and 17:8–13), so, too, on different grounds, does the paragraph concerned with judicial procedure at the central sanctuary (Deut 17:8–13) interlock with the law of the king (17:14–20). Just as the former deliberately makes no mention of the king, so the latter grants the monarch no judicial responsibilities. The radical transformations involved in each case point to the further consequences of the Deuteronomic program of centralization.

---

teronomic program? At the present time, there are no easy answers to this dilemma. Indeed, an additional question must be raised about the criteria altogether for distinguishing between Deuteronomic and Deuteronomistic layers. If, as Dion contends, the apostasy laws of both Deuteronomy 13 and 17:2–7 are Deuteronomistic, why does the Deuteronomistic Historian allude to neither in his condemnation of Jeroboam for having created a cult for the worship of "other gods" (1 Kgs 14:9; cf. 1 Kgs 12:28; see Knoppers, *Two Nations under God*, 2.245)?

98. In other words, the unit was not only practical originally, in a Deuteronomic redaction ascribed to the Josianic period, and then secondarily theologized by the Deuteronomist during the Babylonian Exile, as Rütersworden has suggested (*Gemeinschaft zur Gemeinde*, 94–111). On this point, see the important review by Norbert Lohfink, *TLZ* 113 (1988) 426. From a fresh perspective informed by his work on cuneiform law, Eckart Otto has adopted this model of a two-stage redaction. He argues that in its first, preexilic, Deuteronomic redaction, the legal corpus represented a programmatic legal reform, involving matters of cult, justice, and family law, which was then secondarily revised to become a Deuteronomistic draft constitution for the postexilic community ("Von der Programmschrift einer Rechtsreform zum Verfassungsentwurf des Neuen Israel: Die Stellung des Deuteronomiums in der Rechtsgeschichte Israels," in *Bundesdokument und Gesetz: Studien zum Deuteronomium* [ed. Georg Braulik; HBS 4; Freiburg: Herder, 1995] 92–104). That argument hangs, however, on his assertion of a Deuteronomic core common to both Deuteronomy 13 and 17:2–7, both of which he views as essential to the redactional structure of the Deuteronomic law code. With that premise called into question (see n. 58), the deft reconstruction of two separate redactions and their separate application becomes problematic. Moreover, it is confusing that, in a programmatic legal reform so closely tied to Josiah, there should be no mention whatsoever of the role of the king (see Otto, "Vom Bundesbuch zum Deuteronomium," 266–67). Otto's redactional reconstruction, which denies any Deuteronomic law of the king, is thereby logically inconsistent with his historical claim that the original version of the legal corpus constituted a far-reaching, Josianic cultic, judicial, and legal reform document.

The Eclipse of Royal Judicial Authority (Deut 17:14–20)

In installing a professionalized judiciary at the city gate (Deut 16:18), the authors of Deuteronomy pointedly oust the clan elders from their conventional role as the mediators of judicial authority, precisely in that site. The same issue arises with respect to the Deuteronomic transformation of justice in the central sphere. The Deuteronomic assertion in Deut 17:8–13 that the central sanctuary grants access to supreme judicial authority involves a striking suppression of an alternate conception preserved by other literary sources. How different, for example, is the ideology of the royal psalms: אלהים משפטיך למלך תן וצדקתך לבן מלך "O God, grant the king your judgments; the king's son, your righteousness!" (Ps 72:1). Indeed, that the monarch has a divinely appointed role in the administration of justice represents the standard notion of the literature of the Near East. For example, both in Psalm 72:2, 4 and in Hammurapi's prologue the monarch functions to guarantee a fair trial for the poor, to protect the disadvantaged, and to destroy those who oppress the unprotected.[99] Although in ancient Israel, which understands its law to be divine in origin, the king does not author law, in the context of cuneiform legal history the authority to promulgate law is distinctly monarchic. The great second-millennium cuneiform legal collections attribute the text to a royal speaker.[100]

Although it lies beyond the scope of this volume to provide a detailed reconstruction of the role of the monarch in the Israelite system of justice, a number of points are appropriate to make in light of the impact of Deuteronomy's innovations upon the sequence of topics in chapter 17. Conventionally the monarch represented the supreme legal authority, arbiter, and appellate court.[101] The historiographic sources establish that the king inherits not simply the military function of the judges—leading the tribes in war—but also their judicial role of arbitrating legal disputes (Judg 4:4–5; 1 Sam 7:15–17). So central is the king to the administration of justice that the narratives concerning the establishment of the monarchy give priority to the motif of justice over the more likely historical cause for the institution of kingship, the Philistine threat. Indeed, although the conflicting promonarchical and antimonarchical traditions concerning the founding of the Israelite kingship have long been recognized, there is a striking additional inconsistency that is less widely noted. The redactional incorporation of the Ark Narrative (1 Sam 4:1–7:2) into

---

99. See Roth, *Law Collections*, 76, for the Akkadian and an English translation of the relevant section of the prologue to Hammurapi's Laws (col. 1, ll. 27–39).

100. See Moshe Greenberg, "Some Postulates of Biblical Criminal Law," in *Yehezkel Kaufmann Jubilee Volume* (ed. M. Haran; Jerusalem: Magnes, 1960) 5–28; reprinted in Greenberg, *Studies in the Bible and Jewish Thought* (Philadelphia: JPS, 1995) 25–50.

101. On the judicial function of the king see Roland de Vaux, *Ancient Israel* (London: Darton, Longman & Todd, 1961) 150–52; G. C. Macholz, "Die Stellung des Königs in der israelitischen Gerichtsverfassung," *ZAW* 84 (1972) 157–82; Boecker, *Law and the Administration of Justice*, 40–49; Whitelam, *The Just King*; and Marc Zvi Brettler, *God Is King: Understanding an Israelite Metaphor* (JSOTSup 76; Sheffield: Sheffield Academic Press, 1989) 109–13. In addition to his judicial function, the king also played an important military, executive, and cultic role. For a reconstruction, see de Vaux, *Ancient Israel*, 100–114, 150–52; 376–77.

the account of Samuel's birth and career (1 Sam 1–3; 7:3–17) underscores the extent to which the Philistine threat necessitated the defensive shift from the ad hoc leadership of the "judges" to a monarchy, modeled after the Canaanite city-state, with an attendant standing army. That redactional analysis of the origins of the monarchy largely conforms to modern historical reconstructions; it was a direct response to the expansion of the technologically more advanced Philistines from the coastal littoral into the Shephelah and the hill country of central Judah and Samaria. Nonetheless, an alternative analysis presents the popular demand for a king as filling a judicial, not a military, vacuum. Despite Samuel's exemplary dispensation of justice in his role as circuit-court judge, the sons whom he appoints in his old age fail to follow in his footsteps (1 Sam 8:1–4) and are indicted by the Deuteronomistic Historian for their corruption. In this narrative, all Israel's elders converge upon Samuel at Ramah to request a king as a supreme *judicial* authority, to fill the legal vacuum created by his bribe-taking sons: עתה שׂימה לנו מלך לשׁפטנו "Therefore, appoint a king for us *to dispense justice for us*" (1 Sam 8:5; cf. v. 6).[102]

The narrator's analysis of the founding of the monarchy as a direct response to the failure of Samuel's sons to perform their roles as judges has further support. The Deuteronomistic Historian exegetically appropriates Deut 16:19— the moralizing admonitions directed to judges (which are themselves a Deuteronomic adaptation of Exod 23:6, 8).[103] Thus Deut 16:19 exhorts: לא תטה משׁפט לא תכיר פנים ולא תקח שׁחד ... "*You shall not pervert justice*, you shall not show partiality, *you shall not take bribes . . .*" The Deuteronomistic Historian applies those lemmas to Samuel's sons in the context of their inheriting Samuel's judicial functions (1 Sam 8:1–2). Indeed, the key terms of the lemma from Deut 16:19 are cited chiastically, according to Seidel's law, and the negative commands of the original are rendered in the converted imperfect to signal accomplished—if illicit—fact: ולא הלכו בניו בדרכו ויטו אחרי הבצע ויקחו שׁחד ויטו משׁפט "They did not follow in his footsteps; rather, they sought their own advantage, *they accepted bribes and perverted justice*" (1 Sam 8:3). The indictment of Samuel's sons by the Deuteronomistic Historian echoes the language of Deut 16:19 and is arguably an exegetical adaptation of it to establish their absolute failure to conform to the requirements expected of judges.[104] The new mon-

102. The Hebrew verb can also denote "to rule" or "to govern," but the context favors the judicial denotation here. For a review of the various attempts to clarify the sense of the verb in this verse, see Lyle M. Eslinger, *Kingship of God in Crisis* (Bible and Literature Series 10; Sheffield: Almond, 1985) 254–58.

103. Weinfeld, *Deuteronomy and the Deuteronomic School*, 244–45. Braulik (*Die deuteronomischen Gesetze*, 51 n. 19) and Otto ("Rechtsreformen," 269 n. 96) each refute the argument made by Rüterswörden (*Gemeinschaft zur Gemeinde*, 21–22) that textual dependence does not exist in this case. Schwienhorst-Schönberger's recent reverse claim that Deut 16:19 serves as the source of Exod 23:8 is unconvincing (*Bundesbuch*, 387–88). If, following his analysis, the source text (Deut 16:19) and the interpolation in the Covenant Code (Exod 23:8) are both Deuteronomistic, there is no reason for the interpolation to delete the wisdom motif of its source.

104. Braulik (*Die deuteronomischen Gesetze*, 48–49) argues in contrast that Deut 16:19 presupposes 1 Sam 8:3, as does Buchholz (*Ältesten Israels*, 88–89). Braulik's not considering

arch thus functions in the first instance to dispense justice and only in the second instance to lead the nation in war (1 Sam 8:20).[105]

That the monarch exercises supreme judicial authority is evident not simply in the account of the founding of the monarchy but throughout the Deuteronomistic History. David and Solomon directly and by delegation heard complex legal cases and entertained judicial appeals. Royal prerogative even entitled the monarch to pardon a capital offense that would otherwise require execution by the blood avenger (2 Sam 14:1–24). David is presented as both public prosecutor and judge in Nathan's parable of the ewe lamb, whereby David unwittingly convicts himself of a capital offense (2 Sam 12:1–14). Absalom's designs to exercise supreme judicial authority are no less a usurping assault on his father's throne (2 Sam 15:4) than his subsequent claim on his father's concubines (2 Sam 16:20–22).[106] The king's judicial function, as presupposed by the narratives, is not restricted to being either a final court of appeal (as in the case of the woman from Tekoa in 2 Sam 14:1–24) or a protector of the poor (as in the case of the ewe lamb in 2 Sam 12:1–14). Included among the monarch's judicial functions is the resolution of ambiguous legal cases in which there are no witnesses and in which there exist no empirical criteria for deciding between the competing claims of the two litigants. In other words, the type of cases that, according to both the cuneiform and biblical legal collections, might normally be relegated to a local sanctuary for oracular resolution were remanded to the monarch for his adjudication, according to these narratives.

In his typology of ideal kingship, the Deuteronomistic Historian gives clear priority to such judicial insight over more conventional attributes, such as military leadership. Thus, in the prayer that he attributes to Solomon at the high place of Gibeon, Solomon concedes that he is too inexperienced to lead the nation in war (ואנכי נער קטן לא אדע צאת ובא) but prays, not for martial competence, but for judicial wisdom: ונתת לעבדך לב שמע לשפט את עמך להבין בין טוב לרע "Grant your servant a discerning heart to judge your people and to distinguish between good and bad" (1 Kgs 3:7b, 9a). The fulfillment of the prayer is redactionally illustrated as the Deuteronomistic Historian deftly incorporates

---

the other direction of influence, as suggested here, seems to derive from a set of prior assumptions. He maintains a distinctive block model theory of the redactional history of the legal corpus, according to which Deut 16:18–18:22 represents a late exilic Deuteronomistic stratum, one significantly later than Deut 12:2–16:17. That model, along with others, is still being actively debated in the scholarship. For a critique of Buchholz, see Rüterswörden, "Der Verfassungsentwurf des Deuteronomiums," 317–18.

105. It is curious that Samuel, in responding to the people's request, completely ignores their legitimate concern with judicial probity. He remains completely silent about it, neither acknowledging the corruption of his sons (1 Sam 8:3–4) nor suggesting an alternative form of judicial and military leadership that might satisfy the people's legitimate needs. So concerned is he—or the Deuteronomistic Historian—to point out the abuse of power that he associates with the kingship (1 Sam 8:10–18) that he allows the issue of justice to fall by the wayside.

106. The same assault occurs in the Ugaritic *Kirta* epic (*KTU* 1.16.6:41–54); note Gary N. Knoppers, "Dissonance and Disaster in the Legend of Kirta," *JAOS* 114 (1994) 572–82.

an older tale of two prostitutes who test the acuity of an unnamed king (1 Kgs 3:16–28). The king, now contextually Solomon, is glorified for his "divine wisdom in executing justice" (1 Kgs 3:28). In this idealization of the king in terms of his judicial wisdom, the Deuteronomistic Historian draws extensively on standard Near Eastern royal ideology.[107]

The Israelite and Near Eastern convention that makes the king, historically speaking, central to the administration of justice points to a double anomaly, textually speaking, in the present section of the legal corpus. First, in Deut 17:8–13, the locus for supreme judicial authority is the Temple and its officials. Not a word is said about the monarch, the expected arbiter of judicial authority. Just as in Deut 16:18, where the Deuteronomic authors treat the city gate as if it were a tabula rasa without the elders as its conventional legal historical occupants, so in Deut 17:8–13 they rewrite literary history in designating the central sanctuary—markedly to the exclusion of the Israelite king—as the exclusive source of judicial authority in the central sphere.

Second, in the following unit, Deut 17:14–20, which specifies the duties of the king, not a word is said about his traditional judicial function. Just as Deut 17:8–13 restricts judicial recourse in the central sphere to the cultus, ignoring the role of the king, so does the paragraph devoted to the king suppress just those royal attributes that arguably represented the monarch's greatest source of dignity. Indeed, the depiction of the functions of the king in this unit serves far more to hamstring him than to permit him to exercise any meaningful authority whatsoever. After the introductory specification that the king should not be a foreigner (vv. 14–15), five prohibitions specify what the king should *not* do (vv. 16–17). There remains for the king but a single positive duty: while sitting demurely on his throne to "read each day of his life" from the very Torah scroll that delimits his powers (vv. 18–20). In Deuteronomy's presentation, the king is reduced to a mere titular figurehead of the state, more restricted than potent, more otiose than exercising real military, judicial, executive, and cultic function.[108] The one potent authority is the Torah—the text of Deuteronomy 5–28[109]—in whose original reception,

---

107. Noting this point and showing how Solomon is redactionally aggrandized in conventional Near Eastern terms as possessing superior skills of royal administration as well as encyclopaedic wisdom (1 Kgs 4:1–19; 5:7–8; 5:9–14) is Gary N. Knoppers, *Two Nations under God: The Deuteronomistic History of Solomon and the Dual Monarchies* (2 vols.; HSM 52–53; Atlanta: Scholars Press, 1993–94) 1.83–87. Knoppers extends this analysis to argue that the Deuteronomistic Historian, in aggrandizing Solomon, revamps the Deuteronomic law of the king; see his "The Deuteronomist and the Deuteronomic Law of the King: A Reexamination of a Relationship," *ZAW* 108 (1966) 329–46.

108. Note the interesting suggestion by Christa Schäfer-Lichtenberger that the contraction of royal authority corresponds to a reciprocal realignment of prophetic authority in Deut 18:9–22; see her *Josua und Salomo: Eine Studie zu Autorität und Legitimität des Nachfolgers im Alten Testament* (VTSup 58; Leiden: E. J. Brill, 1994) 103–106. Her approach extends the observations of Lohfink concerning the subordination of all offices to the authority of the Torah ("Ämtergesetze," 313–22).

109. Lohfink, "Ämtergesetze," 318, argues that this is the meaning of the term for the Deuteronomistic author of this passage. Note also Braulik, "Die Ausdrücke für 'Gesetz,'" 36–38.

formulation, transcription, and implementation Deuteronomy's king plays no role whatsoever.

The double anomaly of textual content in each case points to a correlative anomaly of textual sequence. Despite the conventional view that the topic of Deut 16:18–18:22 is "Office-bearers of the theocracy,"[110] the text's sequence does not reflect a concern with administrative organization alone. Were such the case, the textual sequence would be expected to follow the officeholder's rank within the organizational hierarchy and proceed most logically from the officeholder at the top of the hierarchy to the official with the least authority. Indeed, this principle of organizing legal paragraphs in a sequence that reflects social rank, from higher to lower, has long been recognized within Israelite and cuneiform legal collections.[111] Were the arrangement here one of ascending order, the king, not the prophet, would logically be found at the apex of the series; were the order descending, local judicial officals would be found at the end, not the beginning, of the series. The actual arrangement of topics within this unit thus conforms neither to an ascending nor to a descending organization of the administration: local judiciary (Deut 16:18–20; 17:2–7), central justice (Deut 17:8–13), monarch (17:14–20), priests (18:1–8), prophets (18:9–22). Nor are alternative proposals to explain the arrangement convincing.[112] The anomalous arrangement of the text forces a reconsideration of its topical focus, as conventionally understood.

The disorder starts to become intelligible with the recognition that the sequence and selection of topics reflect the authors' drawing the consequences of centralization for both judicial and public administration. Deuteronomy's cultic center eclipses the king both in textual priority (since Deut 17:8–13 precedes 17:14–20) and in claiming supreme judicial authority at royal expense. The centralized cultus usurps the place—textual as well as hierarchical—more conventionally ascribed to the monarch. At the same time, the very retention of the king in this unit, in second place after the account of the centralized judiciary but before the section dealing with the priests (18:1–8), is

110. Driver, *Deuteronomy*, 135, 199, 206; nearly identically, Mayes, *Deuteronomy*, 261–62.

111. In the Israelite context, note the sequence of the goring ox laws in the Covenant Code: death of male or female *adult* (Exod 21:28–30), death of male or female *minor* (Exod 21:31), death of male or female *slave* (Exod 21:32). See Kaufman, "The Structure of the Deuteronomic Law," 116–17, 132–33, 135, 141. On this principle of arrangement within cuneiform law see Petschow, "Systematik," 146–72.

112. Rüterswörden, *Gemeinschaft zur Gemeinde*, 92–93 discovered another principle of organization: according to their means of designation. He proposes that the degree of human involvement in the selection and appointment of the officials decreases steadily as the office becomes one over which God has increasingly sole right of appointment and disposition. Here, the office of prophet logically concludes and anchors the series. Braulik, *Die deuteronomischen Gesetze*, 54–61, elaborates Rüterswörden's idea, suggesting that the officials are also introduced chronologically according to their historical origin. His claim of chronological arrangement, however, problematically associates the professional judiciary of Deut 16:18 with the premonarchic "judge" (p. 55), which was rather an office of ad hoc tribal leadership.

intelligible only in light of the monarch's former role in the judicial system.[113] The resequencing reflects the strategy of the text's authors: they divest the king of his judicial authority and reassign it to the Temple. The authors of Deuteronomy grant pride of place, both judicially and textually, to the cultic center.

113. Lohfink, "Ämtergesetze," 308.

5

The Revisionary Hermeneutics of Deuteronomy

The authors of Deuteronomy radically transformed the religion and society of ancient Judah. The innovation of cultic centralization profoundly changed sacrificial procedure, the festival calendar, judicial procedure, and public administration, including the monarchy. The new vision was as much political as it was religious. It led to a massive reallocation of power and authority, both centrally and locally. At one end of the social spectrum, power relations in the central sphere were reorganized, as the Temple became the exclusive site for cultic activity and consequently usurped even the role of the monarch as the final arbiter of problematic legal cases. At the other end of the spectrum, the authors of Deuteronomy also completely restructured the local sphere. They disrupted the conventional structures of clan piety, based around the local sanctuaries, which they abolished. They displaced the elders from their traditional role in judicial procedure and thereby abrogated their role as mediators of clan values tied to precedent and to continuity with the past. The authors of Deuteronomy also intruded directly into the private domicile. They wrested the original blood rite of Passover out of the hands of the paterfamilias, who was required, instead, to conform to the new demand that Passover be celebrated at the Temple as a pilgrimage sacrifice.

The authors of Deuteronomy sought to eliminate any vestige of popular piety that could jeopardize their new vision of a homogeneous public cultus. Private religion became a matter of public policy in a way that was uncommon in the otherwise religiously tolerant ancient Near East. The authors of Deuteronomy broke down the barriers between public and private and between national and popular religion. In doing so, they directed intense scrutiny toward the family. If you are incited to apostasy—even if by "your brother, your own mother's son, or your son or your daughter, or the wife of your bosom, or your friend who is like yourself"—you must extinguish all feelings of mercy and summarily kill the inciter (Deut 13:7–10). The author of this text converted a demand for absolute political allegiance owed the monarch in neo-Assyrian loyalty oaths, which he used as a source,[1] into a requirement for religious loyalty to the divine Sovereign—but thereby also for religious uniformity. In practical terms, the law established the Deuteronomic Torah as exclusive arbiter of religious authority. It stands to reason that the threat addressed by this law is not restricted to incitement to worship other gods. From the vantage point of the text's authors, heterodoxy included the worship of Yahweh in ways contrary to those prescribed by Deuteronomy—including former Israelite orthodoxy. The law might then conceivably be applied to adherents of traditional Israelite religion who resisted the revisionist program of Deuteronomy: to someone, for example, who sought piously to celebrate the paschal slaughter in the conventional way or who wished to worship Yahweh at one of the local sanctuaries, as envisioned by the altar law of the Covenant Code but prohibited by Deuteronomy.

The authors of Deuteronomy silenced competing—and prior—claims to cultural and religious authority. There is no prophecy—not even that performed by a prophet whose oracles are fulfilled, the conventional touchstone of a prophet's authenticity—but that which conforms to the norms of the Deuteronomic Torah (Deut 13:2–6). The text's authors claimed the right to determine what constitutes true prophecy and what does not. Since the authors were most likely professional scribes associated with Josiah's court, these claims to arbitrate prophecy become ironic, if not audacious. That the authors took the additional step of ascribing the mantle of prophetic authority to their own literary composition by making Moses their pseudepigraphic spokesman only adds to the boldness of the maneuver. They disenfranchised conventional norms of prophecy while asserting the prophetic authority of their own authorial voice.[2]

1. See Moshe Weinfeld, *Deuteronomy and the Deuteronomic School* (Oxford: Clarendon, 1972) 97–100; Paul E. Dion, "Deuteronomy 13: The Suppression of Alien Religious Propaganda in Israel during the Late Monarchical Era," in *Law and Ideology in Monarchic Israel* (ed. Baruch Halpern and Deborah W. Hobson; JSOTSup 124; Sheffield: JSOT Press, 1991) 147–216; and Bernard M. Levinson, "'But You Shall Surely Kill Him!': The Text-Critical and Neo-Assyrian Evidence for MT Deut 13:10," in *Bundesdokument und Gesetz: Studien zum Deuteronomium* (ed. Georg Braulik; HBS 4; Freiburg: Herder, 1995) 54–63. On the intentional Deuteronomic transformation of the neo-Assyrian material, see Bernard M. Levinson, "Recovering the Lost Original Meaning of ולא תכסה עליו (Deuteronomy 13:9)," *JBL* 115 (1996) 615–18.

2. The position taken here challenges the more standard view of the relation between Deuteronomy and prophecy, which emphasizes the continuity between the two. The classical literary critics early in this century often stressed this closeness for apologetic reasons: if the Moses of Deuteronomy could no longer be viewed as an ancient lawgiver, he could be somewhat rehabilitated, now seen as reconfiguring older law in light of prophetic morality; see S. R. Driver, *Deuteronomy* (ICC; 3d ed.; Edinburgh: T. & T. Clark, 1901) xlvii, lvi–lxii. More recent scholarship has formulated the matter in different terms, with the widely held view that Deuteronomy preserves northern prophetic traditions and originates within northern prophetic circles. See E. W. Nicholson, *Deuteronomy and Tradition* (Philadelphia: Fortress, 1967) 69–82; H. Louis Ginsberg, *The Israelian Heritage of Judaism* (New York: Jewish Theological Seminary of America, 1982) 19–24; and Moshe Weinfeld, *Deuteronomy 1–11* (AB 5; New York: Doubleday, 1991) 44–57. Marking a different approach that emphasizes Deuteronomy's trans-

Just as profoundly as they transformed religion and society, the authors of Deuteronomy transformed Israelite literary history. The absence of precedent—of legal and textual justification for their departure from convention—forced the authors of Deuteronomy paradoxically to seek sanction for their new composition from the very literary corpus that they simultaneously displaced. In order to implement and justify the innovation of centralization, they tendentiously revised and expanded the Covenant Code. They forcibly derived their departure from authoritative or prestigious texts from those texts themselves, now redeployed in a major new literary composition. The beginning of Deuteronomy, textually speaking, was therefore the conflict between the Deuteronomic program of centralization and the literary patrimony of its authors, between innovation and the constraints imposed by the existence of those texts.

The way the authors of Deuteronomy chose to give literary expression to their program is remarkable. Given the conflict between the innovation of centralization and the preexisting text of the Covenant Code, a number of literary options were at hand within ancient Israel and the broader Near East. The authors of Deuteronomy could have enacted their legal reform using the technique of the editor of the Hittite Laws, for example, who, when it became necessary to amend older laws, explicitly qualified them as obsolete and as now superceded by a new penalty.[3] More important, they could have chosen sim-

---

formation of conventional prophecy is Joseph Blenkinsopp, *Prophecy and Canon: A Contribution to the Study of Jewish Origins* (Notre Dame: University of Notre Dame Press, 1977) 39–46. See also Blenkinsopp, *The Pentateuch: An Introduction to the First Five Books of the Bible* (New York: Doubleday, 1992) 216–17 for a succinct critique of the claims concerning the prophetic authorship of Deuteronomy.

3. The distinction between the obsolete and the new penalty was technically marked. "Formerly" they would do (*karū*) . . . but "now" (*kinuna*) they do . . . This formula occurs in the Hittite Laws, §§ 7, 9, 19, 25, 51, 54, 57, 58, 59, 63, 67, 69, 81, 91, 92, 94, 101, 119, 121, 122, 123 (fragmentary text), 129, 166–167. On the legal reform involved, see Bernard M. Levinson, "The Human Voice in Divine Revelation: The Problem of Authority in Biblical Law," in *Innovation in Religious Traditions* (ed. Michael A. Williams, Collett Cox, and Martin S. Jaffee; Religion and Society 31; Berlin: Mouton de Gruyter, 1992) 41–43; and the articles by Raymond Westbrook ("What Is the Covenant Code?"), Samuel Greengus ("Some Issues Relating to the Comparability of Laws and the Coherence of the Legal Tradition"), and Eckart Otto ("Aspects of Legal Reforms and Reformulations in Ancient Cuneiform and Israelite Law"), all in *Theory and Method in Biblical and Cuneiform Law: Revision, Interpolation and Development* (ed. Bernard M. Levinson; JSOTSup 181; Sheffield: Sheffield Academic Press, 1994) 22–28, 62–72, 175–82. For the text, see J. Friedrich, *Die hethitischen Gesetze: Transkription, Übersetzung, sprachliche Erläuterung und vollstandiges Wörterverzeichnis* (Documenta et monumenta orientis antiqui 7; 2d ed.; Leiden: E. J. Brill, 1971) 17–21; and, in the most recent translation, Harry A. Hoffner, Jr., "Hittite," in *Law Collections from Mesopotamia and Asia Minor* (ed. and trans. Martha T. Roth; SBLWAW 6; Atlanta: Scholars Press, 1995) 213–47. For suggestive parallels to the Hittite formulary in Rabbinic and Roman law, see Martin S. Jaffee, "The Taqqanah in Tannaitic Literature: Jurisprudence and the Construction of Rabbinic Memory," *JJS* 41 (1990) 204–25.

ply to update the Covenant Code by means of reworking and interpolation.[4] After all, the Covenant Code betrays extended evidence of just such reworking, revision, interpolation, and exegetical activity, much of which preceded the composition of Deuteronomy. The authors of Deuteronomy might more easily have inserted the necessary revisions and corrections directly into the Covenant Code, rather than create an entirely new literary and legal composition. Indeed, certain didactic, theological, and ethical expansions within the Covenant Code and the legal narratives of Exodus (12:24–27a; 13:3–16) betray such an affinity to Deuteronomy that they are labeled "proto-Deuteronomic." If these expansions represent the first literary expression of a scribal group that may later have composed Deuteronomy itself, that only sharpens the question: why did they not merely continue in the more conventional vein?[5] Why did they choose instead to compose an entirely new text?

Why, in other words, does Deuteronomy exist at all? The answer in large measure, of course, is that the transformation of Israelite law and religion called for by Deuteronomy was so profound that simply embedding new material in a preexisting text could not accomplish the necessary changes. Something much more systematic was necessary, because the gap between old text and new need was too great to be spanned by mere ad hoc interpolations.[6] The familiar social world had been irrevocably altered. In response to the neo-Assyrian ravages, Hezekiah had radically transformed Judaean life, desacralizing the countryside and disrupting the established clan lineages and the conventional structures of rural authority, which he replaced with an urbanized, centralized political administration. Recourse to older sureties could no longer suffice; the Covenant Code derived from an entirely different, decentralized social world and could not be made relevant. There was no place in it for a systematic treatment of the cultus or of judicial and political administration, including the monarchy, the priesthood, and the institution of prophecy. What was essential was an entirely new document to accommodate the unprecedented scope of the authors' vision. Moreover, a new literary form was also called for. Deuteronomy, stylized as a treaty between Yahweh and the nation of Israel, abrogated and replaced the political treaty or loyalty oath (*adê*) that had hitherto made Judah the vassal of the neo-Assyrian Empire. The authors of Deuteronomy turned that treaty form against its inventors and made the genre of subjugation an instrument of freedom, both religious and political.

---

4. Frank Crüsemann, *Die Tora: Theologie und Sozialgeschichte des alttestamentlichen Gesetzes* (Munich: Chr. Kaiser, 1992) 235.

5. The expansions in the Covenant Code are pre-Deuteronomic; see Norbert Lohfink, "Gibt es eine deuteronomistische Bearbeitung im Bundesbuch?," *Pentateuchal and Deuteronomistic Studies: Papers Read at the XIIIth IOSOT Congress Leuven 1989* (ed. C. Brekelmans and J. Lust; BETL 94; Louvain: Peeters Press / University Press, 1990) 91–113. On Exod 12:24–27a and 13:3–16, see chapter 3, notes 27, 50.

6. Eckart Otto, *Theologische Ethik des Alten Testaments* (Theologische Wissenschaft 3.2; Stuttgart: W. Kohlhammer, 1994) 181.

But resolving the matter in this way presses yet another question: If a new book, why a new book that looks like an old book? Whether the Mosaic attribution of the legal corpus is original or secondary and Deuteronomistic, the essential point remains: Deuteronomy is stylized not as an overturning, revoking, breach, or alteration of previous Israelite law but rather as continuous with prior teachings and as called for from the very beginning. Discontinuity with classical and authoritative law is presented as continuity; the new code is an elaboration of the old, not its abrogation. Sometimes, indeed, there are clear indications that procedures are to undergo change: what we are doing now, in the fictive time of the text, will not always be the case but will change once God grants peace from enemies roundabout (Deut 12:8–12). Such a convenient *vaticinium ex eventu* explains the introduction of centralization as having been deliberately delayed by divine plan until the necessary preconditions could be met. Alternatively, the Deuteronomistic editors brand the Israelite cultic norms that they wish to abrogate as objectionable practices of the displaced Canaanites (Deut 12:2–3).[7] If these Canaanites did not exist, the authors of Deuteronomy would have found it necessary to invent them: for the prohibited practices involved—worship in a plurality of cultic places (כל המקמות) and the use of cultic pillars (מצבות)—suspiciously resemble former Israelite orthodoxy. After all, Yahweh himself promised his blessing at multiple cultic places (בכל המקום, Exod 20:24), and Moses erected twelve cultic pillars (מצבה) on Mount Sinai, adjacent to the altar, as part of the sacrificial protocol to ratify the covenant (Exod 24:4). These altars and cultic pillars played an important role in popular piety. Archaeology confirms their proliferation throughout ancient Israel; they seem to have been associated with widespread ancestral cults.[8] The prohibition of the cultic post (אשרה, Deut 12:3; 16:21) also represents an inner-Israelite polemic, despite Deuteronomy's representation of it as Canaanite. Asherah, both as goddess and as cult object, was a component of popular piety.[9]

7. The Deuteronomistic Historian employs the same technique elsewhere as well, stigmatizing the orthodox past as Canaanite heterodoxy in Judg 2:6–3:6; see Baruch Halpern, *The First Historians: The Hebrew Bible and History* (San Francisco: Harper & Row, 1988) 134, 139. Halpern elaborates how originally Israelite forms of worship are labeled as foreign in "The Baal (and the Asherah) in Seventh-Century Judah: Yhwh's Retainers Retired," *Konsequente Traditionsgeschichte: Festschrift für Klaus Baltzer* (ed. Rüdiger Bartelmus, Thomas Krüger, and Helmut Utzschneider; OBO 126; Freiburg, Switzerland: Universitätsverlag; Göttingen: Vandenhoeck & Ruprecht, 1993) 115–54.

8. On altar building and pillar raising as components of ancestor worship, see Theodore J. Lewis, *Cults of the Dead in Ancient Israel and Ugarit* (HSM 39; Atlanta: Scholars Press, 1989) 118–20; Elizabeth Bloch-Smith, *Judahite Burial Practices and Beliefs about the Dead* (JSOTSup 123; Sheffield: Sheffield Academic Press, 1992) 113–14, 122–26; and Alan Cooper and Bernard R. Goldstein, "The Cult of the Dead and the Theme of Entry into the Land," *Biblical Interpretation* 1 (1993) 285–303.

9. The inscription from Kuntillat 'Ajrud depicting ithyphallic males and a nude female, entitled "To Yahweh and his Asherah," illustrates the gap between popular and official religion. The cultic post may have represented the Canaanite goddess; see J. Day, "Asherah in the Hebrew Bible and Northwest Semitic Literature" *JBL* 105 (1986) 385–408; W. A. Maier, III, *'Ašerah: Extrabiblical Evidence* (HSM 37; Atlanta: Scholars Press, 1986); and Saul M. Olyan, *Asherah and the Cult of Yahweh in Israel* (SBLMS 34; Atlanta: Scholars Press, 1988). For a

The Canaanite here in Deuteronomy seems more literary trope than historical memory: the authors and editors of the legal corpus stigmatize the orthodoxy from which they depart as foreign and odious. This deft opprobrium conceals the real issue: a polemic against prior Israelite norms of religion, the antiquity and popularity of which threatened the viability of Deuteronomy's innovations. Without explicitly naming and identifying the normative practices that are the actual object of concern, they are branded as non-Israelite and redefined as apostasy. In this sense, ethnicity, both Israelite and Canaanite, becomes a tendentious literary construct: the foreign is the rejected past, whereas the native is the novum that lacks direct historical precedent.

Deuteronomy's Relation to the Covenant Code: A New Approach

In view of the approach advocated here, it becomes possible to reconceptualize the long-standing debate concerning Deuteronomy's dependence upon the Covenant Code. Scholarship has long vacillated between those who assert such dependence but who cannot satisfactorily explain Deuteronomy's independence from the Covenant Code as regards legal content, formulation, and sequence and those who deny dependence but then cannot account for the multiple points of patent, often verbatim, lexical, and topical dependence. Neither of these alternatives is correct; or, from a different perspective, both are. The point is that the authors of Deuteronomy used the Covenant Code dialectically. On the one hand, the Covenant Code was known to and used by the authors of the legal corpus of Deuteronomy, even if not in its present compass or yet redacted into the Sinai pericope; thus, textual dependence exists. On the other hand, the Covenant Code did not constitute a textual source to which the authors of Deuteronomy were bound in language, scope, or substantive legal content. Instead, the authors of Deuteronomy used the Covenant Code as a textual resource in order to pursue their own very different religious and legal agenda. The authors of Deuteronomy employed the garb of dependence to purchase profound hermeneutical independence.

These reflections shed new light upon the authors' casting of Deuteronomy as ancient. The Deuteronomic program of religious, legal, administrative, and ethical innovation was unprecedented. The new norms the Deuteronomic authors sought to implement were consistent neither with previous authoritative texts nor with the iconic, popular piety represented by the distributed cultus. It is tempting to press that point further and to suggest that the Deuteronomic authors represented a sectarian movement within late Judaean society[10]—except

---

stimulating reconsideration of this material, see Baruch Margalit, "The Meaning and Significance of Asherah," *VT* 40 (1990) 264–97.

10. For suggestive remarks along these lines, see M. Smith, *Palestinian Parties and Politics that Shaped the Old Testament* (2d ed.; London: SCM, 1987) 36–42.

that such a label presupposes a notion of "normative" religion that could hardly have existed in late-seventh-century Judah. Be that as it may, the Deuteronomic program was precarious in its originality: it departed from and challenged conventions of thought, belief, and action. For that very reason, the authors of Deuteronomy sought sanction in authoritative or prestigious texts for their innovations. They used the Covenant Code and other legal (and narrative) texts to anchor their program in Israelite tradition. Doing so lent their new vision prestige, credibility, authority, and continuity with a past that they both appropriated and disenfranchised.

Deuteronomy's use of precedent subverts it. The old saw of Deuteronomy as a pious fraud may thus profitably be inverted. Is there not something of an impious fraud—of *pecca fortiter!*—in the literary accomplishment of the text's authors? Deuteronomy is surely one of the most original works of the Hebrew Bible, innovative in its vision of religion, justice, and political structure, as well as in its hermeneutics and textual structure. The fiction concerning the time and place of the text's promulgation, not to mention its Mosaic speaker, aids their endeavor. The authors of Deuteronomy retroject into the past their modernist transformation of tradition. They define their new vision as normative, while troping both the normative tradition and the existing reality from which they depart as deviant. The function of the pseudepigraph is that it displaces not only the previous tradition (the authoritative text) but also that tradition's just claim to priority.[11] The religious norms that preceded Deuteronomy, such as local sacrifice and local celebration of the Passover, are rejected as contrary to divine Torah, which the text of Deuteronomy alone defines and mediates.

Deuteronomy both promotes a radical innovation in ancient Israelite religion and represents a meditation upon what is necessary to accomplish a profound cultural transformation. Its appeal to the Covenant Code, the ways in which it reuses and attempts to situate itself in relation to prior texts, and the fictions it both constructs and deconstructs point to the authors' awareness of the problem of new writing, of revoking old law for the sake of new. In their new literary composition, the authors of Deuteronomy deploy the older lemmas of the Covenant Code in a revised context and, in part, echo—or appropriate—the redactional structure of the older text.[12] Imitation becomes the sincerest form of encroachment.

---

11. See Baruch Halpern, "Sybil, or the Two Nations? Archaism, Kinship, Alienation, and the Elite Redefinition of Traditional Culture in Judah in the 8th–7th Centuries B.C.E.," in *The Study of the Ancient Near East in the Twenty-first Century: The William Foxwell Albright Centennial Conference* (ed. Jerrold S. Cooper and Glenn M. Schwartz; Winona Lake, Ind.: Eisenbrauns, 1996) 333–34.

12. For the congruence in redactional structures, see Eckart Otto, "Vom Bundesbuch zum Deuteronomium: Die deuteronomische Redaktion in Dtn 12–26," in *Biblische Theologie und gesellschaftlicher Wandel: Für Norbert Lohfink* (ed. Georg Braulik, Walter Groß, and Sean McEvenue; Freiburg: Herder, 1993) 260–78.

Deuteronomy's Self-Presentation

As later Deuteronomistic editors reflected upon the relation of the Deuteronomic legal corpus to other collections of law, and as these texts were read in relation to one another, it became necessary to address the question of Deuteronomy's inconsistency with and departure from those texts. For that reason, Deuteronomy everywhere assiduously denies its originality. Deuteronomy consistently asserts its derivative status by presenting itself as either mere explication of preceding legislation (Deut 1:5) or legislative codicil to the original covenant at Sinai/Horeb (Deut 28:69). Deuteronomy presents itself in narrative terms as the recapitulation of the story; in homiletical terms as exhortation to obey previously promulgated statutes; in legal terms as ancillary. Nonetheless, in substantive terms, as Nachmanides and other medieval commentators already recognized, significant difficulties arise the moment the attempt is made to claim the consistency of either the narrative or the legal material in Deuteronomy, let alone the Sinaitic theophany itself, with the material it purports merely to retell.

The reiteration of the past transforms it: that applies as much to Deuteronomy's narratives as to its laws. The rhetoric of the text simultaneously erects fictions of past time and place and breaks down those same fictions. For example, Deuteronomy distinguishes its present, both in the narrative and in the legal corpus, from the past of the previous generation who experienced the exodus, the revelation of law at Horeb, and the wilderness wandering. Within the narrative, Deuteronomy marks itself as taking place היום "today" (i.e., Deut 5:3; 26:16, 18; 29:11, 12, 14 *bis*; 17; and passim) in contradistinction to those earlier events that took place rather בעת ההיא "at that time."[13] No sooner is "this day" distinguished from "at that time," however, than the Mosaic speaker inconsistently insists, "Not with our forefathers did Yahweh make this covenant, but with us, we—these here today—all of us living. Face to face Yahweh spoke *to you* on the mountain out of the fire . . ." (Deut 5:3–4, my emphasis). This "you"—asserted to have been present at Horeb—represents an audacious denial of the facts.[14] The addressees of Moses are actually the new generation that

---

13. See Samuel E. Loewenstamm, "The Formula *Ba'et Hahi'* in the Introductory Speeches in Deuteronomy," *Tarbiz* 38 (1968–69) 99–104 (Hebrew); translated in Loewenstamm, *From Babylon to Canaan: Studies in the Bible and its Oriental Background* (Jerusalem: Magnes, 1992) 42–50. Loewenstamm understands the formula to mark instances where the Deuteronomist merely provides historical details passed over in the earlier narrative account. Similar is the narratological approach of Jean-Pierre Sonnet, who shifts the supplemental model from the editor to the narrator (*"When Moses Had Finished Writing": Communication in Deuteronomy / Deuteronomy as Communication* [Ann Arbor, Mich.: University Microfilms, 1996] 82 n. 77). The revision is forthcoming as Sonnet, *The Book within the Book: Writing in Deuteronomy* (Biblical Interpretation 14; Leiden: E. J. Brill, 1997). More likely, however, the deliberate transformation of those narratives in light of the later ideology of the Deuteronomistic editors is at issue, with the formula marking such revisionist activity.

14. Scholars have dealt with this problem in different ways. Gerhard von Rad argued that the authors of Deuteronomy were striving to reactualize old traditions of election and salvation at a time when Israel was threatened with political and religious disintegration (*Studies in Deuteronomy* [SBT 9; Chicago: Henry Regnery, 1953] 70). Von Rad's assumption of the antiq-

arose after the forty years of wilderness wandering. The sole purpose of that wilderness wandering was to kill off the entire generation of rebellious Israelites who were the actual witnesses to the theophany (Deut 2:14–16). The insistent staccato of repetition suggests that the authors' true appeal is to their own contemporaries in late-seventh-century Judah and, with them, perpetually to every subsequent generation of the text's readers: "us, we—these here today—all of us living."

If the author is boldly revisionary in his claims about the past, so also does he assert hegemony over the future. As with neo-Assyrian loyalty oaths, the covenant in the plains of Moab binds not only those actually party to it but also their progeny, who, unborn, cannot directly assent to it. It thus includes those who are absent: "I make this covenant, with its sanctions, not with you alone, but both with those who are standing here with us this day before Yahweh our God and with those who are not with us here this day" (Deut 29:13–14).[15] For Deuteronomy, presence, or participation in the covenant, and witness, as of the theophany, in themselves have nothing to do with chronology or geography, nothing to do with the past or the future. Literal presence, whether at Sinai/Horeb in the past or on the Plains of Moab in the present, is neither sufficient nor necessary for inclusion in the covenant. Deuteronomy's authors transform both chronology and geography into tropes of human assent. Priority, presence, witness, participation in the covenant—these have nothing to do with literal time and place. They have rather to do with commitment to the Deuteronomic Torah—"Choose life!"—and thereby become matters of hermeneutics.

Revisionary Hermeneutics and Literary History

It seems clear that Israelite authors, preeminently with Deuteronomy, sought to displace the prestige and authority of the literary compositions that preceded them. Within Deuteronomy, the narrator's statement that the divine voice promulgated the Decalogue ולא יסף "but did not continue" (Deut 5:19) is disengenuous. That statement is much more likely a deliberate textual polemic, as Otto Eissfeldt suggested.[16] The denial represents a Deuteronomistic attempt to divest the Covenant Code of its authority by rejecting its Sinaitic pedigree. Of

---

uity of those traditions, however, rests upon his assumption of the amphictyony as the context for their transmission, a belief that recent scholarship has rejected. More recently, a position similar to that suggested here has been proposed by Thomas Römer, "Le Deutéronome à la quête des origines," in *Le Pentateuque: Débats et recherches* (ed. P. Haudebert; LD 151; Paris: Cerf, 1992) 74. Note the challenge to Römer's analysis by Sonnet, *"When Moses Had Finished Writing,"* 14.

15. See "Esarhaddon's Succession Treaty," § 25, ll. 283–301, in the invaluable critical edition of Simo Parpola and Kazuko Watanabe, eds., *Neo-Assyrian Treaties and Loyalty Oaths* (State Archives of Assyria 2; Helsinki: Helsinki University Press, 1988) 40.

16. Otto Eissfeldt, *The Old Testament: An Introduction* (New York: Harper & Row, 1965) 220–23. In some Bible printings, Deut 5:19 appears as Deut 5:22.

course, the Covenant Code was itself only secondarily inserted into the Sinai pericope by clearly evident literary means: its redactors sought to purchase for it an ex post facto revelatory status.[17] Deuteronomy's polemic, although it does not name its object, rewrites literary history. By circumscribing Sinai and silencing the Covenant Code, the redactors of Deuteronomy sought to clear a textual space for Moab as the authentic—and exclusive—supplement to the original revelation (Deut 28:69).

It therefore represents a major irony of literary history that Second Temple editors incorporated both the Covenant Code and the legal corpus of Deuteronomy into the Pentateuch. In doing so, they preserved Deuteronomy alongside the very text that it sought to replace and subvert. An entire trajectory of ongoing textual transformation takes shape as the revising text is itself eventually revised by another literary stratum, only to be revised in turn. The editors of the Deuteronomistic History, for example, do not simply implement but transform Deuteronomic norms. In the narrative of King Josiah's seizing the initiative to celebrate and preside over the first centralized Passover, the Deuteronomistic editors extend to the king a role as defender of the cult that is not ceded him in Deut 17:14–20.[18] The revisionist editors of the Holiness Code rework Deuteronomy in a quite different direction. They abrogate Deuteronomy's innovation of secular slaughter and reject Deuteronomy's transformation of language, denying to זבח "sacrifice" any profane application (Lev 17:2–7).[19] At the same time, in rolling back Deuteronomy's innovation, the authors of

---

17. In the Decalogue, Yahweh proclaims "all these words" (Exod 21:1). That provides the antecedent to the recapitulation by Moses, in the covenant ratification ceremony, of "*all the words of Yahweh* and all the judgments" (Exod 24:3a); to the people's ensuing agreement to perform "*all the words which Yahweh had spoken*" (Exod 24:3b); and to Moses' immediately writing down "*all the words of Yahweh*" (Exod 24:4a). Unaccounted for in these otherwise consistent recapitulations is the reference to "all the judgments" in Exod 24:3a, which is syntactically disruptive in its context. Were it original, it would more logically appear either as "and all the judgments of Yahweh" or "and his judgments." The awkward phrase logically has for its antecedent the superscription to the Covenant Code: "These are *the judgments* that you shall set before them" (Exod 20:1). The function, therefore, of the epexegetical phrase in Exod 24:4 is redactionally to integrate the Covenant Code into the Sinai pericope as a supplement to the Decalogue. See the similar analysis in Eissfeldt, *Old Testament*, 213.

18. Astonishingly, there has been no attempt that I am aware of, by proponents of either the Göttingen or the Cross school, to establish that the various editorial strata that they distinguish within the Deuteronomistic History can also be identified within Deuteronomy itself. Conversely, scholars specializing in Deuteronomy have made little headway in linking the various later (Deuteronomistic) strata that they isolate within the text of Deuteronomy with those in the Deuteronomistic History. There simply seems to be an impasse. The forthcoming Deuteronomy commentary by Timo Veijola (for Das Alte Testament Deutsch) may bridge this gap, because of his work on the Deuteronomistic History. The law of the king in Deut 17:14–20 raises these issues acutely.

19. Alfred Cholewiński, *Heiligkeitsgesetz und Deuteronomium: Eine vergleichende Studie* (AnBib 66; Rome: Pontifical Biblical Institute, 1976) 160–78; and, most recently, Otto, *Theologische Ethik*, 240–42. For a contrasting analysis, arguing that Deuteronomy does not innovate but rather presupposes Leviticus 17 (H), see Jacob Milgrom, *Leviticus 1–16* (AB 3; New York: Doubleday, 1991) 28–29, 713–18.

the Holiness Code presuppose and confirm the more profound innovation of Deuteronomy: centralization itself.[20]

These issues extend further. That late editors included both the Deuteronomistic History and the Chronicler's work in the Hebrew Bible most likely contradicts the intentions of the Chronicler. The designation of Chronicles in the Septuagint and Vulgate as *Paralipomena*, "Omitted Things," is not to the point. It is more reasonable to assume that the intent of the Chronicler was not adventitiously to supplement but rather to draw on the authority of the Deuteronomistic History while, in effect, replacing it for all practical purposes.[21] The Chronicler's real interest was not in the past, as such, but in the present: in justifying a religious, social, and political program for his fifth-century-B.C.E. postexilic community. Ironically, both authors faced similar challenges, lacking sanction or precedent in tradition for the programs they attempted to implement. The Deuteronomistic Historian sought to grant the monarch complete authority over matters of cult and Temple, despite the absence of precedent for such a move in Deuteronomy, his ostensible source.[22] The Chronicler confronted a still more serious problem in seeking warrant for his attempt to configure the postexilic Judaean polity as a Davidide-led royal temple state, following contemporary Achaemenid models.[23] Neither the Pentateuch (the ostensible legal basis of the postexilic theocracy) nor the Deuteronomistic History (the Chronicler's ostensible historiographic source) sufficed: Pentateuchal law envisaged no cultic role for the monarch (Deut 17:14–20), and the Deuteronomistic History reflected the needs of an exilic community requiring a justification for the destruction and assurance that the history of the nation had not come to an abrupt end. The Chronicler's aim, in contrast, was to provide a practical blueprint for the reconstruction of the Second Commonwealth. Never-

20. For the alternative claim that the Holiness Code precedes Deuteronomy, see chapter 3, n. 107.

21. There is a debate within the scholarly literature about whether Chronicles seeks to replace or merely to supplement the Deuteronomistic History. In espousing the latter position, Marc Zvi Brettler, *The Creation of History in Ancient Israel* (London: Routledge, 1995) 22, maintains: "the Chronicler was most likely not writing a history to replace Samuel and Kings, but desired to reshape the way in which these books would be read and remembered. . . . He attempted to supplement them." Brettler's supplemental model does not draw the full implications of his own demonstration of the Chronicler's anachronistic revisions of the Deuteronomistic History: precisely in having the last word, the Chronicler becomes the final mediator of Israel's past and alone provides the charter for the future of the postexilic commonwealth. For a model of how shaping the way earlier books are read and remembered can be tantamount to displacement, see Martin S. Jaffee, "The Pretext of Interpretation: Rabbinic Oral Torah and the Charisma of Revelation," *God in Language* (ed. Robert P. Scharlemann and Gilbert E. M. Ogutu; New York: Paragon, 1987) 73–89.

22. On the originality of the Deuteronomistic Historian, see Gary N. Knoppers, *Two Nations under God: The Deuteronomistic History of Solomon and the Dual Monarchies* (HSM 53; Atlanta: Scholars Press, 1994) 2.229–53.

23. On the type of state that the Chronicler attempts to construct, see Paul E. Dion, "The Civic-and-Temple Community of Persian Period Judaea: Neglected Insights from Eastern Europe," *JNES* 50 (1991) 281–87; and Joel P. Weinberg, *The Citizen-Temple Community* (JSOTSup 151; Sheffield: Sheffield Academic Press, 1992).

theless, in order to claim continuity with past conventions of cultus and monarchy, the Chronicler rewrote his source in light of the new program. The
Chronicler preempted the Deuteronomistic Historian by assuming his identical voice, that of an anonymous authoritative historiographer.

A final irony of literary history took place when later writers harmonized
earlier sources with the very texts that they had originally sought to transform.
For example, in his narrative of Josiah's observance of the Passover, the postexilic Chronicler harmonizes the contradiction between the discrepant Passover laws of Exod 12:9 (which requires that the paschal lamb be roasted *in fire*
and forbids its being boiled) and Deut 16:7 (which stipulates that it must be
boiled) by insisting, "They *boiled* the paschal offering *in fire*, according to the
law" (2 Chr 35:13).[24] In attempting to honor both requirements, the resulting
harmonization conforms to neither. Even more striking is that such harmonistic
exegesis should assert itself as "according to the law"—should thereby present
exegetical law as the original signification of the law. Such attempts pointedly
demonstrate that the exegesis of authoritative Scripture within Scripture itself
acquired authoritative status as Scripture.[25]

The authors of Deuteronomy were thus eventually hoist with their own
petard. Deuteronomy's very achievement of authoritative status led to its displacement: to competing claims to "more" original authority that marshalled
Deuteronomy's arsenal of textual strategies (pseudepigraphy, exegesis, resequencing) against it. The sectarian authors of the Samaritan Pentateuch enlisted
Deuteronomy's distinctive requirement for cultic exclusivity to legitimate their
competing sanctuary on Mount Gerizim. Deuteronomy's rhetoric of displacement was also employed by the authors of the Temple Scroll at Qumran. They
composed a divine pseudepigraph to preempt the prophetic voice of Deuteronomy and harnassed Deuteronomy's lemmas, now revoiced, to sanction their
own sectarian law.[26]

24. See Menahem Haran, *Temples and Temple-Service in Ancient Israel: An Inquiry into
the Character of Cult-Phenomena and the Historical Setting of the Priestly School* (Oxford:
Clarendon, 1978) 322; Isaac Leo Seeligmann, "The Beginnings of Midrash in the Books of
Chronicles," *Tarbiz* 49 (1979–80) 31–32 (Hebrew); Ginsberg, *Israelian Heritage*, 57–58; and
Michael Fishbane, *Biblical Interpretation in Ancient Israel* (Oxford: Clarendon, 1985) 134–37.

25. Identical issues emerge in biblical narrative. The redactor of the flood story attempted
to introduce a harmonization of his discrepant sources concerning the number of animals to be
taken aboard the Ark. In attempting to overcome the two mutually exclusive numbering schemes,
he creates a *tertium quid* consistent with neither. On Gen 7:8–9 see Bernard M. Levinson, "'The
Right Chorale': From the Poetics of Biblical Narrative to the Hermeneutics of the Hebrew Bible,"
in *"Not in Heaven": Coherence and Complexity in Biblical Narrative* (ed. Jason P. Rosenblatt
and Joseph C. Sitterson; Indiana Studies in Biblical Literature; Bloomington: Indiana University Press, 1991) 129–53, at 140.

26. On the Samaritan Pentateuch, see Jeffrey H. Tigay, "Conflation as a Redactional Technique," in *Empirical Models for Biblical Criticism* (ed. Jeffrey H. Tigay; Philadelphia: University of Pennsylvania, 1985) 53–96. For striking examples of textual transformation in the Temple
Scroll, see Michael Fishbane, "Use, Authority and Interpretation of Mikra at Qumran," in *Mikra:
Text, Translation, and Interpretation of the Hebrew Bible in Ancient Judaism and Early Christianity* (ed. Martin J. Mulder; CRINT 2:3; Assen/Maastricht: Van Gorcum; Philadelphia: Fortress, 1988) 339–77 (with extensive bibliography). Disputing that Deuteronomy provided a direct

Revisionist Deuteronomy and the literary history it both manifests and engenders is a call to biblical scholarship to return to the origins of the discipline: to take seriously texts, authors, and interpretation. The authors and editors of Deuteronomy, from the beginning, worked deliberately with texts to transform other texts, to articulate a far-reaching program of cultic, judicial, administrative, ethical, and theological innovation, to advance a new understanding of the past, and to create a new future for the nation. The method advocated here can equally illumine the study of biblical narrative: the study of any text must include a clear sense of its revisionary target.[27] The hermeneutical method, grounded upon diachronic analysis, provides an indispensable means to recover the creativity of ancient Israelite authors and to mark their intellectual accomplishments.

Viewed from this perspective, the legal corpora raise issues of literary history, authorship, voice, and cultural renewal that are central to a theory of literature and to the humanities more broadly. In describing an author's attempt to assert his or her own originality, contemporary literary theory has, in the work of Harold Bloom, turned to psychoanalytic models to clarify the author's struggle for originality.[28] That only begs the question of the origin and appropriateness of Freud's model. It goes against the evidence to find in even the most gripping of the classical Greek tragedies, *Oedipus Rex*, a model of authorship that affords insight into agency and originality. The only insight in that tragedy is into the absence of agency and the inability to originate, because fate's tyranny renders all human desire and initiative futile. The tragic chorus saw that life in their world afforded but one release from continually being subject to fatal reversal (*peripeteia*): "Count no man happy until he is dead!" More is at stake than a matter of literary history. Before Bloom, Kierkegaard also sought to reject all myths of absolute origins—in particular, the Platonic notion of knowledge as the soul's "recollection" (*anagnorisis*) of truths that it possessed prior to embodiment and temporality—urging, rather, biblical "repetition" as a model of consciousness and existence, whereby truth is learned historically. Although Kierkegaard regarded the New Testament as the source of that model, a more appropriate exemplar, it seems to me, both for the psychoanalytical phenomenon and the philosophical one, is that offered by the way Deuteronomy's authors engaged prior texts in order to accomplish

---

source for the Temple Scroll are Hartmut Stegemann, "Is the Temple Scroll a Sixth Book of the Torah—Lost for 2,500 Years?," *Biblical Archaeology Review* 13 (1987) 28–35; and Michael Owen Wise, *A Critical Study of the Temple Scroll from Qumran Cave 11* (Studies in Ancient Oriental Civilization 49; Chicago: Oriental Institute of the University of Chicago, 1990) 35–41.

27. For applications of this principle to the narratives in Deuteronomy, see Levinson, *Hermeneutics of Innovation*, 424–32, and, especially, Brettler, *Creation of History*, 62–78. For a stimulating analysis of how redaction involves revision in the narratives of Genesis, see David M. Carr, *Reading the Fractures of Genesis: Historical and Literary Approaches* (Louisville: Westminster John Knox, 1996).

28. See Harold Bloom, *The Anxiety of Influence: A Theory of Poetry* (London: Oxford University Press, 1973); Bloom, *A Map of Misreading* (Oxford: Oxford University Press, 1975); and Bloom, *Poetry and Repression* (New Haven: Yale University Press, 1976).

their innovative program. They established that priority is not a matter of chronology but a revisionary and sometimes polemical trope in the author's bid to acquire autonomy and independence. There is, after all, no authorship, no originality, no agency, no freedom, no grace, no love, that is not after the fact, that does not come after, that is not belated, that can avoid coming to terms with predecessors and with the burden of the past. That is the significance of "the repetition of this law."

BIBLIOGRAPHY

Aejmelaeus, Anneli. "Die Septuaginta des Deuteronomiums." In *Das Deuteronomium und seine Querbeziehungen*, edited by Timo Veijola, 1–22. Schriften der Finnischen Exegetischen Gesellschaft 62. Göttingen: Vandenhoeck & Ruprecht, 1996.

Albertz, Rainer. *Persönliche Frömmigkeit und offizielle Religion: Religionsinterner Pluralismus in Israel und Babylon.* Stuttgart: Calwer, 1978.

———. *A History of Israelite Religion in the Old Testament Period.* 2 vols. OTL. Louisville: Westminster/John Knox, 1994.

Amsler, Samuel. "Les Documents de la loi et la formation du Pentateuque." In *Le Pentateuque en question: Les Origines et la composition des cinq premiers livres de la Bible à la lumière des recherches récentes*, edited by Albert de Pury, 235–57. Le Monde de la Bible 19. 2d ed. Geneva: Labor et Fides, 1989.

Auerbach, E. "Die Feste im alten Israel." *VT* 8 (1958) 1–14.

Aurelius, Erik. *Der Fürbitter Israels: Eine Studie zum Mosebild im Alten Testament.* ConBOT 27. Stockholm: Almqvist & Wiksell, 1988.

Barr, James. *Holy Scripture: Canon, Authority, Criticism.* Philadelphia: Westminster, 1983.

Barton, John. *Reading the Old Testament: Method in Biblical Study.* Philadelphia: Westminster, 1984.

Beentjes, Pancratius C. "Inverted Quotations in the Bible: A Neglected Stylistic Pattern." *Bib* 63 (1982) 506–23.

Begg, Christopher T. "The Significance of the *Numeruswechsel* in Deuteronomy: The 'Pre-History' of the Question." *ETL* 55 (1979) 116–24.

———. "Contributions to the Elucidation of the Composition of Deuteronomy with Special Attention to the Significance of the *Numeruswechsel*." Ph.D. diss., University of Louvain, 1987.

Begrich, J. "Die priesterliche Torah." In *Werden und Wesen des Alten Testaments*, edited by P. Volz, 63–88. BZAW 66. Berlin: A. Töpelmann, 1936. Reprinted in his *Gesammelte Studien zum Alten Testament*, 232–60. TBü 21. Munich: Chr. Kaiser, 1964.

159

Bewer, Julius A. "The Case for the Early Date of Deuteronomy." *JBL* 47 (1928) 305–21.

Beyerlin, Walter. "Die Paranäse im Bundesbuch und ihre Herkunft." In *Gottes Wort und Gottes Land: Hans-Wilhelm Hertzberg zum 70. Geburtstag*, edited by Henning Graf Reventlow, 9–29. Göttingen: Vandenhoeck & Ruprecht, 1965.

Biale, David. *Gershom Scholem: Kabbalah and Counter-History*. Cambridge, Mass.: Harvard University Press, 1979.

Blenkinsopp, Joseph. *Prophecy and Canon: A Contribution to the Study of Jewish Origins*. Notre Dame: University of Notre Dame Press, 1977.

———. *The Pentateuch: An Introduction to the First Five Books of the Bible*. New York: Doubleday, 1992.

Bloch-Smith, Elizabeth. *Judahite Burial Practices and Beliefs about the Dead*. JSOTSup 123. Sheffield: Sheffield Academic Press, 1992.

Bloom, Harold. *The Anxiety of Influence: A Theory of Poetry*. London: Oxford University Press, 1973.

———. *A Map of Misreading*. Oxford: Oxford University Press, 1975.

———. *Poetry and Repression*. New Haven: Yale University Press, 1976.

Blum, Erhard. *Studien zur Komposition des Pentateuch*. BZAW 189. Berlin: Walter de Gruyter, 1990.

Boecker, Hans Jochen. *Law and the Administration of Justice in the Old Testament and Ancient East*. Minneapolis: Augsburg, 1980.

Braulik, Georg. "Die Ausdrücke für 'Gesetz' im Buch Deuteronomium." *Bib* 51 (1970) 39–66. Reprinted in and cited according to Braulik, *Studien zur Theologie des Deuteronomiums*, 11–38. SBAB 2. Stuttgart: Katholisches Bibelwerk, 1988.

———. *Die Mittel deuteronomischer Rhetorik erhoben aus Deuteronomium 4,1–40*. AnBib 68. Rome: Pontifical Biblical Institute, 1978.

———. "Leidensgedächtnisfeier und Freudenfest: 'Volksliturgie' nach dem deuteronomischen Festkalender (Dtn 16, 1–7)." *TP* 56 (1981) 335–57. Reprinted in and cited according to Braulik, *Studien zur Theologie des Deuteronomiums*, 95–121. SBAB 2. Stuttgart: Katholisches Bibelwerk, 1988.

———. "Die Freude des Festes: Das Kultverständnis des Deuteronomium—die älteste biblische Festtheorie." *Theologisches Jahrbuch 1983* (ed. W. Ernst et al.; Leipzig: St. Benno, 1983) 13–54. Reprinted in and cited according to Braulik, *Studien zur Theologie des Deuteronomiums* (SBAB 2; Stuttgart: Katholisches Bibelwerk, 1988) 161–218.

———. "Zur deuteronomistischen Konzeption von Freiheit und Frieden." In *Congress Volume Salamanca 1983*, edited by J. A. Emerton, 29–39. VTSup 36. Leiden: E. J. Brill, 1985. Reprinted and cited according to Braulik, *Studien zur Theologie des Deuteronomiums*, 219–30. SBAB 2. Stuttgart: Katholisches Bibelwerk, 1988.

———. *Deuteronomium 1–16,17*. Neue Echter Bibel 15. Würzburg: Echter Verlag, 1986.

———. *Die deuteronomischen Gesetze und der Dekalog: Studien zum Aufbau von Deuteronomium 12–26*. SBS 145. Stuttgart: Katholisches Bibelwerk, 1991. An earlier version of chapter 4 is translated as "The Sequence of the Laws in Deuteronomy 12–26 and in the Decalogue." In *A Song of Power and the Power of Song: Essays on the Book of Deuteronomy*, edited by Duane L. Christensen, 313–35. Winona Lake, Ind.: Eisenbrauns, 1993.

———. "Die Funktion von Siebenergruppierungen im Endtext des Deuteronomiums." In *Ein Gott—eine Offenbarung: Festschrift Notker Füglister*, edited by Friedrich V. Reiterer, 37–50. Würzburg: Echter, 1991.

————. *Deuteronomium II: 16,18–34,12.* Neue Echter Bibel 28. Würzburg: Echter Verlag, 1992.

Brekelmans, Chr. "Die sogenannten deuteronomischen Elemente in Gen.-Num.: Ein Beitrag zur Vorgeschichte des Deuteronomiums." In *Volume du Congrès: Genève 1965,* 90–96. VTSup 15. Leiden: E. J. Brill, 1966.

Brett, Mark G. *Biblical Criticism in Crisis? The Impact of the Canonical Approach on Old Testament Studies.* Cambridge: Cambridge University Press, 1991.

Brettler, Marc Zvi. *God Is King: Understanding an Israelite Metaphor.* JSOTSup 76. Sheffield: Sheffield Academic Press, 1989.

————. "Jud 1,1–2,10: From Appendix to Prologue." *ZAW* 101 (1989) 433–35.

————. *The Creation of History in Ancient Israel.* London: Routledge, 1995.

Buchholz, Joachim. Die Ältesten Israels im Deuteronomium. GTA 36. Göttingen: Vandenhoeck & Ruprecht, 1988.

Budd, P. J. "Priestly Instruction in Pre-Exilic Israel." *VT* 23 (1973) 1–14.

Budde, Karl. "Dtn 13 10, und was daran hängt." *ZAW* 36 (1916) 187–97.

Buis, P. *Le Deutéronome.* VS 4. Paris: Beauchesne, 1969.

Caloz, Masséo. "Exode, XIII, 3–16 et son rapport au Deutéronome." RB 75 (1968) 5–62.

Carmichael, Calum M. *The Laws of Deuteronomy.* Ithaca: Cornell University Press, 1974.

————. *Law and Narrative in the Bible: The Evidence of the Deuteronomic Laws and the Decalogue.* Ithaca: Cornell University Press, 1985.

Carr, David M. *Reading the Fractures of Genesis: Historical and Literary Approaches.* Louisville: Westminster John Knox, 1996.

Carroll, Robert P. "The Hebrew Bible as Literature—A Misprision?" *Studia Theologica* 47 (1993) 77–90.

Cartledge, Tony W. *Vows in the Hebrew Bible and the Ancient Near East.* JSOTSup 147. Sheffield: Sheffield Academic Press, 1992.

Cassuto, Umberto. *A Commentary on the Book of Exodus.* Jerusalem: Magnes, 1967.

Cazelles, Henri. Review of *Studien zum Altargesetz Ex 20:24–26,* by Diethelm Conrad. *OrAnt* 11 (1972) 332–34.

Chamberlain, Gary Alan. "Exodus 21–23 and Deuteronomy 12–26: A Form-critical Study." Ph.D. diss., Boston University, 1977.

Childs, Brevard S. *The Book of Exodus.* OTL. Philadelphia: Westminster, 1974.

————. *Introduction to the Old Testament as Scripture.* Philadelphia: Fortress, 1979.

Cholewiński, Alfred. *Heiligkeitsgesetz und Deuteronomium: Eine vergleichende Studie.* AnBib 66. Rome: Pontifical Biblical Institute, 1976.

Christensen, Duane L., ed. *A Song of Power and the Power of Song: Essays on the Book of Deuteronomy.* Winona Lake, Ind.: Eisenbrauns, 1993.

Clarke, E. G. *Targum Pseudo-Jonathan of the Pentateuch: Text and Concordance.* Hoboken, N.J.: Ktav, 1984.

Conrad, Diethelm. *Studien zum Altargesetz Ex 20:24–26.* (Inaugural-Dissertation). Marburg: H. Kombächer, 1968.

Cooper, Alan, and Bernard R. Goldstein. "Exodus and *Maṣṣôt* in History and Tradition." *Maarav* 8 (1992) 15–37.

————. "The Cult of the Dead and the Theme of Entry into the Promised Land." *Biblical Interpretation* 1 (1993) 285–303.

Cross, Frank Moore. *Canaanite Myth and Hebrew Epic: Essays in the History of the Religion of Israel.* Cambridge, Mass.: Harvard University Press, 1973.

Crüsemann, Frank. *Die Tora: Theologie und Sozialgeschichte des alttestamentlichen Gesetzes.* Munich: Chr. Kaiser, 1992.

Dalman, G. *Arbeit und Sitte in Palästina 1.2: Jahresablauf und Tagesablauf: Frühling und Sommer.* BFCT 2.17. Gütersloh: Bertelsmann, 1928.

Daube, David. "The Civil Law of the Mishnah: The Arrangement of the Three Gates." *Tulane Law Review* 18 (1943–44) 351–407.

———. *Studies in Biblical Law.* Cambridge: Cambridge University Press, 1947.

———. "'One from among Your Brethren Shall I Set King over You.'" *JBL* 90 (1971) 480–81.

Davies, Philip R. *In Search of 'Ancient Israel.'* JSOTSup 148. Sheffield: JSOT Press, 1992.

Day, J. "Asherah in the Hebrew Bible and Northwest Semitic Literature." *JBL* 105 (1986) 385–408.

Deller, Karlheinz. "Die Hausgötter der Familie Šukrija S. Ḫuja." In *Studies on the Civilization and Culture of Nuzi and the Hurrians in Honor of Ernest R. Lacheman,* edited by M. A. Morrison and D. I. Owen, 47–76. Winona Lake, Ind.: Eisenbrauns, 1981.

Dillmann, August. *Die Bücher Exodus und Leviticus.* Edited by August Knobel. KeHAT. 2d ed. Leipzig: S. Hirzel, 1880.

———. *Die Bücher Exodus und Leviticus.* Edited by V. Ryssel. KeHAT. 3d ed. Leipzig: S. Hirzel, 1897.

———. *Die Bücher Numeri, Deuteronomium und Josua.* KeHAT. 2d ed. Leipzig: S. Hirzel, 1886.

Dion, Paul E. "Early Evidence for the Ritual Significance of the Base of the Altar." *JBL* 106 (1987) 487–90.

———. "The Civic-and-Temple Community of Persian Period Judaea: Neglected Insights from Eastern Europe." *JNES* 50 (1991) 281–87.

———. "Deuteronomy 13: The Suppression of Alien Religious Propaganda in Israel during the Late Monarchical Era." In *Law and Ideology in Monarchic Israel,* edited by Baruch Halpern and Deborah W. Hobson, 147–216. JSOTSup 124. Sheffield: JSOT Press, 1991.

Dohmen, Christoph. "Was stand auf den Tafeln vom Sinai und was auf denen vom Horeb? Zur Geschichte und Theologie eines Offenbarungsrequisits." In *Vom Sinai zum Horeb: Stationen alttestamentlicher Glaubensgeschichte,* edited by Frank-Lothar Hossfeld, 9–50. Würzburg: Echter, 1989.

———. "Der Sinaibund als Neuer Bund nach Ex 19–34." In *Der Neue Bund im Alten: Studien zur Bundestheologie der beiden Testamente,* edited by Erich Zenger, 51–83. QD 146. Freiburg: Herder, 1993.

Dohmen, Christoph, and Manfred Oeming, *Biblischer Kanon: Warum und Wozu? Eine Kanontheologie.* QD 137. Freiburg: Herder, 1992.

Dorff, Elliot N., and Arthur Rosett. *A Living Tree: The Roots and Growth of Jewish Law.* Albany: State University of New York Press, 1988.

Draffkorn, A. E. "*ILĀNI/ELOHIM.*" *JBL* 76 (1957) 216–24.

Driver, Samuel Rolles. *Deuteronomy.* ICC. 3d ed. Edinburgh: T. & T. Clark, 1901.

———. *The Book of Exodus.* Cambridge Bible for Schools and Colleges. Cambridge: University Press, 1911.

Ehrlich, Arnold B. *Mikra Ki-Pheschuto.* 3 vols. Berlin: M. Poppelauer, 1899–1901. Reprinted with Prolegomenon by H. M. Orlinsky. Library of Biblical Studies. New York: Ktav, 1969 (Hebrew).

Eichler, Barry L. "Literary Structure in the Laws of Eshnunna." In *Language, Literature and History: Philological and Historical Studies Presented to Erica Reiner*, edited by F. Rochberg-Halton, 71–84. AOS 67. New Haven: American Oriental Society, 1987.

Eissfeldt, Otto. *The Old Testament: An Introduction*. New York: Harper & Row, 1965.

Elazar, Daniel J. *Covenant and Polity in Biblical Israel: Biblical Foundations and Jewish Expressions*. New Brunswick: Transaction, 1995.

Elon, Menahem. *Jewish Law: History, Sources, Principles*. 4 vols. Philadelphia: JPS, 1994.

Epstein, Jacob N., and Ezra Z. Melamed, eds. *Mekhilta D'Rabbi Šim'on b. Jochai*. Jerusalem: Mekitze Nirdamim, 1955.

Eslinger, Lyle M. *Kingship of God in Crisis*. Bible and Literature Series 10. Sheffield: Almond, 1985.

Finkelstein, Jacob J. *The Ox That Gored*. Transactions of the American Philosophical Society 71:2. Philadelphia: American Philosophical Society, 1981.

Finkelstein, Louis, ed. *Siphre on Deuteronomium*. New York: Jewish Theological Seminary of America, 1969.

Fischer, Bonifatius et al., eds. *Biblia Sacra Iuxta Vulgatam Versionem. I: Genesis–Psalmi*. 3d ed. Stuttgart: Deutsche Bibelgesellschaft, 1983.

Fishbane, Michael. "Varia Deuteronomica." *ZAW* 84 (1972) 349–52.

———. "Accusations of Adultery: A Study of Law and Scribal Practice in Numbers 5:11–31." *HUCA* 45 (1974) 25–45.

———. *Biblical Interpretation in Ancient Israel*. Oxford: Clarendon, 1985.

———. "Hermeneutics." In *Contemporary Jewish Religious Thought*, edited by A. A. Cohen and P. Mendes-Flohr, 353–61. New York: Charles Scribner's Sons, 1987.

———. "Use, Authority, and Interpretation of Mikra at Qumran." In *Mikra: Text, Translation, and Interpretation of the Hebrew Bible in Ancient Judaism and Early Christianity*, edited by Martin J. Mulder, 339–77. CRINT 2:3. Assen/Maastricht: Van Gorcum; Philadelphia: Fortress, 1988.

———. *The Garments of Torah: Essays in Biblical Hermeneutics*. Bloomington: Indiana University Press, 1989.

Fohrer, Georg. *Überlieferung und Geschichte des Exodus*. BZAW 91. Berlin: Alfred Töpelman, 1964.

Foresti, Fabrizio. "Storia della Redazione di Dtn. 16,18–18,22 e le sue Connessioni con l'Opera Storica Deuteronomistica." *Teresianum Ephemerides Carmeliticae* 39 (1988) 5–199.

Foucault, Michel. "What Is an Author?" In *Textual Strategies*, edited by J. V. Harari, 141–60. Cornell: Ithaca University Press, 1979.

Frankena, R. "The Vassal-Treaties of Esarhaddon and the Dating of Deuteronomy." *OTS* 14 (1965) 122–54.

Friedman, Richard Elliott. *Who Wrote the Bible?* Englewood Cliffs, N.J.: Prentice Hall, 1987.

Friedrich, J. *Die hethitischen Gesetze: Transkription, Übersetzung, sprachliche Erläuterung und vollstandiges Wörterverzeichnis*. 2d ed. Documenta et monumenta orientis antiqui 7. Leiden: E. J. Brill, 1971.

Frymer-Kensky, Tikva. *The Judicial Ordeal in the Ancient Near East*. Ann Arbor, Mich.: University Microfilms, 1977.

———. "Suprarational Legal Procedures in Elam and Nuzi." In *Studies on the Civilization and Culture of Nuzi and the Hurrians in Honor of Ernest R. Lacheman*, edited by M. A. Morrison and D. I. Owen, 115–31. Winona Lake, Ind.: Eisenbrauns, 1981.

———. "The Strange Case of the Suspected Sotah (Numbers v 11–31)." *VT* 34 (1984) 11–26.

Gerbrandt, G. E. *Kingship According to the Deuteronomistic History.* SBLDS 87. Atlanta: Scholars Press, 1986.

Gertz, Jan Christian. *Die Gerichtsorganisation Israels im deuteronomischen Gesetz.* FRLANT 165. Göttingen: Vandenhoeck & Ruprecht, 1993.

———. "Die Passa-Massot-Ordnung im deuteronomischen Festkalender." In *Das Deuteronomium und seine Querbeziehungen,* edited by Timo Veijola, 56–80. Schriften der Finnischen Exegetischen Gesellschaft 62. Göttingen: Vandenhoeck & Ruprecht, 1996.

Ginsberg, H. Louis. *The Israelian Heritage of Judaism.* Texts and Studies of the Jewish Theological Seminary of America 24. New York: Jewish Theological Seminary of America, 1982.

Goldenberg, Robert. "The Problem of Originality in Talmudic Thought." In *From Ancient Israel to Modern Judaism: Intellect in Quest of Understanding, Essays in Honor of Marvin Fox,* edited by Jacob Neusner, Ernest S. Frerichs, and Nahum M. Sarna, 2.19–27. 4 vols. BJS 159, 173–175. Atlanta: Scholars Press, 1989.

Goldstein, Bernard R., and Alan Cooper. "The Festivals of Israel and Judah and the Literary History of the Pentateuch." *JAOS* 110 (1990) 19–31.

Gordon, Cyrus H. "*Elohim* in Its Reputed Meaning of Rulers, Judges." *JBL* 54 (1935) 134–44.

Gramberg, C. P. W. *Kritische Geschichte der Religionsideen des Alten Testaments.* 2 vols. Berlin: Duncker und Humblot, 1829–30.

Greenberg, Moshe. "Some Postulates of Biblical Criminal Law." In *Yehezkel Kaufmann Jubilee Volume,* edited by Menahem Haran, 5–28. Jerusalem: Magnes, 1960. Reprinted in Greenberg, *Studies in the Bible and Jewish Thought* (Philadelphia: JPS, 1995) 25–50.

———. *Ezekiel, 1–20.* AB. Garden City, N.Y.: Doubleday, 1983.

Greengus, Samuel. "Some Issues Relating to the Comparability of Laws and the Coherence of the Legal Tradition." In *Theory and Method in Biblical and Cuneiform Law: Revision, Interpolation and Development,* edited by Bernard M. Levinson, 60–87. JSOTSup 181. Sheffield: Sheffield Academic Press, 1994.

Halbe, Jörn. "*Das Privilegrecht Jahwes Ex 34, 10–26: Gestalt und Wesen, Herkunft und Wirken in vordeuteronomischer Zeit.* FRLANT 114. Göttingen: Vandenhoeck & Ruprecht, 1975.

———. Erwägungen zu Ursprung und Wesen des Massotfestes." *ZAW* 87 (1975) 324–46.

———. "Passa-Massot im deuteronomischen Festkalender: Komposition, Entstehung und Programm von Dtn 16, 1–8." *ZAW* 87 (1975) 147–68.

Halpern, Baruch. "The Centralization Formula in Deuteronomy." *VT* 31 (1981) 20–38.

———. *The First Historians: The Hebrew Bible and History.* San Francisco: Harper & Row, 1988.

———. "Jerusalem and the Lineages in the Seventh Century BCE: Kinship and the Rise of Individual Moral Liability." In *Law and Ideology in Monarchic Israel,* edited by Baruch Halpern and Deborah W. Hobson, 11–107. JSOTSup 124. Sheffield: JSOT Press, 1991.

———. "The Baal (and the Asherah) in Seventh-Century Judah: Yhwh's Retainers Retired." In *Konsequente Traditionsgeschichte: Festschrift für Klaus Baltzer,* edited by Rüdiger Bartelmus, Thomas Krüger, and Helmut Utzschneider, 115–54. OBO 126. Freiburg, Switzerland: Universitätsverlag; Göttingen: Vandenhoeck & Ruprecht, 1993.

———. "Sybil, or the Two Nations? Archaism, Kinship, Alienation, and the Elite Redefinition of Traditional Culture in Judah in the 8th–7th Centuries B.C.E." In *The Study of the Ancient Near East in the Twenty-first Century: The William Foxwell Albright Centennial Conference*, edited by Jerrold S. Cooper and Glenn M. Schwartz, 291–338. Winona Lake, Ind.: Eisenbrauns, 1996.

Haran, Menahem. *Temples and Temple-Service in Ancient Israel: An Inquiry into the Character of Cult-Phenomena and the Historical Setting of the Priestly School*. Oxford: Clarendon, 1978.

Hartman, Geoffrey H. "On the Jewish Imagination." *Prooftexts* 5 (1985) 201–20.

Hoffmann, David Zvi. *Das Buch Deuteronomium Übersetzt und Erklärt*. 2 vols. Berlin: M. Poppelauer, 1913–22.

Hoffmann, Hans-Detlef. *Reform und Reformen. Untersuchung zu einem Grundthema der deuteronomistischen Geschichtsschreibung*. ATANT 66. Zürich: Theologischer Verlag, 1980.

Hoffner, Harry A., Jr. *The Laws of the Hittites*. Ann Arbor, Mich.: University Microfilms, 1963.

———. "Hittite." In *Law Collections from Mesopotamia and Asia Minor*, edited and translated by Martha T. Roth, 213–47. SBLWAW 6. Atlanta: Scholars Press, 1995.

Hoftijzer, J., and K. Jongeling. *Dictionary of the North-West Semitic Inscriptions*. 2 vols. Handbuch der Orientalistik 21. Leiden: E. J. Brill, 1995.

Holladay, John S., Jr. "Religion in Israel and Judah under the Monarchy: An Explicitly Archaeological Approach." In *Ancient Israelite Religion: Essays in Honor of Frank Moore Cross*, edited by Patrick D. Miller, Jr., Paul D. Hanson, and S. Dean McBride, 249–99. Philadelphia: Fortress, 1987.

Hölscher, Gustav. "Komposition und Ursprung des Deuteronomiums." *ZAW* 40 (1922) 161–255.

Honeyman, A. M. "Hebrew קַף 'Basin, Goblet.'" *JTS* 37 (1936) 56–59.

Hoppe, Leslie J. *The Origins of Deuteronomy*. Ann Arbor, Mich.: University Microfilms, 1978.

———. "Elders and Deuteronomy: A Proposal." *Église et théologie* 14 (1983) 259–72.

Hurowitz, Victor Avigdor. "Ancient Israelite Cult in History, Tradition, and Interpretation." Review Article of *Leviticus 1–16*, by Jacob Milgrom. *AJS Review* 19 (1994) 213–36.

Hurvitz, Avi. *A Linguistic Study of the Relationship between the Priestly Source and the Book of Ezekiel*. CahRB 20. Paris: J. Gabalda, 1982.

Hyatt, J. P. *Exodus*. NCBC. Grand Rapids: Eerdmans, 1971.

Ibn Ezra, A. *Commentary on the Torah*. Edited by A. Weiser. 3 vols. Jerusalem: Rav Kook Institute, 1977 (Hebrew).

Jaffee, Martin S. "The Pretext of Interpretation: Rabbinic Oral Torah and the Charisma of Revelation." In *God in Language*, edited by Robert P. Scharlemann and Gilbert E. M. Ogutu, 73–89. New York: Paragon House, 1987.

———. "The Taqqanah in Tannaitic Literature: Jurisprudence and the Construction of Rabbinic Memory." *JJS* 41 (1990) 204–25.

Japhet, Sara. "The Relationship between the Legal Corpora in the Pentateuch in Light of Manumission Laws." In *Studies in Bible, 1986*, edited by S. Japhet, 63–89. ScrHier 31. Jerusalem: Magnes, 1986.

Jeanrond, Werner G. *Text and Interpretation as Categories of Theological Thinking*. New York: Crossroads, 1988.

Johnstone, William. "Reactivating the Chronicles Analogy in Pentateuchal Studies, with Special Reference to the Sinai Pericope in Exodus." *ZAW* 99 (1987) 16–37.

———. "The Decalogue and the Redaction of the Sinai Pericope in Exodus." *ZAW* 100 (1988) 361–85.

Kaufman, Stephen A. "The Structure of the Deuteronomic Law." *Maarav* 1/2 (1978–79) 105–58.

———. "The Temple Scroll and Higher Criticism." *HUCA* 53 (1982) 29–43.

———. "Deuteronomy 15 and Recent Research on the Dating of P." In *Das Deuteronomium: Entstehung, Gestalt und Botschaft*, edited by Norbert Lohfink, 273–76. BETL 68. Louvain: University Press, 1985.

Kaufmann, Yehezkel. *Toledot ha-'emuna ha-yiśre'elit*. 8 vols. in 4 books. Jerusalem: Bialik Institute; Tel Aviv: Dvir, 1937–56 (Hebrew).

———. *The Religion of Israel: From Its Beginnings to the Babylonian Exile*. Translated and abridged by M. Greenberg. Chicago: University of Chicago Press, 1960.

Klein, Michael L. *The Fragment-Targums of the Pentateuch*. AnBib 76. Rome: Pontifical Biblical Institute, 1980.

Kline, Meredith G. *Treaty of the Great King: The Covenant Structure of Deuteronomy*. Grand Rapids: Eerdmans, 1963.

Klostermann, August. *Der Pentateuch: Beiträge zu seinem Verständnis und seiner Entstehungsgeschichte*. Leipzig: A. Deichert, 1907.

Knohl, Israel. "The Priestly Torah versus the Holiness School: Sabbath and the Festivals." *HUCA* 58 (1987) 65–117.

———. *The Sanctuary of Silence: The Priestly Torah and the Holiness School*. Minneapolis: Fortress, 1995.

Knoppers, Gary N. *The Reign of Solomon and the Rise of Jeroboam*. Vol. 1 of *Two Nations under God: The Deuteronomistic History of Solomon and the Dual Monarchies*. HSM 52. Atlanta: Scholars Press, 1993.

———. *The Reign of Jeroboam, the Fall of Israel, and the Reign of Josiah*. Vol. 2 of *Two Nations under God: The Deuteronomistic History of Solomon and the Dual Monarchies*. HSM 53. Atlanta: Scholars Press, 1994.

———. "Dissonance and Disaster in the Legend of Kirta." *JAOS* 114 (1994) 572–82.

———. "Jehoshaphat's Judiciary and 'the Scroll of YHWH's Torah.'" *JBL* 113 (1994) 59–80.

———. "The Deuteronomist and the Deuteronomic Law of the King: A Reexamination of a Relationship." *ZAW* 108 (1996) 329–46.

———. "Prayer and Propaganda: Solomon's Dedication of the Temple and the Deuteronomist's Program." *CBQ* 57 (1995) 229–54.

Köhler, Ludwig. *Hebrew Man*. London: SCM, 1956.

Krinetzki, Günter. *Rechtsprechung und Amt im Deuteronomium: Zur Exegese der Gesetze Dtn 16,18–20; 17,8–22*. Frankfurt: Peter Lang, 1994.

Kugel, James L. "On the Bible and Literary Criticism." *Prooftexts* 1 (1981) 217–36.

———. "Early Interpretation: The Common Background of Late Forms of Biblical Exegesis." In *Early Biblical Interpretation*, edited by James L. Kugel and Rowan A. Greer, 9–106. Philadelphia: Westminster, 1986.

L'Hour, J. "Une législation criminelle dans le Deutéronome." *Bib* 44 (1963) 1–28.

Laaf, Peter. *Die Pascha-Feier Israels: Eine literarkritische und überlieferungsgeschichtliche Studie*. BBB 36. Bonn: Peter Hanstein, 1970.

Lafont, Sophie. "Ancient Near Eastern Laws: Continuity and Pluralism." In *Theory and Method in Biblical and Cuneiform Law: Revision, Interpolation and Development*, edited by Bernard M. Levinson, 91–118. JSOTSup 181. Sheffield: Sheffield Academic Press, 1994.

Lauterbach, Jacob Z., ed. *Mekilta De-Rabbi Ishmael*. 3 vols. Philadelphia: JPS, 1933–35.

Lehmann, Manfred R. "Biblical Oaths." *ZAW* 81 (1969) 74–92.

Leiman, Sidney Z. *The Canonization of Hebrew Scripture: The Talmudic and Midrashic Evidence*. Connecticut Academy of Arts and Sciences Transactions 47. Hamden, Conn.: Archon, 1976.

Lemke, Werner K. "The Synoptic Problem in the Chronicler's History." *HTR* 58 (1965) 349–63.

Levenson, Jon D. *Sinai and Zion: An Entry into the Jewish Bible*. Minneapolis: Winston, 1985.

———. "The Sources of Torah: Psalm 119 and the Modes of Revelation in Second Temple Judaism." In *Ancient Israelite Religion: Essays in Honor of Frank Moore Cross*, edited by Patrick D. Miller, Jr., Paul D. Hanson, and S. Dean McBride, 559–74. Philadelphia: Fortress, 1987.

———. "The Hebrew Bible, the Old Testament, and Historical Criticism." In idem, *The Hebrew Bible, the Old Testament, and Historical Criticism: Jews and Christians in Biblical Studies*, 1–32. Louisville: Westminster/John Knox, 1993.

Levine, Baruch A. *Leviticus*. JPS Torah Commentary. Philadelphia: JPS, 1989.

Levinson, Bernard M. "Calum M. Carmichael's Approach to the Laws of Deuteronomy." *HTR* 83 (1990) 227–57.

———. "McConville's *Law and Theology in Deuteronomy*." *JQR* 80 (1990) 396–404.

———. *The Hermeneutics of Innovation: The Impact of Centralization upon the Structure, Sequence, and Reformulation of Legal Material in Deuteronomy*. Ann Arbor, Mich.: University Microfilms, 1991.

———. "'The Right Chorale': From the Poetics of Biblical Narrative to the Hermeneutics of the Hebrew Bible." In *"Not in Heaven": Coherence and Complexity in Biblical Narrative*, edited by Jason P. Rosenblatt and Joseph C. Sitterson, 129–53. Indiana Studies in Biblical Literature. Bloomington: Indiana University Press, 1991.

———. "The Human Voice in Divine Revelation: The Problem of Authority in Biblical Law." In *Innovation in Religious Traditions*, edited by Michael A. Williams, Collett Cox, and Martin S. Jaffee, 35–71. Religion and Society 31. Berlin: Mouton de Gruyter, 1992.

———. "The Case for Revision and Interpolation within the Biblical Legal Corpora." In *Theory and Method in Biblical and Cuneiform Law: Revision, Interpolation and Development*, edited by Bernard M. Levinson, 37–59. JSOTSup 181. Sheffield: Sheffield Academic Press, 1994.

———. "'But You Shall Surely Kill Him!': The Text-Critical and Neo-Assyrian Evidence for MT Deut 13:10." In *Bundesdokument und Gesetz: Studien zum Deuteronomium*, edited by Georg Braulik, 37–63. HBS 4. Freiburg: Herder, 1995.

———. "Recovering the Lost Original Meaning of עליו תכסה ולא (Deuteronomy 13:9)." *JBL* 115 (1996) 601–20.

Lewis, Theodore J. *Cults of the Dead in Ancient Israel and Ugarit*. HSM 39. Atlanta: Scholars Press, 1989.

Lieberman, Saul J. *Hellenism in Jewish Palestine*. 2d. ed. New York: Jewish Theological Seminary of America, 1962.

Lieberman, Stephen J. "Canonical and Official Cuneiform Texts: Towards an Understanding of Assurbanipal's Personal Tablet Collection." In *Lingering Over Words: Studies in Ancient Near Eastern Literature in Honor of William J. Moran*, edited by Tzvi Abusch, John Huehnergard, and Piotr Steinkeller, 305–36. HSM 37. Atlanta: Scholars Press, 1990.

Liedke, G. *Gestalt und Bezeichnung alttestamentlicher Rechtssätze. Eine formgeschichtlich-terminologische Studie*. WMANT 39. Neukirchen-Vluyn: Neukirchener Verlag, 1971.

Lockshin, Martin I. "Tradition or Context: Two Exegetes Struggle with Peshat." In *From Ancient Israel to Modern Judaism: Intellect in Quest of Understanding, Essays in Honor of Marvin Fox*, edited by Jacob Neusner, Ernest S. Frerichs, and Nahum M. Sarna, 2.173–86. 4 vols. BJS 159, 173–75. Atlanta: Scholars Press, 1989.

Loewenstamm, Samuel E. *The Evolution of the Exodus Tradition*. Jerusalem: Magnes, 1992.

———. "The Formula *Ba'et Hahi'* in the Introductory Speeches in Deuteronomy." *Tarbiz* 38 (1968–69) 99–104 (Hebrew). Translated in Loewenstamm, *From Babylon to Canaan: Studies in the Bible and its Oriental Background* (Jerusalem: Magnes, 1992) 42–50.

Lohfink, Norbert. *Das Hauptgebot: Eine Untersuchung literarischer Einleitungsfragen zu Dtn 5–11*. AnBib 20. Rome: Pontifical Biblical Institute, 1963.

———. "Die Sicherung der Wirksamkeit des Gotteswortes durch das Prinzip der Schriftlichkeit der Tora und durch das Prinzip der Gewaltenteilung nach den Ämtergesetzen des Buches Deuteronomium (Dt 16,18–18,22)." In *Testimonium Veritati: Festschrift Wilhelm Kempf*, edited by H. Wolter, 143–55. Frankfurter Theologische Studien 7. Frankfurt: Knecht, 1971. Reprinted and cited according to Lohfink, *Studien zum Deuteronomium und zur deuteronomistischen Literatur I*, 305–23. SBAB 8. Stuttgart: Katholisches Bibelwerk, 1990. Translated as "Distribution of the Functions of Power: The Laws Concerning Public Offices in Deuteronomy 16:18–18:22." In *A Song of Power and the Power of Song: Essays on the Book of Deuteronomy*, edited by Duane L. Christensen, 336–52. Winona Lake, Ind.: Eisenbrauns, 1993.

———. "Deuteronomy." *IDBSup*, 229–32. Nashville: Abingdon, 1976.

———. "Kerygmata des deuteronomistischen Geschichtswerks." In *Die Botschaft und die Boten: Festschrift für Hans Walter Wolff zum 70. Geburtstag*, edited by J. Jeremias and L. Perlitt, 87–100. Neukirchen-Vluyn: Neukirchener Verlag, 1981. Reprinted in and cited according to Lohfink, *Studien zum Deuteronomium und zur deuteronomistischen Literatur II*, 125–42. SBAB 12. Stuttgart: Katholisches Bibelwerk, 1991.

———. "Lectures on Deuteronomy 12–14." Unpublished Internal Course Material. Rome: Pontifical Biblical Institute, 1983.

———. "Zur deuteronomischen Zentralisationsformel." *Bib* 65 (1984) 297–328. Reprinted in and cited according to Lohfink, *Studien zum Deuteronomium und zur deuteronomistischen Literatur II*, 147–77. SBAB 12. Stuttgart: Katholisches Bibelwerk, 1991.

———. "Zur neueren Diskussion über 2 Kön 22–23." In *Das Deuteronomium: Entstehung, Gestalt und Botschaft*, edited by Norbert Lohfink, 24–48. BETL 68. Louvain: University Press, 1985. Translated as "Recent Discussion on 2 Kings 22–23: The State of the Question." In *A Song of Power and the Power of Song: Essays on the Book of Deuteronomy*, edited by Duane L. Christensen, 36–61. Winona Lake, Ind.: Eisenbrauns, 1993.

———. "חרם *ḥāram.*" *TDOT* 5 (1986) 180–99.

———. "The Cult Reform of Josiah of Judah: 2 Kings 22–23 as a Source for the History of Israelite Religion." In *Ancient Israelite Religion: Essays in Honor of Frank Moore Cross*, edited by Patrick D. Miller, Jr., Paul D. Hanson, and S. Dean McBride, 459–75. Philadelphia: Fortress, 1987.

———. Review of *Von der politischen Gemeinschaft zur Gemeinde*, by Udo Rütersworden. *TLZ* 113 (1988) 425–30.

———. "Dtn 12,1 und Gen 15,18: Das dem Samen Abrahams geschenkte Land als der Geltungsbereich der deuteronomischen Gesetze." In *Die Väter Israels: Festschrift für Josef Scharbert*, edited by A. R. Müller, 183–210. Stuttgart: Katholisches Bibelwerk, 1989. Reprinted in and cited according to Lohfink, *Studien zum Deuteronomium und zur deuteronomistischen Literatur II*, 257–85. SBAB 12. Stuttgart: Katholisches Bibelwerk, 1991.

———. "Die *ḥuqqîm ûmišpāṭîm* und ihre Neubegrenzung durch Dtn 12,1." *Bib* 70 (1989) 1–29. Reprinted in and cited according to Lohfink, *Studien zum Deuteronomium und zur deuteronomistischen Literatur II*, 229–56. SBAB 12. Stuttgart: Katholisches Bibelwerk, 1991.

———. "Das deuteronomische Gesetz in der Endgestalt—Entwurf einer Gesellschaft ohne marginale Gruppen." *BN* 51 (1990) 25–40.

———. "Das Deuteronomium: Jahwegesetz oder Mosegesetz? Die Subjektzuordnung bei Wörtern für 'Gesetz' im Dtn und in der dtr Literatur." *TP* 65 (1990) 387–91.

———. "Gibt es eine deuteronomistische Bearbeitung im Bundesbuch?" In *Pentateuchal and Deuteronomistic Studies: Papers Read at the XIIIth IOSOT Congress Leuven 1989*, edited by C. Brekelmans and J. Lust, 91–113. BETL 94. Louvain: Peeters Press/University Press, 1990.

———. "2 Kön 23,3 und Dtn 6,17." *Bib* 71 (1990) 34–42.

———. *Die Väter Israels im Deuteronomium: Mit einer Stellungnahme von Thomas Römer.* OBO 111. Freiburg, Switzerland: Universitätsverlag; Göttingen: Vandenhoeck & Ruprecht, 1991.

———. "Zum rabbinischen Verständnis von Dtn 12,1." In *Studien zum Deuteronomium und zur deuteronomistischen Literatur II*, 287–92. SBAB 12. Stuttgart: Katholisches Bibelwerk, 1991.

———. "Deutéronome et Pentateuque: État de la recherche." In *Le Pentateuque: Débats et recherches: XIVᵉ congrès de l'ACFEB, Angers (1991)*, edited by P. Haudebert, 35–64. LD 151. Paris: Cerf, 1992.

———. "Opfer und Säkularisierung im Deuteronomium." In *Studien zu Opfer und Kult im Alten Testament*, edited by Adrian Schenker, 15–43. Forschungen zum Alten Testament 3. Tübingen: J. C. B. Mohr (Paul Siebeck), 1992.

———. Review of *Deuteronomy 1–11*, by Moshe Weinfeld. *TLZ* 118 (1993) 127–30.

———. "Gab es eine deuteronomistische Bewegung?" In *Jeremia und die "deuteronomistische Bewegung"*, edited by Walter Groß, 313–82. BBB 98. Weinheim: BELTZ Athenäum, 1995.

———. "Kultzentralisation und Deuteronomium." Review Article of *Kultzentralisation: Entstehung und Theologie von Dtn 12*, by Eleonore Reuter. *Zeitschrift für Altorientalische und Biblische Rechtsgeschichte* 1 (1995) 117–48.

———. "Fortschreibung? Zur Technik von Rechtsrevisionen im deuteronomischen Bereich, erörtert an Deuteronomium 12, Ex 21,2–11 und Dtn 15,12–18." In *Das Deuteronomium und seine Querbeziehungen*, edited by Timo Veijola, 127–71. Schriften der Finnischen Exegetischen Gesellschaft 62. Göttingen: Vandenhoeck & Ruprecht, 1996.

Loretz, Otto. *Habiru-Hebräer: Eine sozio-linguistische Studie über die Herkunft des Gentiliziums ʿibrî vom Appellativum ḫabiru.* BZAW 160. Berlin: Walter de Gruyter, 1984.

McBride, S. Dean, Jr. "The Deuteronomic Name Theology." Ph.D. diss., Harvard University, 1969.

———. "Deuteronomium." *TRE* 7 (1982) 531–43.

———. "Polity of the Covenant People: The Book of Deuteronomy." *Int* 41 (1987) 229–44. Reprinted in *A Song of Power and the Power of Song: Essays on the Book of Deuteronomy*, edited by Duane L. Christensen, 62–77. Winona Lake, Ind.: Eisenbrauns, 1993.

McConville, J. G. *Law and Theology in Deuteronomy.* JSOTSup 33. Sheffield: JSOT Press, 1984.

Macholz, G. C. "Die Stellung des Königs in der israelitischen Gerichtsverfassung." *ZAW* 84 (1972) 157–82.

———. "Zur Geschichte der Justizorganisation in Juda." *ZAW* 84 (1972) 314–40.

McKenzie, D. A. "Judicial Procedure at the Town Gate." *VT* 14 (1964) 100–104.

Mackenzie, Roderick A. F. "The Formal Aspect of Ancient Near Eastern Law." In *The Seed of Wisdom: Essays in Honor of T. J. Meek*, edited by W. S. McCullough, 31–44. Toronto: University of Toronto Press, 1964.

McKenzie, Steven L. *The Chronicler's Use of the Deuteronomistic History.* HSM 33. Atlanta: Scholars Press, 1985.

———. *The Trouble with Kings: The Composition of the Book of Kings in the Deuteronomistic History.* VTSup 42. Leiden: E. J. Brill, 1991.

———. "The Books of Kings in the Deuteronomistic History." In *The History of Israel's Traditions: The Heritage of Martin Noth*, edited by Steven L. McKenzie and M. Patrick Graham, 281–307. JSOTSup 182. Sheffield: Sheffield Academic Press, 1994.

Maier, W. A., III. *ʾAšerah: Extrabiblical Evidence.* HSM 37. Atlanta: Scholars Press, 1986.

Malul, Meir. *Studies in Mesopotamian Legal Symbolism.* AOAT 221. Kevelaer: Butzon & Bercker; Neukirchen-Vluyn: Neukirchener Verlag, 1988.

Margalit, Baruch. "The Meaning and Significance of Asherah." *VT* 40 (1990) 264–97.

Marks, Herbert. Review of *Biblical Interpretation in Ancient Israel*, by Michael Fishbane. *Yearbook of Comparative and General Literature* 35 (1986) 152–55.

Matthews, Victor H. "Entrance Ways and Threshing Floors: Legally Significant Sites in the Ancient Near East." *Fides et Historia* 19 (1987) 25–40.

Mayes, A. D. H. "The Period of the Judges and the Rise of the Monarchy." In *Israelite and Judaean History*, edited by J. H. Hayes and J. M. Miller, 297–304. Philadelphia: Westminster, 1977.

———. *Deuteronomy.* NCBC. London: Marshall, Morgan & Scott, 1979.

———. "On Describing the Purpose of Deuteronomy." *JSOT* 58 (1993) 13–33.

Meier, Samuel A. *Speaking of Speaking: Marking Direct Discourse in the Hebrew Bible.* VTSup 46. Leiden: E. J. Brill, 1992.

Meir, R. Samuel ben (Rashbam). *Commentary on the Pentateuch.* Edited by David Rosin. Breslau: Schottelaender, 1881 (Hebrew).

Merendino, Rosario Pius. *Das deuteronomische Gesetz: Eine literarkritische, gattungs- und überlieferungsgeschichtliche Untersuchung zu Dt 12–26.* BBB 31. Bonn: Peter Hanstein, 1969.

Mettinger, Tryggve N. D. *The Dethronement of Sabaoth: Studies in the Shem and Kabod Theologies.* Lund: CWK Gleerup, 1982.

Midrash rabbah ha-mevu'ar, vol. 2, *Shemot rabbah*. 2 vols. Jerusalem: Makhon ha-midrash ha-mevu'ar, 1983 (Hebrew). Translated as *Midrash Rabbah Exodus* by S. M. Lehrman. London: Soncino, 1983.

Milgrom, Jacob. "The Alleged 'Demythologization' and 'Secularization' in Deuteronomy." *IEJ* 23 (1973) 156–61.

———. "Profane Slaughter and a Formulaic Key to the Composition of Deuteronomy." *HUCA* 47 (1976) 1–17.

———. "The Ideological and Historical Importance of the Office of Judge in Deuteronomy." In *Isac* [*sic*] *Leo Seeligmann Volume: Essays on the Bible and the Ancient World*, edited by Alexander Rofé and Yair Zakovitch, 3.129–40. Jerusalem: E. Rubinstein, 1983.

———. "Ethics and Ritual: The Foundations of the Biblical Dietary Laws." In *Religion and Law: Biblical-Judaic and Islamic Perspectives*, edited by E. B. Firmage, B. G. Weiss, and J. W. Welch, 159–91. Winona Lake, Ind.: Eisenbrauns, 1990.

———. *Leviticus 1–16*. AB 3. New York: Doubleday, 1991.

———. "Lex Talionis and the Rabbis." *Bible Review* 12:2 (April 1996) 16, 48.

Miller, Patrick D. *Deuteronomy*. Interpretation, a Bible Commentary for Teaching and Preaching. Louisville: John Knox, 1990.

Minnette de Tillesse, G. "Sections 'tu' et sections 'vous' dans le Deutéronome." *VT* 12 (1962) 29–87.

Moore, G. F. "The Vulgate Chapters and the Numbered Verses in the Hebrew Bible." *JBL* 12 (1893) 73–78. Reprinted, *The Canon and Masorah of the Hebrew Bible*, edited by Sidney Z. Leiman, 815–820. New York: Ktav, 1974.

Morgan, Donn Farley. *The So-Called Cultic Calendars in the Pentateuch: A Morphological and Typological Study*. Ann Arbor, Mich.: University Microfilms, 1974.

Morrow, William S. "The Composition of Deuteronomy 14:1–17:1." Ph.D. diss., University of Toronto, 1988.

———. *Scribing the Center: Organization and Redaction in Deuteronomy 14:1–17:13*. SBLMS 49. Atlanta: Scholars Press, 1995.

Nachmanides (R. Moses ben Nachman). *Commentary on the Torah*. Edited by Charles B. Chavel. 2 vols. Jerusalem: Rav Kook Institute, 1959 (Hebrew). Translation by Charles B. Chavel. 5 vols. New York: Shilo, 1971–76.

Nicholson, Ernest W. *Deuteronomy and Tradition*. Philadelphia: Fortress, 1967.

Nicolsky, N. M. "Pascha im Kulte des jerusalemischen Tempels." *ZAW* 45 (1927) 171–90.

Niehr, Herbert. *Rechtsprechung in Israel: Untersuchungen zur Geschichte der Gerichtsorganisation im Alten Testament*. SBS 130. Stuttgart: Katholisches Bibelwerk, 1987.

Nielsen, Eduard. *Deuteronomium*. Handbuch zum Alten Testament 1.6. Tübingen: J. C. B. Mohr (Paul Siebeck), 1995.

Noth, Martin. *Exodus*. OTL. Philadelphia: Westminster, 1962.

———. *Numbers*. OTL. Philadelphia: Westminster, 1968.

Olyan, Saul M. *Asherah and the Cult of Yahweh in Israel*. SBLMS 34. Atlanta: Scholars Press, 1988.

Orlinsky, Harry M. *Notes on the New Translation of the Torah*. Philadelphia: JPS, 1970.

Osumi, Yuichi. *Die Kompositionsgeschichte des Bundesbuches Exodus 20,22b–23,33*. OBO 105. Freiburg, Switzerland: Universitätsverlag; Göttingen: Vandenhoeck & Ruprecht, 1991.

Otto, Eckart. *Das Mazzotfest in Gilgal*. BWANT 107. Stuttgart: W. Kohlhammer, 1975.

———. *Jerusalem—die Geschichte der Heiligen Stadt: Von den Anfängen bis zur Kreuzfahrerzeit*. Stuttgart: W. Kohlhammer, 1980.

————. *Wandel der Rechtsbegründungen in der Gesellschaftsgeschichte des antiken Israel: Eine Rechtsgeschichte des "Bundesbuches" Ex XX 22–XXIII 13*. StudBib 3. Leiden: E. J. Brill, 1988.

————. "Die rechtshistorische Entwicklung des Depositenrechts in altorientalischen und altisraelitischen Rechtskorpora." *Zeitschrift der Savigny-Stiftung für Rechtsgeschichte, Romanistische Abteilung* 105 (1988) 1–31.

————. "פסח *pāsaḥ/paesaḥ*." *TWAT* 6 (1989) 659–82.

————. *Körperverletzungen in den Keilschriftrechten und im Alten Testament: Studien zum Rechtstransfer im Alten Orient*. AOAT 226. Kevelaer: Butzon & Bercker; Neukirchen-Vluyn: Neukirchener Verlag, 1991.

————. "Soziale Verantwortung und Reinheit des Landes: Zur Redaktion der kasuistischen Rechtssätze in Deuteronomium 19–25." In *Prophetie und geschichtliche Wirklichkeit im alten Israel: Festschrift für Siegfried Hermann*, edited by Rüdiger Liwak and Siegfried Wagner, 290–306. Stuttgart: W. Kohlhammer, 1991.

————. "שבע/שבועות *šaeba'/šābûʿôt*." *TWAT* 7 (1992) 1000–1027.

————. "Rechtsreformen in Deuteronomium XII–XXVI und im Mittelassyrischen Kodex der Tafel A (KAV 1)." In *Congress Volume: Paris, 1992*, edited by J. A. Emerton, 239–73. VTSup 61. Leiden: E. J. Brill, 1995.

————. "Vom Bundesbuch zum Deuteronomium: die deuteronomische Redaktion in Dtn 12–26." In *Biblische Theologie und gesellschaftlicher Wandel: Für Norbert Lohfink*, edited by Georg Braulik, Walter Groß, and Sean McEvenue, 260–78. Freiburg: Herder, 1993.

————. "Zur Kompositionsgeschichte des alttestamentlichen 'Bundesbuches' Ex 20,22b–23,33." Review Article of *Die Kompositionsgeschichte des Bundesbuches Exodus 20,22b–23,33*, by Yuichi Osumi. *WZKM* 83 (1993) 149–65.

————. "Die Torah in Israels Rechtsgeschichte." Review Article of *Die Tora: Theologie und Sozialgeschichte des alttestamentlichen Gesetzes*, by Frank Crüsemann. *TLZ* 118 (1993) 904–10.

————. "Town and Rural Countryside in Ancient Israelite Law: Reception and Redaction in Cuneiform and Israelite Law." *JSOT* 57 (1993) 3–22.

————. "Aspects of Legal Reform and Reformulation in Ancient Cuneiform and Israelite Law." In *Theory and Method in Biblical and Cuneiform Law: Revision, Interpolation and Development*, edited by Bernard M. Levinson, 160–96. JSOTSup 181. Sheffield: Sheffield Academic Press, 1994.

————. "Del libro de la Alianza a la ley de Santidad: La reformulación del derecho israelita y la formación del Pentateuco." *EstBib* 52 (1994) 195–217.

————. "Vom Rechtsbruch zur Sünde: Priesterliche Interpretationen des Rechts." *Jahrbuch für Biblische Theologie* 9 (1994) 25–52.

————. Review of *Die Deuteronomischen Gesetze und der Dekalog*, by Georg Braulik. *TLZ* 119 (1994) 15–17.

————. *Theologische Ethik des Alten Testaments*. Theologische Wissenschaft 3.2. Stuttgart: W. Kohlhammer, 1994.

————. "Von der Gerichtsordnung zum Verfassungsentwurf: Deuteronomische Gestaltung und deuteronomistische Interpretation im 'Ämtergesetz' Dtn 16,18–18,22." In *"Wer ist wie du, HERR, unter den Göttern?" Studien zur Theologie und Religionsgeschichte Israels für Otto Kaiser*, edited by Ingo Kottsieper et al., 142–55. Göttingen: Vandenhoeck & Ruprecht, 1995.

————. "Von der Programmschrift einer Rechtsreform zum Verfassungsentwurf des Neuen Israel: Die Stellung des Deuteronomiums in der Rechtsgeschichte Israels."

In *Bundesdokument und Gesetz: Studien zum Deuteronomium,* edited by Georg Braulik, 93–104. HBS 4. Freiburg: Herder, 1995.

———. "שער *Ša'ar.*" *TWAT* 8 (1995) 358–403.

———. "Diachronie und Synchronie im Depositenrecht des 'Bundesbuches.'" *Zeitschrift für Altorientalische und Biblische Rechtsgeschichte* 2 (1996) 76–85.

———. "Treueid und Gesetz: Die Ursprünge des Deuteronomiums im Horizont neuassyrischen Vertragsrechts." *Zeitschrift für Altorientalische und Biblische Rechtsgeschichte* 2 (1996) 1–52.

Otto, Eckart, and Tim Schramm. *Festival and Joy.* Nashville: Abingdon, 1980.

Palmer, Richard E. *Hermeneutics: Interpretation Theory in Schleiermacher, Dilthey, Heidegger, and Gadamer.* Northwestern University Studies in Phenomenology and Existential Philosophy. Evanston, Ill.: Northwestern University Press, 1969.

Parpola, Simo, and Kazuko Watanabe, eds. *Neo-Assyrian Treaties and Loyalty Oaths.* State Archives of Assyria 2. Helsinki: Helsinki University Press, 1988.

Paton, Louis Bayles. "The Case for the Post-Exilic Origins of Deuteronomy." *JBL* 47 (1928) 322–57.

Patrick, Dale. *Old Testament Law.* Atlanta: John Knox, 1985.

Perlitt, Lothar. "Der Staatsgedanke im Deuteronomium." In *Language, Theology, and the Bible: Essays in Honour of James Barr,* edited by Samuel E. Balentine and James Barton, 182–98. Oxford: Clarendon, 1994.

Peshitta Institute, ed. *The Old Testament in Syriac according to the Peshitta Version.* 1.1. Leiden: E. J. Brill, 1977.

Petschow, Herbert. "Zur Systematik und Gesetzestechnik im Codex Hammurabi." *ZA* 57 (1965) 146–72.

Phillips, A. *Ancient Israel's Criminal Law: A New Approach to the Decalogue.* New York: Schocken, 1970.

Polka, Brayton. *The Dialectic of Biblical Critique: Interpretation and Existence.* New York: St. Martin's, 1986.

———. *Truth and Interpretation: An Essay in Thinking.* New York: St. Martin's, 1990.

Polzin, Robert. *Moses and the Deuteronomist: A Literary Study of the Deuteronomic History.* New York: Seabury, 1980.

Preuß, Horst Dietrich. *Deuteronomium.* ErFor 164. Darmstadt: Wissenschaftliche Buchgesellschaft, 1982.

———. "Zum deuteronomistischen Geschichtswerk." *TRu* 58 (1993) 229–64, 341–95.

Pritchard, James B. *Ancient Near Eastern Texts Relating to the Old Testament.* 3d ed. Princeton: Princeton University Press, 1969.

Pury, Albert de, and Thomas Römer. "Le Pentateuque en question: Position du problème et brève histoire de la recherche." In *Le Pentateuque en question: Les Origines et la composition des cinq premiers livres de la Bible à la lumière des recherches récentes,* edited by Albert de Pury, 9–80. Le Monde de la Bible 19. 2d ed. Geneva: Labor et Fides, 1991.

Rabin, Chaim. "Discourse Analysis and the Dating of Deuteronomy." In *Interpreting the Hebrew Bible. Essays in Honour of E. I. J. Rosenthal,* edited by J. A. Emerton and S. C. Reif, 171–78. Cambridge: Cambridge University Press, 1982.

Rad, Gerhard von. *Studies in Deuteronomy.* SBT 9. Chicago: Henry Regnery, 1953.

———. *Deuteronomy.* OTL. Philadelphia: Westminster, 1966.

———. *The Problem of the Hexateuch and Other Essays.* New York: McGraw Hill, 1966.

Rakover, N. *A Bibliography of Jewish Law.* Jerusalem: Harry Fischel Institute for Research in Jewish Law, 1975.

Ramban. *See* Nachmanides.

Rashbam. *See* Meir, R. Samuel ben.

Rawidowicz, Simon. "On Interpretation." *PAAJR* 26 (1957) 83–126. Reprinted, with abridged notes, in Rawidowicz, *Studies in Jewish Thought,* 45–80. Philadelphia: JPS, 1974.

Reuter, Eleonore. "'Nimm nichts davon weg und füge nichts hinzu!' Dtn 13,1, seine alttestamentlichen Parallelen und seine altorientalischen Vorbilder." *BN* 47 (1989) 107–14.

———. *Kultzentralisation: Entstehung und Theologie von Dtn 12.* BBB 87. Frankfurt: Anton Hain, 1993.

Reviv, Hanoch. *The Elders in Ancient Israel: A Study of a Biblical Institution.* Jerusalem: Magnes, 1989.

Roberts, B. J. *The Old Testament Text and Versions.* Cardiff: University of Wales, 1951.

Rochberg-Halton, Francesca. "Canonicity in Cuneiform Texts." *JCS* 36 (1984) 127–44.

Rofé, Alexander. "The Strata of Law about the Centralization of Worship in Deuteronomy and the History of the Deuteronomic Movement." In *Congress Volume, Uppsala 1971,* 221–26. VTSup 22. Leiden: E. J. Brill, 1972.

———. Review of *Deuteronomy and the Deuteronomic School,* by Moshe Weinfeld. *Christian News from Israel* 24 (1974) 204–09.

———. "The Law about the Organization of Justice in Deuteronomy (16:18–20; 17:8–13)." *Beth Miqra* 65 (1976) 199–210 (Hebrew; English abstract).

———. "The Arrangement of the Laws in Deuteronomy." *ETL* 64 (1988) 265–87.

———. *Introduction to Deuteronomy: Part I and Further Chapters.* 2d rev. ed. Jerusalem: Akademon, 1988 (Hebrew).

———. "The Vineyard of Naboth: The Origin and Message of the Story." *VT* 38 (1988) 89–104.

Römer, Thomas. "Le Deutéronome à la quête des origines." In *Le Pentateuque: Débats et recherches: XIVᵉ congrès de l'ACFEB, Angers (1991),* edited by P. Haudebert, 65–98. LD 151. Paris: Cerf, 1992.

———. "The Book of Deuteronomy." In *The History of Israel's Traditions: The Heritage of Martin Noth,* edited by Steven L. McKenzie and M. Patrick Graham, 178–212. JSOTSup 182. Sheffield: Sheffield Academic Press, 1994.

Rose, Martin. *Der Ausschließlichkeitsanspruch Jahwes: Deuteronomische Schultheologie und die Volksfrömmigkeit in der späten Königszeit.* BWANT 106. Stuttgart: W. Kohlhammer, 1975.

Roth, Martha T. *Law Collections from Mesopotamia and Asia Minor.* SBLWAW 6. Atlanta: Scholars Press, 1995.

Rothschild, Hava Tirosh. "Continuity and Revision in the Study of Kabbalah." Review Article of *Kabbalah: New Perspectives,* by Moshe Idel. *AJS Review* 16 (1991) 161–92.

Rüterswörden, Udo. *Von der politischen Gemeinschaft zur Gemeinde: Studien zu Dt 16,18–18,22.* BBB 65. Frankfurt: Athenäum, 1987.

———. "Der Verfassungsentwurf des Deuteronomiums in der neueren Diskussion: Ein Überblick." In *Altes Testament Forschung und Wirkung: Festschrift für Henning Graf Reventlow,* edited by Peter Mommer and Winfried Thiel, 313–28. Berlin: Peter Lang, 1994.

Said, Edward W. *Beginnings: Intention and Method.* New York: Basic Books, 1975.

Sanders, James A. *Torah and Canon.* Philadelphia: Fortress, 1972.

————. "Adaptable for Life: The Nature and Function of Canon." In *Magnalia Dei, the Mighty Acts of God: Essays on the Bible and Archeology in Memory of G. Ernest Wright*, edited by F. M. Cross, W. Lemke, and P. Miller, 531–60. Garden City, N.Y.: Doubleday, 1976.

————. *From Sacred Story to Sacred Text: Canon as Paradigm.* Philadelphia: Fortress, 1987.

Sarna, Nahum M. "Psalm 89: A Study in Inner Biblical Exegesis." In *Biblical and Other Studies*, edited by A. Altmann, 29–46. Brandeis University Studies and Texts 1. Cambridge, Mass.: Harvard University Press, 1963.

Schäfer-Lichtenberger, Christa. *Josua und Salomo: Eine Studie zu Autorität und Legitimität des Nachfolgers im Alten Testament.* VTSup 58. Leiden: E. J. Brill, 1994.

Schmitt, G. *Du sollst keinen Frieden schließen mit den Bewohnern des Landes: Die Wegweisung gegen die Kanaanäer in Israels Geschichte und Geschichtsschreibung.* BWANT 91. Stuttgart: Kohlhammer, 1970.

Scholem, Gershom. "Revelation and Tradition as Religious Categories in Judaism." In his *The Messianic Idea in Judaism*, 282–303. New York: Schocken, 1971.

Schwienhorst-Schönberger, Ludger. *Das Bundesbuch (Ex 20,22–23,33): Studien zu seiner Entstehung und Theologie.* BZAW 188. Berlin: Walter de Gruyter, 1990.

Seebaß, Horst. "Vorschlag zur Vereinfachung literarischer Analysen im dtn Gesetz." *BN* 58 (1991) 83–98.

Seeligmann, Isaac Leo. "Hebräische Erzählung und biblische Geschichtsschreibung." *Theologische Zeitschrift* 18 (1962) 305–25.

————. "The Beginnings of Midrash in the Books of Chronicles." *Tarbiz* 49 (1979–80) 14–32 (Hebrew; English summary, ii–iii).

Segal, J. B. *The Hebrew Passover: From the Earliest Times to* A.D. *70.* London Oriental Series 12. London: Oxford University Press, 1963.

Segert, Stanislav. "Genres of Ancient Israelite Legal Sentences: 1934 and 1974." *WZKM* 68 (1976) 131–42.

Seidel, Moshe. "Parallels between Isaiah and Psalms." *Sinai* 38 (1955–56) 149–72, 229–40, 272–80, 335–55. Reprinted in Seidel, *Hiqrei Miqra*, 1–97. Jerusalem: Rav Kook Institute, 1978 (Hebrew).

Seitz, Gottfried. *Redaktionsgeschichtliche Studien zum Deuteronomium.* BWANT 93. Stuttgart: Kohlhammer, 1971.

Shaver, Judson R. *Torah and the Chronicler's History Work: An Inquiry into the Chronicler's References to Laws, Festivals, and Cultic Institutions in Relationship to Pentateuchal Legislation.* BJS 196. Atlanta: Scholars Press, 1989.

Skweres, Dieter Eduard. *Die Rückverweise im Buch Deuteronomium.* AnBib 79. Rome: Pontifical Biblical Institute, 1979.

Smith, Jonathan Z. "Sacred Persistence: Toward a Redescription of Canon." In *Imagining Religion: From Babylon to Jonestown*, 36–52. Chicago Studies in the History of Judaism. Chicago and London: University of Chicago Press, 1982.

Smith, Morton. "Pseudepigraphy in the Israelite Literary Tradition." In *Pseudepigrapha I: Pseudopythagorica—Lettres de Platon—Littérature pseudépigraphique juive*, edited by Kurt von Fritz, 191–215. Fondation Hardt. Entretiens sur l'antiquité classique 18. Geneva: Vandoeuvres, 1971.

————. *Palestinian Parties and Politics That Shaped the Old Testament.* 2d ed. London: SCM Press, 1987.

Sonnet, Jean-Pierre. *"When Moses Had Finished Writing": Communication in Deuteronomy / Deuteronomy as Communication.* Ann Arbor, Mich.: University Microfilms, 1996. Revision forthcoming as Sonnet, *The Book within the Book: Writing in Deuteronomy*. Biblical Interpretation 14. Leiden: E. J. Brill, 1997.

Sperber, Alexander. *The Bible in Aramaic Based on Old Manuscripts and Printed Texts. 1: The Pentateuch According to Targum Onkelos*. Leiden: E. J. Brill, 1959.

Sprinkle, Joseph M. *The "Book of the Covenant": A Literary Approach*. JSOTSup 174. Sheffield: JSOT Press, 1994.

Stegemann, Hartmut. "Is the Temple Scroll a Sixth Book of the Torah—Lost for 2,500 Years?" *Biblical Archaeology Review* 13 (1987) 28–35.

Stern, Philip D. *The Biblical Ḥerem: A Window on Israel's Religious Experience*. BJS 211. Atlanta: Scholars Press, 1991.

Steymans, Hans Ulrich. "Eine assyrische Vorlage für Deuteronomium 28,20–44." In *Bundesdokument und Gesetz: Studien zum Deuteronomium*, edited by Georg Braulik, 119–41. HBS 4. Freiburg: Herder, 1995.

Suzuki, Yoshihide. "The 'Numeruswechsel' in Deuteronomy." Ph. D. diss. Claremont Graduate School, 1982.

———. "Deuteronomic Reformation in View of the Centralization of the Administration of Justice." *AJBI* 13 (1987) 22–58.

Talmon, Shemaryahu. "Double Readings in the Massoretic Text." *Textus* 1 (1960) 144–84.

———. "The Textual Study of the Bible—a New Outlook." In *Qumran and the History of the Biblical Text*, edited by F. M. Cross and S. Talmon, 321–400. Cambridge, Mass.: Harvard University, 1975.

———. "The Presentation of Synchroneity and Simultaneity in Biblical Narrative." In *Studies in Hebrew Narrative Art Throughout the Ages*, edited by J. Heinemann and S. Werses, 9–26. ScrHier 27. Jerusalem: Magnes, 1978. Reprinted in Talmon, *Literary Studies in the Hebrew Bible: Form and Content, Collected Studies*, 112–33. Jerusalem: Magnes; Leiden: E. J. Brill, 1993.

Thompson, Thomas L. *Early History of the Israelite People: From the Written and Archaeological Sources*. Studies in the History of the Ancient Near East 4. Leiden: E. J. Brill, 1992.

———. "Palestinian Pastoralism and Israel's Origins." *SJOT* 6 (1992) 1–13.

Tigay, Jeffrey H. "Conflation as a Redactional Technique." In *Empirical Models for Biblical Criticism*, edited by Jeffrey H. Tigay, 53–96. Philadelphia: University of Pennsylvania, 1985.

Tomback, Richard S. *A Comparative Semitic Lexicon of the Phoenician and Punic Languages*. SBLDS 32. Missoula: Scholars Press, 1978.

Tov, Emanuel. "Glosses, Interpolations, and Other Types of Scribal Additions in the Text of the Hebrew Bible." In *Language, Theology, and The Bible: Essays in Honour of James Barr*, edited by Samuel E. Balentine and John Barton, 40–66. Oxford: Clarendon, 1994.

van der Toorn, Karel. *Sin and Sanction in Israel and Mesopotamia: A Comparative Study*. SSN 22. Assen/Maastricht: Van Gorcum, 1985.

Van Seters, John. *Abraham in History and Tradition*. New Haven: Yale University Press, 1975.

———. "The Place of the Yahwist in the History of Passover and Massot." *ZAW* 95 (1983) 167–82.

———. "Etiology in the Moses Tradition: The Case of Exodus 18." In *Biblical and Other Studies in Memory of S. D. Goitein*, edited by R. Ahroni, 355–61. HAR 9. Columbus: Department of Judaic and Near Eastern Languages and Literatures, Ohio State University, 1985.

———. "'Comparing Scripture with Scripture': Some Observations on the Sinai Pericope of Exodus 19–24." In *Canon, Theology, and Old Testament Interpretation: Essays in Honor of Brevard S. Childs,* edited by G. M. Tucker, D. L. Peterson, and R. R. Wilson, 111–30. Philadelphia: Fortress Press, 1988.

———. *The Life of Moses: The Yahwist as Historian in Exodus–Numbers.* Louisville: Westminster/John Knox, 1994.

Vaux, Roland de. *Ancient Israel: Its Life and Institutions.* London: Darton, Longman & Todd, 1961.

Veijola, Timo. "Wahrheit und Intoleranz nach Deuteronomium 13." *ZTK* 92 (1995) 287–314.

———. "The History of Passover in the Light of Deuteronomy 16, 1–8." *Zeitschrift für Altorientalische und Biblische Rechtsgeschichte* 2 (1996) 53–75.

Viberg, Åke. *Symbols of Law: A Contextual Analysis of Legal Symbolic Acts in the Old Testament.* ConBOT 34. Stockholm: Almqvist & Wiksell, 1992.

Wacholder, Ben Zion. *The Dawn of Qumran: The Sectarian Torah and the Teacher of Righteousness.* Cincinnati: Hebrew Union College Press, 1983.

Waltke, Bruce K., and M. O'Connor. *An Introduction to Biblical Hebrew Syntax.* Winona Lake, Ind.: Eisenbrauns, 1990.

Wambacq, B. N. "Les Origines de la *Pesaḥ* israélite." *Bib* 57 (1976) 206–24.

———. "Les Maṣṣôt." *Bib* 61 (1980) 31–54.

Weinberg, Joel P. "Das *bēit 'ābōt* im 6.–4. Jahrhundert v.u.Z." *VT* 23 (1973) 400–14.

———. *The Citizen-Temple Community.* JSOTSup 151. Sheffield: Sheffield Academic Press, 1992.

Weinfeld, Moshe. "The Reorientation in the Understanding of the Divinity and of the Cultus in the Book of Deuteronomy." *Tarbiz* 31 (1961–62) 1–17 (Hebrew, English summary).

———. "Deuteronomy—The Present State of Inquiry." *JBL* 86 (1967) 249–62. Reprinted in *A Song of Power and the Power of Song: Essays on the Book of Deuteronomy,* edited by Duane L. Christensen, 21–35. Winona Lake, Ind.: Eisenbrauns, 1993.

———. *Deuteronomy and the Deuteronomic School.* Oxford: Clarendon, 1972.

———. "Elders." *Encyclopedia Judaica* 6.578–80. Jerusalem: Encyclopedia Judaica, 1972.

———. "Ordeal of Jealousy." *Encyclopedia Judaica* 12.1449–50. Jerusalem: Encyclopedia Judaica, 1972.

———. "The Loyalty Oath in the Ancient Near East." *UF* 8 (1976) 379–414.

———. "Judge and Officer in Ancient Israel and in the Ancient Near East." *Israel Oriental Studies* 7 (1977) 65–88.

———. *Deuteronomy 1–11.* AB 5. New York: Doubleday, 1991.

Weissblueth, S. "'In Every Place Where I Mention My Name I Will Come to You and Bless You.'" *Beth Mikra* 30 (1984/85) 173–78 (Hebrew).

Welch, Adam C. *The Code of Deuteronomy: A New Theory of Its Origin.* New York: George H. Doran [1924].

Wellhausen, Julius. *Prolegomena to the History of Israel.* Edinburgh: Adam & Charles Black, 1885. Reprinted, New York: Meridian, 1957.

———. *Die Composition des Hexateuchs und der historischen Bücher des Alten Testaments.* 4th ed. Berlin: Walter de Gruyter, 1963.

Westbrook, Raymond. "Biblical and Cuneiform Law Codes." *RB* 92 (1985) 247–64.

————. *Studies in Biblical and Cuneiform Law*. CahRB 26. Paris: Gabalda, 1988.

————. "What Is the Covenant Code?" In *Theory and Method in Biblical and Cunei-form Law: Revision, Interpolation and Development*, edited by Bernard M. Levinson, 15–36. JSOTSup 181. Sheffield: Sheffield Academic Press, 1994.

Whitelam, Keith W. *The Just King: Monarchical Judicial Authority in Ancient Israel*. JSOTSup 12. Sheffield: JSOT Press, 1979.

Wiener, Harold M. "The Arrangement of Deuteronomy 12–26." *JPOS* 6 (1926) 185–95. Republished in Wiener, *Posthumous Essays*, 26–36. Edited by H. Loewe. London: Oxford, 1932.

————. *The Altars of the Old Testament*. Beigabe zur orientalistischen Literatur-Zeitung. Leipzig: J. C. Hinrichs, 1927.

Williams, Ronald J. *Hebrew Syntax: An Outline*. 2d ed. Toronto: University of Toronto Press, 1976.

Williamson, Hugh G. M. "History." In *It Is Written: Scripture Citing Scripture: Es-says in Honour of Barnabas Lindars*, edited by D. A. Carson and H. G. M. Williamson, 25–38. Cambridge: Cambridge University Press, 1988.

Wilson, Robert R. *Prophecy and Society in Ancient Israel*. Philadelphia: Fortress, 1980.

————."Enforcing the Covenant: The Mechanisms of Judicial Authority in Early Israel." In *The Quest for the Kingdom of God: Studies in Honor of George E. Mendenhall*, edited by H. B. Huffmon, F. A. Spina, and A. R. W. Green, 59–75. Winona Lake, Ind.: Eisenbrauns, 1983.

————. "Israel's Judicial System in the Preexilic Period." *JQR* 74 (1983) 229–48.

Wise, Michael Owen. *A Critical Study of the Temple Scroll from Qumran Cave 11*. Chicago: Oriental Institute of the University of Chicago, 1990.

Wright, George Ernest. "The Book of Deuteronomy." Vol. 2 of *Interpreter's Bible*. Nashville: Abingdon-Cokesbury, 1953.

Yadin, Yigael. *The Temple Scroll*. 3 vols. Jerusalem: Israel Exploration Society, 1977–83.

Yaron, Reuven. *The Laws of Eshnunna*. 2d ed. Jerusalem: Magnes; Leiden: E. J. Brill, 1988.

————. "'Enquire Now about Hammurabi, Ruler of Babylon.'" *Legal History Review* 49 (1991) 223–38.

Yeivin, Israel. *Introduction to the Tiberian Masorah*. SBLMasS 5. [Missoula:] Schol-ars Press, 1980.

Author Index

Pages where substantial discussion occurs are in italics.

Subject Index

Aaron, 19, 113
Abimelek, 32 n.18, 81 n.87
Abraham, 4, 32 n.18
Absalom, 140
Achaemenid models of royal authority, 126 n.73, 154
adê (loyalty oath). *See* cuneiform law: vassal treaty
altar, as site for theophany, 5, 31, 31 n.17, 49–51
altar law of the Covenant Code, 8, 31–38, 46, 49, 145
altars, local. *See* local altars
ambiguous legal cases, 113–14, 117, 127–30
Amoraim, 47
amphictyony, 57 n.9, 95 n.117
Ämtergesetze. See Laws of Public Officials
ancestor worship, 148 n.8. *See also* popular piety
Angel of Destruction, 58
anthology, redactional, 28
apostasy, laws of
  as an abomination, 102
  incitement to, 103–104, 108, 118, 120, 132, 144–46
  paradigmatic function of, 124

question of literary sequence, 99
relation of Deut 13:7–12 and 17:2–7, 101–104, 108, 118–23, 131–33
represent series of exegetical reformulations, 122–23 and notes
as transgression against the Decalogue, 133–35
apotropaic ritual(s), 5, 58–59, 58 n.15, 60 n.25, 61–62, 72, 79, 87. *See also* blood
archaeology, 63, 148
Ark Narrative, 138–39
Asherah. *See under* popular piety
Ashurbanipal, 63
association of words or ideas. *See under* editorial devices
Assyria. *See* cuneiform law: vassal treaty; neo-Assyrian crisis
astral worship, 135, 135 n.93
authorship
  denial of, 47
  impediments to, 5–6, 13–17, 28, 33–34, 41–43, 46–48, 53–54, 109–10, 146–50
  models of, 27, 156–57
  See also exegesis; originality; texts; textual authority

Index of Scriptural and Other Sources

Sources are arranged in the following order: The Bible, Ancient Near Eastern Literature, Versions, Targums, Dead Sea Scrolls, Pseudepigrapha, Rabbinic Literature

The Bible

Genesis
4:7   60 n.25
7:8–9   155 n.25
9:4   60
12:6   31 n.16
12:7–8   4 n.3, 31 n.17
18:14   129 n.80
18:18   129 n.80
19:16   118n
20:13   32 n.18, 33 n.20, 114n (from 113 n.43)
24:1–3   112 n.38
28:11   31 n.16
31:53   114n (from 113 n.43)
35:1–7   4 n.3
35:7   114n (from 113 n.43)
50:16   42 n.44

Exodus
4:24–26   59 n.17
6:10–11   20n (from 19 n.54)
6:12–25   19
6:13   19, 20n (from 19 n.54)
6:14–25   19, 19 n.53
6:26–27   20n (from 19 n.54)
6:27–28   19
6:29   20n (from 19 n.54)
6:30   19
12   58 n.15
12–13   12, 66 n.43
12:1–13   62, 84
12:1–14   61 n.28, 62
12:1–28   61 n.27
12:3   54 n.1, 57, 57 n.10, 72, 72 n.68
12:5   72
12:6   62, 73 n.71, 77 n.79
12:6–8a   84
12:8   83, 83 n.94, 84, 84n (from 83 n.94), 87
12:8–9   61, 79

12:9   73 n.70, 155
12:10   86–87
12:13   58 n.16
12:14–20   68
12:15   67 n.48
12:21   54 n.1, 57, 57n.10, 62, 72, 72 n.68, 73 n.71, 79
12:21–23   61, 65, 87
12:21–27   61 n.28
12:22   59–60, 59 n.22, 74, 77 nn.78–79, 87
12:23   58, 60 n.25, 62
12:24–27a   12 n.31, 61, 62 n.30, 65, 72, 147
12:26–27   78 n.81
12:29–30   68
12:30–31   77 n.78
12:33   78 n.81
12:39   78 n.81
13   70
13:1–2   93 n.113